The Criminal Law Library

OFFENCES AGAINST PROPERTY

The Criminal Law Library

Editor-in-Chief:
Rt. Hon. Lord Elwyn-Jones, PC, CH

The Criminal Law Library—No. 7

OFFENCES AGAINST PROPERTY

JACQUES PARRY, BCL, MA(Oxon),
Barrister of the Middle Temple

WATERLOW PUBLISHERS

First edition 1989
© Jacques Parry 1989

Waterlow Publishers
Paulton House
8 Shepherdess Walk
London N1 7LB
A division of Pergamon Professional & Financial Services PLC

ISBN 0 08 033070 3

British Library Cataloguing in Publication Data

Parry, Jacques
    Offences against property.—(Criminal law
    library).
    1. England. Property. Law
    I. Title II. Series
    344.2064

Typeset by
Exe Valley Dataset Ltd, Exeter, Devon

Printed in Great Britain by
BPCC Wheatons, Exeter, Devon

Preface

The central subject of this book is that of criminal liability for dealings with the property of others which are either unauthorised or authorised only as a result of deception or threats. Also included are certain offences which, though not confined to such dealings, will typically involve them (*e.g.* blackmail, making off without payment and damaging property with disregard for danger to life), but *not* offences of deception (other than that of obtaining property by deception) or other dishonest conduct not directly involving the property of others (*e.g.* forgery, false accounting or corruption). These offences, among others, are dealt with in the companion volume on *Fraud* by Anthony J. Arlidge Q.C. and myself (hereinafter referred to by its title alone). However, the intention is that each work should stand in its own right, and that matters properly within the scope of both (*e.g.* obtaining property by deception, and certain aspects of theft) should be dealt with in both.

I have attempted to state the law as at 1 January 1989, but it has proved possible to insert brief references to a few later decisions.

J.H.P.

Contents

Contents

Table of Cases

Criminal proceedings are listed under the name of the defendant unless the prosecution was brought by a named individual. Paragraph references in bold type indicate that the case in question is discussed in the text.

Table of Statutes

Paragraph references in bold type indicate that the provision in question is quoted (in full or in part) in the text.

CHAPTER 1

Stealing

THEFT

1.01 The basic offence of dishonestly acquiring property is theft. Section 1(1) of the Theft Act 1968 provides:

> "A person is guilty of theft if he dishonestly appropriates property belonging to another with the intention of permanently depriving the other of it; and 'thief' and 'steal' shall be construed accordingly."

The offence was proposed by the Criminal Law Revision Committee[1] as a replacement for the old offence of larceny. It is triable either way[2] and is punishable on conviction on indictment with ten years' imprisonment.[3] Five elements must be proved:

(a) the charge must relate to certain *property*;
(b) that property must *belong* to a person other than the defendant;
(c) the defendant must *appropriate* it;
(d) he must *intend permanently to deprive* the other person of it; and
(e) he must act *dishonestly*.

We shall discuss each of these elements in turn.

Property

1.02 Theft cannot be committed in the abstract: the prosecution must point to some item of property which they allege to have been stolen. "Property" is defined for this purpose by section 4(1) of the 1968 Act:

> " 'Property' includes money and all other property, real or personal, including things in action and other intangible property."

This apparently circular definition simply means that if a thing falls within the concept of property for the purposes of the general law then it constitutes "property" for the purposes of the Theft Act too, and can therefore be stolen. But section 4 goes on to provide that certain things,

---

1 Cmnd. 2977.
2 Magistrates' Courts Act 1980 s. 17(1), Sch. 1.
3 Theft Act 1968 s. 7.

though qualifying as property, can be stolen only in certain circumstances. For this reason (among others) it will be convenient to distinguish three types of property:

(a) tangible movables;
(b) corporeal land; and
(c) intangible property.

We shall then examine some cases on or near the borderline between what is property and what is not.

Tangible movables

1.03 It goes without saying that tangible property other than land can be stolen.[4] The only qualification to this relates to wild creatures and their carcases, which are property but can be stolen only in certain circumstances:[5] in effect (though the Act itself does not make the connection) there are situations where other forms of property would "belong to another" but wild creatures and their carcases do not. These restrictions are therefore discussed in the context of the general question of when property is regarded as belonging to another.[6]

Corporeal land

1.04 Section 4(1) expressly provides that the term "property" includes real property. Real property can therefore be stolen. Incorporeal hereditaments (*i.e.* legal rights over land, such as easements) are a form of intangible property and can be stolen to the same extent as any other such property.[7] The physical land itself, however, can be stolen only in certain circumstances. Section 4(2) provides in part as follows:

"A person cannot steal land,[8] or things forming part of land and severed from it by him or by his direction, except in the following cases, that is to say—
(*a*) when he is a trustee or personal representative, or is authorised by power of attorney, or as liquidator of a company, or otherwise, to sell or dispose of land belonging to another, and he appropriates the land or anything forming part of it by dealing with it in breach of the confidence reposed in him; or
(*b*) when he is not in possession of the land and appropriates anything forming part of the land by severing it or causing it to be severed, or after it has been severed; or

4 But not everything which is tangible is property: see *infra*, para. 1.13.
5 s. 4(4).
6 *Infra*, paras. 1.61 f.
7 *Infra*, para. 1.12.
8 "Land" does not include incorporeal hereditaments: s. 4(2).

(c) when, being in possession of the land under a tenancy, he appropriates
the whole or part of any fixture or structure let to be used with the
land."

In order to see the effect of this provision it may be helpful to distinguish
two situations: the appropriation of entire areas of land, and the
severance from the land of things forming part of it.

Areas of land

1.05 One effect of section 4(2) is that the land itself, as distinct from
things forming part of it, cannot normally be stolen at all. Squatting, even
if intended to be permanent, is not theft;[9] nor is the dishonest moving of
boundary fences and the like. The only case where an entire area of land
can be stolen is that of a trustee or personal representative, or other
person authorised to sell or dispose of land belonging to another, who
appropriates the land by "dealing with it in breach of the confidence
reposed in him". Thus an agent authorised to sell land for a stipulated
minimum price can be guilty of stealing the land if he dishonestly sells it
to an associate for less than that price. But he must be authorised to sell
or dispose of the land, not merely to arrange for its sale or disposal by
the owner or a third party. Nor is it clear that he can be guilty if he does
precisely what he is authorised to do, but he does it dishonestly—*e.g.* by
selling at an undervalue when the price has been left to his discretion. But
the difficulty is nothing to do with the fact that the property disposed of
is land and not personality: the agent is clearly dealing with the land "in
breach of the confidence reposed in him", in the sense that (even if
technically within his authority) his act constitutes a breach of his
fiduciary duty to his principal. The problem is the more general one of
whether such a disposal is an *appropriation* of the property, and it is
examined in that context.[10]

Things forming part of the land

1.06 *Fixtures and chattels.* Alternatively things forming part of the land
may in certain circumstances be stolen by detaching them from the land.
In determining whether a particular thing is a fixture, and therefore part
of the land, the maxim "*quicquid plantatur solo, solo cedit*" should not be
taken literally: an object is not necessarily a fixture just because it is fixed
to the ground. *Prima facie* it will be,[11] but the prosecution may rebut this
inference (and thus avoid the restrictions imposed by section 4(2)) by
showing that the object was affixed not to improve the realty but for the
more convenient use of the object itself. Thus a tapestry may remain a

 9 But *cf. infra*, paras. 7.61 ff.
10 *Infra*, paras. 1.92 ff.
11 *Holland v. Hodgson* (1872) L.R. 7 C.P. 328.

chattel even when nailed to a wall, because it has to be fixed to a wall if it is to be properly appreciated.[12] Conversely an object which is *not* affixed to the land is *prima facie* a chattel,[13] though it may exceptionally become part of the realty if so regarded by the occupier.[14]

1.07 *Fiduciaries.* If the thing appropriated *is* part of the land, and is severed from it by the defendant or by his direction, the basic rule is that he does not thereby steal it; nor, it would seem, does he steal it by appropriating it after it has been severed.[15] But this rule is subject to three exceptions which denude it of most of its significance. The first exception is that a trustee, personal representative, or other person authorised to sell or dispose of land belonging to another, can steal something forming part of the land if he appropriates it by dealing with it in breach of the confidence reposed in him. Such a person can be charged with theft even if he appropriates the land itself;[16] *a fortiori* if he appropriates only things forming part of it.

1.08 *Persons not in possession.* By virtue of section 4(2)(*b*), things forming part of the land can also be stolen by any person who is not in possession of the land if he appropriates the thing in question by severing it or causing it to be severed; and such a person can steal a thing which did form part of the land until it was severed, whoever severed it,[17] if he then appropriates it. "Possession" is not defined, and is presumably to be interpreted in the light of established principles of common law. In that case a person is not in possession merely because he is in residence, *e.g.* as a lodger, relative or guest of the occupier: possession means *exclusive* possession. Nor is he in possession if he owns the land but has granted exclusive possession to another, *e.g.* under a tenancy.[18] Therefore a lessor can steal things forming part of the land which he has let.

1.09 A person who *is* in possession, on the other hand, is not caught by section 4(2)(*b*). If he is in possession under a tenancy he may fall within section 4(2)(*c*);[19] but he may have possession under a licence rather than

12 *Leigh v. Taylor* [1902] A.C. 157.
13 *Berkley v. Poulett* (1976) 241 E.G. 911, 242 E.G. 39.
14 *Hamp v. Bygrave* (1982) 266 E.G. 720.
15 It might perhaps be argued that once the thing is severed from the land it is no longer a thing "forming part of land" and therefore falls outside s. 4(2). But s. 4(2) (*b*) envisages an appropriation of a thing "forming part of the land . . . after it has been severed".
16 *Supra*, para. 1.05.
17 If it were severed by someone other than the defendant (otherwise than by his directions), s. 4(2) would not apply at all. If it were severed by the defendant, or by his directions, the exception in s. 4(2)(*b*) would apply.
18 *Cooper v. Crabtree* (1882) 20 Ch.D. 589.
19 *Infra*, para. 1.11.

a tenancy, or he may be squatting with no title other than a possessory one. In such a case he is caught by neither paragraph (*b*) nor paragraph (*c*), and (unless he is a fiduciary within paragraph (*a*)) can appropriate things forming part of the land with impunity. The prosecution may therefore wish to argue that he was not in possession at the material time after all. In the case of a licensee they might contend that the agreement did not give him *exclusive* possession: if it did, it would normally constitute a tenancy rather than a licence,[20] and section 4(2)(*c*) would apply. If the defendant claims to have been squatting, the prosecution may argue that he either did not have the requisite intention to exclude all others (including the true owner) or did not evince that intention to the world at large; in either case he would not be in possession but only a trespasser,[21] and section 4(2)(*b*) would apply. Alternatively a charge of criminal damage might be possible.[22]

1.10 Section 4(2)(*b*), which constitutes an exception to the basic rule that things forming part of the land cannot be stolen, is itself subject to a sub-exception created by section 4(3):

"A person who picks mushrooms growing wild on any land, or who picks flowers, fruit or foliage from a plant growing wild on any land, does not (although not in possession of the land) steal what he picks, unless he does it for reward or for sale or other commercial purpose.
   For purposes of this subsection 'mushroom' includes any fungus, and 'plant' includes any shrub or tree."

Thus it is not theft to pick

(a) wild mushrooms or other fungus, or
(b) flowers, fruit or foliage from a wild plant, shrub or tree.

Any other form of appropriation, such as the uprooting of plants or the stripping of branches from a tree, is not protected by section 4(3). If done by someone not in possession of the land it can therefore constitute theft by virtue of section 4(2)(*b*)—though a charge of criminal damage might be more appropriate. By way of sub-sub-exception, it is provided that even the picking of wild mushrooms, or of flowers, fruit or foliage from wild plants, can be theft if done for reward or for sale or other commercial purpose. It may be that a defendant who picks such items in order to sell them is not caught by this rule unless the intended sale can be described as a "commercial purpose"; but the wording seems to imply either that sale is deemed to be a commercial purpose *per se* or that it is sufficient even if it is not a commercial purpose. In any event a person picking items

20 *Street v. Mountford* [1985] A.C. 809.
21 *Powell v. McFarlane* (1977) 38 P. & C.R. 452.
22 *Infra*, paras. 6.02 ff.

for sale on a non-commercial basis (*e.g.* for charity) is unlikely to be regarded as dishonest.

1.11 *Persons in possession under a tenancy.* A person in possession of land cannot steal things forming part of the land by virtue of section 4(2)(*b*), but may be caught instead by section 4(2)(*c*)—provided firstly that he is in possession under a tenancy[23] and not as a licensee or squatter, and secondly that he appropriates a fixture or structure let to be used with the land (or part of such a fixture or structure). This does not include things which form part of the land but are not fixtures or structures (*e.g.* plants); nor does it include fixtures or structures whose function is purely ornamental, because they are not let to be *used* with the land.

Intangible property

1.12 Section 4(1) expressly provides that for the purposes of the offence of theft the term "property" includes things in action and other intangible property. It follows that it is possible to steal not only tangible things (*e.g.* movables and corporeal land) but also incorporeal rights over tangible things (*e.g.* easements)[24] and abstract rights which do not relate to any specific tangible thing at all, whether they technically qualify as "things in action" (*e.g.* debts) or not (*e.g.* export quotas which can be bought and sold).[25] In the case of intangible property particular difficulties arise from the requirements of appropriation and of intention permanently to deprive, and these difficulties will be considered in due course.[26] But if the defendant succeeds in actually depriving another person of his rights, there is no problem. In *Kohn*[27] a director who fraudulently drew cheques on his company's bank account was held to have stolen the debt owed to the company by the bank and represented by the credit balance in the account. Because he was the agent for the company, with authority to write cheques on its behalf, the cheques were not forgeries: they were valid company cheques, and when they were presented the effect was to reduce the credit balance outstanding and thus to deprive the company of its property.[28] Similarly, it was held, the drawing of a cheque on an

---

23 *i.e.* a tenancy for years or any less period, including an agreement for a tenancy and a statutory tenancy: s. 4(2).
24 Incorporeal hereditaments do not constitute "land" for the purposes of s. 4(2) and can therefore be stolen to the same (limited) extent as other intangible property.
25 *Attorney-General of Hong Kong v. Chan Nai-Keung* [1987] 1 W.L.R. 1339; *infra,* para. 1.94.
26 *Infra,* paras. 1.71, 1.110.
27 (1979) 69 Cr.App.R. 395.
28 For fuller discussion of the application of the law of theft to the misappropriation of bank balances, see *Fraud* paras. 3.05 ff.; E. Griew, "Stealing and Obtaining Bank Credits" [1986] Crim.L.R. 356.

account which is already overdrawn can amount to the theft of the account-holder's right (if any) to have his cheques honoured up to an agreed overdraft limit. If he has an overdraft limit of £300 and the account is already overdrawn by £100, any dishonest drawing on the account will deprive him of some or all of his right to the other £200 (which is itself an item of property).[29] But if he had no right to overdraw any further, there would be no property to be stolen.[30]

Borderline cases

The human body

1.13 Since section 4 does not extend the concept of property but merely defines it in terms of the civil law, it follows that a thing which the civil law does not regard as property cannot be stolen at all. The only important tangible object falling into this category appears to be the human body:[31] people are not property, and therefore kidnapping is not theft.[32] The same rule applies to a corpse[33] (unless, perhaps, it has been preserved for scientific purposes);[34] but things removed from the body of a living person presumably belong to that person if to no-one else. The removal itself, if effected without authority, would of course be more appropriately charged as an assault.

Intangibles

1.14 Intangible commodities, however valuable, do not necessarily qualify as property. One cannot steal services,[35] whether those of a human being or of a machine: therefore the misuse of computer time is not theft. Another example is electricity. People pay for the right to use electricity, and that right is doubtless a form of intangible property; but electricity itself is not, and therefore cannot be stolen.[36] The dishonest use of electricity is an offence,[37] but is not theft.

1.15 A more controversial case is that of information.[38] Certainly there can be property which consists in the right to the exclusive *use* of

---

29 This was conceded in *Chan Man-Sin* [1988] 1 W.L.R. 196.
30 Except that consisting in the bank's right to repayment of the existing overdraft, which would not of course be affected by further drawings.
31 See A.T.H. Smith, "Stealing the Body and its Parts" [1976] Crim.L.R. 622.
32 But it is an offence at common law: *D.* [1984] A.C. 778. See also Child Abduction Act 1984.
33 *Handyside's Case* 2 East P.C. 652. It is an offence at common law to remove a body from a grave without lawful authority: *Sharpe* (1857) Dears. & B. 160.
34 *Doodeward v. Spence* (1908) 6 C.L.R. 406.
35 But one can obtain them by deception: Theft Act 1978 s. 1(1), *infra*, para. 2.33.
36 *Low v. Blease* [1975] Crim.L.R. 513.
37 Theft Act 1968 s. 13: *infra*, para. 5.61.
38 See *Fraud*, paras. 3.10ff.

information: copyright is an example, and a copyright can in certain circumstances be stolen.[39] But this would involve proof both that the copyright was appropriated and that the defendant intended (or at any rate can be deemed to have intended) permanently to deprive the copyright owner of it. These matters may be as hard to prove as in the case of any other intangible property. Nor is a person who infringes a copyright guilty of stealing the infringing copy, because the copy does not belong to the owner of the copyright.[40] The question therefore arises whether, irrespective of the copyright position, information itself can be property and can therefore be stolen. In *Oxford v. Moss*,[41] where the Divisional Court held that it could not, authorities to the contrary[42] were not referred to. The point cannot therefore be regarded as settled. But even if a higher court were to conclude that information can indeed constitute property, a charge of stealing information would require proof of an intention (actual or constructive) permanently to deprive of it the person to whom it "belongs". In *Lloyd, Bhuee and Ali*[43] the Court of Appeal held that it was not theft to borrow feature films without authority in order to make pirate copies, because the films were returned and there was never any intention permanently to deprive their owner of them. The court has been criticised for ignoring the possibility that the appellants might have stolen the images making up the films, as distinct from the physical material on which those images were stored.[44] But in order to secure a conviction on this basis it would have to be shown not only that the images were themselves a form of property distinct from the copyright in them (*Oxford v. Moss* notwithstanding), but also that their owner was intended to be permanently deprived of them. The court took the view that one is not permanently deprived of one's property, even constructively, merely because it loses some (but not all) of its value. This view would seem to rule out a charge of theft in such circumstances, whether framed as a theft of the physical medium or of the images or other information stored thereon.

39   *Pace* Lord Denning M.R. in *Rank Film Distributors Ltd v. Video Information Centre* [1982] A.C. 380 at p. 409. Infringement of copyright may also be an offence under s. 107 of the Copyright, Designs and Patents Act 1988 (formerly s. 21 of the Copyright Act 1956): see G. McFarlane, *A Practical Introduction to Copyright* (1982) pp. 111 ff., and *Copyright through the Cases* (1986) section 10.
40   *Storrow and Poole* [1983] Crim.L.R. 332: s. 18(1) of the Copyright Act 1956 merely gave the copyright owner certain civil remedies *as if* he were the owner of the infringing copy. See now Copyright, Designs and Patents Act 1988 s. 99.
41   (1978) 68 Cr.App.R. 183.
42   *Green v. Folgham* (1823) 1 Sim. & Stu. 398; *Re Keene* [1922] 2 Ch. 475; *Exchange Telegraph Co. Ltd v. Howard* (1906) 22 T.L.R. 375.
43   [1985] Q.B. 829.
44   G. McFarlane, "Theft of Intangible Property" (1985) 135 N.L.J. 650.

Identification of the property

1.16 On a charge of theft the prosecution must be able to prove not only that some property was dishonestly appropriated, but also what that property was. A person charged with stealing a number of items may be convicted of stealing only some of them.[45] Moreover there is no need to identify the property stolen in the sense of distinguishing it from similar property which was not stolen: thus a person who is responsible for handling money over a period of time, but is unable to account for the full amount received, may be charged with theft of the deficiency even if it cannot be proved exactly which money he stole.[46] Similarly a person who by mistake is issued with two cheques instead of one, and cashes them both, may be charged with stealing the excess even if there is no way of proving which cheque he was entitled to and which he was not.[47] But the indictment must contain "such particulars as may be necessary for giving reasonable information as to the nature of the charge",[48] and this requirement will not be satisfied unless the property alleged to have been stolen is described, in general terms at least. The prosecution may therefore be in difficulty if they can prove that the defendant must have stolen one of two items, but cannot prove which: *e.g.* where he is employed to sell goods and cannot account for the full price of all the goods which are missing, but there is no evidence to suggest whether he stole the goods or sold them and stole the proceeds.[49] Strictly speaking neither charge can be proved beyond reasonable doubt. All the prosecution can do is to charge the possibility which seems more likely to represent the truth (in most cases, theft of the proceeds) and hope that the court will regard any objection as unduly technical.

Belonging to another

1.17 Property cannot be stolen unless it "belongs" to someone other than the prospective thief.[50] This excludes not only property which has never belonged to anyone other than the defendant, such as the rights conferred on him by a cheque drawn in his favour,[51] but also property which has ceased to belong to another before[52] the moment when the

---

45 *Machent v. Quinn* [1970] 2 All E.R. 255.
46 *Tomlin* [1954] 2 Q.B. 278.
47 *Davis* [1988] Crim.L.R. 762.
48 Indictment Rules 1971 r. 5(1).
49 The point arose on the facts of *Tomlin, supra,* but seems to have been overlooked.
50 But a person who appropriates property which he wrongly believes to belong to someone else might be convicted of an attempt: *infra,* para. 1.189.
51 As distinct from the cheque itself.
52 It is not in itself a defence that the property ceases to belong to the other *at* the moment of appropriation: *Lawrence* [1972] A.C. 626. But in that case the owner's consent to what the defendant does might prevent it from being an appropriation at all: *infra,* paras. 1.73 ff.

defendant appropriates it. Sometimes it is clear beyond doubt that by the time of the alleged appropriation the property no longer belongs to its original owner in any sense: in one reported case the defendant had eaten it.[53] Other cases can involve the determination of fine points of civil law. From time to time judges refer to the desirability of keeping the civil law firmly in its place and not allowing it to complicate the law of theft.[54] But such a separation could only be maintained if theft were defined without reference to the concepts of property law (which it is not), and the criminal courts have frequently been called upon to apply such concepts for the purpose of determining whether the property appropriated "belonged" to a person other than the appropriator. In *Walker*,[55] for example, the seller of a video recorder was charged with stealing it by reselling it to a third party, after the buyer had first returned it to him for repair and then taken out a summons for the recovery of the price. His conviction was quashed because the jury had not had explained to them the possibility that the buyer's conduct might have amounted to a rescission of the contract, in which case the ownership of the recorder would have reverted to the seller.

1.18 More often the defendant is a purported buyer of goods who has absconded without troubling to pay for them, and the question arises whether title to the goods had already passed to him under a contract of sale. If it had, his action will not normally be an appropriation of property belonging to another but only the evasion of a debt.[56] In *Edwards v. Ddin*[57] the defendant had filled his petrol tank at a garage and driven off without paying. It was held, applying what is now section 18 of the Sale of Goods Act 1979, that it could not have been intended that the petrol should continue to belong to the seller even after it had been pumped into the buyer's tank, because even if the buyer failed to pay for it the seller would be unable to get it back: it would of course be irretrievably mixed with the petrol already in the tank. In *Davies v. Leighton*[58] the opposite conclusion was reached where a customer in a supermarket had had goods wrapped and priced by an assistant but had left without paying for them at the checkout. The seller would have had no difficulty in repossessing the goods, and there was no reason to suppose that title was intended to pass until they were paid for. These cases do not establish any point of general principle: they are merely

53 *Corcoran v. Whent* [1977] Crim.L.R. 52.
54 Most notably Lord Roskill in *Morris* [1984] A.C. 320 at p. 334.
55 [1984] Crim.L.R. 112.
56 Which might still be an offence, *e.g.* that of making off without payment contrary to s. 3 of the Theft Act 1978: *infra*, paras. 5.46 ff.
57 [1976] 1 W.L.R. 942.
58 (1978) 68 Cr.App.R. 4.

applications, on particular facts, of the fundamental requirement that the property in question must have belonged to another at the time of the appropriation. But they also illustrate how issues of property and contract law can be as crucial in a criminal case as in a civil one.

1.19   The indictment or information should identify the person to whom the property is alleged to have belonged; but it is immaterial that that person is incorrectly identified, provided that the defendant is not thereby prejudiced.[59] If necessary the property can be described as belonging to a person unknown.[60]

1.20   Section 5 of the Theft Act 1968 defines the expression "belonging to another" for the purposes of the offence of theft. It provides in effect that property belongs to a person other than the defendant in six different situations.

Proprietary interests

1.21   Section 5(1) provides, in part, as follows:

"Property shall be regarded as belonging to any person . . . having in it any proprietary right or interest (not being an equitable interest arising only from an agreement to transfer or grant an interest)."

This is the most obvious example of property belonging to another, and in the vast majority of cases it will be unnecessary to look any further. Property belongs not only to a person who is its sole owner but also to anyone who has any proprietary right or interest in it. Since there is no requirement that the property should *not* belong to the defendant himself, but only that it *should* belong to someone else, it follows that property which is jointly owned by one or more persons can be stolen by one or more of those persons from any or all of the other joint owners.[61] The Theft Act contains no counterpart to section 10(2)(c) of the Criminal Damage Act 1971, which provides that property belongs to a person who has a charge on it; but a charge is surely a proprietary right or interest.

Equitable interests

1.22   The victim's interest in the property need not be a legal one: it is expressly provided that an equitable interest will suffice. Thus a trustee, although the sole owner at law, can nevertheless steal the trust property, because the beneficiaries have a proprietary (albeit only equitable) interest

59   *Etim v. Hatfield* [1975] Crim.L.R. 234.
60   Indictment Rules 1971 r. 8.
61   *Bonner* [1970] 1 W.L.R. 838.

in it. It therefore belongs to them as well as to him.[62] A recently established application of this principle, apparently unforeseen by the framers of the Theft Act,[63] is the case where property is transferred by mistake and the transferee is accordingly deemed to hold it on trust for the transferor: the transferee can therefore steal it if he dishonestly takes advantage of the mistake.[64]

1.23 The question whether particular property is subject to a trust can be a difficult one. The problem has arisen in the context of persons in a fiduciary position who abuse that position so as to make a secret profit. It was until recently thought that such a person holds the profit on a constructive trust for the person to whom his fiduciary duty is owed, at any rate if he obtains it by misusing property or confidential information which (in either case) has been entrusted to him. The authorities for this theory consisted almost entirely of *obiter dicta* in cases where the issue was not so much whether the fiduciary was a trustee of the profit as whether he was liable to account for it at all;[65] and the theory has now been firmly rejected, at any rate as far as the law of theft is concerned, in *Attorney-General's Reference (No. 1 of 1985)*.[66] The reference arose out of a case where the manager of a public house, employed by the brewery to sell only their beer, had fraudulently sold his own beer and kept the proceeds. It was held that he was not guilty of stealing the proceeds because they did not belong to the brewery, even in equity: he was liable to account for his profit, but he was not a trustee of it. The decision was confirmed by the House of Lords in *Cooke*,[67] a case involving essentially similar facts.

1.24 It would be otherwise if the property in question were not just obtained through the defendant's misuse of his position and of his employer's property, but actually represented property entrusted to him. The court pointed out in the *Attorney-General's Reference*:

> "There is a clear and important difference between on the one hand a person misappropriating specific property with which he has been entrusted, and on the other hand a person in a fiduciary position who uses that position to make a secret profit for which he will be held accountable. Whether the former is within section 5, we do not have to decide." [68]

---

62 For the position where there is no beneficiary with a proprietary interest, see *infra*, para. 1.29.
63 *Cf.* s. 5(4); *infra*, paras. 1.40 ff.
64 *Shadrokh-Cigari* [1988] Crim.L.R. 465.
65 *e.g. Parker v. McKenna* (1874) L.R. 10 Ch.App. 96; *Cook v. Deeks* [1916] 1 A.C. 554; *Boardman v. Phipps* [1967] 2 A.C. 46.
66 [1986] Q.B. 491; see also *infra*, para. 1.31.
67 [1986] A.C. 909.
68 At p. 503.

It is submitted that the former case clearly *is* within section 5, and that it makes no difference if the property appropriated is not the property originally entrusted to the defendant but represents the proceeds of that property: not only does it fall within section 5(3),[69] but it is subject to a constructive trust in the employer's favour and therefore belongs to him by virtue of section 5(1). This principle is well established[70] and is unaffected by the *Attorney-General's Reference*.

1.25 *Agreements to transfer or grant an interest*   There is however an exception to the rule that property subject to a trust belongs to the person entitled to it in equity: this is not so if the trust arises only from an agreement to transfer or grant an interest in the property. If an owner of property contracts to sell it, and the property is of such a character that a decree of specific performance will be available in the event of his subsequently failing to do so, the purchaser acquires an equitable interest in the property as soon as the contract is made: "equity regards that as done which ought to be done". In the absence of specific provision for this situation, the property would be regarded as belonging not only to the seller but also, by virtue of his equitable interest, to the buyer. It would follow that if the seller dishonestly appropriated it, intending that the buyer should never have it, he would be stealing it. But the law stops short of thus treating as theft what is effectively no more than a breach of contract: for the purposes of the Act the property does not yet belong to the buyer, his equitable interest notwithstanding, and it cannot therefore be stolen from him. If, however, the effect of the contract is actually to pass the legal title to the buyer, as against merely imposing on the seller an obligation to pass it (if, in other words, it is a sale rather than an agreement to sell),[71] the property does not immediately belong to the buyer and can be stolen from him. Whether or not this is the effect of the contract depends on the intentions of the parties,[72] but, unless a different intention appears, an unconditional contract for the sale of specific goods in a deliverable state is presumed to be intended as a sale with immediate effect.[73]

Property belonging to the defendant's company
1.26 There is one situation where it might perhaps be argued that property should not be regarded as belonging to anyone other than the defendant, although it is technically owned by another person: *viz.* where

---

69   *Infra*, paras. 1.30 ff.
70   See *Fraud*, para. 4.02.
71   Sale of Goods Act 1979 s. 2(4), (5).
72   *Ibid.*, s. 17.
73   *Ibid.*, s. 18 rule 1.

that person is a company wholly owned by the defendant himself.[74] It might be said that in reality, as against legal theory, a company's property is the property of the shareholders, and that if they act unanimously they cannot therefore be guilty of stealing it. But this would be an over-simplification. A person's own property is by no means interchangeable with that of his wholly-owned company: for one thing, the company's creditors have an interest only in the latter. In *Attorney-General's Reference (No. 2 of 1982)*[75] it was apparently assumed that such property did belong to another for the purposes of a theft charge, and it is submitted with respect that the assumption was correct. Whether the defendant's dealings with the property can be an appropriation of it, or dishonest, is another matter.[76]

Possession or control

1.27 Section 5(1) also provides:

"Property shall be regarded as belonging to any person having possession or control of it . . ."

Thus the Act reflects the law's traditional emphasis on the protection of possession as well as title. Property can be stolen from a person who has no proprietary interest in it but only possession; and there is no need even to investigate the obscurities of the concept of possession, since the wider and less technical notion of control will also suffice. In *Woodman*[77] the appellant had appropriated a quantity of scrap metal from a disused factory. The owners of the factory had sold all the scrap metal on the site to a third party some two years before, but, unbeknown to the site owners, the third party had left some of it behind. It was held that even if the site owners were not in *possession* of the residue, because they did not know it was there, there was ample evidence that they were at any rate in *control* of it by virtue of their control of the site on which it lay.

". . . we think that in ordinary and straightforward cases if it is once established that a particular person is in control of a site such as this, then *prima facie* he is in control of articles which are on that site." [78]

Control of the site was easy to infer since the owners had surrounded it with a barbed-wire fence and a number of notices warning that trespassers would be prosecuted; but any evidence of an intention to exclude others would probably be sufficient to establish control.

74 See *Fraud*, para. 4.06.
75 [1984] Q.B. 624.
76 *Infra*, paras. 1.93 f., 1.152 f.; *Fraud* paras. 4.26 ff.
77 [1974] Q.B. 754.
78 At p. 758.

1.28 Even so, control of a site does not necessarily involve control of any articles upon it: it merely raises a presumption to that effect. In *Woodman* the court went on to say:

> "There has been some mention in argument of what would happen if in a case like the present, a third party had come and placed some article within the barbed-wire fence and thus on the site. The article might be an article of some serious criminal consequence such as explosives or drugs. It may well be that in that type of case the fact that the article has been introduced at a late stage in circumstances in which the occupier of the site had no means of knowledge would produce a different result from that which arises under the general presumption to which we have referred . . ." [79]

Even if the occupier of a site does have control of articles lost or abandoned there, it does not follow that it is theft for a finder to appropriate them: such an appropriation may be permissible as a matter of civil law, provided that the occupier has not manifested an intention to exercise exclusive control over both the land and things upon it, and provided also that the finder is not a trespasser.[80] The occupier might perhaps *be* in control of the article in question, by virtue of the presumption laid down in *Woodman*, without necessarily manifesting such an *intention* to exercise exclusive control as would entitle him to the article as against a finder lawfully on the premises. In that case the finder would be legally entitled to keep the article even though it "belonged" to the occupier. If he knew that he was so entitled, he would not be dishonest;[81] if he did not, the question would arise whether one can steal by taking property which one is legally entitled to take. It has indeed been held that even an *owner* of property can steal it from someone who has no right to withhold it from him;[82] but it is submitted that an appropriation in such circumstances cannot properly be regarded as dishonest.[83]

Trust property

1.29 Section 5(2) provides:

> "Where property is subject to a trust, the persons to whom it belongs shall be regarded as including any person having a right to enforce the trust, and an intention to defeat the trust shall be regarded accordingly as an intention to deprive of the property any person having that right."

---

79 *Ibid.*
80 *Parker v. British Airways Board* [1982] Q.B. 1004. In *Hibbert v. McKiernan* [1948] 2 K.B. 142 a trespasser on a golf course was held to have stolen lost golf balls from the golf club: a trespasser has no right to lost property as against the occupier. The position would no doubt be the same under the Theft Act.
81 s. 2(1)(*a*): *infra*, para. 1.144.
82 *Turner (No. 2)* [1971] 1 W.L.R. 901.
83 *Infra*, paras. 1.154 ff.

In most cases involving trust property it will be unnecessary to invoke this subsection because the property will belong to the beneficiaries by virtue of section 5(1).[84] Charitable trusts, however, do not have identifiable beneficiaries with proprietary interests in the trust property; they can, on the other hand, be enforced by the Attorney-General. By virtue of section 5(2) property subject to such a trust is therefore deemed to belong to the Attorney-General, and an intention to defeat the objects of the trust is deemed to be an intention permanently to deprive him of the property. It can therefore be stolen by even a sole trustee, although there is no-one else with a proprietary interest or possession or control.

Property to be dealt with in a particular way

1.30   Section 5(3) provides:

> "Where a person receives property from or on account of another, and is under an obligation to the other to retain and deal with that property or its proceeds in a particular way, the property or proceeds shall be regarded (as against him) as belonging to the other."

This provision too adds little to section 5(1), because, where a person holds property subject to the obligation described, the person to whom the obligation is owed will usually have at least an equitable interest in the property. But this is not invariably so: it is possible to have a personal right that certain property shall be dealt with in a particular way without thereby having a proprietary interest in it.[85] The effect of section 5(3) is that an infringement of such a right can amount to theft, provided that the property is received by the defendant from or on account of the person whose right is infringed. In other words, a person who holds property in a fiduciary capacity can steal it even if he is not a trustee. Before the subsection can apply, two requirements must be satisfied: firstly, the defendant must have received property from or on account of another person; secondly, he must be under an obligation to that person to retain and deal with the property or its proceeds in a particular way.

Receipt from or on account of another
1.31   More precisely, the first requirement is that the property appropriated must

(a) have itself been received by the defendant *from* the person to whom it is alleged to belong, or
(b) have been received by him *on that person's account*, or
(c) be the *proceeds* of *other* property received by him from that person or on his account.

---

84   *Supra*, para. 1.22.
85   *e.g. Palmer v. Carey* [1926] A.C. 703.

Property is not received on another person's account merely because the defendant is obliged to account to him for it, *e.g.* because it is obtained by a breach of fiduciary duty;[86] and this is so even if the person from whom the property is received *thinks* that the defendant is receiving it on a third person's account. In *Attorney-General's Reference (No. 1 of 1985),*[87] where the manager of a tied public house had sold his own beer instead of his employers', the Court of Appeal rejected the Crown's argument that the proceeds of the sales were deemed to belong to the employers by virtue of section 5(3).

> "Whether that argument is correct or not depends on whether [the manager] can properly be said to have received property (*i.e.*, the payment over the counter for the beer he has sold to the customer) 'on account of' the employers. We do not think he can. He received the money on his own account as a result of his private venture. No doubt he is in breach of his contract with the employers; no doubt he is under an obligation to account to the employers at least for the profit he has made out of his venture, but that is a different matter. The fact that A may have to account to B for money he has received from X does not mean necessarily that he received the money on account of B." [88]

Even if the manager had received the money on his employers' account, section 5(3) would still not have applied because the court went on to hold that his obligation to account for the money was a purely personal one: he did not hold it as trustee or otherwise in a fiduciary capacity.[89] The case therefore did not satisfy the second requirement, to which we now turn.

Obligation to deal with the property in a particular way

1.32   The second requirement for the application of section 5(3) is that the defendant must be under an obligation to the person in question[90] to retain and deal with the property[91] in a particular way. We must consider firstly what sort of obligation this must be, secondly what it is that the defendant must be obliged to do, and thirdly the factors which will determine whether the requisite obligation does in fact exist.

---

86 *Powell v. MacRae* [1977] Crim.L.R. 571; *cf. Cullum* (1873) L.R. 2 C.C.R. 28.
87 [1986] Q.B. 491.
88 At p. 501.
89 *Supra*, para. 1.23.
90 *i.e.* the person from whom or on whose account the property in question (or the property of which it is the proceeds) was received. An obligation owed to any other person will not suffice: see *Fraud*, para. 4.12.
91 *Quaere* whether it would suffice if the property in question were the proceeds of the property originally received from that person or on his account, and the obligation owed to him extended only to the original property and not to its proceeds. It is submitted that the alternative "or proceeds" in the clause "the property or proceeds shall be regarded . . . as belonging to the other" applies only if there is an obligation to retain and deal with the proceeds (as well as, or instead of, the property originally received) in a particular way.

1.33 *Nature of the obligation.* The "obligation" referred to in section 5(3) must be a legal obligation: expectations which are not legally enforceable do not count.[92] It follows that, once the first requirement is found to be satisfied, it will be necessary to determine the defendant's rights and obligations in civil law. Notwithstanding earlier *dicta* suggesting that it is for the jury to decide what amounts to an obligation for this purpose,[93] the correct procedure was laid down in *Mainwaring and Madders:*[94]

> "Whether or not an obligation arises is a matter of law, because an obligation must be a legal obligation. But a legal obligation arises only in certain circumstances, and in many cases the circumstances cannot be known until the facts have been established. It is for the jury, not the judge, to establish the facts, if they are in dispute.
>
> What, in our judgment, a judge ought to do is this: if the facts relied upon by the prosecution are in dispute he should direct the jury to make their findings on the facts, and then say to them: 'If you find the facts to be such-and-such, then I direct you as a matter of law that a legal obligation arose to which section 5(3) applies.' " [95]

1.34 The requirement that the obligation be a legally enforceable one must be qualified in one respect. In *Meech*[96] it was held that an obligation may exist for this purpose although it is unenforceable on the grounds of illegality, at any rate if the defendant was unaware of the illegality when he assumed the obligation. Meech was charged with stealing the proceeds of a cheque which had been entrusted to him by one McCord. McCord had obtained the cheque by means of a forged instrument; but Meech did not know this when he accepted the cheque, and it was held that he was therefore under an obligation to McCord to deal with the proceeds as requested. It was immaterial that any attempt by McCord to enforce that obligation could have been thwarted with a plea of *ex turpi causa*.

> "The question has to be looked at from Meech's point of view, not McCord's. Meech plainly assumed an 'obligation' to McCord which, on the facts then known to him, he remained obliged to fulfil and, on the facts as found, he must be taken at that time honestly to have intended to fulfil. The fact that on the true facts if known McCord might not and indeed would not subsequently have been permitted to enforce that obligation in a civil court does not prevent that 'obligation' on Meech having arisen. The argument confuses the creation of the obligation with the subsequent discharge of that obligation either by performance or otherwise. That the obligation might have become impossible of performance by Meech or of enforcement by McCord on grounds of illegality or for reasons of public policy is irrelevant." [97]

92   Subject to what is said *infra* at paras. 1.34 ff.
93   *Hall* [1973] Q.B. 126; *Hayes* (1977) 64 Cr.App.R. 82.
94   (1981) 74 Cr.App.R. 99.
95   At p. 107.
96   [1974] Q.B. 549.
97   At p. 554 f.

1.35 The implications of this reasoning are obscure. It is not clear which factor the court regarded as crucial—the peculiar status of an obligation tainted by illegality, or Meech's initial ignorance of the facts. The court may have taken the view that illegality does not nullify an obligation altogether but converts it into a kind of quasi-obligation, binding (and therefore within section 5(3)) but unenforceable. But it is hard to see how an obligation which is not legally enforceable can properly be described as a legal obligation at all,[98] or (if it can) why the court thought it relevant whether the illegality was known to the appellant. If the subsection can be brought into play either by an obligation which is binding in every sense or by one which is vitiated by illegality, it hardly matters whether the defendant thinks that what he has undertaken is the former or knows that it is the latter. On the other hand it would be contrary to principle to treat the defendant's knowledge as not just relevant but crucial, so that an obligation vitiated by illegality would be sufficient if (and only if) he thought it were fully binding. Either such an obligation is the kind of obligation contemplated by section 5(3) or it is not. If it is not, it is surely immaterial that the defendant thinks he is under the kind of obligation which is.[99] The subsection requires him to *be* under an obligation, not just to *believe* that he is under one.

1.36 Even if it were analytically sound to treat the defendant's mis-apprehensions as a substitute for the binding obligation which section 5(3) requires, this would not in itself be sufficient to justify the decision, since Meech had discovered the truth before he appropriated the proceeds of the cheque. If the court had been prepared simply to equate an obligation tainted by illegality with one not so tainted, this development would have presented no difficulty: the obligation would at all material times have been the kind of obligation contemplated by section 5(3), and Meech would have known that it was. But the court again appears to shy away from saying simply that the requisite obligation did exist throughout:

> "The answer to the . . . contention is that Meech being under the initial obligation already mentioned, the proceeds of the cheque continued as between him and McCord to be deemed to be McCord's property . . ."[1]

In other words, the property continued to belong to McCord by virtue of section 5(3) even if the obligation ceased to exist when Meech discovered the truth. As the court had earlier said in connection with the argument that Meech was never under a legal obligation at all (to which the relevance of the remark is, with respect, not apparent):

98 *Cf. Gilks* [1972] 1 W.L.R. 1341; *infra*, para. 1.42.
99 Except that he might then be guilty of an attempt: *infra*, para. 1.189.
1 At p. 556.

"The opening words of section 5(3) clearly look to the time of the creation of or the acceptance of the obligation by the bailee and not to the time of performance by him of the obligation so created and accepted by him." [2]

But this interpretation is by no means inevitable. The subsection could equally be construed as requiring that the defendant must be under the obligation at the time when the property is alleged to belong to another, *i.e.* (because it is the only time at which that question is relevant) at the time of the dishonest appropriation. This interpretation is supported by *Brewster*,[3] where it appeared that the appellant's initial obligation to his clients in respect of money received on their account might have been discharged by the clients' agreement to his treating the money as his own. It was held that it was for the jury to decide whether the clients had in fact agreed to abandon their rights in this respect. The court apparently assumed that there could be no conviction if the obligation no longer existed at the time of the dishonest appropriation. It is submitted with respect that the assumption was right.

1.37 *Content of the obligation.* The obligation which must exist, before section 5(3) can come into play, is an obligation to retain and deal with the property received, or with its proceeds, in a particular way. It is not sufficient if the obligation is merely to account for the value of the property or (where the property is money) for an equivalent sum, as in the case of a fiduciary who dishonestly makes a secret profit:[4] there must be "an obligation to keep in existence a separate fund".[5] If the defendant is not required to deal with any specific property in a particular way, it cannot be unlawful for him to deal with any particular property in some other way. Thus in *Hall*[6] the subsection was held not to apply to a travel agent who had accepted payment for air tickets but failed either to provide the tickets or to refund the money: he was of course under an obligation to provide the tickets, but not to preserve a separate fund for that purpose. Subject to the law of bankruptcy,[7] he was entitled to use the money in any way he chose.

1.38 On the other hand there need not be an obligation to preserve the original property *in specie*: an obligation to retain and deal with the *proceeds* of that property is enough. The subsection may apply to a sum of money even though the recipient is expected to put it in a bank account. Nor does it matter that he is entitled to put it in his own account rather

2   At p. 555.
3   (1979) 69 Cr.App.R. 375.
4   *Attorney-General's Reference (No. 1 of 1985)* [1986] Q.B. 491; *supra*, para. 1.23.
5   *Robertson* [1977] Crim.L.R. 629, *per* Judge Rubin Q.C.
6   [1973] Q.B. 126.
7   Insolvency Act 1985 ch. VII.

than a separate one.[8] In *Davidge v. Bunnett*[9] the appellant had been convicted of stealing money entrusted to her by her flat-mates for the purpose of paying the gas bill. It was held that the money belonged to the others by virtue of section 5(3), although the appellant would have been entitled to pay it into her own bank account (had she had one) and to pay the bill with her own cheque. Her obligation in that event would presumably have been to ensure that the bill was paid within a reasonable time and that until then the account remained in credit at least to the extent of her flat-mates' contributions—thus keeping the fund in existence, albeit as an unidentifiable part of the larger fund represented by the credit balance. If, like Hall, she had been entitled to draw on the account for her own purposes so as to reduce the balance below the sum contributed by the others, or to pay that sum into an account which was already overdrawn so that the fund would be automatically depleted, it would seem that section 5(3) could not have applied.

1.39 *Incidence of the obligation.* Whether or not the required obligation exists in any particular case is of course a matter of civil law. Such an obligation may be imposed by the general law: thus it was argued (unsuccessfully) in *D.P.P. v. Huskinson*[10] that a recipient of housing benefit was legally obliged to use it directly for the payment of rent. The question turned solely on the construction of the legislation under which the benefit was paid. More often the property will have been received by the defendant under an agreement between himself and the person from whom (or on whose account)[11] he receives it, and the extent of his obligations will then depend on the terms of that agreement. In the absence of other evidence as to the parties' intentions, the crucial factor is likely to be the nature of the relationship existing between them. Property transferred between parties dealing at arm's length, *e.g.* as an advance payment for goods or services, will normally become the property of the transferee to treat as his own even if it is given to him for a specific purpose such as the purchase of necessary equipment, unless there is a clear understanding that he is obliged to use it for that purpose and that purpose alone.[12] But if the transferee is in a fiduciary position *vis-à-vis* the transferor, and the property is transferred to him for a specific purpose of the transferor's, it will be easy to infer that he has undertaken a legal obligation to use it for that purpose—in other words, that he holds it in his capacity as a fiduciary. This situation must be distinguished from

8   *Banyard and Lacey* [1958] Crim.L.R. 49; *Yule* [1964] 1 Q.B. 5.
9   [1984] Crim.L.R. 297.
10 [1988] Crim.L.R. 620.
11 Or both, in which case the necessary obligation may be imposed by either. This point was apparently overlooked in *Lewis v. Lethbridge* [1987] Crim.L.R. 59.
12 *Jones* (1948) 33 Cr.App.R. 11; *cf. Hughes* [1956] Crim.L.R. 835.

that of the fiduciary who abuses his position so as to obtain property from a third party on his own account, and who is therefore liable to account for it to his principal. Section 5(3) has no application here, because the fiduciary has received the property neither from the principal nor on his account; nor does he hold it in his capacity as fiduciary.[13]

Property got by another's mistake

1.40 Section 5(4) provides:

"Where a person gets property by another's mistake, and is under an obligation to make restoration (in whole or in part) of the property or its proceeds or of the value thereof, then to the extent of that obligation the property or proceeds shall be regarded (as against him) as belonging to the person entitled to restoration, and an intention not to make restoration shall be regarded accordingly as an intention to deprive that person of the property or proceeds."

The main objective of the subsection was to reverse the controversial decision in *Moynes v. Cooper*,[14] where a wages clerk inadvertently paid an employee his wages in full although he had already received some of them in advance. The employee was held not to have stolen the money by dishonestly keeping it on discovering the mistake, because it became his money when he received it. Under section 5(4) it would be deemed still to belong to his employer, and the Court of Appeal has confirmed that he could now be convicted of theft.[15]

Mistake

1.41 The first requirement for the application of section 5(4), that the defendant should get property "by another's mistake", is self-explanatory. The nature of the mistake appears to be immaterial, provided of course that it is sufficient to generate the obligation to make restoration which is the second requirement. It is not necessary that the defendant should be aware of the mistake at the time when he acquires the property, provided that he has discovered it before the time of the appropriation relied upon; nor is it necessary that he should have contributed towards it. If he has *deliberately* contributed to it, by misrepresentation or otherwise, he will be guilty of a deception and should be charged accordingly[16]—thus avoiding the difficult issue of whether section 5(4) applies to such a case.[17]

13 *Attorney-General's Reference (No. 1 of 1985)* [1986] Q.B. 491; *supra*, para. 1.31.
14 [1956] 1 Q.B. 439.
15 *Attorney-General's Reference (No. 1 of 1983)* [1985] Q.B. 182; *infra*, para. 1.44.
16 *Infra*, ch. 2.
17 *Infra*, paras. 1.56 ff.

Obligation to make restoration

1.42   *Nature of the obligation.* The second prerequisite for the application
of section 5(4) is that the mistake must result in the defendant being under
an obligation to make restoration. As in the case of the obligation
required by section 5(3), it is clear that this obligation must be binding
in law and not just in honour. In *Gilks*[18] the appellant's bookmaker had
inadvertently paid him more than he had actually won. He kept the
money. There is an obvious similarity between these facts and those of
Moynes v. Cooper,[19] for which section 5(4) was primarily designed, and
it was argued that by virtue of the subsection the money still belonged to
the bookmaker. The argument was rejected.[20] The appellant may or may
not have been morally bound to return the money but he was not *legally*
obliged to do so, because wagering transactions are legally unenforceable
and the court will not examine the state of accounts between a bookmaker
and his client.[21] In the absence of an obligation binding in law, section
5(4) could have no application.

1.43   *Content of the obligation.* The obligation which must exist in order
to bring section 5(4) into play is an obligation to make restoration, in
whole or in part, of the property obtained *or* of its proceeds *or* of its
value. It is this third possibility which gives the subsection its importance.
If the mistake results in the defendant being obliged to make restoration
of the very property originally obtained, or of any property identifiable
as the proceeds of that property, a dishonest appropriation of that
property or its proceeds with intent to evade that obligation is itself an
infringement of another person's rights in respect of the property; it is
therefore not surprising that it should be treated as theft. Indeed, such a
case would normally fall within section 5(3). But section 5(4) goes further:
unlike section 5(3), its application is not confined to trustees and other
fiduciaries. Although it requires the defendant to be under a legal
obligation in consequence of his acquisition of the property by another's
mistake, this need only be an obligation to make restoration of the
property's *value*, as against an obligation to deal with the property itself
(or even its proceeds) in a particular way. Provided that he gets the
property by another's mistake, and is therefore obliged to make
restoration of its value, it is deemed to belong to the person entitled to
such restoration; the defendant will therefore be stealing it if he
dishonestly appropriates it (or its proceeds)[22] with the intention not to

18   [1972] 1 W.L.R. 1341.
19   [1956] 1 Q.B. 439; *supra*, para. 1.40.
20   But the appeal was dismissed on other grounds: *infra*, para. 1.54.
21   *Morgan v. Ashcroft* [1938] 1 K.B. 49.
22   It is arguable that the *proceeds* of the property originally obtained belong to another
     only if there is an obligation to make restoration of those proceeds, *i.e.* not just of the
     property's value; but this construction is perhaps somewhat strained.

make restoration. It is immaterial that as a matter of civil law he commits no wrong in keeping it but only in failing to pay for it, or that the property which he steals is property which the civil law regards as his to deal with as he will.

1.44 The startling implications of section 5(4) were demonstrated in *Attorney-General's Reference (No. 1 of 1983)*,[23] where the facts were essentially similar to those of *Moynes v. Cooper*[24] in that the defendant's employers had inadvertently paid her a sum of money by way of wages to which she was not in fact entitled, and which she kept after discovering the error. There was a difference in that in this case the wages were paid not in cash but by direct transfer into the defendant's bank account, but this did not affect the result. The effect of the credit to the defendant's account (assuming that the account was not overdrawn) was that the bank's indebtedness to her was increased by the amount thus credited. This additional debt was an item of intangible property and was therefore capable of being stolen.[25] As a matter of civil law it was, despite the mistake, property belonging to the defendant herself and to no-one else;[26] but it was property acquired by her as a result of another's mistake, and, though not obliged to restore the property itself or its proceeds, she was under an obligation to make restoration of its value—in other words, to repay an equivalent sum. Therefore, by virtue of section 5(4), her right to claim the sum in question from her bank was deemed to be property belonging to her employers; therefore, had it been proved that she had dishonestly appropriated that property, she could have been convicted of stealing it. The conclusion is inevitable but nonetheless remarkable. The defendant's conduct in retaining the money was not an interference with any proprietary right still vested in her employers,[27] but simply a failure to pay a debt. It may be doubted whether there was any pressing need to bring such conduct within the criminal law, and indeed the court expressed the view that in such circumstances it might well be inappropriate to prosecute.

1.45 This is not to say that the subsection turns the mere non-payment of such a debt into theft: all it does is to create a legal fiction that the property obtained and its proceeds[28] belong to the person entitled to restoration, and that the intention not to make restoration is an intention

23 [1985] Q.B. 182.
24 [1956] 1 Q.B. 439; *supra*, para. 1.40.
25 *Supra*, para. 1.12.
26 Assuming she was not a trustee of it: *cf. infra*, para. 1.50.
27 Subject to n. 26, *supra*.
28 Subject to n. 22, *supra*.

to deprive him of it. It must in addition be proved that the defendant
dishonestly appropriated the property or its proceeds, *i.e.* that he
dishonestly[29] assumed a right to it by keeping it or dealing with it as
owner.[30] He will not have done so if he has already disposed of it, and of
any proceeds, before he realises the mistake. Since his fault (if any) lies
not in anything done to the property itself but rather in his decision not
to repay its value, it is hard to see why it should make any difference
whether the property or its proceeds are still in his hands when he reaches
that decision. But such anomalies are bound to result if what is really no
more than the evasion of a personal liability is treated as theft.

1.46 *Obligations in quasi-contract.* Different kinds of mistake on the part
of a transferor of property can give rise to a bewildering variety of legal
consequences, which may or may not include an obligation on the part
of the transferee to make restoration either of the property itself or of its
proceeds or its value.[31] Perhaps the most important of these possibilities
for present purposes (in that it is arguably the only case where reliance
on section 5(4) is both necessary and possible) is that of liability under
the law of quasi-contract, which (*inter alia*) requires a person to pay for
property transferred to him by mistake if he would otherwise be unjustly
enriched. The obligation thus imposed is an obligation to make
"restoration" (*i.e.* restitution)[32] of the property's value (or, where the
property is money, of an equivalent sum). The property itself, and any
proceeds thereof, will therefore be deemed to belong to the transferor by
virtue of section 5(4). This is not to say that the subsection will come into
play whenever property is transferred by mistake. In every such case the
transferee will have been enriched if he is not required to pay for the
property; whether that enrichment would be "unjust" is another matter.
The question is not simply whether it would be in some sense unfair for
him to keep the property for nothing, but whether the circumstances (and
in particular the nature of the mistake) bring the case within the category
of situations in which the common law permits recovery. The notion of
unjust enrichment is not in fact a *test* of liability at all, but only another
way of expressing the conclusion that restitution is available in a
particular case. But the point is largely academic. In practice almost any
mistake which induces one person to transfer property to another will
give rise to a claim in quasi-contract, at any rate if the recipient discovers

---

29 In view of the clear intention that the subsection should cover the evasion of liability
    in restitution, dishonesty is presumably not negated in this context by the mere fact
    that the defendant's conduct is not itself unlawful as a matter of civil law: *infra*, para.
    1.159.
30 s. 3(1); *infra*, para. 1.104.
31 See Glanville Williams, "Mistake in the Law of Theft" [1977] C.L.J. 62.
32 *Attorney-General's Reference (No. 1 of 1983)* [1985] Q.B. 182 at p. 189.

the mistake while he still has the property or its proceeds—as he must if there is to be any question of his stealing them.

1.47 Where the property transferred by mistake is money, the person paying it is *prima facie* entitled to claim repayment of an equivalent sum by means of an action for money had and received.[33] It is sometimes said that the mistake must be as to a "fundamental" or "essential" fact,[34] but this terminology is somewhat misleading because the expression "fundamental mistake" is usually reserved for the sort of mistake which has the effect of nullifying a transaction altogether. Where money is paid under the latter type of mistake (*e.g.* a mistake of identity) the payee does not acquire ownership of it and can therefore be convicted of stealing it without reference to section 5(4);[35] but even if the mistake is less drastic he may still be liable in quasi-contract to repay an equivalent amount, and in that case the money will continue to belong to the payer by virtue of section 5(4). Thus the defendant in *Moynes v. Cooper*[36] would now be guilty of theft.[37] For this purpose it is enough if the payment was made in consequence of a misapprehension on the part of the payer as to some circumstance which was material to him and which the payee knew (or should have known) to be material.[38] In principle it ought to be sufficient if the misapprehension is only *one* of the reasons for making the payment, and not necessarily the main one.[39] The money need not have been paid under the impression that it is legally due,[40] though this will almost certainly be sufficient. The reason for the "almost" is that on one view a mistake of *law* is not enough,[41] at any rate where the payee is unaware of the mistake at the time of receiving the money.[42] But it may be that where a mistake of law is treated as being insufficient it is really on the grounds that the money is paid by way of submission to an honest claim—*i.e.* the payer takes the risk that his interpretation of the law may be wrong.[43]

---

33 *Kelly v. Solari* (1841) 9 M. & W. 54.
34 *Morgan v. Ashcroft* [1938] 1 K.B. 49 at p. 77, *per* Scott L.J.; *Norwich Union Fire Insurance Society Ltd v. William H. Price Ltd* [1934] A.C. 455 at p. 463, *per* Lord Wright; *Attorney-General's Reference (No. 1 of 1983)* [1985] Q.B. 182 at p. 189.
35 *Infra*, paras. 1.52 ff.
36 [1956] 1 Q.B. 439; *supra*, para. 1.40.
37 *Attorney-General's Reference (No. 1 of 1983)* [1985] Q.B. 182.
38 *Kleinwort, Sons & Co. v. Dunlop Rubber Co.* (1907) 97 L.T. 263; *Kerrison v. Glyn, Mills, Currie & Co.* (1911) 81 L.J.K.B. 465; *R. E. Jones Ltd v. Waring & Gillow Ltd* [1926] A.C. 670; *Colonial Bank v. Exchange Bank of Yarmouth, Nova Scotia* (1885) 11 App.Cas. 84; Goff and Jones, *The Law of Restitution* (3rd ed.) p. 89.
39 *Cf. infra*, para. 2.28 (deception), *Barton v. Armstrong* [1976] A.C. 104 (duress).
40 *Barclays Bank Ltd v. W. J. Simms Son & Cooke (Southern) Ltd* [1980] Q.B. 677.
41 *Bilbie v. Lumley* (1802) 2 East 469.
42 *Ward & Co. v. Wallis* [1900] 1 Q.B. 675 at p. 678, *per* Kennedy J. He must of course discover the mistake at some stage if his keeping of the money is to be dishonest.
43 Goff and Jones, *op. cit.* ch. 4.

1.48   There is one possible difficulty in applying section 5(4) to money
paid under a mistake of fact. It has been said that a person who pays
money under such a mistake must make a demand for repayment before
commencing an action to recover the money, because until he makes such
a demand he has no cause of action in quasi-contract.[44] If this were so it
would follow that the recipient who dishonestly keeps the money before
the payer has even discovered the mistake, let alone demanded the money
back, would not yet be under an obligation to make restoration. But
section 5(4) refers to a person who *is* under such an obligation, not a
person who may subsequently incur one.[45] This interpretation would drive
a coach and horses through the subsection, which is obviously not
intended to apply only where the recipient refuses to repay the money
after the mistake has been discovered and a demand for repayment
made.[46] It is submitted that even if the defendant is not technically liable
to repay the money until it is demanded, he is nevertheless under an
obligation to make restoration within the meaning of section 5(4).

1.49   Where the property transferred by mistake is something other than
money, and the mistake is not "fundamental" in the sense of nullifying
the transfer altogether (in which case there is no need to invoke section
5(4)),[47] the transferor may be able to claim its value by way of the
quasi-contractual action of *quantum valebat*. Direct authority is lacking,
but it is likely that the obligation to make restoration will be imposed
whenever the mistake has induced the transferor to make the transfer and
the transferee has become aware of the mistake while he still has the
property or its proceeds.[48]

1.50   *Obligations under trusts.* The law of quasi-contract is not, however,
the only source of restitutionary obligations. An alternative ground of
liability was established in *Shadrokh-Cigari*,[49] where the appellant had
been convicted of stealing certain banker's drafts issued in his favour on
an account in the name of his ward. The drafts would not have been
issued had the account not been accidentally credited with a payment of
£286,000 instead of £286. It was held, following the decision of Goulding
J. in *Chase Manhattan Bank N.A. v. Israel-British Bank (London) Ltd*,[50]
that because of the mistake the bank issuing the drafts retained an

44   *Freeman v. Jeffries* (1869) L.R. 4 Ex. 189, *per* Martin and Bramwell BB.
45   *Cf.* the argument that the subsection does not apply to property to which the defendant
       has acquired a voidable title which has not yet been rescinded: *infra*, para. 1.58.
46   Indeed it is debatable whether it does apply in such a case: an open refusal, inviting
       challenge by legal action, is arguably not dishonest.
47   *Infra*, paras. 1.52 ff.
48   Goff and Jones, *op. cit.*, pp. 150 f.
49   [1988] Crim.L.R. 465.
50   [1981] Ch. 105.

equitable interest in them. Therefore they did belong to another although they were issued to the appellant. If these decisions are correct, they would seem at first sight to render section 5(4) redundant: the mistaken transferor apparently retains an equitable interest in the property transferred, in which case it still belongs to him by virtue of section 5(1), and it is unnecessary to invoke section 5(4). But the court recognised in *Shadrokh-Cigari* that section 5(4) would also apply, since the appellant was under an obligation to make restoration of the drafts or their proceeds or value. There is no obvious advantage for the prosecution in showing that the property literally belongs to another, as against being deemed to do so: if the defendant is clearly liable in quasi-contract, thus bringing the case within section 5(4), there seems little purpose in attempting to establish that he is a trustee as well. Only where the property is not obtained "by another's mistake" does the possibility of a trust become significant.

1.51 There is, moreover, a difficulty in applying the trust concept to facts such as those of *Shadrokh-Cigari* itself. The value of the drafts lay in the rights which they conferred upon the appellant—rights against the issuing bank. The bank could not of course own rights against itself, either at law or in equity. The only property in which it could have retained an equitable interest was the documents representing those rights, not the rights themselves. If the charge is properly to reflect the gravamen of what has been done, it must relate to the rights rather than the documents; and the rights cannot belong to another under section 5(1) but only under section 5(4). In *Davis*[51] the Court of Appeal professed itself unable to understand how the rights conferred on the appellant by a cheque issued to him in error could have been stolen by him, with or without the help of section 5(4); but it is not clear why the court thought that the subsection makes no difference. It has been argued that section 5(4) can have no more application than section 5(1), because the person conferring the rights cannot be entitled to "restoration" of rights which he never had in the first place.[52] But section 5(4) envisages the "restoration" not only of the property itself but also of its proceeds and its value, neither of which will previously have belonged to the person to whom the subsection deems the property and its proceeds to belong. It is submitted that in this situation, if in no other, section 5(4) applies where section 5(1) does not.

1.52 *Fundamental mistake.* Another situation where it may not be strictly necessary to invoke section 5(4) (though it will usually apply) is

51 [1988] Crim.L.R. 762.
52 J. C. Smith, [1988] Crim.L.R. at p. 467.

that in which the mistake made by the person transferring the property to the defendant is "fundamental" in the narrowest sense of the word: *i.e.* its effect is that the transferor retains not only the beneficial ownership of the property but the legal title as well. The attempted transfer of ownership is completely void. The property therefore continues to belong to the transferor in every sense; but since the transferee is obviously under an obligation to return it (*i.e.* he will otherwise be liable in the tort of conversion), the prosecution will normally have little incentive to try to bring such a case within section 5(1) rather than section 5(4). Precisely what kinds of mistake the civil law regards as fundamental in this sense is far from clear. Broadly speaking a mistake as to the identity of the transferee is sufficient, but a mistake as to his attributes is not. In other words it is sufficient if A intends to transfer property to B and transfers it to C by mistake,[53] but not if he actually intends to transfer it to C—even if he intends to do so only because he wrongly believes that C has some or all of the attributes of B.[54] Similarly a transfer of property X is void if the transferor intended to transfer property Y instead.[55]

1.53 In the context of the criminal law, however, the concept of fundamental mistake has been stretched a good deal further. In *Williams (Jean-Jacques)*[56] it was held that a schoolboy who knowingly exchanged obsolete foreign banknotes at a bureau de change was guilty of stealing the proceeds, because as a result of the cashier's mistake the proceeds never became the appellant's property at all. The reasoning is arguably open to criticism in more than one respect. In the first place it is doubtful whether a sale of goods can be rendered completely void merely because the buyer is mistaken as to the attributes of the goods, even if his mistake is such that he thinks they are something essentially different from what they actually are. In *Bell v. Lever Brothers Ltd*[57] the House of Lords thought that this might be the effect if such a misapprehension were shared by both parties, but apparently not if one of them knew the truth.[58] On the other hand it is hard to see why in principle this should make any difference. On the contrary, if the effect of declaring the sale void is to release the buyer from a bad bargain, the argument for such a result would seem stronger where the seller knows that the buyer is mistaken than when he does not. But even if the agreement was void, it does not

53 *Cundy v. Lindsay* (1878) 3 App.Cas. 459.
54 *Lewis v. Averay* [1972] 1 Q.B. 198.
55 *Lancs and Yorks Railway Co. v. MacNicoll* (1918) 118 L.T. 596; *The Nordborg* [1939] P. 121 at p. 126.
56 [1980] Crim.L.R. 589.
57 [1932] A.C. 167.
58 The fact that the seller knows the buyer is mistaken about the goods does not in itself invalidate the sale if the mistake is not fundamental: *Smith v. Hughes* (1871) L.R. 6 Q.B. 597.

follow that the payment of the price was also void. The cashier intended
to pass the ownership of the money to the appellant. There was no
mistake about the money he was paying or the person to whom he was
paying it. The appellant may have been liable to repay the money, but
the conclusion that it never became his money at all is hard to accept.

1.54 The point was not crucial in *Williams* because if the appellant *was*
liable to repay the money, and dishonestly kept it, he was guilty of theft
by virtue of section 5(4); there was no need to assert that he never *owned*
the money. In *Gilks*,[59] however, this conclusion was essential to the
dismissal of the appeal. The appellant had kept money paid to him in
error by his bookmaker. It was held that section 5(4) did not apply
because any obligation to return the money was binding on the appellant
in honour only and not in law,[60] but that this was immaterial because the
mistake invalidated the payment altogether and the money was therefore
still the bookmaker's. These two conclusions are not easy to reconcile: if
the money was still the bookmaker's, the appellant must surely have been
under a legal obligation to give it back. His refusal to do so would be a
conversion.[61] But it is submitted with respect that the court was wrong in
holding that the money did still belong to the bookmaker. His mistake
was not as to the appellant's identity or as to the money being paid out,
but over the amount which the appellant had won and to which he was
in honour (though not in law) entitled. The Court of Appeal had
previously held in the civil case of *Morgan v. Ashcroft*,[62] which *Gilks*
purported to follow, that there are two reasons why an inadvertent
over-payment on the part of a bookmaker is irrecoverable: firstly that the
court will not take an account as between the parties to a wagering
transaction, and secondly that a payment under an unenforceable
agreement is regarded in the eyes of the law as a voluntary payment.[63] It
would seem to follow from the latter ground that the bookmaker's
mistake does not prevent the ownership of the money from passing to the
payee. As authority for the proposition that it does, the court which
decided *Gilks* relied on the old criminal case of *Middleton*;[64] but that case
did concern a mistake of identity, and the money was handed over under
the impression that the recipient was legally entitled to it.

1.55 The point of general principle decided by *Gilks* is that if the
defendant has obtained the property in question by another's mistake,

59 [1972] 1 W.L.R. 1341.
60 *Supra*, para. 1.42.
61 See Glanville Williams [1977] C.L.J. at p. 73.
62 [1938] 1 K.B. 49.
63 For this interpretation of the second *ratio* see *Barclays Bank Ltd v. W. J. Simms, Son & Cooke (Southern) Ltd* [1980] Q.B. 677 at p. 698, *per* Robert Goff J.
64 (1873) L.R. 2 C.C.R. 38.

but for some reason is not under a legal obligation to make restoration
and is therefore not caught by section 5(4), the prosecution may
nevertheless fall back on section 5(1) if the mistake is so fundamental as
to prevent the ownership of the property from passing—in other words,
that a person in possession of another's property may be guilty of stealing
it even if the law requires him neither to return it nor to pay for it. This
proposition is itself questionable;[65] its application to the facts of the case,
doubly so. Section 5(4) is drafted in extremely wide terms, with the result
that property obtained by another's mistake generally *will* be caught by
it. If even section 5(4) is not wide enough to serve the purpose, a case
would need to be quite exceptional (more so, it is submitted, than *Gilks*)
for section 5(1) to be available as an alternative. The rule of thumb for
the prosecutor in such a case is, or should be, that it is section 5(4) or
nothing.

1.56 *Voidable transfers.* A less drastic effect of a mistake on the part of
a transferor of property is that the title conferred on the transferee,
though valid for the time being, is voidable at the instance of the
transferor. A common example is that of property sold under a contract
which is voidable for misrepresentation, fraudulent or otherwise, or for
breach of a duty of disclosure. Provided that he acts promptly, and before
the property has been sold or pledged to an innocent third party,[66] the
seller may rescind the contract by giving notice to the buyer (or, if the
buyer has gone to ground, to an appropriate body such as the police).[67]
The effect of a valid rescission is that the contract is avoided *ab initio* and
title to the property reverts to the seller. For the purposes of the law of
theft we must therefore distinguish between an appropriation of the
property by the transferee after the rescission and an appropriation while
the contract is still on foot.

1.57 At first sight the position after the contract has been rescinded is
simple: the property once again belongs to the seller, so that an
appropriation of it by the buyer (such as a resale to a third party) can
amount to theft.[68] The difficulty is that the seller may have succeeded in
rescinding the contract without notifying the buyer, *e.g.* by reporting the
fraud to the police. In that case the buyer will not know that the property
is no longer his; and in general the law of theft requires not only that the
property appropriated should in fact belong to someone other than the

---

65   *Infra*, paras. 1.154 ff.
66   Sale of Goods Act 1979 s. 23.
67   *Car and Universal Finance Co. Ltd v. Caldwell* [1965] 1 Q.B. 525.
68   Conversely an appropriation by the seller, after regaining possession, would not:
     Walker [1984] Crim.L.R. 112.

defendant, but that the defendant should realise that it does.[69] One
solution would be to argue that the fraudulent buyer presumably expects
the seller to retain some sort of claim to the property, and that he should
not escape liability merely because he is unfamiliar with the finer points
of the law of contract. Alternatively the prosecution might point out that
he must have realised that the seller *might* have gone to the police by the
time of the appropriation relied upon. He may not appreciate the legal
significance of the seller's going to the police; but on principle it ought to
be sufficient if he either knows that certain events have occurred, as a
result of which (though he need not know this) the property now belongs
to another, or if he at least realises that those events *may* have occurred.
Recklessness, in the sense of the actual awareness of a possibility, ought
to be enough.

1.58 A more difficult question is that of whether property obtained
under a voidable contract is property belonging to the person from whom
it is obtained even *before* he rescinds the contract. Since at this stage he
has neither title nor possession nor control, the only basis on which it
might be said that the property belongs to him is section 5(4). Can it be
said that the transferee "is under an obligation to make restoration . . .
of the property or its proceeds or of the value thereof"? Strictly speaking
he is under no such obligation unless and until the contract is rescinded.
If he is guilty of fraud he is of course liable to the transferor in the tort
of deceit; but his liability under that head is to pay compensation for the
transferor's loss, not to make restoration of the property or its proceeds
or value. He is not obliged to do the latter unless and until the transferor
asks him to. To put it at its highest he is under a potential or contingent
obligation, which is only another way of saying that he is not under an
obligation yet. This view is to some extent supported by *Kaur v. Chief
Constable for Hampshire*,[70] where the appellant had bought a pair of shoes
in a manner which arguably amounted to fraud. Her conviction of theft
was quashed. It was said that section 5(4) did not apply because she was
not under any obligation to make restoration of the shoes at the moment
when she picked them up after paying for them: even if the contract of
sale was voidable, it had not yet been avoided.[71] In *Morris*[72] Lord Roskill
said that he thought *Kaur* had probably been wrongly decided, but it is
not clear why. The decision seems entirely consistent with the reasoning
in *Morris*.[73] It cannot be assumed that in Lord Roskill's view section 5(4)
should have been applied.

69 *Infra*, para. 1.149.
70 [1981] 1 W.L.R. 578.
71 At p. 584.
72 [1984] A.C. 320 at p. 334.
73 *Infra*, para. 1.82.

1.59 We have seen, however, that in certain circumstances a mistake on the part of a transferor gives him a claim in quasi-contract against the transferee, so that the latter is under an obligation to make restoration of the property's value, and section 5(4) comes into play.[74] This must be so even if there is technically no liability in quasi-contract until payment is demanded, because otherwise the subsection would be toothless.[75] If, on the other hand, it does *not* come into play where the property is transferred under a contract which the mistake renders voidable, a difficult question arises. If the circumstances are such that the transferor's mistake *would* have given rise to liability in quasi-contract (and thus triggered section 5(4)) had it induced him to transfer the property without entering into a contract (*e.g.* because he wrongly supposed that he was legally obliged to transfer it), is the operation of the subsection excluded because he does enter into a contract? It is one thing to say that the subsection does not catch property *merely* because it has been transferred under a voidable contract; to say that the very existence of such a contract *precludes* reliance on the subsection, when it would otherwise apply, is perhaps another. The existence or otherwise of a contract, particularly a voidable one, hardly affects the culpability of the defendant's conduct one way or the other. Admittedly it would seem that the availability of the contractual remedy of rescission leaves no room for liability in quasi-contract, and the wording of section 5(4) clearly includes the latter but apparently not the former. Since it is hard to justify the subsection's presence in the Act at all, there is something to be said for confining it to cases falling squarely within its terms. But a distinction between contractual and non-contractual transfers would seem equally indefensible, and is unlikely to have been intended.

Corporations sole

1.60 Section 5(5) provides:

"Property of a corporation sole shall be regarded as belonging to the corporation notwithstanding a vacancy in the corporation."

Wild creatures

1.61 Wild creatures, tamed or untamed, are regarded as property for the purposes of the Act and can therefore be stolen.[76] But they can be stolen only in certain circumstances, and the effect of these restrictions (though this is not how the Act expresses it) is that the requirement that

74 *Supra*, para. 1.40.
75 *Supra*, para. 1.48.
76 s. 4(4).

the property should "belong to another" is stricter in the case of wild creatures and their carcases than for other forms of property. The object is to ensure that poaching, which is adequately dealt with by other legislation,[77] does not amount to theft as well. Section 4(4) provides:

> ". . . a person cannot steal a wild creature not tamed nor ordinarily kept in captivity, or the carcase of any such creature, unless either it has been reduced into possession by or on behalf of another person and possession of it has not since been lost or abandoned, or another person is in course of reducing it into possession."

Wild creatures at large do not belong to anyone in any sense, but when taken they become the property of the landowner.[78] In the absence of provision to the contrary, a poacher would therefore be guilty of theft as soon as he first appropriated the creature after the initial taking. Section 4(4) excludes that possibility. In effect if not in terms, it provides that a wild creature (or its carcase) does not belong to another merely because that other has a proprietary interest in it, which would normally suffice by virtue of section 5(1). It can be stolen only in four situations, all of them essentially variations on the theme of possession or control: *viz.* where

(*a*) the creature is or was tamed (whether or not kept in captivity);
(*b*) the creature is or was ordinarily kept in captivity (even if still wild, and even if not in captivity at the time of the appropriation);
(*c*) the creature or its carcase is in the possession of another (even a trespasser), provided that
    (i) that other acquired possession of it *either* by himself reducing (*i.e.* taking) it into possession *or* by someone else's doing so on his behalf (*e.g.* not if it has been abandoned on his land by a trespasser), and
    (ii) he has not since then lost or abandoned possession; or
(*d*) the creature or its carcase is in the course of being reduced into possession by another.

1.62 But it must be repeated that section 4(4) is not expressed as an exception to the terms of section 5: it represents an additional requirement. In other words a wild creature, or the carcase of a wild creature, which technically belongs to another under section 5(1) nevertheless cannot be stolen unless it falls within one of the four categories above; but on the other hand it is not sufficient that the creature does fall within one of those categories if it does not also fall within section 5, because property cannot be stolen unless it belongs to another. A creature which

---

77 *Infra*, paras. 7.72 ff.
78 *Blades v. Higgs* (1865) 11 H.L.Cas. 621.

is in the course of being reduced into possession by another person, for example, is not yet *in* that person's possession. If it is not in his control either, and no-one has a proprietary interest in it, the requirements of section 5 may not be satisfied. In that case the question whether the additional requirements of section 4(4) are satisfied becomes academic.

Appropriation

Ordinary meaning and extended meaning

1.63 The property in question must be "appropriated" by the defendant. The *Oxford English Dictionary* defines "appropriate" as "to take for one's own, to take to oneself". An appropriation of property in the ordinary sense would therefore involve taking possession of it, or obtaining ownership of it, or otherwise dealing with it in such a way as to deprive its owner of it and to make it effectively one's own. But section 3(1) of the Theft Act 1968 begins by giving the word an extended meaning:

"Any assumption by a person of the rights of an owner amounts to an appropriation . . ."

With one possible exception which is discussed below,[79] this phrase would seem wide enough to cover any act falling within the word's ordinary meaning: its importance lies in the possibility that it may include others too. We shall examine two examples of conduct which, though not an appropriation in the ordinary sense, may arguably be caught by section 3(1): firstly an act which infringes the owner's rights over his property without itself depriving him of it, and secondly an act which does not infringe his rights at all.

Acts not depriving the owner of the property

1.64 Section 3(1), at first sight straightforward enough, proves on closer examination to be regrettably obscure. The "rights of an owner" presumably include all the rights conferred on an owner by virtue of his ownership—the right to possess the property, to use it, to dispose of it, to damage or destroy it, and so on. Obviously one cannot do all these things at once. What then is an "assumption" of the rights of an owner? Does the expression refer only to what might be loosely described as an assumption of *all* the rights of an owner—*i.e.* an act which itself deprives the owner of his property and makes it *de facto* that of the defendant? If so, it is no more than a restatement of the ordinary meaning of the word "appropriate". Or does it extend to an "assumption" of *any* of the rights of an owner—*i.e.* to any act which, on the part of an owner, would constitute an exercise of any of those rights? On this latter view an

79 Paras. 1.73 ff.

appropriation of property need not itself have the effect of depriving the property's owner of it, though it would not of course amount to theft unless done with the intention of depriving the owner at some stage.

1.65 The issue arose for consideration by the House of Lords in *Morris* and *Anderton v. Burnside*.[80] In each of these consolidated appeals the appellant had switched the price labels of two items on display in a supermarket with a view to buying the more expensive item for the price of the cheaper, and the question before the House was whether this was an appropriation for the purposes of a charge of theft. The defence argued that it was not caught by section 3(1), because a customer who switches price labels is not assuming *all* the rights of an owner over the more expensive item: he is not yet making it effectively his own, only preparing to obtain it by deception. It might be otherwise if he simply secreted it about his person in order to remove it without paying for it at all. On this view the opening words of section 3(1) would add little or nothing, since only an appropriation in the ordinary sense would qualify as an "assumption . . . of the rights of an owner". The House, while conceding that this construction might have some force if the phrase were read literally and out of context, held it to be inconsistent with expressions used elsewhere in the Act.[81]

> "It follows therefore that it is enough for the prosecution if they have proved in these cases the assumption by the defendants of *any* of the rights of the owner of the goods in question, that is to say, the supermarket concerned . . ."[82]

Therefore the appellants had been rightly convicted of theft, though the view was expressed that if (as in one of the cases before the House) the defendant is not apprehended until after he has paid the lower price at the check-out, it might be preferable "in the interests of simplicity" to charge an obtaining by deception instead.[83]

1.66 On the other hand their Lordships declined to take this reasoning to its logical conclusion. Only the supermarket staff, as agents of the owner, are entitled to alter the pricing of the goods on display; a customer who does so is presumably therefore "assuming" one of the rights of an

---

80 [1984] A.C. 320, hereinafter referred to simply as *Morris*.
81 *viz.* "any later assumption of a right" later in s. 3(1) (*infra*, para. 1.104); "no later assumption by him of rights" in s.3(2) (*infra*, para. 1.105); and s.2(1)(*a*), which provides that an appropriation of property belonging to another is not dishonest if done in the belief that the defendant has in law the right to deprive the other of it (*infra*, para. 1.144). The relevance of this last provision is, with respect, not apparent.
82 At p. 332, *per* Lord Roskill, with whose speech the remainder of their Lordships agreed. It should be noted however that s. 3(1) refers to the rights of *an* owner, not those of *the* owner.
83 At p. 335; see *infra*, ch. 2.

owner, in the sense that he is doing something which, if done by the owner or his agent, would be an exercise of one of those rights. If an assumption of *any* of the rights of an owner is sufficient, it would seem to follow that label-switching is *per se* an "assumption of the rights of an owner", and therefore an appropriation. But Lord Roskill (with whom the rest of their Lordships agreed) thought otherwise:

> ". . . if a shopper with some perverted sense of humour, intending only to create confusion and nothing more both for the supermarket and for other shoppers, switches labels, I do not think that that act of label switching alone is without more an appropriation, though it is not difficult to envisage some cases of dishonest label-switching which could be."[84]

In the cases before the House, his Lordship went on, the appropriation consisted not in the label-switching alone but in the combination of that act *and* the removal of the desired item from the shelf. He offered no explanation for this assertion, and it is hard to suggest one. Obviously the label-switching joker does not commit theft, but that is because he does not intend to deprive the supermarket of the goods and he is not dishonest; it is scarcely necessary to insist in addition that his act is not an appropriation. Moreover Lord Roskill's analysis fails to make it clear whether there is an appropriation even by a dishonest customer, who does intend to buy the more expensive item at the lower price, if he is arrested after switching the labels but before removing the more expensive item from the shelf. Is this one of the cases, which his Lordship thought it "not difficult to envisage", where an act of dishonest label-switching "could be" an appropriation in itself? But if so, why did the appellants in *Morris* appropriate the goods only by switching the labels *and* removing the goods from the shelves? If, as we have seen, the appropriation may be an assumption of *any* of the rights of an owner, and need not itself be the act which deprives the owner of his property, what is the additional significance of the removal from the shelf?

1.67 One possible explanation (ventured with no great confidence) is that, unlike the switching of the labels, the removal of the goods from the shelf is an overt and unequivocal demonstration of the defendant's intention to keep them for himself. This distinction is admittedly dubious: just as a customer *might* switch the labels in order to create confusion, so he *might* remove articles from the shelf in order to create confusion by hiding them or replacing them on the wrong shelves. Neither scenario is more obviously fanciful than the other. A more serious objection is that Lord Roskill himself went out of his way to reject the suggestion, made by Webster J. in *Eddy v. Niman*,[85] that appropriation must be an "overt"

---

84 At p. 332.
85 (1981) 73 Cr.App.R. 237 at p. 241.

act.[86] It is of course true that theft need not be "overt" in the literal sense of being public or unconcealed—on the contrary, it is usually committed in secret—but Webster J. was presumably using the word in its secondary sense, well established in the language of the criminal law,[87] to denote the outward (but not necessarily public) manifestations of criminal intent, as distinct from the mere formation of such intent in the defendant's mind. In this sense Lord Roskill would probably agree.[88] Perhaps, then, a possible interpretation of his reasoning is that an unauthorised interference with property (not amounting to an appropriation in the ordinary sense) is not in itself sufficient, even if the intention to deprive can be proved by other evidence; but it may be sufficient if *either* it is itself unequivocal evidence of that intention *or* it is accompanied by further acts which are. Pending further elucidation by the courts, however, this can be no more than speculation.

Acts not affecting the property
1.68 According to *Morris*, one effect of extending the concept of appropriation so as to include "any assumption . . . of the rights of an owner" is that an infringement of an owner's rights over his property can amount to an appropriation of the property even if the owner is not *ipso facto* deprived of it, though such an act cannot be theft unless accompanied by an intention to deprive him of it at some later stage. What is more debatable is whether even the extended meaning is wide enough to cover an act which, though it might loosely be described as an assumption of the rights of an owner, does not *infringe* the owner's rights in any way because it has no effect on his property. The point may indeed be academic: even if such an act can be an appropriation, it is suggested below that it ought not to be regarded as dishonest.[89] But if that argument is rejected there is still the question of whether such an act can be an appropriation. The most recent authorities suggest that it can; but it must be said that the implications of this view have scarcely been addressed.

1.69 In *Rogers v. Arnott*[90] the defendant, lawfully in possession of a tape-recorder belonging to another, had demonstrated it to a third party and offered to sell it to him. This was held to constitute the old offence of larceny by a bailee. Would it now amount to theft? It is questionable whether a mere offer to sell property, or for that matter a completed contract to do so, can fairly be described either as an appropriation in

86 At p. 334.
87 Especially in relation to the inchoate offences of attempt and conspiracy: see *Fraud* para. 12.48.
88 *Cf. infra*, para. 1.104.
89 Paras. 1.154 ff.
90 [1960] 2 Q.B. 244.

the ordinary sense or as an "assumption . . . of the rights of an owner". It is true that the right to sell property is one of the rights of an owner, and that a person who purports to sell another's property is in one sense "assuming" that right. On the other hand the phrase "the rights of an owner" is ambiguous. It might be construed as referring only to the *freedoms* conferred by ownership (*i.e.* the right to deal with the property without incurring liability to others) and not to the *powers* thereby conferred (*i.e.* the ability to alter the distribution of legal rights, *e.g.* by transferring ownership to another). *Morris* establishes that one can assume the rights of an owner by doing something which only the owner may lawfully do, *i.e.* by infringing his rights as an owner; to say that one can do so without infringing his rights at all, merely by purporting to exercise one of his powers, is another matter altogether. A purported sale of another's property, transferring neither possession nor ownership, is not an infringement of that person's rights,[91] and arguably therefore is not an "assumption . . . of the rights of an owner".

1.70 It should be noted that the case of *Pitham and Hehl*,[92] which at first sight appears to support the view that there is an appropriation in this situation, is clearly unsatisfactory whether that view be right or wrong. The appellants had entered a house and removed the furniture after a third man had purported to sell the furniture to them. They knew that he had no right to sell it, and they were clearly guilty of burglary,[93] but they were acquitted of burglary and convicted of handling instead. These convictions could be upheld only if the furniture had already been stolen before the appellants took it away; but upheld they were. The furniture was stolen, it was held, not when the appellants removed it but when the third man offered it to them, thus assuming the rights of an owner. This reasoning extends the concept of appropriation beyond anything previously suggested. Even if *Rogers v. Arnott* is still good law, it is distinguishable: the defendant in that case was making a genuine offer to sell the tape-recorder. He had no right to sell it, and this may indeed have been the basis on which he offered it,[94] but he did have a limited interest in it by virtue of his possession and he was offering to sell such interest as he had. In *Pitham* the third man had no greater interest in the furniture than the appellants did, and the purported purchase appears to have been no more than a payment for his assistance in bringing the furniture to their attention. They were not really buying it at all: they were stealing

91 *Lancashire Waggon Co. Ltd v. Fitzhugh* (1861) 6 H. & N. 502.
92 (1976) 65 Cr.App.R. 45.
93 *Infra*, paras. 7.02 ff.
94 The price asked was less than half of the tape recorder's real value. The prospective purchaser did in fact know that the defendant had no right to sell it (he was a police officer acting on a tip-off), but it is not clear whether the defendant knew that he knew.

it. The third man was no doubt an accessory to their theft, but to treat his offer as itself amounting to theft is to put form before substance. It is submitted with great respect that the case is wrongly decided.

1.71 If the facts of *Rogers v. Arnott* would now constitute theft, it presumably makes no difference whether the property in question is physically present at the scene of the offending transaction or is elsewhere[95] or has no physical existence at all,[96] provided that the defendant intends the owner to lose it permanently or can be deemed so to intend;[97] and recent authority does indeed suggest that the intangible property can be appropriated by an act which leaves the property (*i.e.* the owner's rights) entirely unaffected. This view was at first rejected in *Kohn*,[98] where a company director was held to have stolen the company's bank balance by drawing cheques for his own purposes, and it was said that the theft was complete only when the account was debited and not when the cheques were drawn. This dictum was applied in *Doole*,[99] and it is submitted with respect that it is correct. The drawing of a cheque without authority may of course be a breach of contract, but it does not infringe the owner's proprietary rights over the balance of the account. In *Wille*,[1] however, it was pointed out that this view had been criticised as being inconsistent with the wording of section 3(1); the point was left open "as there appears to be force in the criticism",[2] and it was held that a credit balance could be stolen by means of a cheque which the bank had no mandate to honour. Similarly in *Chan Man-Sin v. Attorney-General of Hong Kong*[3] the Privy Council held that the appellant had stolen a company's credit balance by forging cheques which were honoured by the bank. In this case, unlike *Kohn*, the unauthorised cheques were not binding on the company and did not affect its rights against the bank.[4] Therefore, it was argued, the appellant had neither appropriated the company's property nor had any intention of depriving the company thereof.[5] It was held that this was an appropriation within the extended meaning given to that term by the Hong Kong counterpart of section 3(1), because it was an "assumption . . . of the rights of an owner".

"The owner of the chose in action consisting of a credit with his bank or a contractual right to draw on an account has, clearly, the right as owner to

95 *Cf. Bloxham* (1943) 29 Cr.App.R. 37 (held to be not even attempted larceny).
96 *Supra*, para. 1.12.
97 *Infra*, paras. 1.108 ff. If he does not intend the purchaser to get and keep the property, he will of course be obtaining the purchase price by deception: *infra*, Ch. 2.
98 (1979) 69 Cr.App.R. 395 at p. 407.
99 [1985] Crim.L.R. 450.
1 (1987) 86 Cr.App.R. 296.
2 At p. 301.
3 [1988] 1 W.L.R. 196.
4 *Tai Hing Cotton Mill Ltd v. Liu Chong Hing Bank Ltd* [1986] A.C. 80.
5 On the latter point see *infra*, para. 1.134.

draw by means of a properly completed negotiable instrument or order to
pay and it is, in their Lordships' view, beyond argument that one who draws,
presents and negotiates a cheque on a particular bank account is assuming
the rights of the owner of the credit in the account or (as the case may be)
of the pre-negotiated right to draw on the account up to the agreed figure
. . .

It is, in their Lordships' view, entirely immaterial that the end result of
the transaction may be a legal nullity, for it is not possible to read into
[section 3(1)] any requirement that the assumption of rights there envisaged
should have a legally efficacious result." [6]

It was thought unnecessary to decide whether the appropriation occurred
when the cheques were presented, or when the transactions were
completed by the making of consequential entries in the relevant
accounts. It was apparently not suggested that the appropriation might
have consisted in the *drawing* of the cheques. But there can hardly be a
material distinction between the unauthorised drawing of the cheque and
the unauthorised (and ineffective) debiting of the account. Neither affects
the owner's property; each is an "assumption" of his rights only in the
loosest possible sense. Yet their Lordships assume it to be "beyond
argument" that it is the loosest possible sense which is intended.

1.72   The same question has arisen in the context of territorial jurisdiction, and again the courts' latest pronouncement suggests a dramatic
widening of the concept of appropriation. In *Tomsett*[7] one of the
appellants sent a telex from London purporting to instruct a bank in New
York to transfer $7,000,000 to an account held by the other appellant at
another bank, also in New York. Their convictions of conspiracy to steal
were quashed. A conspiracy to commit an offence is not indictable in
England and Wales unless the full offence would have been committed
there,[8] and the intended theft would have been committed in New York.
This was because the money to be stolen was in New York, and it was
assumed that an appropriation of property can be effected only in the
place where the property is. If an appropriation necessarily involves some
effect on the property, this assumption would seem self-evidently correct.
But in *R. v. Governor of Pentonville Prison ex p. Osman*[9] the Divisional
Court rejected it and held on essentially similar facts that the appropriation was complete when the telex was sent: that act was itself a
"usurpation" of the rights of the person actually entitled to the money.

6   At pp. 199 f.
7   [1985] Crim.L.R. 369.
8   *Board of Trade v. Owen* [1957] A.C. 602.
9   [1988] Crim.L.R. 611.

Therefore the theft was committed in the country from which the telex was sent (although the court did not rule out the possibility that it might *also* be committed in the country where the telex was received). But if the sending of the telex is itself an appropriation of the money, it follows that the sender has stolen the money even if the message is ignored or never arrives. Nobody but a lawyer, and few lawyers at that, would regard the mere sending of the telex as more than an attempt to steal the money.[10] We seem to have reached the point where the defendant need not have done anything *to* the property at all, provided he has done *something* (or, perhaps, some act which is more than merely preparatory) with the intention of depriving its owner of it. To extract such a result from the wording of section 3(1) is a remarkable feat of interpretation.

Consent of person to whom property belongs

1.73 A question which has generated immense confusion is that of whether an act can be an appropriation, in either the ordinary or the extended sense of the word, if it is done with the consent of the person to whom the property belongs. Under the old law of larceny, it was expressly required that the taking of the property be "without the consent of the owner"; no such express requirement appears in section 1(1) of the Theft Act 1968, and in *Lawrence v. Metropolitan Police Commissioner*[11] the House of Lords held that it is not implied. The appellant, a taxi-driver, had falsely told an Italian passenger that his destination was far away and that the journey would be very expensive. The passenger tendered £1, which was nearly twice the correct fare, and made no protest when the driver took a further £6 from the passenger's open wallet. The House of Lords affirmed the driver's conviction of stealing the £6, rejecting the argument that the taking of the money could not be theft because it was done with the owner's consent:

> "I see no ground for concluding that the omission of the words 'without the consent of the owner' was inadvertent and not deliberate, and to read the subsection as if they were included is, in my opinion, wholly unwarranted. Parliament by the omission of these words has relieved the prosecution of the burden of establishing that the taking was without the owner's consent. That is no longer an ingredient of the offence."[12]

1.74 This statement must now be regarded with extreme caution. It is no doubt true that once the express requirements of section 1(1) are satisfied, there is no further, implied requirement that the owner of the

10 But the attempt would not be indictable in England if the full offence would not have been: Criminal Attempts Act 1981 s. 1(1), (4).
11 [1972] A.C. 626.
12 At pp. 631 f., *per* Viscount Dilhorne, with whose speech the remainder of their Lordships agreed.

property must not have consented to what is done; but if he does consent it now appears that the express requirements of section 1(1) are *not* satisfied. In a number of cases since *Lawrence* it has been held, asserted or assumed that an act authorised by the person to whom property belongs cannot be regarded as an appropriation of that property. In *Meech*[13] the appellant had cashed a cheque for another man but kept the proceeds; the Court of Appeal held that he did not steal the money when he withdrew it from the bank (even if he had already decided to keep it) but only when he dealt with it in a manner inconsistent with his instructions. In *Skipp*[14] the appellant, posing as a haulage contractor, had collected three loads and made off with them; the Court of Appeal held that he had committed not three thefts but one, because not until all three consignments had been loaded (and probably not until he deviated from the route to their appointed destination) did he do anything with them which he was not authorised to do. In *Hircock*[15] the appellant had obtained a car on hire-purchase by deception, intending to sell it and keep the proceeds; the Court of Appeal held, or at any rate assumed, that he did not steal the car when he first obtained it (because under the hire-purchase agreement he was entitled to take possession of it) but only when he sold it. In *Eddy v. Niman*[16] the defendant took articles from the shelves of a supermarket and placed them in one of the wire baskets provided, intending to remove them from the store without paying, but changed his mind and left without them; the Divisional Court held that he had not stolen them. He had done no more than any customer was authorised to do, and his dishonest intention could not convert an authorised act into an "assumption . . . of the rights of an owner".

1.75   These decisions, though hard to reconcile with the House of Lords' decision in *Lawrence*, were in effect approved by the House in *Morris*.[17] The prosecution, not content to establish that property can be appropriated without the owner being thereby deprived of it, sought further to argue that the act of appropriation need not even be inconsistent with the owner's rights. On this view there would be an appropriation of goods on display in a supermarket not only by the dishonest customer who hides them under his coat or switches the price labels, but also by the honest one who puts them in the basket or trolley provided with the intention of paying for them. The honest customer would not of course be guilty of theft because he would not have the necessary *mens rea*, but he would

13   [1974] Q.B. 549.
14   [1975] Cr.Im.L.R. 114.
15   (1978) 67 Cr.App.R. 278.
16   (1981) 73 Cr.App.R. 237.
17   [1984] A.C. 320; *supra*, para. 1.65.

be committing the *actus reus*. It was unnecessary for the House to express an opinion on this argument, but Lord Roskill went out of his way to do so:

"If one postulates an honest customer taking goods from a shelf to put in his or her trolley to take to the checkpoint there to pay the proper price, I am unable to see that any of these actions involves any assumption by the shopper of the rights of the supermarket. In the context of section 3(1), the concept of appropriation in my view involves not an act expressly or impliedly authorised by the owner but an act by way of adverse interference with or usurpation of those rights. When the honest shopper acts as I have just described, he or she is acting with the implied authority of the owner of the supermarket to take the goods from the shelf, put them in the trolley, take them to the checkpoint and there pay the correct price, at which moment the property in the goods will pass to the shopper for the first time. It is with the consent of the owners of the supermarket, be that consent express or implied, that the shopper does these acts . . . I do not think that section 3(1) envisages any such act as an 'appropriation', whatever may be the meaning of that word in other fields such as contract or sale of goods law."[18]

1.76   The importance of this passage lies not in the proposition that the honest customer does not appropriate the goods by handling them in the authorised manner, but in its implied corollary that *no* customer does—however dishonest his intentions. This is clear from his Lordship's approval of *Eddy v. Niman*,[19] where a shopper was held not to have stolen goods merely by placing them in the wire basket with the intention of stealing them. If this is correct it must apply equally to any prospective purchaser of goods who is authorised to take possession of the goods before paying for them, such as a motorist buying petrol at a self-service garage. In *McHugh*[20] it was assumed that such a person would be stealing the petrol if at the time when he put it into his tank he had no intention of paying for it; but he is authorised to put the petrol in his tank, just as the supermarket shopper is authorised to put the goods in the basket, and it seems that his action in doing so cannot therefore be theft. Nor does he steal the petrol if he does in fact drive off without paying, because once in his tank it is no longer property belonging to another.[21] The appropriate charge in such a case, if deception cannot be proved, is one of making off without payment.[22]

1.77   Lord Roskill's statement was *obiter*, but it has since been applied by the Court of Appeal. In *Fritschy*[23] the appellant, at the owner's request,

18   At p. 332.
19   (1981) 73 Cr.App.R. 237; *supra*, para. 1.74.
20   (1976) 64 Cr.App.R. 92.
21   *Edwards v. Ddin* [1976] 3 All E.R. 705.
22   Theft Act 1978 s. 3; *infra*, paras. 5.46 ff.
23   [1985] Crim.L.R. 745.

had collected a number of Krugerrands from bullion dealers in England and taken them to Switzerland. The jury were directed that he would be guilty of stealing them if, when he collected them, he had the dishonest intention of keeping them for himself. His conviction was quashed. What he had done within the jurisdiction, though done with dishonest intent, was exactly what the owner of the property had authorised him to do: it was not an "adverse interference with or usurpation of" the owner's rights. He may have stolen the Krugerrands in Switzerland, by dealing with them otherwise than in accordance with his instructions, but not in England.

Consent and the ordinary meaning of "appropriation"
1.78 Lord Roskill's dictum in *Morris*, and the Court of Appeal's decisions to the same effect, raise a number of difficulties. In the first place it is not clear how the restriction thus imposed on the scope of the concept of appropriation can be extracted from the wording of the Act. It may be that an act authorised by the person to whom the property belongs cannot be regarded as an "assumption . . . of the rights of an owner" and therefore does not qualify as an appropriation by virtue of section 3(1); but (as Lord Roskill himself pointed out,[24] without examining the implications of the remark) section 3(1) is not an exhaustive definition. It says only that an assumption of the rights of an owner is an appropriation, not that nothing else is. To take possession of another's property with the intention of keeping it, with or without his consent, is surely to appropriate it in the ordinary sense; if so, such an act should in principle be an appropriation within the meaning of section 1(1), whether or not it is also an assumption of the rights of an owner. It would not necessarily follow that the owner's consent would in such a case be immaterial: it might render the defendant's act lawful as a matter of civil law and therefore (arguably) not dishonest.[25] But a rule that an authorised act cannot even be an appropriation would seem, with respect, to go too far. Nor does such a rule fit easily with the wording of section 2(1)(*b*), which provides that a person's appropriation of property belonging to another is not to be regarded as dishonest "if he appropriates the property in the belief that he would have the other's consent if the other knew of the appropriation and the circumstances of it". This implies that if the owner did consent to the defendant's act it would not automatically follow that the act was not an appropriation at all.

The problem of Lawrence
1.79 The rule laid down in *Morris* is hard to reconcile with the House

---

24 [1984] A.C. 320 at p. 331.
25 *Infra*, paras. 1.154 ff.

of Lords' earlier decision in *Lawrence*,[26] where, it will be recalled, a
taxi-driver was held to have stolen money from a passenger's wallet
although the passenger let him take it. Lord Roskill made light of the
difficulty.

> "In the leading speech, Viscount Dilhorne expressly accepted the view of the
> Court of Appeal (Criminal Division) in that case that the offence of theft
> involved four elements, (1) a dishonest (2) appropriation (3) of property
> belonging to another, (4) with the intention of permanently depriving the
> owner of it. Viscount Dilhorne also rejected the argument that even if these
> four elements were all present there could not be theft within the section if
> the owner of the property in question had consented to the acts which were
> done by the defendant. That there was in that case a dishonest appropriation
> was beyond question and the House did not have to consider the precise
> meaning of that word in section 3(1)."[27]

1.80 Lawrence must indeed have appropriated his passenger's money,
since the House of Lords upheld his conviction of theft and that decision
still stands. What is not clear, let alone "beyond question", is how he can
be said to have appropriated it within the restricted meaning now assigned
to that word by *Morris*. The passenger saw that Lawrence was taking the
money from the wallet, and raised no objection. If this was not "an act
expressly or impliedly authorised by the owner", it must be because that
expression is narrower than it might seem. Clearly it requires qualification
in some way which Lord Roskill left unexplained, and we must consider
what the nature of such qualification might be. There are, it is suggested,
two main possibilities. On the one hand it may be that an act is not
"authorised" for this purpose if the owner's apparent authority is
procured by fraud; alternatively, it may be necessary to draw a distinction
between positive authorisation of the defendant's act and passive
acquiescence in it.

1.81 *Consent vitiated by fraud.* There is an obvious distinction between
the conduct of a dishonest taxi-driver who exacts an excessive fare from
a gullible passenger and that of a dishonest shopper who takes articles
from a supermarket shelf intending not to pay for them, but placing them
for the moment in the basket or trolley provided. All the supermarket's
customers have authority to do what the dishonest customer does, and
his authority to do it is quite unconnected with his dishonest intentions;
the taxi-driver's authority to take the money, on the other hand, is
procured only by his deception as to the amount properly payable. A
possible way of reconciling Lord Roskill's dictum with the decision in
Lawrence, therefore, is by construing the former as implicitly confined to

26 [1972] A.C. 626; *supra*, para. 1.73.
27 [1984] A.C. 320 at p. 331.

consent legitimately obtained, and as having no application to a consent procured by fraud. On this view consent vitiated by fraud is not real consent, and does not therefore preclude an appropriation.

1.82 Some support for this view may perhaps be derived from Lord Roskill's criticism of the decision in *Kaur v. Chief Constable for Hampshire*,[28] where the appellant had bought a pair of shoes at the price marked on one of them, knowing that this was an error and that the correct price was a higher one marked on the other shoe. Her conviction of theft was quashed. In *Morris* Lord Roskill said he was disposed to the view that *Kaur* had been wrongly decided. This remark was left unexplained and seems inconsistent with his Lordship's earlier statement that an authorised act is not an appropriation. Clearly he cannot have thought that Kaur stole the shoes by picking them up (albeit with the dishonest intention of buying them at the lower price if possible) because picking them up was something which any customer was authorised to do.[29] Perhaps he meant that she stole them by buying them and taking them away: this too was an authorised act in the sense that the cashier agreed to sell her the shoes, but it is arguable that Kaur procured the transaction by fraud in presenting the shoes at the cash desk without pointing out the discrepancy between the two prices. In *Kaur* itself Lord Lane C.J. said that it "was not a case where there was any deception at all",[30] but he seems to have meant only that the appellant had not herself altered the price labels (as in *Morris*). Whether it can be a deception to buy goods which one knows to be wrongly priced is not clear. There is much to be said for the view that this is not deception but only non-disclosure: the civil law does not regard it as a misrepresentation to make a contract on terms which one knows the other party would not accept if he were in possession of all the facts, nor is there any general duty to make disclosure of material facts of which one knows the other party to be unaware.[31]

1.83 On the other hand there is authority for the view that such conduct does involve deception for the purposes of the criminal law. In *Williams (Jean-Jacques)*[32] a schoolboy had bought obsolete Jugoslavian banknotes which were worthless except as collectors' items. He took them to a bureau de change and said to the cashier either "Will you change these notes?" or "Can I cash these in?" The cashier paid him a total of over a

---

28 [1981] 1 W.L.R. 578.
29 *Cf.* his Lordship's approval of *Eddy v. Niman* (1981) 73 Cr.App.R. 237.
30 [1981] 1 W.L.R. 578 at p. 582.
31 *Smith v. Hughes* (1871) L.R. 6 Q.B. 597.
32 [1980] Crim.L.R. 589.

hundred pounds for notes which had cost him only seven. The Court of Appeal not only upheld a conviction of theft (on the ground that the mistake was so fundamental as to invalidate the payment altogether,[33] thus circumventing the argument that the cashier had authorised the appellent to take the money) but also criticised the recorder's ruling that there was no evidence of any false representation and that charges of obtaining the money by deception could therefore not be left to the jury. It would have been open to the jury to find that the appellant had represented that he believed the notes to be valid currency in Jugoslavia. Presumably Kaur represented that she believed the price she was charged to be the correct price; and if this was the reason for Lord Roskill's dissatisfaction with the decision, it suggests that his remarks on the effect of consent were not intended to apply to a consent obtained by fraud.

1.84 But any attempt to justify *Lawrence* solely on the basis of the deception is open to various objections. In the first place it would mean that virtually[34] any case of obtaining property by deception contrary to section 15(1) of the Theft Act 1968[35] would also be theft, since any consent which might be given would necessarily be vitiated by the deception and would not therefore prevent the defendant's act from being an appropriation. Indeed this conclusion was accepted by the Court of Appeal (though not, at least not in so many words, by the House of Lords) in *Lawrence*[36] itself: the court thought that this was the consequence of the omission from the definition of theft of the words "without the consent of the owner" which had formerly been part of the definition of larceny. But it was not the intention of the Criminal Law Revision Committee in framing the Act: they envisaged that conduct which would formerly have constituted the old offence of obtaining property by false pretences would in future amount to obtaining property by deception but not to theft.[37] Had it been intended that every obtaining by deception should also be theft, section 15 would have been unnecessary and would presumably have been omitted from the Act.

1.85 Moreover, with the exception of *Lawrence* itself (where the Court of Appeal and the House of Lords agreed that the owner's consent was not a defence at all, even if *not* obtained by deception), the authorities do not support the view that it is theft to obtain property with the owner's consent if that consent is procured by fraud. Admittedly this view seems

---

33 *Supra*, para. 1.53.
34 There would be an exception in the case of land, which can be the subject of an offence under s. 15(1) but cannot normally be stolen: *supra*, paras. 1.04 ff.
35 *Infra*, ch. 2.
36 [1971] 1 Q.B. 373.
37 Cmnd. 2977 para. 38; *cf. infra*, para. 1.88.

the only explanation of Lord Roskill's remarks on *Kaur*,[38] but he did not expressly suggest any such distinction. Had he intended to exclude cases of deception from his statement that authorised acts are not appropriations, he would surely have done so in a less oblique manner. Not only did he abstain from any such qualification, but he referred without disapproval to the decision in *Skipp*[39] that a person does not steal property by deceiving the owner into letting him take it away. *Hircock*[40] is another decision to the same effect. If these cases are inconsistent with *Lawrence*, they must of course be wrongly decided; but to dismiss two decisions of the Court of Appeal in such a way would be a counsel of despair.

1.86   The suggested distinction based on the presence or absence of the element of deception not only runs counter to the authorities but is also, it is submitted, unsound in principle. Once it is accepted that the owner's consent is a defence to a charge of theft, it is hard to see any logical justification for denying that defence merely because the consent is procured by deception: consent is consent, however obtained. The point may perhaps be illustrated by a comparison with the offence of rape, an essential element of which is the victim's lack of consent. If she consents to what is done, it is not rape. There is no rule that a consent obtained by fraud does not count.[41] Fraud as to a fundamental fact, such as the nature of the act,[42] may mean that what appears to be consent is really no consent at all; but if the woman does consent, it matters not that she does so only because she has been deceived. At common law her consent was a defence even if the defendant procured it by impersonating her husband;[43] this particular rule has now been reversed by statute,[44] but it demonstrates that fraud in itself does not nullify consent. If it did, the offence of procuring intercourse by false pretences[45] would be largely redundant.

1.87   Similarly, to take a closer analogy, it was held in *Whittaker v. Campbell*[46] that a person does not take a conveyance "without having the consent of the owner" for the purposes of section 12(1) of the Theft Act 1968 if he deceives the owner into letting him take it. The court expressly denied the existence of any general principle that fraud vitiates consent.

38 *Supra*, para. 1.82.
39 [1975] Crim.L.R. 114; *supra*, para. 1.74.
40 (1978) 67 Cr.App.R. 278; *supra*, para. 1.74.
41 *Clarence* (1888) 22 Q.B.D. 23 at p. 44, *per* Stephen J.
42 *e.g. Flattery* (1877) 2 Q.B.D. 410.
43 *Barrow* (1868) L.R. 1 C.C.R. 156.
44 Sexual Offences Act 1956 s. 1(2).
45 Sexual Offences Act 1956 s. 3.
46 [1984] Q.B. 318; *infra*, para. 5.12.

It is true that a fraud of this type might formerly have amounted to larceny by a trick,[47] although that offence too required a taking without the consent of the owner; but this rule is now recognised to have been anomalous. In reality the owner does consent.[48] To hold otherwise was no more than a device for the creation of a new form of larceny to which the owner's consent was no defence. It is also true that a person who sells property by deceiving the purchaser as to the nature of the property sold may be guilty of stealing the purchase price if the mistake thus induced is sufficiently fundamental to render the payment void:[49] in such a case the purchaser's apparent consent is no consent at all. Similarly a person who obtains property by deceiving the owner into transferring it to him may be guilty of stealing it if the result of the deception is that the owner does not even realise that that is what he is doing, so that his apparent consent to the transfer is void on the grounds of *non est factum*.[50] But these situations are exceptional. It would be most unwise for a prosecutor to assume that the obtaining of property by deception can always be charged as theft. On the contrary, the safe and appropriate course, when deception can be established, is to charge an offence of deception.[51]

1.88 A more subtle version of the distinction discussed above is the theory that Lord Roskill's dictum in *Morris* does not apply to the obtaining of *possession* by deception, but does rule out a charge of theft where the owner is deceived into transferring *ownership*; in other words, that what under the old law would have been larceny by a trick is now theft as well as obtaining property by deception contrary to section 15(1), while what would formerly have been obtaining by false pretences is not theft but an offence under section 15(1) alone. This is certainly what the Criminal Law Revision Committee intended:[52] in effect, obtaining by false pretences was to be extended so as to include the territory formerly occupied by larceny by a trick, but not *vice versa*. The Act clearly achieves the former objective, by defining an "obtaining" of property to include the obtaining of possession or control as well as that of ownership;[53] what is doubtful is whether the distinction between obtaining possession and obtaining ownership, no longer crucial to the deception offence, still marks the boundary of theft. The Act draws no such distinction, unless it is somehow implicit in the definition of appropriation. Perhaps obtaining the possession of another's property is an "assumption . . . of

47 *Pear* (1779) 1 Leach 212.
48 *Du Jardin v. Beadman Bros Ltd* [1952] 2 Q.B. 712.
49 *Williams (Jean-Jacques)* [1980] Crim.L.R. 589; *supra*, para. 1.53.
50 *Davies* [1982] 1 All E.R. 513.
51 *Infra*, ch. 2.
52 Cmnd. 2977, para. 38; see J.C. Smith, [1981] Crim.L.R. at p. 678.
53 s. 15(2).

the rights of an owner", whereas obtaining the ownership of it is not.[54]
But this is to burden that expression with a weight of meaning which it
was surely never intended to bear:

> ". . . whatever the word 'appropriates' means it cannot sensibly be made to
> include the consensual transfer of possession while excluding the consensual
> transfer of ownership."[55]

Nor would such a distinction be satisfactory even if it could somehow be
extracted from the wording of the Act. It would admittedly have the merit
of providing section 15 with an independent function (because an
obtaining of ownership by deception would not be caught by section 1 as
well as by section 15) but the other objections to a distinction based on
the presence or absence of deception apply here with at least equal force.
Lord Roskill drew no such distinction. On the contrary, he cast no doubt
on the correctness of *Skipp*[56] and *Hircock*[57] which decide that a consent
procured by deception is a defence not only where the defendant obtains
the ownership of the property but also where he obtains possession alone.
And the distinction between obtaining possession and obtaining ownership is at least as artificial and illogical a line of demarcation as that
between consent procured by deception and consent not so procured. It
does not even explain *Lawrence*, because if the passenger consented to
anything it was surely to the driver's acquiring *ownership* of the money,
not just possession. But this brings us to an alternative explanation: *viz.*
that he consented to neither.

1.89   *Authority and acquiescence.* An alternative explanation of the
apparent inconsistency between *Lawrence* and *Morris* is that when Lord
Roskill said that an authorised act is not an appropriation he was using
the notion of authority in a strict sense, referring to a positive prior
consent as distinct from mere acquiescence or subsequent ratification. In
this sense it would appear that Lawrence's passenger did not authorise
him to extract £6 from the passenger's wallet: he merely failed to protest
when he saw what Lawrence was doing. If, the moment before Lawrence
took the money, the passenger had been asked by an officious bystander
(in Italian) whether he consented to the driver taking £6 from his wallet,
he would probably have replied not "Oh, of course" but something to
the effect of "Well, I'm not sure—is the fare really as much as that?"
Viscount Dilhorne himself appears to have regarded this distinction, or
one very like it, as material:

54 J.C. Smith, [1981] Crim.L.R. at p. 677.
55 Glanville Williams, [1981] Crim.L.R. at pp. 668 f.
56 [1975] Crim.L.R. 114.
57 (1978) 67 Cr.App.R. 278.

"My Lords, in cross-examination, [the passenger], when asked whether he had consented to the money being taken, said that he had 'permitted'. He gave evidence through an interpreter and it does not appear that he was asked to explain what he meant by the use of that word. He had not objected when the £6 was taken. He had not asked for the return of any of it. It may well be that when he used the word 'permitted', he meant no more than that he had allowed the money to be taken. It certainly was not established at the trial that he had agreed to pay to the appellant a sum far in excess of the legal fare for the journey and so had consented to the acquisition by the appellant of the £6."[58]

The sense of this important passage is unfortunately obscured by the wording of the last sentence. The point, it is submitted, is not merely that the passenger never agreed to pay "a sum far in excess of the legal fare" (in the sense that he did not realise that the total of £7 *was* far in excess of the legal fare) but that he never *agreed* to pay the extra £6 at all. He merely failed to resist or protest when the appellant took it. This distinction was admittedly not crucial to the decision. Viscount Dilhorne went on to say, in effect, that even if the appellant *had* taken the precaution of obtaining the passenger's consent to the taking of the money he would still have been stealing it; and the decision seems to be based on this latter view, rather than on the narrower ground that he did not in fact obtain the passenger's consent at all. The reasoning in *Lawrence* cannot stand with that of *Morris*, and Lord Roskill did not say that it could. What he said was that in *Lawrence* there clearly was an appropriation: in other words, the result was right although the reasoning was wrong. If the dicta in *Morris* are correct, it is submitted that *Lawrence* must now be regarded as a decision turning on its own special facts.

1.90 It should be noted that the distinction between authority and acquiescence is not the same as that between a delivery by the owner to the defendant and a taking by the defendant with the owner's prior consent. It has been rightly pointed out that for criminal liability to turn on such a distinction would be absurd.[59] It does not follow that it is not an appropriation to take property without prior consent, merely because the owner raises no objection. Nor should it make any difference in principle whether the owner becomes aware of the taking, and raises no objection, at some later time or at the very moment when it is done. In neither case is the taking "authorised" in the strictest sense of the word.

The limits of authority
1.91 Even if an act authorised by the owner is not an appropriation, it obviously does not follow that a person authorised to deal with another's

58 [1972] A.C. 626 at p. 631.
59 Glanville Williams, [1981] Crim.L.R. at p. 669.

property can never steal it: he is immune from a theft charge only as long as he stays within the limits of the authority granted to him. When a bank issues a customer with a cash card it authorises him to withdraw money from the bank's cash dispensers, but (in the absence of agreement to the contrary) only while his account is in credit; using the card when the account is overdrawn is an act going beyond the user's authority and may therefore be an appropriation of the cash.[60] In *Skipp*[61] the appellant was not guilty of theft when he obtained goods by posing as a genuine haulage contractor, but he did steal them as soon as he left the route to their appointed destination. Similarly in *McPherson*[62] a supermarket customer was held to have stolen goods by removing them from the shelf and putting them in her shopping bag. The decision was approved in *Morris*, presumably on the ground that although the first act was authorised the second was not. Customers are not normally permitted to carry goods in their own bags but only in the receptacles provided by the store. In *Pilgram v. Rice-Smith*[63] an assistant at a supermarket meat counter fraudulently underpriced meat which she served to a friend, who took it to the check-out and paid only the price thus certified to be payable. Both were held guilty of theft. The decision is not inconsistent with *Morris*, because the assistant was not authorised to hand the meat over without pricing it correctly. A more dubious example of the same principle is *Monaghan*,[64] where a supermarket cashier was held to have stolen a sum of money received from a customer by putting it in the till without ringing it up, intending to remove it[65] later. It might be said that the case is on all fours with *Pilgram v. Rice-Smith*: the cashier was not authorised to put the money in the till without ringing it up. But the two cases are distinguishable. Rice-Smith literally dealt with the meat in an unauthorised manner by marking it with the wrong price, whereas what Monaghan did with the money itself was entirely correct. Her duty was to put it in the till and that is exactly what she did. She failed to *record* the fact that she had done so, and was no doubt guilty of false accounting,[66] but in the light of *Morris* her conviction of theft is hard to justify.

1.92 *Agents.* In each of these cases, with the possible exception of *Monaghan*, the defendant dealt with the property in an unauthorised way.

60 *Cf. Kennison v. Daire* (1986) 160 C.L.R. 129 (High Court of Australia).
61 [1975] Crim.L.R. 114.
62 [1973] Crim.L.R. 191.
63 [1977] 1 W.L.R. 671.
64 [1979] Crim.L.R. 673.
65 Or, more likely, other money amounting to the same sum—in which case she did not intend to deprive her employer of the money which she was held to have appropriated. This point was apparently overlooked.
66 Theft Act 1968 s. 17; see *Fraud*, paras. 6.41 ff.

What is less clear is whether an act which would otherwise be authorised
can be deemed to be unauthorised, and therefore an appropriation, solely
on the grounds that it is done with dishonest intent.[67] The shoplifter's
removal of the goods from the supermarket shelf is objectively an
authorised act, and does not become an appropriation merely because it
is done with the dishonest intention of keeping the goods without paying
for them. On the other hand it is sometimes said that an agent authorised
to deal with another's property on that person's behalf can be guilty of
stealing the property if he uses it for purposes of his own, even if what he
does is on the face of it within the scope of his authority, because every
agent's authority is implicitly confined to acts done *bona fide* in the
interests of his principal. In *Attorney-General of Hong Kong v. Chan
Nai-Keung*[68] the Privy Council said:

> "So long as an agent is acting within the scope of his authority in selling the
> property of his principal, he is not assuming any rights of the owner, but
> merely exercising rights which the owner has conferred upon him. But an
> agent authorised to sell can have no authority to sell dishonestly against the
> owner's interest. Thus, for example, if an agent in purported exercise of his
> authority dishonestly sells the principal's property to a third party at an
> undervalue he clearly exceeds his authority and thereby assumes the rights
> of the owner in a way which amounts to an appropriation . . ."[69]

At first sight this may seem no more than common sense, but it is
submitted with respect that it is an over-simplification. The fiduciary duty
of an agent is not the same as, but is more demanding than, his duty not
to exceed his authority. Whether he acts within his authority depends on
what he does; whether he acts in breach of his fiduciary duty may depend
in addition on his reasons for doing it. In *Hambro v. Burnand*[70] it was
held by the Court of Appeal that a transaction entered into by a Lloyd's
underwriter on behalf of his syndicate was within his actual authority
although he had made it for his own purposes rather than those of the
syndicate. It was precisely the sort of transaction which he was expressly
authorised to make, and the fact that he had made it for a fraudulent
purpose did not take it outside the scope of that authority. Similarly in
Moore v. I. Bresler Ltd[71] a company was held liable for offences
committed by its agents although the offences amounted to a fraud on
the company itself, because the fraudulent transactions effected by its
agents were within the authority conferred upon them.

---

67 For a fuller discussion of this point see *Fraud*, paras. 4.22 ff.
68 [1987] 1 W.L.R. 1339. The question of appropriation was not argued: see *infra*, para.
    1.94.
69 At p. 1343.
70 [1904] 2 K.B. 10.
71 [1944] 2 All E.R. 515.

"The sales undoubtedly were fraudulent, but they were sales made with the authority of the respondent company by these two men as agents for the respondent company."[72]

Of course it may be that in order to achieve his fraudulent purpose an agent must deal with his principal's property in a way which (irrespective of his motives) is simply not what he is authorised to do, *e.g.* by disposing of the property at an undervalue; and in that case the problem of the principal's consent does not arise. But it is submitted that it is entirely possible for an agent to defraud his principal by means of an act in relation to the principal's property which is within the authority conferred upon him. And in that case it would seem that he is not guilty of theft.

1.93 *Company controllers.* Even if the argument advanced above is wrong, and it is impossible for an agent of a natural person to defraud that person in a manner authorised by him, there is a further difficulty in applying this proposition to the agents of corporations.[73] An agent who has fraudulently misapplied a company's funds may (depending on his seniority within the company)[74] be able to argue that he is not just an agent but the company's "directing mind", its *alter ego,* and that anything which he does with the company's property is necessarily authorised by the company. The argument is more compelling than in the case of an agent of a natural person, because natural persons have minds of their own: it can safely be assumed that no-one would knowingly consent to a fraud on himself, and it is tempting (though not necessarily logical) to infer that a fraud by an agent on his human principal must therefore in fact be unauthorised. But a corporate person has no mind other than that with which its human controllers choose to invest it. If they choose to conduct their own fraudulent transactions in the company's name, those transactions will have been authorised by the company. Of course it may be that the giving of such authority is *ultra vires* the company and therefore of no effect, but this will not be so merely because the transaction in question is a fraud on the company itself. A transaction may be *intra vires* even if it is not entered into *bona fide* in the interests of the company, provided either that the making of such transactions is one of the company's objects or that the particular transaction in question is reasonably incidental to the pursuit of those objects.[75]

---

72 At p. 516, *per* Viscount Caldecote C.J.
73 What follows is only an outline of the nature of the problem, which in view of the decision in *Attorney-General of Hong Kong v. Chan Nai-Keung* [1987] 1 W.L.R. 1339 (*infra*, para. 1.94) may well be of no more than academic interest. For fuller discussions see G.R. Sullivan, "Company Controllers, Company Cheques and Theft" [1983] Crim.L.R. 512; Janet Dine, "Another View" [1984] Crim.L.R. 397; Sullivan, "A Reply" *ibid.* at p. 405; *Fraud* paras. 4.26 ff.
74 See *Tesco Supermarkets Ltd v. Nattrass* [1972] A.C. 153.
75 *Re Horsley & Weight Ltd* [1982] Ch. 442; *Rolled Steel Products (Holdings) Ltd v. British Steel Corporation* [1986] Ch. 246.

1.94   Whether this inconvenient principle will be applied by the criminal courts is another matter. A majority of the House of Lords appeared to accept it in *Tarling (No. 1) v. Government of the Republic of Singapore*,[76] since they thought it would not be theft for the chairman of a company to buy its property at an undervalue. In *Attorney-General's Reference (No. 2 of 1982)*,[77] however, the Court of Appeal rejected the argument that a director's misuse of his company's property cannot be dishonest. It did not consider the more fundamental question of whether such conduct can be an appropriation,[78] but its reasoning (*viz.* that fraud on a company, even by a director, cannot be regarded as having been effected by the company itself) would apply equally to the issue of appropriation. In *Attorney-General of Hong Kong v. Chan Nai-Keung*[79] the defendant had general authority to sell property belonging to a company of which he was a director, but sold it at a gross undervalue. The Court of Appeal of Hong Kong quashed his conviction of theft (under a provision identical to section 1(1) of the Theft Act) on the grounds that he was the *alter ego* of the company and that the company had sold its own property. The Privy Council found the Court of Appeal's reasoning "difficult to understand" and restored the conviction.

> "If the proposition . . . is that the director of a company who has a general authority to sell the company's property cannot be guilty of theft if he sells the property even dishonestly and in fraud of the company, it is clearly erroneous . . . "[80]

But, as in the *Attorney-General's Reference*, it was not argued that the defendant's conduct was not an appropriation—only that it was not dishonest. Even on this latter point the Privy Council omitted to explain how its reasoning could be reconciled with the provisions of section 2(1).[81] It did not adopt the reasoning in the *Attorney-General's Reference* but simply treated that case as authority for the general proposition that any conduct which would formerly have constituted the offence of fraudulent conversion is now theft. It is hardly to be supposed that when the question directly arises for decision the criminal courts will retract the assumption made in both the *Attorney-General's Reference* and *Chan Nai-Keung*, that fraudulent dealings with a company's property by its controllers in the name of the company are an appropriation of that property.[81a] But it has yet to be explained how that proposition can be reconciled with *Morris*.

76 (1978) 70 Cr.App.R. 77.
77 [1984] Q.B. 624; *infra*, para. 1.152.
78 The argument took place before the decision in *Morris*, and the point was conceded by the defence.
79 [1987] 1 W.L.R. 1339.
80 At p. 1342.
81 *Infra*, paras. 1.142 ff.
81a The prediction in the text proved correct in *Philippou*, The Times 6 April 1989.

Consent under compulsion

1.95 We have already considered the argument that a consent obtained by fraud is not a real consent and does not prevent the act thus authorised from being an appropriation, and it was submitted that fraud in itself does not have this effect unless the mistake thereby induced is fundamental.[82] Another possibility is that the owner's apparent consent may have been procured not by fraud but by threats, and again it is arguable that a consent thus extorted is of no effect. Obviously a person who induces another to hand over his property by threatening him with immediate personal violence is guilty of theft, and indeed of robbery.[83] It is commonly said that a contract procured by duress is not void but only voidable,[84] but it can hardly make any difference whether the defendant insists on dressing the robbery up as a contract by providing some nominal consideration for the property he obtains. Since he is well aware that the victim will repudiate the transaction as soon as the immediate threat is past, there is no sense in treating it as even provisionally valid.

1.96 When a consent apparently given by the victim of a fraud is regarded as invalid, it is not the fraud itself which invalidates it but rather the mistake thereby induced. It follows that an apparent consent given under a fundamental mistake is equally invalid whether the mistake is attributable to fraud or is self-induced.[85] Similarly, it would seem, an apparent consent given only out of fear is equally invalid whether or not the fear is induced by the defendant's conduct. In *Bruce*[86] the appellants had surrounded a lone passenger in a railway compartment and, without actually threatening him, frightened him into handing over some money. They were acquitted of robbery but convicted of theft. On appeal it was argued that if they had not put the victim in fear and were therefore not guilty of robbery, then he must have given them the money voluntarily, in which case they were not guilty even of theft. The Court of Appeal rejected the argument as fallacious.

"The taking of [the] money was not necessarily the innocent receipt of a gift or loan if it was not robbery. It could have been a dishonest appropriation by takers who had not intended to put a timid man in fear but knew that they had done so and took advantage of his timidity and stole his money."[87]

Thus it seems that an apparent consent is invalid if given only out of fear of violence, whether or not that fear is aroused by such threats or other deliberate conduct as would justify a conviction of robbery.

82 *Supra*, paras. 1.81 ff.
83 *Infra*, paras. 1.170 ff.
84 *e.g. Lynch v. D.P.P. for Northern Ireland* [1976] A.C. 653 at pp. 680, 695.
85 *e.g. Gilks* [1972] 1 W.L.R. 1341; *supra*, para. 1.54.
86 [1975] 1 W.L.R. 1252.
87 At pp. 1256 f.

1.97   These considerations apply only to the normal situation where the victim's fear of violence is his sole reason for entering into the transaction at all. If he is also influenced by other potential benefits over and above the avoidance of personal injury, he is still entitled to repudiate the transaction[88] but it can hardly be void *ab initio* because he may prefer not to.[89] Presumably, therefore, the obtaining is not an appropriation.

1.98   More significantly, threats to inflict harm other than personal injury do not vitiate a transaction at all unless they constitute illegitimate pressure amounting to compulsion of the victim's will. The victim must have no practical choice open to him other than entering into the transaction, and the threats depriving him of such choice must be illegitimate in view of either the sanction threatened or the nature of the demand. Even then the transaction is not void but voidable.[90] It is submitted that the obtaining of property by threats cannot fairly be regarded as theft if the threats are not such as to render the transaction even voidable. If the civil law does not regard them as improper it would seem inappropriate for the criminal law to intervene.[91] More doubtful, perhaps, is the intermediate case where the transaction is rendered voidable but not void, either because the threat is only one of the factors influencing the victim or because it is a threat of something less than personal violence; but it is submitted that in either case there is such a consent as to prevent the obtaining of the property from being an appropriation. Like a transaction procured by deception but not rendered void by fundamental mistake, the transaction is fully valid unless and until the victim chooses to rescind it. To deem it somehow invalid even before he has done so would be contrary to principle. If such a case merits prosecution at all the appropriate charge is one of blackmail.[92]

1.99   Like the person who apprehends violence, a person who has to choose between parting with his property and some less appealing alternative may be put in this dilemma by circumstances other than direct threats. Unlike the fear of violence, however, other forms of pressure cannot have precisely the same effect, whether they result from threats or from other circumstances, because where they do result from threats they

88   *Barton v. Armstrong* [1976] A.C. 104.
89   In *Barton v. Armstrong, supra*, the Privy Council granted a declaration that the deeds in question were "void" as against the victim of the duress, but this clearly did not mean that they had been void all along. The victim had demonstrated his wish to repudiate them by seeking the declaration.
90   *Pao On v. Lau Yiu Long* [1980] A.C. 614 at p. 636; *Universe Tankships Inc. of Monrovia v. International Transport Workers' Federation* [1983] 1 A.C. 366 at p. 400, *per* Lord Scarman.
91   *Cf. infra*, paras. 1.154 ff.
92   *Infra*, paras. 3.02 ff.

do not necessarily vitiate the victim's consent even if they leave him no real choice: the threats must also be "illegitimate" in view of either the sanction threatened or the nature of the demand.[93] This latter requirement can have no application where the defendant neither threatens the victim with any sanction nor makes any demand, but simply places him in a position where disastrous consequences are inevitable unless he parts with his property. Nor can the validity of the victim's consent depend solely on the availability of a practical alternative course of action, because it can hardly be right that a consent extracted by threats is less likely to be invalid than one obtained by other forms of pressure.

1.100   The problem arose, but appears to have gone unrecognised, in *Navvabi*.[94] The appellant had drawn cheques in favour of a casino, guaranteeing them with a cheque card and thus imposing upon his bank an obligation to honour them. He had neither funds nor an overdraft facility and was therefore not authorised to use the cheque card. The Court of Appeal quashed his conviction of stealing the bank's money by delivering the cheques and tendering the cheque card, on the ground that those acts merely gave the payee of the cheques a contractual right to a specified sum of money: no identifiable property was lost by the bank until the cheques were presented and honoured. It was conceded that the appellant could properly have been convicted of stealing the money paid by the bank if the prosecution had relied upon an appropriation at the time when the bank paid it, rather than the time when he drew the cheques. The court doubted whether this concession was correct, and it has been argued that it was not.

> "Even if (as, of course, would not be the fact) the bank had paid the casino in cash, it could hardly be said that the particular banknotes were being appropriated by the appellant. The bank, which was the owner, would have been acting as such in handing over the notes; and the casino would have acted quite properly receiving the ownership (not 'assuming' it) when it took possession of them. Neither the bank nor the casino was, in any sense, acting as the agent of the appellant and these acts could not be attributed to him."[95]

1.101   An alternative view is that the appellant deliberately deprived the bank of its money, just as if he had broken into the vaults and taken it. The difference is that the bank consented to hand the money over; but that difference is immaterial if the bank's consent was effectively nullified by the absence of any practicable alternative. There is an analogy with the reasoning in *Beck*,[96] where the deception involved in the appellant's

---

93   *Universe Tankships Inc. of Monrovia v. International Transport Workers' Federation* [1983] A.C. 366 at pp. 400 f., *per* Lord Scarman.
94   [1986] 1 W.L.R. 1311.
95   J.C. Smith, [1987] Crim.L.R. at p. 58.
96   [1985] 1 W.L.R. 22.

use of forged traveller's cheques was held to have been the cause of his bank's accepting them. The chain of causation was not broken by the fact that the bank paid up in the knowledge that the traveller's cheques were forgeries, because its decision to do so was not genuinely voluntary: in commercial terms it had no choice. Similarly the decision whether to honour a cheque guaranteed by a cheque card is, to a bank proposing to remain in business, no decision at all. It has no choice. But the reasoning adopted in *Beck* was rejected in *Bevan*,[97] where an appellant who misused a cheque card in essentially the same way as Navvabi was held to have obtained a pecuniary advantage (*viz.* being allowed to borrow by way of overdraft) by deception.[98] The fact that the bank could not realistically have refused to honour the cheques, and thereby to let the appellant overdraw, did not mean that it had not "allowed" him to do so.

> "When the appellant's bank received a request by the paying bank for reimbursement in respect of a cheque drawn by the appellant, it of course readily complied. The bank's motive was no doubt the protection of its own reputation, as well as its contractual obligation owed directly to the paying bank . . . But reimbursement by the appellant's bank was nevertheless an act of will; when it took place the appellant was allowed by the bank to borrow money on overdraft; and the overdraft was consensual, since the appellant had impliedly requested it and the bank had, albeit reluctantly, agreed."[99]

It has been rightly pointed out that the appellant's bank, "far from allowing him to borrow, simply recognised that he had already 'helped himself' to the money".[1] But in that case perhaps Navvabi did appropriate the bank's money after all. If, on the other hand, the reasoning in *Bevan* is right, then Navvabi's bank voluntarily paid the money to his order, and in the light of *Morris* this could not be an appropriation on his part. Indeed it was said in *Bevan*, on the authority of *Navvabi*, that the appellant was clearly not guilty of stealing from the bank.[2]

Entrapment

1.102 Where the owner of property allows another to have easy access to it with a view to catching him if he steals it, the owner may expect or even hope that it will be taken but he does not thereby consent to the taking; the suspect therefore commits theft if he falls into the trap. If, however, the owner goes further and instructs an employee to hand the property over to the suspected thief, feigning disloyalty, the suspect's

97 (1987) 84 Cr.App.R. 143.
98 Theft Act 1968 s. 16(2)(*b*); *Fraud*, para. 3.38.
99 At p. 148.
1 J. C. Smith, [1987] Crim.L.R. at p. 130.
2 (1987) 84 Cr.App.R. 143 at p. 146.

receipt of the property is now authorised by the owner[3] and is presumably therefore not an appropriation but only an attempt to appropriate.[4] The would-be thief has failed in his objective and a charge of attempted theft would seem adequate, just as a confidence trickster is guilty only of an attempt to obtain money by deception if his intended victim sees through the fraud and pays up only in order to trap him;[5] but it would not be surprising if the requirement of an unauthorised act were to be qualified in such a way as to permit a conviction of the full offence.

Property got by another's mistake
1.103   Lord Roskill's dictum must be subject to at least one exception if the Act is not to be reduced to absurdity: *viz.* where the defendant has acquired both ownership and possession of the property in question, but under section 5(4) it is deemed to belong to another because the defendant got it by another's mistake and is under an obligation to make restoration, in whole or in part, of the property or its proceeds or of the value thereof.[6] The typical example is that of a person who is inadvertently paid more money than is in fact due to him, and dishonestly keeps the excess on discovering the mistake. His keeping of the money will almost always be authorised by the person to whom the obligation is owed, because that person will usually be the one who mistakenly gave it to him in the first place; that person may of course discover the mistake before the defendant does, and demand repayment, but in that case a refusal on the defendant's part will hardly be dishonest. A literal application of *Morris* would render section 5(4) virtually redundant, which is unlikely to have been the intention of Parliament. In this respect, as in others, the subsection must be regarded as anomalous and exceptional.

Appropriation after acquiring property without stealing it

The general rule
1.104   After defining appropriation in general terms, section 3(1) goes on:

". . . and this includes, where [a person] has come by the property (innocently or not) without stealing it, any later assumption of a right to it by keeping or dealing with it as owner."

A person may "come by" property innocently if the acquisition is not dishonest, *e.g.* if he finds it and believes that its owner cannot reasonably

3 *Turvey* [1946] 2 All E.R. 60.
4 Criminal Attempts Act 1981 s. 1(2), (3); *Shivpuri* [1987] A.C. 1.
5 *Mills* (1857) 1 Dears & B. 205; see *Fraud*, para. 2.22.
6 *Supra*, paras. 1.40 ff.

be traced,[7] or picks it up in a shop and forgets to pay for it. If he subsequently assumes a right to it by keeping it or dealing with it as owner, that subsequent appropriation will be theft if done dishonestly and with the intention permanently to deprive. The same applies if the original acquisition was not innocent but was not theft either, *e.g.* if the defendant originally intended merely to borrow the property without authority but then decides to keep it for good. A "dealing with the property as owner" might amount to an appropriation either in the ordinary sense (*e.g.* disposing of the property) or in the extended sense (*e.g.* using it after deciding not to return it). It is arguable that "keeping" is even wider in that it includes passive retention of the property without any positive act at all. But this interpretation was rejected in *Broom v. Crowther*,[8] where the defendant was held not to have appropriated an article merely by allowing it to remain in his bedroom after discovering that it was stolen. Similarly in *Ditch and Ward*[9] it was held that if a person has come into possession of goods, otherwise than by an act of his or with which he is concerned, he does not appropriate them if he merely decides to keep them and does nothing more. It would be strange if the making of a decision could in itself amount to theft; but the word "keeping" must mean something. Perhaps it denotes a failure to return the property such as would render the defendant liable in conversion. This would be consistent with the view advanced below, that only acts which are unlawful as a matter of civil law can amount to theft.[10]

The bona fide *purchaser*

1.105 To this general rule there is one exception. Section 3(2) provides:

"Where property or a right or interest in property is or purports to be transferred for value to a person acting in good faith, no later assumption by him of rights which he believed himself to be acquiring shall, by reason of any defect in the transferor's title, amount to theft of the property."

If in good faith a person buys property which has been obtained by fraud, he will probably obtain a good title to the property because the seller will probably have had a voidable one.[11] Even if the buyer subsequently finds out about the fraud and keeps the property anyway, he will not be stealing it because he will not be appropriating property belonging to another: the property now belongs to him. But if the seller has no title to the property at all, *e.g.* because it has been stolen, even a *bona fide* purchaser will normally acquire no title either: *nemo dat quod non habet*. If he then

---

7   s. 2(1)(*c*), *infra*, para. 1.146.
8   (1984) 148 J.P. 592; see J.R. Spencer, [1985] Crim.L.R. at p. 93.
9   28 February 1986, unreported (C.A.).
10 *Infra*, paras. 1.154 ff.
11 Sale of Goods Act 1979 s. 23.

discovers that the property is stolen, but keeps it or otherwise deals with it as owner, section 3(2) shields him from the full rigour of section 3(1). His assumption of rights which he thought he was acquiring when he bought the property does not amount to theft. The fact that he now knows he did *not* acquire those rights is immaterial. But this exemption is hedged about with qualifications. It applies only if the defendant gave value for the property, or for the right or interest in it which he thought he was acquiring, and only if he did so in good faith; the latter requirement is probably not satisfied if he suspected that the goods might be stolen.[12] Moreover section 3(2) only protects him from a charge of *stealing* the property by *himself* assuming the rights of an owner over it, *e.g.* by keeping it. He can still be guilty of other offences, or of stealing in other ways. If he sells the goods to someone who does not know they are stolen, he will probably be guilty of obtaining the price by deception;[13] and if he dishonestly undertakes their retention, removal, disposal or realisation for the benefit of another person, or assists in their retention, removal, disposal or realisation by another person, he will be guilty of handling them.[14] Selling the goods is not in itself a disposal or realisation for the benefit of another person,[15] but if the purchaser knows that they are stolen then *he* will be guilty of both handling and theft,[16] and the seller will be a party to those offences. It might perhaps be argued that to charge him in such circumstances would be contrary to the spirit of section 3(2), but the subsection is itself something of a concession to human frailty and it may be legitimate to confine it strictly to its terms.

Successive appropriations

1.106 There is no reason why the same property should not be the subject of successive appropriations, and therefore successive thefts, from different victims. Since property belongs to a person who has possession or control of it, albeit without title,[17] it follows that property which has already been stolen by one person may be stolen from him by another. It is also clear that there can be successive appropriations from the *same* victim: a person who "comes by" property belonging to another will almost invariably be appropriating it, and section 3(1) makes it clear that he can subsequently appropriate it again.[18] It is more doubtful whether such successive appropriations can constitute successive *thefts*. Section

12 This was the view of the justices in *Broom v. Crowther* (1984) 148 J.P. 592.
13 s. 15(1), *infra*, Ch. 2.
14 s. 22(1), *infra*, paras. 4.02 ff.
15 *Bloxham* [1983] 1 A.C. 109; *infra* para. 4.42.
16 *Infra*, para. 4.75.
17 s. 5(1); *supra*, para. 1.27.
18 *Supra*, para. 1.104.

3(1) says that a person can appropriate property by dealing with it after coming by it if he came by it "without stealing it", which would seem to imply that if he did steal it at that point then he does not steal it again by dealing with it as owner. If, for example, he first acquires the property and then disposes of it, the disposal may be an appropriation (and therefore a theft) if the acquisition was not a theft; if it *was* a theft, it seems that the disposal is not an appropriation at all. In *Meech*[19] one of the appellants had withdrawn money from a bank on behalf of another man, whereupon the other appellants pretended (with his connivance) to rob him of it. It was argued on their behalf that the money was stolen by the first appellant when he withdrew it from the bank with the intention of defrauding its owner, and that it could not therefore have been stolen again at the time of the bogus robbery. The Court of Appeal rejected the argument that the money was stolen when it was withdrawn,[20] but accepted the implied assumption that only if it were not stolen at that stage could it be stolen later. If this is right it may follow that a person who steals property abroad cannot steal it again even if he appropriates it (*e.g.* by disposing of it) within the jurisdiction.[21] But it might be argued that such a person has come by the property "without stealing it" and is therefore still eligible to steal it by virtue of section 3(1). An offence committed abroad is not merely an offence over which the English courts have no jurisdiction: it is not an offence under English law at all.[22] Possibly a person who steals property abroad is not "stealing" it within the meaning of the Act.[23]

The duration of an appropriation

1.107 The problem of successive appropriations must be distinguished from that of whether an appropriation is instantaneous or continues over a period of time. For the purposes of theft itself the issue is largely academic (except for drafting purposes), but it is a real one in the case of robbery (where the defendant must use or threaten force "immediately before or at the time of" stealing)[24] and in that of handling stolen goods (where the act of handling must be done "otherwise than in the course of the stealing").[25] The difference is that on a robbery charge it is the

19 [1974] Q.B. 549.
20 *Supra*, para. 1.74.
21 *Cf. Figures* [1976] Crim.L.R. 744.
22 *Treacy v. D.P.P.* [1971] A.C. 537 at p. 559, *per* Lord Diplock; *D.P.P. v. Stonehouse* [1978] A.C. 55 at p. 90, *per* Lord Keith.
23 In the absence of express provision to the contrary, *e.g.* s. 24(1) (*infra*, para. 4.05), which however applies only to the provisions of the Act relating to goods which have already been stolen.
24 *Infra*, para. 1.175.
25 *Infra*, para. 4.72.

prosecution who may need to allege that the stealing continued over a period of time, while on a handling charge it is the defence. Oddly enough, stealing seems to go on for longer in robbery cases[26] than in those of handling.[27]

Intention permanently to deprive

1.108 The defendant must have appropriated the property with the intention of permanently depriving of it the person to whom it belongs. If he has no such intention, he may be guilty of other offences[28] but he is not guilty of theft. The requirement may conveniently be analysed in terms of four issues. Firstly, when is a person to whom property belongs "deprived" of it? Secondly, when is such deprivation permanent? Thirdly, what is an intention to bring permanent deprivation about? And finally, in which circumstances may a person who does not literally intend to cause permanent deprivation nevertheless be deemed so to intend?

Deprivation

Tangible property

1.109 An owner of tangible property is obviously deprived of it if he loses possession of it, even if he retains ownership; and presumably *vice versa*. It seems that he is also deprived of it for the purposes of the Act if he has already lost possession and is prevented from regaining it, since a person who dishonestly receives goods which have already been stolen can be convicted not only of handling stolen goods (which does not require an intention permanently to deprive) but also of theft (which does).[29]

Intangible property

1.110 Intangible property, on the other hand, consists solely of legal rights.[30] It cannot be possessed, and its owner cannot therefore be deprived of it by being dispossessed. He is not *literally* deprived of it unless he loses his rights. This may indeed be the effect of an appropriation if the appropriator is authorised to dispose of the property on the owner's behalf.[31] In *Koln*[32] a director who fraudulently drew cheques on his company's bank account was held to have stolen the debt owned to the company by the bank and represented by the credit balance in the account. The company was not entitled to have the sums

---

26   *Hale* (1978) 68 Cr.App.R. 415; *infra*, para. 1.176.
27   *Pitham and Hehl* (1977) 65 Cr.App.R. 45; *infra*, para. 4.73.
28   *Infra*, ch. 5.
29   *Stapylton v. O'Callaghan* [1973] 2 All E.R. 782; *infra*, para. 4.75.
30   *Supra*, para. 1.12.
31   Though the existence of such authority may mean that there is no appropriation: *supra*, paras. 1.92 ff.
32   (1979) 69 Cr.App.R. 395.

in question restored to the account when the fraud was discovered, and was permanently deprived of the money. But it seems that even if the company's rights against the bank had been unaffected the intention permanently to deprive would nevertheless have been deemed to exist.[33]

Permanent deprivation

1.111 The defendant's intention must be to deprive the victim *permanently* of his property. This requirement is obviously not literally satisfied if his intention is to return the property at some later stage, though in certain circumstances a temporary deprivation may be deemed to be permanent.[34] But it is not in itself a defence that he intends to (or does) replace the property with other property of equivalent value, even if the two are for all practical purposes interchangeable. Thus a person who "borrows" money without authority intends to deprive the owner permanently even if he intends to "pay it back", unless his intention is to return the same notes or coins and not just others to the same value.[35] If he has a defence it will be on the grounds not that he had no intention permanently to deprive but that he did not act dishonestly.[36]

1.112 A person to whom property "belongs" in the sense that he has a limited interest in it, such as a right to possession for a limited period under a contract of hire, may be deprived of it permanently even though he had no right to keep it permanently in the first place. Thus a person who takes such property, even with the intention of returning it to the owner once the period of hire has expired, can be guilty of stealing it from the hirer.

Intention

1.113 The defendant must *intend* permanently to deprive. The precise meaning of this requirement may vary according to the circumstances. In particular, there is a distinction between an intention to *act* in a certain way and an intention that one's actions shall result in certain *consequences*. In the present context the latter type takes the form of an appropriation intended to cause permanent deprivation in itself, without the need for any further action on the defendant's part; the former is represented by the more common case where he intends to cause permanent deprivation by dint of what he intends to do (or to refrain from doing) after the initial appropriation.

---

33 *Infra*, paras. 1.133 f.
34 *Infra*, paras. 1.126 ff.
35 *Halstead v. Patel* [1972] 1 W.L.R. 661; *Velumyl* [1989] Crim.L.R. 299.
36 *Infra*, paras. 1.138 ff.

Appropriation itself intended to cause permanent deprivation

1.114 Clearly the defendant intends permanently to deprive of the property the person to whom it belongs if he intends the act of appropriation itself, without any further action on his part, to have that effect. Where the appropriation puts the property not only out of the victim's control but also out of the defendant's (*e.g.* where it consists in a disposal of the property) there is no question of the defendant's doing anything further by way of depriving the victim of it: the only issues are, firstly, what consequences he intends to flow from the appropriation itself, and secondly, whether those consequences would involve permanent deprivation. Thus a person who throws another's property down a well may be guilty of stealing it if, but only if, he intends that as a result of that action the owner shall not get the property back. The consequences which a person "intends" to bring about by his conduct include those which it is his purpose to bring about, and in order to achieve which he acts as he does; if there are other consequences which it is not his purpose to bring about, but which he knows are virtually certain to result from his action, it may be legitimate for a jury to infer that he intended them too.[37] Thus the person who throws property down a well may be regarded as intending permanently to deprive its owner of it if he knows that the owner will be unable to get it back, even if his motive in doing so is not to deprive the owner of it but to see how deep the well is. A person who knows that his conduct *may* result in the owner of property being permanently deprived of it, though the likelihood of this result falls short of a virtual certainty, does not literally intend that result; but he might be deemed to intend it.[38]

Intention as to subsequent conduct

1.115 We have seen that the act of appropriation need not itself deprive the victim of the property at all.[39] Therefore, even if the appropriation is not itself intended to deprive the victim permanently without further action on the defendant's part, it may nevertheless amount to theft if *either* it does itself deprive the victim, and the defendant intends to ensure that the deprivation thus effected becomes permanent, *or* it does not itself deprive the victim but is done with the intention of depriving him later and doing so with permanent effect. We shall consider these alternatives in turn.

1.116 *Intention to render deprivation permanent.* Where the appropriation itself has the effect of depriving the victim of the property for the

---

37 *Moloney* [1985] A.C. 905; *Nedrick* [1986] 1 W.L.R. 1025; *infra*, paras. 6.14 ff.
38 *Infra*, paras. 1.126 ff.
39 *Supra*, paras. 1.64 ff.

time being, the question is whether at the time of the appropriation the defendant's intention is to act (or to refrain from acting) in such a way as to render that deprivation permanent. What is required in this context is not only an intention that a certain consequence (*sc.* permanent deprivation) shall result from the defendant's conduct, but also an intention to *act* (or to refrain from acting) at some later stage in such a way as to bring that consequence about. Discussion of the nature of intention in the criminal law has tended to concentrate on the former type, sometimes to the virtual exclusion of the latter; but the two are quite distinct. The existence or otherwise of the former type depends partly on the defendant's purpose in acting as he does, and partly on his perception of the likelihood that the consequences in question will ensue; that of the latter on the plans (if any) which he has already formulated at the relevant time (*i.e.,* in the context of theft, that of the appropriation) with regard to his conduct thereafter. A well-known dictum of Asquith L.J. in a civil case incorporates both types:

> "If the plaintiff did no more than entertain [this] idea . . . ; if she got no further than to contemplate it as a (perhaps attractive) possibility, then one would have to say (and it matters not which way it is put) either that there was *no* evidence of a positive 'intention', or the word 'intention' was incapable as a matter of construction of applying to anything so tentative, and so indefinite. An 'intention' to my mind connotes a state of affairs which the party 'intending' . . . does more than merely contemplate: it connotes a state of affairs which, on the contrary, he decides, so far as in him lies, to bring about, and which, in point of possibility, he has a reasonable prospect of being able to bring about, by his own act of volition."[40]

His Lordship was not of course attempting an exhaustive definition: his point was that a person cannot be said to "intend" a state of affairs to come about unless he has either done an act which may itself have that effect or has at least decided to do so at a later stage. Merely contemplating the possibility of acting in a particular way is not enough: he must have made up his mind that he will do so. Thus a person who has not decided whether or not to steal, even if the opportunity should present itself, does not intend to steal.[41] Similarly a person who appropriates another's property by taking it under his own control, and thereby depriving its owner of it, does not thereby steal it unless he has made up his mind to act thereafter in such a way that the owner will not get it back (*e.g.* by keeping it for good, destroying it or disposing of it to a third party who will not return it to its owner).

---

40 *Cunliffe v. Goodman* [1950] 2 K.B. 237 at p. 253. The second sentence was cited with approval by Lord Hailsham L.C. in *Hyam* [1975] A.C. 55 at p. 74, and applied by the Court of Appeal in *Mohan* [1976] Q.B. 1.
41 *Hargreaves* [1985] Crim.L.R. 243.

1.117 This principle must however be qualified in one important respect. It is possible to intend to act in a particular way without making up one's mind that one will definitely do so, come what may. An intention to do something if, and only if, certain conditions are fulfilled is an intention to do it. Thus a man would be guilty of burglary contrary to section 9(1)(*a*) of the Theft Act 1968, which requires an intention to commit (*inter alia*) theft or rape,[42] if he entered a building as a trespasser with the intention of stealing a particular article should it be there, or (probably) of having sexual intercourse with a woman whether or not she should consent.[43] It would seem to follow that it would be theft to appropriate a garment with the intention of trying it on later and keeping it only if it should turn out to be a good fit, or to appropriate a work of art with the intention of having it examined and keeping it only if it should turn out to be authentic.

1.118 However, two decisions of the Court of Appeal suggest that an intention to keep the property appropriated only if certain conditions should prove to be satisfied is not sufficient on a charge of theft (as against attempted theft) unless those conditions *are* satisfied. In *Easom*[44] the appellant had rifled through the handbag of a woman sitting next to him in a cinema but found nothing of any value and left the contents as he found them. Unfortunately for him, the woman was a police officer; but his conviction of stealing the contents was quashed.

> "In every case of theft the appropriation must be accompanied by the intention of permanently depriving the owner of his property. What may be loosely described as a 'conditional' appropriation will not do. If the appropriator has it in mind merely to deprive the owner of such of his property as, on examination, proves worth taking and then, finding that the booty is valueless to the appropriator, leaves it ready to hand to be repossessed by the owner, the appropriator has not stolen. If a dishonest postal sorter picks up a pile of letters, intending to steal any which are registered, but, on finding that none of them are, replaces them, he has stolen nothing . . . "[45]

This last proposition is clearly correct, if only because a postal sorter has authority to pick up letters, and his doing what he is authorised to do cannot amount to an appropriation even if he does it with a secret dishonest intention.[46] But the court apparently meant that his intention to keep any letters which are registered is not an intention to keep the letters he picks up, because those letters are not registered. Similarly

42 *Infra*, paras. 7.24 ff.
43 *Infra*, para. 7.31.
44 [1971] 2 Q.B. 315.
45 At p. 319.
46 *Morris* [1984] A.C. 320; *supra*, para. 1.75.

Easom's intention to keep any valuable articles he might find was not an intention to keep the worthless ones he did find. On a suitably drawn indictment he might properly have been convicted of attempting to steal the valuable articles which were not there, but he had not stolen the worthless ones which were. This reasoning was endorsed in *Bayley and Easterbrook*,[47] where the appellants had appropriated a box containing two pieces of valuable railway equipment. They did not know what it contained until they opened it, whereupon they decided that they had no use for the contents. They therefore returned both the contents and the box. Their convictions of attempted theft were upheld[48] but the court added that they had rightly been acquitted of theft.

1.119   In both these cases the court took the view that although the appellants had intended to steal they had not succeeded in doing so, because what they had taken was something they did not want. A person who appropriates property in the hope that it is something he wants is not guilty of stealing it if it is in fact something he does not want. Strictly speaking this rule is not entirely logical. Such a person does intend to keep the property he appropriates: his intention is conditional on the property being what he wants, but it is intention nonetheless. If he did not intend to steal he could not be guilty of an attempt, which (as *Bayley* confirms) he is. It may be said that what he intends to steal is not the property he in fact appropriates but some other property which is not there. But this will not do, because in neither of the cases is it suggested that he would not be guilty of theft if the property *were* what he wanted, even if he did not know it yet. The court in *Easom* said that the dishonest postal sorter would not be guilty of theft if none of the letters he picked up were registered: if one of them were, it is submitted that (subject to the question of appropriation) he would be guilty of stealing it as soon as he picked up the pile. But if this is right then it follows that he intends to keep all the letters, including the ones which are not registered. His intention when he picks them up is exactly the same whether some of them are registered or all of them or none of them, because by definition his intention cannot depend on circumstances as yet unknown to him: it is simply an intention to keep any letters which are registered and to replace any which are not. Whether any of them *are* registered will determine what course of action is dictated by this intention, but it cannot affect the intention itself. Logically, therefore, the sorter is stealing all the letters, registered or not, because he intends (conditionally, but that is immaterial) to keep them all.

47   [1980] Crim.L.R. 503.
48   *Infra*, para. 1.124.

1.120 On the other hand the apparently logical conclusion seems repugnant to common sense. It would bring the law into disrepute to convict people of stealing worthless rubbish. Moreover a person cannot on any view be convicted of theft unless he appropriates *something* which he thinks may be what he wants. If he takes a box, intending to open it later and examine the contents, and to return the box alone if the contents are valuable but to return both box and contents if they are not, it would be absurd that his liability should hinge on whether the box contained worthless rubbish or nothing at all. It makes good practical sense that if what he has taken is not what he wants then he should be convicted not of theft but only of an attempt.

1.121 Let us assume, then, that the property which the defendant has appropriated is something which he would choose to keep if he knew what it was: otherwise, as we have just seen, he cannot be guilty of more than an attempt. But even if what he has taken is something he would want, it does not follow that he intends to keep it before he knows what it is. It is true that an intention to keep property on certain conditions is an intention to keep it. Therefore, it may be said, an intention to keep property on condition that it should prove to be what one wants is an intention to keep it. But there are conditions and conditions. Suppose the defendant has not the slightest idea what his booty might be, and his intention is simply to examine it at the first opportunity and then to decide whether to keep it or return it. If it is in fact valuable, it cannot be argued that what he intends to keep is not *this* property but some other property which he has not taken. But there is another, quite different objection: can it be said in these circumstances that he *intends* to keep any property at all?

1.122 The passage quoted from *Easom* above suggests not, and it was applied in *Husseyn*.[49] The appellant in that case had been caught tampering with the door of a van which contained a holdall which in turn contained valuable sub-aqua equipment, and he was convicted of attempting to steal the sub-aqua equipment.[50] The difficulty faced by the prosecution was that the appellant had not known what was in the holdall, and he would not have taken its contents had he inspected them and found them to be of no value. The Court of Appeal concluded that he had not therefore intended to steal.

"The learned judge said that the jury could infer that what the [appellant was] about was to look into the holdall and, if its contents were valuable, to steal it. In the view of this Court that was a misdirection . . .

49 (1977) 67 Cr.App.R. 131; otherwise *Hussein*.
50 See *Attorney-General's References (Nos. 1 and 2 of 1979)* [1980] Q.B. 180 at p. 189.

The direction of the learned judge in this case . . . must be wrong, for it cannot be said that one who has it in mind to steal only if what he finds is worth stealing has a present intention to steal."[51]

This statement, and the dictum in *Easom* on which it was based, were almost universally condemned as amounting to a "rogues' charter". Lord Scarman, who had delivered the judgment in *Husseyn*, subsequently explained:

> "In *Easom* . . . Edmund Davies L.J. emphasised that in a case of theft the appropriation must be accompanied by the intention of permanently depriving the owner of his property . . . All that *Hussein* decided was that the same intention must be proved when the charge is one of attempted theft. Unfortunately in *Hussein* the issue of intention was summed up in such a way as to suggest that theft, or attempted theft, could be committed by a person who has not yet formed the intention which the statute defines as a necessary part of the offence. An intention to steal can exist even though, unknown to the accused, there is nothing to steal; but, if a man be in two minds as to whether to steal or not, the intention required by the statute is not proved."[52]

1.123 His Lordship thus acknowledged that the difficulty to which he had referred in *Husseyn* would equally have arisen if the appellant had got as far as picking the holdall up, though still unaware of what it contained, and had accordingly been charged with actually stealing its contents. But in *Attorney-General's References (Nos. 1 and 2 of 1979)*[53] his dictum was explained away on a ground which (although the court asserted otherwise) could apply only to the requirement of intention to steal in inchoate offences such as attempted theft, and not to the element of intention permanently to deprive in the full offence of theft.[54] The court went on to hold that an intention to keep property if it should prove to be worth stealing is nonetheless an intention to keep it. This proposition is applicable not only to attempted theft but also to theft, and contradicts not only what Lord Scarman said in *Husseyn* but also (on one interpretation, at least) what he subsequently claimed to have meant. But it is too ambiguous to be applied without clarification. The court's reasoning equates an intention to keep property if it satisfies some objective criterion, *e.g.* that of being genuine rather than counterfeit, with an intention to keep it if it is "worth stealing". The latter intention, it seems, is just as much an intention permanently to deprive (or, if the property is not actually appropriated, an intention to steal) as the former. But this is tantamount to saying that a person may form an intention to

---

51 At p. 132.
52 *D.P.P. v. Nock* [1978] A.C. 979 at p. 1000.
53 [1980] Q.B. 180.
54 See *infra*, para. 1.183.

do something without ever making up his mind that he will, or even
making up his mind that he will do it if certain objective criteria should
prove to be satisfied. An intention to keep an article if it turns out to be
an article of a particular type is nonetheless a (conditional) intention to
keep it. The criterion is an objective one: either the article is of the type
in question or it is not, and if it is then the decision to keep it has already
been taken. No further deliberation is required. An intention to consider
the matter with an open mind at some later stage, and *then* to decide
whether to keep the article, is not an intention to keep it at all—not even
a conditional one.[55] To describe the latter intention as being an intention
to keep the property on condition that it should prove to be "worth
stealing", and therefore as constituting an intention to steal because even
a conditional intention is an intention, is to play with words. Husseyn
doubtless did intend to steal the contents of the holdall if they proved to
be "worth stealing"; but the question of whether they *were* worth stealing
was not one to which the answer would become apparent as soon as he
inspected them. It would depend, for example, whether he himself had
any use for sub-aqua equipment, and (if not) how easily, and at what
price, and with how much risk, he would expect to be able to dispose of
it. These were questions which he *might* have considered and resolved
before trying to get into the van, but doubtless he had not done so because
he did not know what was in it. He would therefore have had to address
his mind to them if he had succeeded in getting into the van and opening
the holdall. Having considered them, he would then have had to make
up his mind whether, in the light of these factors, the equipment was
"worth stealing"—in other words, whether to steal it. To say that he
intended all along to steal the contents, if they were worth stealing, is no
more than a somewhat tendentious way of saying that he intended first
to inspect them and then to decide whether or not to steal them; and an
intention to decide later whether or not to do a thing is not an intention
to do it.

1.124 Admittedly there is no longer any likelihood of a judge being criticised on appeal for ignoring this difficulty. In *Bayley and
Easterbrook*[56] the appellants had taken a box whose contents proved on
inspection to be of no use to them. They were convicted of attempted
theft after a direction that it would be sufficient if they had taken the box
dishonestly and with the already-formed intention of keeping its contents,
whatever they might be, if of value to them. Their appeals were dismissed
on the grounds that they "did intend to steal whatever was in the box;
whether they would keep the contents or any of them would depend on

55   *Hargreaves* [1985] Crim.L.R. 243.
56   [1980] Crim.L.R. 503.

what they were."[57] In other words it was sufficient if the appellants intended to inspect the contents and then to decide whether or not to keep them, though this state of mind had to be decently wrapped up as an "already-formed intention" of keeping them. It does not follow that the point is now of purely academic interest. At the heart of the approved solution, it is submitted, lies a serious ambiguity; and while that ambiguity need not be clarified by the judge, there is no reason why it should not be drawn to the jury's attention by the defence.

1.125 *Intention to deprive later.* Where the appropriation does not itself have the effect of depriving the victim of the property, the intention which must be proved is an intention to do something at a later stage which will not only deprive him of it but will do so permanently—with or without some further action on the defendant's part at some yet later stage. If, for example, the appropriation consists in the switching of price labels in a supermarket,[58] it must be proved that the defendant intended first to remove the more expensive article from the supermarket, and then to keep it or otherwise ensure that the supermarket would not get it back. In this case the act of appropriation will be of some assistance in effecting the intended act of deprivation, since the defendant will be able to buy the article more cheaply as a result of having switched the labels; but it is not clear whether this is essential. It would be surprising if it were not. A person does not steal his neighbour's lawn-mower by using it without permission but with the intention of returning it; it can hardly make any difference that he intends to take it again, and this time for good, when the owner goes on holiday.

Constructive intention permanently to deprive

1.126 Section 6(1) of the Theft Act 1968 provides:

> "A person appropriating property belonging to another without meaning the other permanently to lose the thing itself is nevertheless to be regarded as having the intention of permanently depriving the other of it if his intention is to treat the thing as his own to dispose of regardless of the other's rights; and a borrowing or lending of it may amount to so treating it if, but only if, the borrowing or lending is for a period and in circumstances making it equivalent to an outright taking or disposal."

It has been said that section 6 merely gives "illustrations" of what can amount to an intention permanently to deprive, that it is a misconception

---

57 This reasoning, like that in the *Attorney-General's References,* ignores the fact that a person could not at that time be convicted of attempting to steal something which was not there: *Haughton v. Smith* [1975] A.C. 476; *Partington v. Williams* (1975) 62 Cr.App.R. 220. The rule was abolished by the Criminal Attempts Act 1981 s. 1(2): *infra,* para. 1.188.
58 *Cf. Morris* [1984] A.C. 320; *supra,* para. 1.65.

to interpret it as "watering down" the definition of theft in section 1(1),[59] and that it does not enlarge the scope of that definition and is purely expository.[60] But if anything is clear about this section it is that in certain circumstances a person who does not literally intend permanently to deprive is nevertheless *deemed* so to intend. The Court of Appeal has confirmed that this is so.[61] The section did not appear in the Criminal Law Revision Committee's draft Bill, and was inserted during the Bill's passage for the sole purpose of ensuring that the requirement of intention permanently to deprive would be interpreted in the same way for the purposes of theft as it had been in the case of larceny.[62] The Court of Appeal has indicated that it should if possible be interpreted as doing no more than that, and indeed that in the vast majority of cases it need not be referred to at all.[63] Yet the draftsman could hardly have concealed the section's objectives more effectively had he tried.

1.127 Subsection (1) begins with the cryptic statement that it is sufficient if the defendant intends to treat "the thing itself" (as distinct from the "property", whatever that distinction may signify) as his own to dispose of regardless of the rights of the person to whom the property belongs. It then leaves the reader wrong-footed (artfully disguising the drift of what follows with the conjunction "and" instead of the logical "but") by saying in effect that if the defendant's intention is to "borrow" or "lend" the "thing", then it does not matter whether his intention is to treat it as his own to dispose of regardless of the other's rights after all: instead (". . . if, but only if . . ."), the question is whether the borrowing or lending is for a period and in circumstances making it equivalent to an outright taking or disposal. Thus the criterion of an intention to treat the thing as the defendant's own to dispose of regardless of the other's rights is strictly relevant *only* where his intention is to do something *other* than a "borrowing" or a "lending", because borrowings and lendings are subject *only* to the criterion of whether they are equivalent to an outright taking or disposal. It would therefore seem reasonable to deal first with borrowings and lendings, and then to consider what is left to be governed by the criterion of an intention to treat the thing as one's own to dispose of regardless of the other's rights. It is here assumed (not because the wording makes it clear but because no other reading would make sense) that some such words as "respectively" or "as the case may be" are to be implied at the end of the subsection, so that the reference is to a

59 *Warner* (1970) 55 Cr.App.R. 93 at p. 97.
60 *Coffey* [1987] Crim.L.R. 498.
61 *Lloyd* [1985] Q.B. 829 at p. 834.
62 See J.R. Spencer, "The Metamorphosis of Section 6 of the Theft Act" [1977] Crim.L.R. 653.
63 *Lloyd* [1985] Q.B. 829 at p. 835.

borrowing which is equivalent to an outright *taking* or a *leading* which is equivalent to an outright *disposal.*

Borrowing equivalent to outright taking
1.128   By a "borrowing" of a thing the section presumably means a taking of possession without the permission of the person to whom the thing belongs but with the intention of returning it to him later. If the defendant appropriates it with the intention of "borrowing" it in this sense, his intention may be deemed to be an intention permanently to deprive (because technically it is deemed to be an intention to treat the thing as his own to dispose of regardless of the other's rights, which in turn is deemed to be an intention permanently to deprive) if the borrowing which he intends to effect would be for a period and in circumstances making it equivalent to an outright taking. In *Lloyd, Bhuee and Ali*[64] the Court of Appeal attempted to explain when this requirement would be satisfied.

> "This half of the subsection, we believe, is intended to make it clear that a mere borrowing is never enough to constitute the necessary guilty mind unless the intention is to return the 'thing' in such a changed state that it can truly be said that all its goodness or virtue has gone . . ."[65]

The "goodness or virtue" may have gone from the thing by the time of its return either because of what has been done to it in the meantime (*e.g.* an appropriation of an animal with the intention of killing it and returning the carcase) or because of the period which will then have elapsed (*e.g.* an appropriation of a season ticket with the intention of returning it only when it has expired). The requirement was not satisfied in *Lloyd* itself, where the appellants had borrowed feature films from a cinema for the purpose of making pirate copies before returning the originals. It could not be said that all the value had been taken from the films before they were returned, and indeed the court took the view that the films themselves (as distinct from the copyright owners' wider commercial interests) had not diminished in value at all. The point was misunderstood in *Bagshaw*,[66] where it was suggested that a defendant who had dishonestly obtained a number of gas cylinders might properly have been convicted of stealing them if his intention were to keep them until all the gas had been used. Even when the cylinders were empty they would not have lost their value, because they could be refilled and used again. If that were the defendant's intention he would be stealing the gas but not the cylinders.

---

64   [1985] Q.B. 829.
65   At p. 836.
66   [1988] Crim.L.R. 321.

1.129   The interpretation of the second part of section 6(1) which was put forward in *Lloyd* may however be unduly restrictive. In *Coffey*[67] the appellant had obtained certain machinery by deception with the intention of exerting pressure on its owner, with whom he had been in dispute, by keeping the machinery until he got what he wanted. It was not clear exactly what he wanted, nor what he proposed to do with the machinery if he did not get whatever it was. His conviction of obtaining property by deception[68] was quashed on the grounds that the summing up was defective, but the Court of Appeal thought that he could properly have been convicted had the jury taken the view that the intended detention of the machinery was "equivalent to an outright taking". Apparently this was a possible conclusion although there was no question of the machinery being drained of its "goodness" before it was returned. The court thought there were two views of the facts which might justify such a conclusion. If the jury had thought that the appellant might have intended eventually to return the machinery even if he did not get what he wanted, they would nevertheless have been entitled to convict if they were sure that he intended to keep it for such a long time as to make the detention equivalent to an outright taking. If, on the other hand, they had thought that his intention was to keep the machinery for good unless he did get what he wanted, they would again have been entitled to convict—but only if they thought that he had regarded this outcome as sufficiently likely to make his intended conduct equivalent to an outright taking. This last qualification is surprising. It would not seem unreasonable to say that a person is effectively taking property outright if his intention is to keep it permanently unless its owner complies with certain conditions, even if he thinks that the owner will probably do so. In *Barnett and Reid*[69] it was said that the taking of property by way of security would normally amount to an intention permanently to deprive,[70] though there might be rare circumstances in which it would not.

Lending equivalent to outright disposal
1.130   A "lending" of a thing is presumably a parting with the possession of it on the terms that it is to be returned either to the lender or to the person to whom it belongs. A person who appropriates property with the intention of lending it will not intend the owner permanently to lose it if his intention is to lend it on the basis that it is to be returned to the owner. If his intention is to lend it on the basis that it is to be returned to him

---

67   [1987] Crim.L.R. 498.
68   *Infra*, ch. 2.
69   21 July 1987, Criminal Appeal Office transcript nos. 5818/C3/86, 5819/C3/86, at p. 5.
70   The court appeared to think that this was the effect of the first part of s. 6(1) rather than the second: *cf. infra*, para. 1.131.

rather than the owner, he may or may not have the necessary intention: it depends what he intends to do with the property when he gets it back. But in either case he may be deemed to have the intention permanently to deprive if the intended lending would be for such a period or in such circumstances as to make it equivalent to an outright disposal. This might be so if he intended that the property should have lost all its "goodness" before it was returned, or that it should be kept by the borrower for a sufficiently long period. These possibilities are perhaps unlikely to arise.

Otherwise treating property as one's own to dispose of
1.131 Where the defendant intends neither to borrow nor to lend the property, but does not intend the owner permanently to lose the thing itself, he may be deemed to have the intention permanently to deprive only if his intention is to treat the thing as his own to dispose of regardless of the owner's rights. In *Lloyd*[71] this provision was explained as follows:

> ". . . the first part of section 6(1) seems to us to be aimed at the sort of case where a defendant takes things and then offers them back to the owner for the owner to buy if he wishes. If the taker intends to return them to the owner only upon such payment, then, on the wording of section 6(1), that is deemed to amount to the necessary intention permanently to deprive . . . There are other cases of similar intent: for instance, 'I have taken your valuable painting. You can have it back on payment to me of £X,000. If you are not prepared to make that payment, then you are not going to get your painting back.' "[72]

The only real difference between these examples is that in the former the owner is apparently not intended to realise that he is buying his own property back, whereas in the latter he is. This distinction can hardly be crucial to the defendant's liability for appropriating the property in the first place, though it will of course determine whether his subsequent attempt to obtain the money is an offence of deception or of blackmail. In *Coffey*[73] the retention of another's property with a view to inducing him to comply with the appellant's demands was regarded as a case where the first part of section 6(1) might usefully have been "illustrated" by the second. But the second part does not *illustrate* the first at all: it lays down a different requirement which, in cases of borrowing and lending, must be satisfied *instead* of that laid down by the first part. Admittedly it does this by deeming a case satisfying the second requirement to have satisfied the first, but if a case is governed by the second part of the subsection, then the only way it *can* satisfy the first requirement is by satisfying the second. The court does not appear to have considered whether the

71 [1985] Q.B. 829.
72 At p. 836.
73 [1987] Crim.L.R. 498; *supra*, para. 1.129.

appellant intended to "borrow" the property at all; yet strictly speaking it is this which determines which part of the subsection applies.

1.132 *Documents returned to owner after use.* The explanation put forward in *Lloyd* may justify the application of the first part of section 6(1) to cases where defendants have appropriated (or obtained by deception) documents of various types with the intention that the documents should find their way back to their owners only after being used to secure some form of financial advantage. One such case is *Duru,*[74] where a person who obtained cheques by deception was held to have done so with the intention of permanently depriving their owners of them, although once the cheques had been presented and honoured the owners would be able to get them back from the bank. The court thought it unnecessary to invoke section 6(1) but added that if necessary the appellant could have been regarded as intending to treat the cheques as his own to dispose of regardless of the other's rights, because on its return to the drawer after being honoured a cheque is no longer a thing of value. It might perhaps be said that all the "goodness" has gone out of it. But this explanation seems unconvincing in the case of *Downes,*[75] where the appellant had sold Inland Revenue tax vouchers to a third party who he knew would use them to perpetrate a fraud on the Revenue. Although the fraud would necessarily involve returning the vouchers to the Revenue, it was held that the appellant intended permanently to deprive the Revenue of them because his intention was to treat them as his own to dispose of regardless of the Revenue's rights. It was expressly stated that the case was governed by the first part of section 6(1) and not the second. Both cases can be explained along the lines suggested in *Lloyd*: both owners were to get their documents back only by "paying" for them, in *Duru* by a reduction in the credit balance of the account on which the cheques were drawn and in *Downes* by demanding less tax from the third party presenting the vouchers. Cases where the owner is intended to get his property back only at some cost to himself are highly likely to be caught by section 6(1). The doubtful cases are those where the *only* loss he is intended to suffer is the temporary loss of the property itself.

1.133 *Effective deprivation of intangible property.* Another possible application of the first part of section 6(1) is in the context of intangible property. Although it is clear that such property can be stolen,[76] its characteristics pose particular difficulties as regards the requirement of an intention permanently to deprive. A person who without authority

74 [1974] 1 W.L.R. 2.
75 (1983) 77 Cr.App.R. 260.
76 *Supra*, para. 1.12.

arranges for funds to be transferred from other people's bank accounts to his own, for example, is likely to be charged with stealing the other customers' money; but, unlike the fraudulent agent who abuses his authority to draw on his principal's account,[77] he has not diminished the other customers' rights against the bank (*i.e.* their property) at all. They are still entitled to payment in full of the sums originally due. The defendant may hope that they will not notice the discrepancy or claim their money back, but if he appreciates the legal position then he does not literally intend to deprive them of their rights.

1.134 In *Doole*[78] the Court of Appeal was disinclined to accept the implications of this reasoning, and in *Chan Man-Sin v. Attorney-General of Hong Kong*[79] it was firmly rejected by the Privy Council. In the latter case, already discussed in connection with the requirement of appropriation, the appellant was held to have stolen the credit balances in the bank accounts of certain companies by drawing forged cheques which were honoured by the companies' bank. He had not only appropriated the companies' property but had done so with intent to deprive them thereof. Their Lordships thought this would be so not only if he intended the forgery of the cheques to remain undetected, but even if he did not. In the latter case he would be caught by the Hong Kong counterpart of section 6(1).

> "Quite clearly here the defendant was purporting to deal with the companies' property without regard to their rights."[80]

This is the whole of their Lordships' reasoning on the point, and it is, with respect, wholly unconvincing. The appellant may have been "purporting" to deal with the companies' property without regard to their rights, but he neither did so in fact nor intended to do so. He did not interfere with the companies' property, or (which comes to the same thing) with their rights, in any way. This hardly amounts to acting regardless of their rights. In any event the first part of section 6(1) does not come into play in every case where a person deals with another's property without regard to the other's rights, but only where he intends to treat it as his own *to dispose of* regardless of those rights. The appellant in *Chan Man-Sin* made no attempt to dispose of the property at all. It is confidently predicted that this casual misreading of the subsection will not be the last word on the subject.

77 *e.g. Kohn* (1979) 69 Cr.App.R. 395, *supra*, para. 1.110.
78 [1985] Crim.L.R. 450.
79 [1988] 1 W.L.R. 196.
80 At p. 199.

1.135 *Purported disposals.* A yet more dubious possibility for the application of the first part of section 6(1) is the case of a defendant who purports to sell property belonging to another, knowing that the owner will be deprived of the property neither in theory nor (because the defendant has no intention of delivering it) in effect. We have seen that it is doubtful whether such an act amounts even to an appropriation, because although it may be a fraud on the intending purchaser it does not infringe the rights of the owner.[81] If it *is* an appropriation it is equally doubtful whether it is done with an intention permanently to deprive. The defendant's intention is that the owner shall not be deprived of the property at all, let alone permanently. It has been suggested that the defendant intends to treat the property as his own to dispose of and can therefore be deemed to have an intention permanently to deprive by virtue of section 6(1).[82] But it is hard to see in what sense he is treating it as his own to dispose of *regardless of the owner's rights,* as the subsection requires, if he knows that those rights will remain entirely unaffected.

1.136 *Owner put at risk of permanent loss.* It is possible that the first part of section 6(1) catches a defendant whose intention is to dispose of the property appropriated in such a way that the owner may or may not get it back, *e.g.* by abandoning it or entrusting it to a highly unreliable intermediary. If so, the effect would be to dilute the requirement of an *intention* to bring about permanent deprivation: mere recklessness would be sufficient. Alternatively it might be said that the defendant intends to bring about a situation in which the owner is put at risk of being permanently deprived of the property, and that by virtue of section 6(1) that situation is deemed to be one in which the owner *is* permanently deprived.

1.137 The application of section 6(1) to cases where the owner is merely put at risk of losing the property for good might be defended by reference to section 6(2), which in effect deems the defendant to have the intention permanently to deprive if he puts the owner at risk in one particular way. Section 6(2) provides:

> "Without prejudice to the generality of subsection (1) above, where a person, having possession or control (lawfully or not) of property belonging to another, parts with the property under a condition as to its return which he may not be able to perform, this (if done for purposes of his own and without the other's authority) amounts to treating the property as his own to dispose of regardless of the other's rights."

81 *Supra,* paras. 1.69 f.
82 J.C. Smith, *The Law of Theft* (5th ed.) para. 26.

The subsection is primarily designed to catch the defendant who has possession of another's property and pledges it without authority: the "condition as to its return" is the redemption of the pledge. But the subsection does not say that a person who parts with property in the circumstances described is deemed to have the intention permanently to deprive the other of it: it says that he is thereby treating the property[83] as his own to dispose of regardless of the other's rights, which in turn means that an *intention* to act in such a way is deemed to be an intention permanently to deprive by virtue of the first part of section 6(1). Therefore a person who pledges another's property, certain that he will be able to redeem it, is not caught by section 6(2): he does not *intend* to part with the property under a condition as to its return which he may not be able to perform, because he thinks he will be able to perform it, and section 6(2) does not therefore deem him to intend to treat the property as his own to dispose of regardless of the other's rights. But section 6(2) is to be read without prejudice to the generality of section 6(1), and such a person might be regarded as intending to treat the property as his own to dispose of regardless of the other's rights without reference to section 6(2). Section 6(2) would then be exposed as redundant, but perhaps it is there only for the avoidance of doubt. It might however be argued that "lending" in section 6(1) includes a pledge, in which case the only question would be whether the pledge was intended to be for a period or in circumstances making it equivalent to an outright disposal. That would in turn depend on whether, and if so how soon, the defendant expected to be able to redeem the pledge.[84] If he thought he could do so without difficulty, then the pledge could hardly be equivalent to an outright disposal.

Dishonesty

1.138 An appropriation of property belonging to another, even if effected with the intention of permanently depriving the property's owner of it, is not theft unless it is also dishonest. The word "dishonestly" in section 1(1) corresponds to the requirement in the old offence of larceny that the property be taken "fraudulently and without a claim of right made in good faith".[85] The change of terminology does not appear to have been intended by the Criminal Law Revision Committee to mark a change of substance.

" 'Dishonestly' seems to us a better word than 'fraudulently'. The question 'Was this dishonest?' is easier for a jury to answer than the question 'Was

---

83   Not, as s. 6(1) would have it, the "thing". The difference is unexplained and probably inexplicable.
84   *Cf. Coffey* [1987] Crim.L.R. 498; *supra*, para. 1.129.
85   Larceny Act 1916 s. 1(1).

this fraudulent?'. 'Dishonesty' is something which laymen may easily recognise when they see it, whereas 'fraud' may seem to involve technicalities which have to be explained by a lawyer."[86]

This probably means simply that a requirement of 'dishonesty' is less likely to confuse a jury by hinting at the existence of requirements which do not in fact exist. Alternatively it may have been thought that a requirement of fraud did involve "technicalities" which need not be carried over into the new offence of theft. But nowhere in the report is it suggested that, conversely, the new requirement of dishonesty might involve elements which had *not* been essential to the old requirement of fraud.

The test of dishonesty

1.139 Exactly what the latter requirement did involve was unfortunately not as clear as the Committee apparently supposed. One view was that in the context of larceny the requirement of fraud added nothing, because larceny also required the absence of a claim of right, and a taking without a claim of right must necessarily be fraudulent. In *Williams*[87] the Court of Criminal Appeal denied that the requirement of fraud was redundant, but the definition of it there proposed (*viz.* that the taking must be intentional, under no mistake, and with knowledge that the thing taken was the property of another person)[88] would seem to require nothing which was not already involved in the requirement that the property be taken without a claim of right. But Lord Goddard C.J., speaking for the court, also said:

> "It is one thing if a person with good credit and with plenty of money uses somebody else's money which may be in his possession and which may have been entrusted to him or which he may have had the opportunity of taking, merely intending to use those coins instead of some of his own which he has only to go to his room or to his bank to obtain. No jury would then say that there was any intent to defraud or any fraudulent taking.
>
> It is quite another matter if the person who takes the money is not in a position to replace it at the time but only has a hope or expectation that he will be able to do so in the future . . ."[89]

This passage implied that even a taking of property without a claim of right might not be fraudulent (or at any rate that a jury might refuse to find it so) if it did not prejudice the owner's interests in any way. The passage was relied upon in *Cockburn*,[90] where the manager of a shop was charged with stealing from the till. He claimed to have intended to replace

86   Cmnd. 2977 para. 39.
87   [1953] 1 Q.B. 660.
88   At p. 666.
89   [1953] 2 W.L.R. 937 at p. 942.
90   [1968] 1 W.L.R. 281.

the money before it was missed, and he apparently had good grounds for expecting to be able to do so. His conviction was affirmed. It was pointed out that the passage quoted above did not appear in the official report of *Williams* and had probably been deleted by Lord Goddard himself when he came to revise the judgment. The court described it as "an extremely dangerous and most misleading statement" and expressed the hope that it would in future be disregarded, and went on to assert that even a taking which attracted no moral obloquy and did no harm at all might nevertheless be technically larcenous.

1.140 But this view was in turn criticised by a full Court of Appeal in the post-1968 case of *Feely*,[91] and the need for dishonesty in the ordinary sense of the word was reaffirmed.

> "It is possible to imagine a case of taking by an employee in breach of instructions to which no one would, or could reasonably, attach moral obloquy; for example, that of a manager of a shop, who having been told that under no circumstances was he to take money from the till for his own purposes, took 40p from it, having no small change himself, to pay for a taxi hired by his wife who had arrived at the shop saying that she only had a £5 note which the cabby could not change. To hold that such a man was a thief and to say that his intention to put the money back in the till when he acquired some change was at the most a matter of mitigation would tend to bring the law into contempt. In our judgment a taking to which no moral obloquy can reasonably attach is not within the concept of stealing either at common law or under the Theft Act 1968."[92]

In other words, the requirement of fraud had involved an element of moral turpitude all along, and the substitution of a requirement of "dishonesty" had served merely to emphasise the point. Moreover it had recently been held by the House of Lords that the meaning of an ordinary English word in a statutory provision is a question of fact.[93] "Dishonestly" is an ordinary English word; therefore it is wrong for the jury to be directed that certain conduct is as a matter of law dishonest. They must be invited to decide whether *they* think it is. They may well think it is not dishonest if, as in the case of the 40p for the cab fare, there is no risk of loss or inconvenience to the owner; they are entitled to think so even if there is.

1.141 But a jury cannot be expected to tackle the issue without any guidance as to how they might do so, or what standards of honesty they ought to apply. In *Feely* it was said that a jury should apply "the current standards of ordinary decent people",[94] which were assumed to be

91 [1973] Q.B. 530.
92 At p. 539.
93 *Brutus v. Cozens* [1972] A.C. 854.
94 At p. 538.

adequately represented by the standards of the jury themselves. But in other cases it has been suggested that the crucial question is whether the defendant himself thinks his conduct dishonest.[95] Clearly it would be absurd if an alleged thief had to be acquitted whenever it appeared that his conduct had not been dishonest according to his own moral values, however warped or non-existent they might be; and this conclusion was ingeniously avoided in *Ghosh*.[96]

> "In determining whether the prosecution has proved that the defendant was acting dishonestly, a jury must first of all decide whether according to the ordinary standards of reasonable and honest people what was done was dishonest. If it was not dishonest by those standards, that is the end of the matter and the prosecution fails.
>
> If it was dishonest by those standards, then the jury must consider whether the defendant himself must have realised that what he was doing was by those standards dishonest. In most cases, where the actions are obviously dishonest by ordinary standards, there will be no doubt about it. It will be obvious that the defendant himself knew that he was acting dishonestly. It is dishonest for a defendant to act in a way which he knows ordinary people consider to be dishonest, even if he asserts or genuinely believes that he is morally justified in acting as he did. For example, Robin Hood or those ardent anti-vivisectionists who remove animals from vivisection laboratories are acting dishonestly, even though they may consider themselves to be morally justified in doing what they do, because they know that ordinary people would consider these actions to be dishonest."[97]

Thus the test is partly objective and partly subjective. It is objective in that it is the standards of ordinary, reasonable people which are relevant, not those of the defendant himself; it is subjective in that he must have *realised* that his conduct was dishonest in that objective sense. But the jury need not be directed on this latter requirement unless the defendant has raised the issue: in the absence of any evidence to the contrary, it may be assumed that he knows what sort of conduct ordinary people believe to be dishonest.[98] Even so, it is debatable whether a person who appropriates another's property, without a claim of right and with the intention of permanently depriving the owner of it, ought to be acquitted of theft just because ordinary people would not say he had acted dishonestly. A rule that he must be acquitted even if they *would* say so, provided that he did not realise they would, surely goes too far.[99]

95 *Boggeln v. Williams* [1978] 1 W.L.R. 873; *Landy* [1981] 1 W.L.R. 355. The latter case concerned the offence of conspiracy to defraud and was explained in *McIvor* [1982] 1 W.L.R. 409 as being confined to that context, but the distinction was rejected in *Ghosh, infra.*
96 [1982] Q.B. 1053.
97 At p. 1064.
98 *Roberts* (1986) 84 Cr.App.R. 117; *Cowan*, 7 November 1986, Criminal Appeal Office transcript no. 7890/C/85; *Barnett and Reid* 21 July 1987, Criminal Appeal Office transcript nos. 5818/C3/86, 5819/C3/86.
99 See the compelling arguments marshalled by E. Griew in "Dishonesty: the Objections to *Feely* and *Ghosh*" [1985] Crim.L.R. 341.

Dishonesty excluded

1.142 Some members of the Criminal Law Revision Committee thought that there was no need to define dishonesty at all,[1] and to some extent *Ghosh* has proved them right. But the Act does provide a partial and somewhat negative definition of the concept, in the sense that certain states of mind are expressly excluded from it. A person who acts in one of these states of mind does not act dishonestly, whatever ordinary people may think. Section 2(1) provides:

"A person's appropriation of property belonging to another is not to be regarded as dishonest—

(a) if he appropriates the property in the belief that he has in law the right to deprive the other of it, on behalf of himself or of a third person; or

(b) if he appropriates the property in the belief that he would have the other's consent if the other knew of the appropriation and the circumstances of it; or

(c) (except where the property came to him as trustee or personal representative) if he appropriates the property in the belief that the person to whom the property belongs cannot be discovered by taking reasonable steps."

1.143 It would of course be rare for ordinary people to think it dishonest to appropriate property in any of the circumstances described. Only if they might think so could the appropriation be dishonest under the *Ghosh* test, and only then could section 2(1) have any practical effect. Indeed it has been said that there is no need to direct the jury on section 2(1)(a), because a defendant who can invoke it will not be dishonest under the *Ghosh* test anyway.[2] The same reasoning would presumably apply to paragraphs (b) and (c). But it would be unwise to conclude that the subsection is entirely redundant. There may be exceptional circumstances in which a defendant falls within its terms although an ordinary person might say that his conduct was dishonest. Such a defendant would be entitled to an acquittal. On the other hand it was said in *Attorney-General's Reference (No. 2 of 1982)*[3] that section 2(1) does not apply unless the belief is an honest one. It is true of course that the defendant cannot secure an acquittal merely by *claiming* to have held one of the beliefs specified in the subsection, because it may be clear that in truth he believed no such thing; but if the statement that the belief must be an honest one means only that it must actually have been held, it adds nothing. If, however, it lays down an additional requirement, that the defendant must not only hold the belief in question but must also hold it *honestly*, it cannot be right. There would be no sense in a provision to

1 Cmnd. 2977 para. 39.
2 *Kell* [1985] Crim.L.R. 239; *cf. Woolven* (1983) 77 Cr.App.R. 231.
3 [1984] Q.B. 624, following a dictum in *Lawrence* [1971] 1 Q.B. 373 at p. 377.

the effect that it is not dishonest to do certain things unless they are done dishonestly. Either the subsection is meaningless or the dictum in the *Attorney-General's Reference* is. It is submitted with respect that it is the latter.

Belief in legal right to deprive
1.144 If the defendant thinks, albeit wrongly and entirely without justification, that in law he has the right to deprive of the property the person to whom it belongs, his appropriation of it is not dishonest. It is neither necessary nor sufficient that he should think he is the *owner* of the property: it is not sufficient because even an owner can steal his property from someone who has a right to keep it from him (*e.g.* a hirer),[4] and it is not necessary because one may have a right to deprive another of property even if one is not the owner (*e.g.* if one has the owner's authority to do so). In any event the question is not whether the defendant would have had a right to deprive the other person of the property if the facts had been as he supposed them to be, but simply whether he *thought* he had a right to do so. He may think that he has such a right because he is mistaken about either the facts or the law, or both. Thus it is not dishonest to take money from another person's wallet if the taker thinks not only that the money is legally due to him but also that the law gives him a right to take it. This is so even if he knows he has no right to get the money in the way that he does. If he thinks he would be entitled to take it by stealth, it is not dishonest for him to take it by force instead.[5] But the use or threat of force might amount to an assault, or to blackmail.[6]

Belief that consent would be given
1.145 If the defendant knows that the person to whom the property belongs has not consented to the appropriation, but thinks that he would consent to it if only he knew the circumstances, the appropriation is not dishonest. It has been said that the belief must be "an honest belief in a true consent, honestly obtained",[7] which is doubly[8] puzzling because the defendant need not believe that consent *has* been given at all,[9] only that it *would* be if the circumstances were known. But clearly it is not sufficient that he believes he could have procured the requisite consent by deception: he must believe that the person to whom the property belongs

4 *Quaere* whether he can steal it from someone who does not have such a right: *infra*, paras. 1.154 ff.
5 *Robinson* [1977] Crim.L.R. 173.
6 *Infra*, paras. 3.02 ff.
7 *Attorney-General's Reference (No. 2 of 1982)* [1984] Q.B. 624 at p. 641.
8 *Cf. supra*, para. 1.143.
9 Though this would surely suffice: *infra*, para. 1.151.

would have consented if he had known *all* the circumstances, including the real object of the appropriation.[10]

Belief that the owner cannot reasonably be discovered

1.146   Under section 2(1)(*c*) a person's appropriation of property is not dishonest if he does it in the belief that the person to whom the property belongs cannot be discovered by taking reasonable steps. The most likely application of this provision is in the case of property lost by its owner and found by the defendant. A finder of lost property may adopt various methods of tracing the owner: he may take it to the police, place advertisements, make enquiries in such quarters as may be suggested by the nature of the property or by such clues as it may bear, and so on. Some of the steps open to him may be reasonable, in the sense that the value of the property and the chances of thereby tracing its owner justify the effort and expense involved; others may not. The effect of section 2(1)(*c*) is that he does not steal the property if he keeps it or disposes of it in the belief that there are no steps open to him which it would be reasonable for him to take, or that such steps as *are* reasonable have already been taken. The defence is available even if a course of action still open to him *might* lead to the tracing of the owner, if that possibility is so slim as to be out-weighed by the difficulty and cost of the steps required: the owner cannot be discovered by taking *reasonable* steps if the only steps which might lead to his discovery are steps which in all the circumstances (including the likelihood of success) it would be unreasonable to expect the defendant to take. On the other hand it is not necessarily a defence that a particular line of enquiry holds out little hope of success, if it is so easily pursued that it would be reasonable to try it anyway: in that case it is not true to say that the owner *cannot* be discovered by taking reasonable steps, although it is true that he probably will not be.

1.147   But the question is not whether the person to whom the property belongs can in fact be discovered by taking reasonable steps: it is whether the defendant *thinks* he can. It is not clear quite how subjective this test is. Clearly it is irrelevant that the owner might be discovered by taking certain steps if the possibility of taking those steps (or of their leading to the owner) has not occurred to the defendant at all. Similarly it is immaterial that certain steps are in fact so likely to succeed (or so easy to take, or both) as to make it reasonable to take them, if it would not *in fact* be reasonable to take them were they as unlikely to succeed (or as hard to take, or both) as the defendant thinks they are. What is doubtful is whether it is a defence that he *thinks* it would not be reasonable to take

10   *Lawrence* [1971] 1 Q.B. 373 at p. 377.

them, if objectively (and even assuming the steps to be as onerous and as unlikely to succeed as he thinks they are) it *would* be reasonable. Must the court assess what it is "reasonable" for him to do on the basis not only of the facts and probabilities as he perceives them, but also of his own opinions as to what is and is not reasonable? The fact that he attaches more importance to his own convenience than others might, or less importance to an owner's interest in the return of his property, may make him less socially aware than others, but scarcely dishonest. By analogy with *Ghosh*, however, it might perhaps be sufficient if he knew that most people would think it reasonable to take certain steps, even if he personally might disagree.

1.148 The defence is not available at all to a defendant who has obtained the property in question as trustee or personal representative. A person acting in one of these capacities is not entitled to keep property for himself, or to dispose of it for his own purposes, even if the person beneficially entitled to it cannot be traced.

Dishonesty arguably excluded

Belief that the property does not belong to another
1.149 It is not expressly provided that it is not dishonest to appropriate property which does in fact belong to another, under the impression that it does not; but this must surely be implied. In *Small*[11] the appellant had taken a car which, he claimed, he thought had been abandoned. He was convicted of theft after a direction that such a belief would be a defence only if there were reasonable grounds for it. His conviction was quashed on the grounds that if he thought the car had been abandoned, but had no reasonable grounds for thinking so, the first limb of the *Ghosh* test might be satisfied but the second was not. It may with respect be doubted whether even the first limb was satisfied. The defendant's awareness or otherwise of the circumstances is relevant not just to the issue of whether he *knew* that other people would think his conduct dishonest, but to that of whether they would in fact think so. Taking a car which one foolishly believes to have been abandoned is not dishonest by anyone's standards. In any case there is no need to invite a perverse verdict by confusing the jury with the dishonesty issue: if the defendant thinks the property has been abandoned he does not intend to deprive anyone of it, permanently or otherwise.

1.150 On the other hand it is not essential that the defendant should be certain that the property belongs to another. To appropriate property in

11 [1988] R.T.R. 32.

the knowledge that it *probably* belongs to another is something which many people would regard as dishonest, even if there is a possibility that the property may have been abandoned or that it may belong to the appropriator alone. If the property does indeed belong to another the appropriation of it might therefore be theft, provided that there is an intention permanently to deprive that person of it. It would not of course be sufficient if the defendant intended to keep the property only on condition that it turned out *not* to belong to anyone else. But if he intended to keep it anyway, it might be said that this was an intention permanently to deprive of it anyone to whom it might belong. An intention to do a thing if certain conditions are fulfilled is still an intention to do it,[12] and it would seem sufficient that the defendant intends to deprive another person of the property he appropriates should there be anyone to be deprived. Similarly it has been suggested that a person who buys stolen goods, knowing that they are probably stolen, may be guilty of stealing the goods from their true owner even if he is not guilty of handling them.[13] This view is open to the objection that a buyer who suspects that the goods may be stolen, but thinks that they probably are not, also intends to deprive the true owner of them *if* they are stolen; and no-one suggests that this should be theft.[14] Perhaps the answer is that the buyer who knowingly takes a small risk of the goods being stolen is not dishonest, because most people would have no compunction in doing the same.

Belief that consent has been given

1.151 Nor is it expressly provided that it is not dishonest to appropriate property belonging to another under the mistaken impression that the person to whom it belongs has consented to the appropriation. The omission is surprising, particularly since such a defence is expressly conferred in the case of other offences of taking property (*e.g.* taking a conveyance[15] and removing articles from places open to the public)[16] and of damaging it;[17] but again it must surely be implied. In *Barnett and Reid*[18] it was said that

"It is clearly not dishonest if you take, believing you have consent",[19]

but no authority was cited. In *Kell*[20] this was regarded as being the effect

12 *Supra*, para. 1.117.
13 J.R. Spencer, "Handling, Theft and the *Mala Fide* Purchaser" [1985] Crim.L.R. 92. See also Glanville Williams, [1985] Crim.L.R. 432 at p. 438 and Spencer's reply at p. 440.
14 E. Griew, *The Theft Acts 1968 and 1978* (5th ed.) para. 2–98.
15 Theft Act 1968 s. 12(6); *infra*, para. 5.18.
16 Theft Act 1968 s. 11(3); *infra*, para. 5.45.
17 Criminal Damage Act 1971 s. 5(2)(*a*); *infra*, para. 6.42.
18 21 July 1987, Criminal Appeal Office transcript nos. 5818/C3/86, 5819/C3/86.
19 At p. 7.
20 [1985] Crim.L.R. 239.

either of the *Ghosh* test or of section 2(1)(*a*). No doubt the *Ghosh* test would normally suffice, because an appropriation in such circumstances could seldom be dishonest on any view. But it is submitted that such a belief, like those expressly listed in section 2(1), is a complete defence whether or not the jury happen to think that it ought to be. Normally, too, it will fall within section 2(1)(*a*), because if the defendant did have the owner's consent to his appropriation of the property he would have a legal right to deprive the owner of it: this is perhaps a curious way of putting it, because the phrase "the right to deprive" has connotations of depriving the owner against his will, but it is probably not confined to that context. Difficulty arises only in the exceptional case where, although the defendant may have thought that he had the owner's consent, it is not clear *either* that a jury would think this meant his conduct was not dishonest *or* that he thought it gave him a legal right to act as he did.

1.152   Such a case was *Attorney-General's Reference (No. 2 of 1982)*,[21] where it was argued that an appropriation by company directors of their company's property cannot be dishonest if their position empowers them to act as the company's *alter ego*, because what they do is necessarily done with the company's consent. It is in fact debatable whether there is even an appropriation in such a case, because according to *Morris*[22] an act to which the owner does in fact consent is not an appropriation; but the *Attorney-General's Reference* was argued just before the decision in *Morris*, and it was conceded that there would be an appropriation. The only issue was that of dishonesty. The defence argued that, however dishonest a director's conduct might be in the ordinary sense of the word, it could not be technically dishonest for the purposes of a theft charge because such a conclusion was ruled out by section 2(1)(*b*). The director not only *thinks* that he would have the company's consent to the appropriation: he *knows* that he would, because he is himself empowered to grant it. The argument was rejected, partly on the grounds that the "belief" referred to must be an honest belief[23] and partly because the defence position was in any event self-contradictory.

> "The essence of the defendants' argument is the alleged identity, in all respects, and for every purpose, between the defendants and the company. It is said, in effect, that their acts are necessarily the company's acts; that their will, knowledge and belief are those of the company, and that their consent necessarily implies consent by the company. But how then can the company be regarded as 'the other' for the purposes of *this* provision [*sc.* section 2(1)(*b*)]? One merely has to read its wording to see that it cannot be

---

21   [1984] Q.B. 624; *cf. Attorney-General of Hong Kong v. Chan Nai-Keung* [1987] 1 W.L.R. 1339, *supra*, para. 1.94.
22   [1984] A.C. 320; *supra*, para. 1.75.
23   *Supra*, para. 1.143.

given any sensible meaning in a context such as the present, where the mind and will of the defendants are also treated in law as the mind and will of 'the other'."[24]

It might equally be said, of course, that it is inconsistent for the prosecution to argue both that the company's property is property belonging to another and that the company is not a person other than the defendant for the purposes of section 2(1)(*b*).

1.153 A more straightforward reason for rejecting the argument would have been that the wording of section 2(1)(*b*) simply did not apply to the situation envisaged. The fraudulent director does not believe that the company *would* consent to his depredations *if* it knew the circumstances: he believes (rightly or wrongly) that, through him, it *does* know the circumstances and it *does* consent. On this view the provision which applies to a defendant who thinks that he does have the owner's consent is not section 2(1)(*b*) but section 2(1)(*a*). But that provision applies only where the defendant thinks he has a right to deprive the owner of the property. A company director has a right to make fraudulent disposals of company property only if "right" means "power" rather than "freedom": he *can* make such disposals and they may well be valid, but he will be liable to the company for breach of fiduciary duty. It is submitted that this cannot sensibly be regarded as a right to deprive the company for the purposes of section 2(1)(*a*). And in that case the director falls between the two stools of section 2(1)(*a*) and (*b*), and is left to the mercy of the *Ghosh* test. It may be thought that this would be the right outcome in such a case, but it would have been achieved at the cost of consistency and common sense. If a person is not dishonest when he thinks that the owner *would* consent to the appropriation if he knew the circumstances, he cannot possibly be dishonest when he thinks that the owner does know the circumstances and does consent.[25] The way to deal with company fraud is to devise offences which take account of the peculiarities of company law, not to draw irrational distinctions in the law of theft.

Conduct otherwise lawful
1.154 Perhaps more controversially, it is submitted that there is one situation in which the element of dishonesty may be negatived by the actual circumstances of the appropriation (as distinct from the defendant's perception of those circumstances). This is where his conduct gives rise to no liability as a matter of civil law.[26] If the reason for this is that

24 At p. 642.
25 *Cf. supra*, para. 1.151.
26 See G. Williams, "Theft, Consent and Illegality" [1977] Crim.L.R. 127, 205, 327.

he has the consent of the person to whom the property belongs, there is no appropriation;[27] but even if he has no such consent to what he does, it does not follow that he incurs civil liability by doing it. There are many situations in which one may lawfully take property owned or possessed by another person without his consent. It has already been suggested that conduct which does not infringe the rights of the person to whom the property belongs cannot properly be regarded as an appropriation;[28] even if it can, it is submitted that it cannot properly be regarded as dishonest. Usually, no doubt, it would not be so regarded under the *Ghosh* test; but here too the question is whether that is the only shield available, or whether a defendant whose conduct is otherwise lawful is entitled to be acquitted of theft as a matter of law, even if a jury might think it somehow "dishonest" of him to stand on his legal rights.

1.155 There is some distinctly unsatisfactory authority to the effect that the lawfulness of the defendant's conduct is not in itself a defence. In *Bonner*[29] it was held that a member of a partnership can be convicted of stealing the partnership's property (which of course belongs to the other partners as well as to him) whether or not his appropriation of it amounts to an actionable conversion;[30] but the defence had argued that there could be no appropriation in such a case, not that an appropriation could not be dishonest. In any event the misappropriation of partnership property by one of the partners must inevitably give rise to *some* civil liability, if only for breach of the partnership agreement. In *Gilks*[31] the appellant had been collecting his winnings from a betting shop when he was inadvertently paid more than he had in fact won. He kept the money. It was held that although he had no legal obligation to pay the money back[32] (and section 5(4) therefore did not apply)[33] he was still guilty of stealing it, because the effect of the mistake was that the money still belonged to the bookmaker. But this is self-contradictory. If the money was still the bookmaker's, the appellant surely *was* obliged to pay it back: his failure to do so was a conversion. If his action had been otherwise lawful (*i.e.* if the money had become his) he would not have been guilty of theft (because by the time he appropriated the money it would no longer have belonged to another). The court thought that he *was* guilty of theft because the money did *not* become his. But in that case he *was* obliged to pay it back and his action in keeping it *was* unlawful (and incidentally

27 *Supra*, paras. 1.73 ff.
28 *Supra*, paras. 1.68 ff.
29 [1970] 1 W.L.R. 838.
30 Which it now does: Torts (Interference with Goods) Act 1977 s. 10.
31 [1972] 1 W.L.R. 1341.
32 *Morgan v. Ashcroft* [1938] 1 K.B. 49.
33 *Supra*, para. 1.42.

section 5(4) did apply). The case may perhaps be explained on the basis that the court's opinion that section 5(4) did not apply was *obiter* (since the appeal was dismissed on another ground) and wrong. It does not decide that otherwise lawful conduct can be theft.

1.156 Perhaps the strongest authority against the view here advanced is *Turner (No. 2)*.[34] The appellant, having arranged for a garage to carry out repairs on his car, had surreptitiously removed the car from outside the garage without paying for the repairs. His conviction of theft was affirmed. The decision was justifiable on the facts because the garage clearly had a lien on the car for the price of the repairs. The appellant therefore had no right to repossess the car without paying the bill, and by doing so he committed the tort of conversion. But the court felt unable to deal with the case on this basis because it was not the basis on which he had been convicted. The jury had been directed not to consider the question of the lien; and had there been no lien the appellant would have been legally entitled to take the car back.[35] It would still have "belonged" to the garage for the purposes of the law of theft, because the garage had possession or control of it,[36] but in the absence of a lien the garage would have had no right that its owner should refrain from taking it away. This, it was held, was immaterial. The appellant had appropriated a car which belonged to another and he had intended permanently to deprive the other of it. Whether he was guilty of theft therefore depended solely on whether he had acted dishonestly; and whether he had acted dishonestly depended solely on what he *thought* he was entitled to do.

"The whole test of dishonesty is the mental element of belief. No doubt, though the defendant may for certain purposes be presumed to know the law, he would not at the time have the vaguest idea whether he had in law a right to take the car back again, and accordingly when one looks at his mental state, one looks at it in the light of what he believed. The jury were properly told that if he believed that he had a right, albeit there was none, he would nevertheless fall to be acquitted."[37]

Yet although he was assumed to have had such a right, he was dishonest because he did not know that he had it.

1.157 It is submitted with respect that there are several reasons to doubt the correctness of this decision. Firstly, the assertion that "the whole test of dishonesty is the mental element of belief" is simply untrue. According to *Ghosh* the test is *partly* the mental element of belief, but partly also an

34 [1971] 1 W.L.R. 901.
35 Strictly speaking he would have had to terminate the bailment first, by notice to the bailee. But his criminal liability can hardly turn on a formality such as this.
36 s. 5(1); *supra*, para. 1.27.
37 At pp. 904 f.

objective element determined by reference to the moral standards of ordinary people. If the defendant's conduct is not in fact dishonest according to those standards, it does not become dishonest just because he thinks it is. But even if it is not in fact *unlawful* according to the objective standards of the civil law, *Turner* says it can still be dishonest (and therefore criminal) if he thinks it *is* unlawful. It can hardly be a defence that his conduct is objectively honest but not that it is objectively lawful. Indeed it might be said that no reasonable person could regard it as dishonest to do what the civil law permits, and that the possibility of such a finding is therefore ruled out by *Ghosh*. Secondly, a comparison of the *Turner* rule with section 2(1)(*a*) reveals a startling anomaly: the defendant cannot be dishonest if he *thinks* he has a right to act as he does, but he can be if (unbeknown to him) he actually does have such a right. Such a distinction defies explanation. Ignorance of the law may not be a defence, but it can hardly be a ground for criminal liability. Thirdly and most fundamentally, for the law of theft to prohibit conduct which is otherwise lawful would be to exceed its proper function. Its purpose is the imposition of penal sanctions for those infringements of proprietary rights which are too serious to be remediable by civil sanctions alone—not for conduct which (though arguably "dishonest" in some loose, extra-legal sense) does not infringe proprietary rights and is not remediable by civil sanctions at all. It ought not to be used as a blunderbuss against targets left unscathed by the precision weaponry of the civil law.

1.158 It has however been suggested by Professor J. C. Smith that it may indeed be legitimate to deploy the law of theft against conduct permissible in the civil law.

> "Where the civil law gives a positive right, the exercise of that right certainly cannot properly be held to amount to a criminal offence. To do so would be, in effect, to alter the civil law. On the other hand, the mere fact that P has no civil remedy should not inhibit the court from finding that D has stolen P's property if the definition of theft is satisfied. For example, if D dishonestly and without authority offers to sell P's property to E, D may not yet be guilty of any civil wrong against P but it would be strange to say that the civil law gave D a 'right' to do such an act; and it is submitted that, if the words of s. 1 fit D's act, he should be convicted of theft."[38]

It is submitted with respect that the distinction here proposed is of doubtful validity. A person has a right to do something if no-one else has any right that he should refrain from doing it, *i.e.* if his doing of it would give rise to no civil remedy: *ubi remedium ibi jus*. It is admittedly somewhat negative to define a right in terms of the absence of remedy, but that is the essence of a right in the sense of a liberty to do something

38   *The Law of Theft* (5th ed.) para. 20.

(as distinct from claims in respect of the conduct of others, and powers to effect changes in existing rights and duties). A right to do something is no more than the absence of a duty not to do it. Such rights cannot be divided into those which are "positive" and those which are merely negative: if anything, they are *all* negative. Elsewhere Professor Smith distinguishes between a "mere liberty or power" and "an express authority or right in the strict sense".[39] In the context of *powers* the problem does not arise: clearly one may steal by exercising a power over another's property, *e.g.* by passing good title to a third party, if one has a duty not to do so. What is here challenged is the assumption that an "express authority" is somehow essentially different from a "mere liberty" and can alone be described as a "right in the strict sense". A liberty has exactly the same effect whether it is expressly conferred or exists only because it has never been taken away. In either case, it means simply that its holder may act in the manner in question without fear of legal sanctions. If it would be wrong to impose criminal sanctions for doing a thing where a liberty to do it has been expressly conferred, it must be equally wrong where the same liberty exists for any other reason.

1.159 It must however be conceded that in certain contexts the Act does reveal a clear intention that otherwise lawful conduct may be regarded as dishonest. One example is that of a person who receives goods which have been obtained by deception in such circumstances that he acquires a good, though voidable, title. Clearly he can be convicted of handling stolen goods,[40] although that offence also requires dishonesty and he commits no civil wrong. Even in the context of theft itself, the defence here proposed cannot be available where the defendant has got property by another's mistake and is under an obligation to make restoration of its value. In such a case it is expressly provided that the property is deemed to belong to the person entitled to restoration.[41] This provision would be pointless if the defendant could still escape liability on the grounds that he is not dishonest because he commits no civil wrong by keeping the property. But it would be dangerous to generalise from such an anomalous provision. It is submitted that these exceptional cases do not substantially affect the argument advanced above as it relates to the offence of theft.

Dishonesty not excluded

1.160 Two situations are expressly mentioned in the Act only to make

---

39 *Ibid.*, para. 112.
40 S. 22(1); *infra*, para. 4.02.
41 S. 5(4); *supra*, para. 1.40.

it clear that in these cases dishonesty is not necessarily excluded: whether it exists in any particular such case will therefore fall to be determined under the *Ghosh* test.

No view to gain
1.161   Section 1(2) provides:

> "It is immaterial whether the appropriation is made with a view to gain, or is made for the thief's own benefit."

Thus it may be sufficient (provided the jury think fit) if the defendant intends someone else to benefit from the appropriation rather than himself, or if he intends that no-one shall benefit but that the owner shall suffer loss.

Willingness to pay
1.162   Section 2(2) provides:

> "A person's appropriation of property belonging to another may be dishonest notwithstanding that he is willing to pay for the property."

Doubtless it would not be dishonest to take an article from a temporarily unattended shop, leaving the price on the counter, even in the knowledge that the proprietor would not approve. But it is not in itself a defence that the owner of the property is intended to receive its value in full. Thus it may be dishonest to write unauthorised cheques on another person's account even if they are used for the payment of debts actually owed by that person, so that he receives a benefit (*viz.* the payment of his debts) corresponding to his loss.[42]

Jurisdiction

1.163   In general an act does not amount to an offence under the law of England and Wales unless it is done *in* England or Wales. In the case of theft this means that the defendant must not only appropriate the property but must do so within the jurisdiction. This rule can give rise to difficulties if at the time of the alleged theft the property is in one country and the defendant in another; but these difficulties are simply one aspect of the more general question, discussed above,[43] of what constitutes an appropriation. Even when the issue is not *whether* the defendant appropriated the property but *where* he did so, it is the scope of the concept of appropriation which is likely to prove crucial.

42   *Sobel* [1986] Crim.L.R. 261.
43   Paras. 1.63 ff.

Mail

1.164 The general rule is subject to an exception in the case of thefts of or from mail bags. Section 14(1) of the Theft Act 1968 provides:

"Where a person—
(a) steals or attempts to steal any mail bag[44] or postal packet in the course of transmission as such between places in different jurisdictions in the British postal area,[45] or any of the contents of such a mail bag or postal packet; or
(b) in stealing or with intent to steal any such mail bag or postal packet or any of its contents, commits any robbery, attempted robbery or assault with intent to rob;
then, notwithstanding that he does so outside England and Wales, he shall be guilty of committing or attempting to commit the offence under this Act as if he had done so in England or Wales, and he shall accordingly be liable to be prosecuted, tried and punished in England and Wales without proof that the offence was committed there."

Thus a person who steals mail from a train going from Glasgow to London can be charged with theft in England without proof that the train had crossed the border when he committed the theft; and if the mail were en route to Belfast he could be charged in England although the mail would never have reached England at all.

Nuclear material

Stealing

1.165 When section 1(1)(c) of the Nuclear Material (Offences) Act 1983 is brought into force, any act[46] done in relation to or by means of nuclear material, which would have amounted to an offence of theft, robbery,[47] burglary,[48] aggravated burglary[49] or assault with intent to rob[50] had it been done within the jurisdiction, will amount to that offence notwithstanding that it is done outside the jurisdiction. Proceedings for an offence under the Act which would not be an offence apart from the Act[51] may not be begun except by or with the consent of the Attorney-General.[52] "Nuclear material" is defined as material which, within the meaning of the Convention on the Physical Protection of Nuclear Material,[53] is nuclear material used for peaceful purposes.[54] The Con-

44 Including any article serving the purpose of a mail bag: s. 14(3).
45 *i.e.* the several jurisdictions of England and Wales, of Scotland, of Northern Ireland, of the Isle of Man and of the Channel Islands: s. 14(2).
46 Including an omission: s. 1(2).
47 *Infra*, paras. 1.170 ff.
48 *Infra*, paras. 7.02 ff.
49 *Infra*, paras. 7.44 ff.
50 *Infra*, para. 1.190.
51 Disregarding the provisions of the Internationally Protected Persons Act 1978 and the Suppression of Terrorism Act 1978.
52 s. 3(1)(a).
53 Opened for signature at Vienna and New York on 3 March 1980: s. 5(4).
54 s. 6(1).

vention's elaborate definition of nuclear material is set out in the Schedule
to the Act and is not here reproduced. If in any proceedings a question
arises whether any material was used for peaceful purposes, a certificate
issued by or under the authority of the Secretary of State and stating that
it was, or was not, so used at a time specified in the certificate will be
conclusive of that question;[55] and a document purporting to be such a
certificate will be presumed to be one unless the contrary is proved.[56]

Threats to steal
1.166 Threatening to seal property is not normally an offence in
itself,[57] but threats to steal nuclear material are (or will be when the
1983 Act is brought into force) an exception. Section 2(4) provides in
effect that a person commits an offence if, in order to compel a State,
international governmental organisation or person to do or abstain from
doing any act, he threatens that he or any other person will steal nuclear
material. This includes a threat to obtain nuclear material outside the
jurisdiction in circumstances which would amount to theft under English
law by virtue of section 1(1)(*c*).[58] The offence will be punishable on
conviction on indictment with imprisonment for a term not exceeding
fourteen years *and* not exceeding the term of imprisonment to which a
person would be liable for the offence constituted by doing the act
threatened[59] at the place where the conviction occurs and at the time of
the offence to which the conviction relates.[60]

Spouses
1.167 Proceedings for stealing property belonging to the defendant's
spouse must be instituted by or with the consent of the Director of Public
Prosecutions.[61] But this requirement does not apply where the spouses are
charged jointly or where by virtue of any judicial decree or order
(wherever made) they are at the time of the offence under no obligation
to cohabit.

Evidence
Despatch and receipt of goods
1.168 Section 27(4) of the Theft Act 1968 allows the admission in

55 s. 6(2).
56 s. 6(3).
57 *Cf.* threats to destroy or damage property: Criminal Damage Act 1971 s. 2, *infra*, paras.
6.80 f. A threat to steal might amount to blackmail (*infra*, paras. 3.02 ff.), but of course
the blackmailer usually obtains property by threats rather than threatening to obtain
property.
58 s. 2(7).
59 See s. 2(6)(*b*).
60 s. 2(5).
61 Theft Act 1968 s. 30(4). The consent of a Crown Prosecutor is deemed to be that of
the Director: Prosecution of Offences Act 1985 s. 1(7).

evidence of statutory declarations regarding the despatch, receipt or non-receipt of goods alleged to have been stolen in the course of transmission. It provides:

> "In any proceedings for the theft of anything in the course of transmission (whether by post or otherwise), or for handling stolen goods from such a theft, a statutory declaration made by any person that he despatched or received or failed to receive any goods or postal packet, or that any goods or postal packet when despatched or received by him were in a particular state or condition, shall be admissible as evidence of the facts stated in the declaration, subject to the following conditions:
>
> (a) a statutory declaration shall only be admissible where and to the extent of which oral evidence to the like effect would have been admissible in the proceedings; and
>
> (b) a statutory declaration shall only be admissible if at least seven days before the hearing or trial a copy of it has been given to the person charged, and he has not, at least three days before the hearing or trial or within such further time as the court may in special circumstances allow, given the prosecutor written notice requiring the attendance at the hearing or trial of the person making the declaration."

Recent possession

1.169 Possession of recently stolen goods is evidence that the possessor either stole them or received them knowing them to be stolen; but if the prosecution cannot prove which, the defendant is likely to be convicted of handling rather than theft. The so-called "doctrine of recent possession" is therefore discussed in the context of the offence of handling.[62]

AGGRAVATED THEFT

Robbery

1.170 Section 8(1) of the Theft Act 1968 redefines the common law offence of robbery. It provides:

> "A person is guilty of robbery if he steals, and immediately before or at the time of doing so, and in order to do so, he uses force on any person or puts or seeks to put any person in fear of being then and there subjected to force."

Robbery is punishable on conviction on indictment with life imprisonment.[63]

Stealing

1.171 The element of stealing is essential: robbery is an aggravated form of theft. If the defendant is not guilty of theft, then he is not guilty of

---

62   *Infra*, para. 4.60.
63   s. 8(2).

robbery. If, for example, he appropriates property belonging to another in the belief that he has a legal right to deprive the other of it, the appropriation is not dishonest;[64] therefore it is not theft; therefore it is not robbery, even if it is effected by force and the defendant knows that he has no right to get the property in that way.[65] In this case the appropriate charge is one of assault or possibly blackmail.[66] Similarly he must have actually appropriated the property and not just attempted or evinced an intention to do so. In these cases he might be charged with attempted robbery, assault with intent to rob,[67] or blackmail. But any unauthorised handling of property can amount to an appropriation.[68] A person who grabs a woman's handbag and attempts to wrest it away by force is therefore guilty of robbery even if he is unsuccessful.[69]

Use or threat of force

1.172 A person commits robbery only if, as well as stealing, he does one of the following:

(a) he *uses* force on any person; or

(b) he puts any person in *fear* of being then and there subjected to force; or

(c) he *seeks* to put any person in fear of being then and there subjected to force.

"Force" is an ordinary English word, and whether a particular action amounts or would amount to a use of force is therefore a question for the jury. A jury is entitled to find that it is a use of force on a person to nudge him off balance so that an accomplice can pick his pocket,[70] or to put one's hand over his mouth to stop him calling for help,[71] or even to wrench the property out of his unresisting grasp.[72] It is hard to agree that a reasonable jury might regard this last example as a use of force at all, let alone as a use of force *on a person*. Certainly the Criminal Law Revision Committee did not think so.[73] But it now seems that it is robbery if a jury thinks it is; and if it is left up to them they may well think so, because if they think that the victim has been "robbed" in the popular sense of the word (which need not involve force at all) they may be reluctant to find that an element of the statutory definition has not been proved.

---

64 s. 2(1)(*a*); *supra*, para. 1.144.
65 *Skivington* [1968] 1 Q.B. 166; *Robinson* [1977] Crim.L.R. 173.
66 *Infra*, paras. 3.02 ff.
67 *Infra*, para. 1.190.
68 *Supra*, paras. 1.64 ff.
69 *Corcoran v. Anderton* (1980) 71 Cr.App.R. 104.
70 *Dawson* (1977) 64 Cr.App.R. 170.
71 *Hale* (1978) 68 Cr.App.R. 415.
72 *Clouden* [1987] Crim.L.R. 56.
73 Cmnd. 2977 para. 65.

1.173 The defendant need not actually use force on the victim: it is sufficient if he puts him in fear that he will do so, or seeks to put him in such fear. A mere threat of force is sufficient, whether or not the victim is frightened and whether or not he believes that the threat will be carried out if he does not co-operate, provided only that (with or without the help of the threat) the defendant does succeed in stealing.[74] It is also sufficient if he seeks to put the victim in fear without making any express threat. But he must at least seek to put the victim in fear of being subjected to force *then and there*. A threat to use force on him on some subsequent occasion, or (it seems) immediately to take him elsewhere and then use force on him, would not suffice. Nor would it be sufficient if one person were put in fear that force would then and there be used on another, *e.g.* if the defendant told a woman that unless she gave him money he would injure the baby in her arms. All these cases could however be charged as blackmail.

The force and the stealing

1.174 The required relationship between the use or threat of force and the stealing has two aspects. The defendant must use or threaten force

   (*a*) either
       (i) immediately before stealing or
       (ii) at the time of stealing, *and*
   (*b*) in order to steal.

Immediately before or at the time of stealing

1.175 The defendant must use or threaten force and he must steal, and he must do the one immediately before or at the time of doing the other. What is "immediately before" the theft is a question of degree which can no doubt be left to the jury, but they will probably be encouraged to disregard a delay which is not such as to divide the force and the theft into entirely distinct transactions. Moreover a threat can obviously continue to operate on the mind of the victim after it is made. It must be sufficient if the defendant keeps the victim in a state of fear for some time up to and including the moment of the theft.[75]

1.176 Force used or threatened *after* the theft is not sufficient; but what might at first sight appear to have been done after the theft may be regarded as having been contemporaneous with it. In *Hale*[76] two men had forced their way into a woman's house and taken her jewellery, then

---

74 *Cf.* the offence of blackmail, which is complete on the making of a demand with menaces: *infra*, paras. 3.02 ff.
75 *Cf. Donaghy* [1981] Crim.L.R. 644.
76 (1978) 68 Cr.App.R. 415.

threatened her and tied her up before making their getaway. It was held that they had used and threatened force "at the time of" stealing the jewellery, although they were already guilty of stealing it before they used or threatened force, because the stealing was still in progress.

> "In the present case there can be little doubt that if the appellant had been interrupted after the seizure of the jewellery box the jury would have been entitled to find that the appellant and his accomplice were assuming the rights of an owner at the time when the jewellery box was seized. However, the act of appropriation does not suddenly cease. It is a continuous act and it is a matter for the jury to decide whether or not the act of appropriation has finished."[77]

Thus there may be a point at which the defendant has already stolen for the purposes of a charge of theft, but is still stealing for the purposes of robbery. How long after the initial appropriation this may be will depend on the circumstances, but clearly there must come a point where any reasonable jury would say that the stealing is over and done with.

In order to steal

1.177 The force must also be used or treatened *in order* to steal and not for some other purpose such as deterring the victim from revealing the theft, inducing him to provide evidence that there was no theft,[78] or sheer sadism. But it may be used or threatened in order to steal even after the original theft has been committed, provided that the defendant is continuing to steal and and the use or threat of force is intended to enable him to go on doing so.[79] There is no requirement that his action in using or threatening force should in fact enable or assist him to steal: it is sufficient that he thinks it may, and that that is the reason (or at least *a* reason) why he does it.

Force by one and theft by another

1.178 If one person steals with the assistance or encouragement of another, both are guilty of theft. If the second person uses or threatens force immediately before or at the time of the theft, and in order to facilitate it, he is guilty of robbery. The person actually appropriating the property will also be guilty of robbery if the use or threat of force was with *his* assistance or encouragement; but it is not sufficient that he took the opportunity of stealing when the victim had been rendered powerless by others without the complicity of the thief.[80]

Force on one and theft from another

1.179 There is no requirement that the victim of the force or the threat

77   At p. 418.
78   *Cf. Shendley* [1970] Crim.L.R. 49.
79   *Hale* (1978) 68 Cr.App.R. 415; *supra*, para. 1.176.
80   *Harris*, The Times 4 March 1988.

be the same person as the victim of the theft. Provided that the force is used or threatened immediately before or at the time of stealing and in order to do so, robbery may therefore be committed by using force on one person and stealing from another. This possibility may be combined with the previous one. Thus if A uses force on B so as to enable C to steal from D, A and C may both be guilty of robbery.

Theft with a firearm

1.180   A person who commits theft,[81] or attempts to do so or aids or abets another to do so, and who at the time of doing so (or of being arrested for doing so) has in his possession a firearm or imitation firearm, is guilty of an offence under section 17(2) of the Firearms Act 1968 unless he shows that he had it in his possession for a lawful object. The offence is punishable on conviction on indictment with life imprisonment or a fine or both.[82] A "firearm" is defined for this purpose as including

(a) a lethal barrelled weapon of any description from which any shot, bullet or other missile can be discharged, and

(b) a "prohibited weapon", *i.e.* any weapon of whatever description (whether lethal or not) designed or adapted for the discharge of any noxious liquid, gas or other thing.[83]

A weapon is "lethal" not only if it is designed to kill but also if it is capable of doing so if misused;[84] but there must be evidence both that a shot, bullet or other missile could in fact be fired from the weapon in question (or that it could be adapted so as to be capable of firing one)[85] and that a missile so fired might, if the weapon were misused, cause an injury from which death might result.[86] An "imitation firearm" is defined as any thing which has the appearance of being a firearm of type (*a*) above, whether or not it is capable of discharging any shot, bullet or other

81 Firearms Act 1968 Sch. 1. He must be guilty of the offence even if he has the firearm only when he is arrested: *Baker* [1962] 2 Q.B. 530.
82 Sch. 6 Pt I as amended by Criminal Justice Act 1988 s. 44(3). For offences committed before s. 44 came into force (*viz.* before 29 September 1988: s. 171(6)) the maximum remains at 14 years (s. 44(4)); but this would seem not to apply to a person who commits theft before that date and has a firearm in his possession when he is arrested on or after it.
83 s. 5(1)(*b*). An electric stun device designed to cause pain and temporary incapacity by inflicting an electric shock is a weapon designed for the discharge of a noxious thing: *Flack v. Baldry* [1988] 1 W.L.R. 393. The term "prohibited weapon" also includes automatic firearms and certain other weapons which are clearly within the definition of a "firearm" set out above: s. 5(1)(*a*), Firearms (Amendment) Act 1988 s. 1(1), (2).
84 *Read v. Donovan* [1947] K.B. 326; *Moore v. Gooderham* [1960] 1 W.L.R. 1308; *Thorpe* [1987] 1 W.L.R. 383.
85 *Cafferata v. Wilson* [1936] 3 All E.R. 149; *Freeman* [1970] 1 W.L.R. 788.
86 *Grace v. D.P.P.*, [1989] Crim.L.R. 365.

missile.[87] The test is whether the thing looked like a firearm at the time when the defendant had it with him.[88]

Burglary by stealing

1.181 Under section 9(1)(*b*) of the Theft Act 1968 a person is guilty of burglary if (*inter alia*) he enters a building as a trespasser and steals anything in the building, or enters part of a building as a trespasser and steals anything in that part. This form of the offence is therefore an aggravated form of theft. There is in turn an aggravated form of burglary which is committed if the burglar has with him a firearm, imitation firearm, weapon of offence or explosive. Burglary and aggravated burglary are discussed below.[89]

INTENT TO STEAL

1.182 Several offences involve, or may involve, an element of intention to steal. This element by definition consists of an intention not only dishonestly to appropriate property belonging to another but also permanently to deprive of it the person to whom it belongs. This latter intention is an element of the offence of theft itself,[90] and much of the discussion of it in that context is equally relevant here. In particular it is essential that at the time of the alleged offence the defendant should have made up his mind to steal; but here too it is sufficient that he has decided to do so if certain conditions are satisfied, and one of those conditions may be that he should find property which is "worth stealing".[91] Where he is alleged only to have intended to steal and not to have actually stolen, however, the fact that he did not know what was there to be stolen is one which must be borne in mind when drafting the indictment. It is wrong to allege that he intended to steal particular property if he had no idea that that property might be there. This was the explanation advanced in *Attorney-General's References (Nos. 1 and 2 of 1979)*[92] for the much-criticised dictum in *Husseyn*[93] that a person who intends to steal only if what he finds is worth stealing does not have a present intention to steal. Husseyn, it was pointed out in the *Attorney-General's References,* had been charged with attempting to steal specific articles contained in a

87 s. 57(4).
88 *Morris and King* (1984) 79 Cr.App.R. 104.
89 Paras. 7.02 ff., 7.44 ff.
90 *Supra,* paras. 1.108 ff.
91 *Attorney-General's References (Nos. 1 and 2 of 1979)* [1980] Q.B. 180; *supra,* para. 1.123.
92 [1980] Q.B. 180.
93 (1978) 67 Cr.App.R. 131; *supra,* para. 1.122.

holdall inside a van into which he had tried to gain entry; and since he had not known what was there, it could not be said that he had intended to steal those specific articles. Therefore he had not attempted to steal them. Had he been charged with attempting to steal "some or all of the contents" of the van, there would have been no difficulty.[94] This is not what the dictum meant, but it had to be explained away somehow. The inconvenient rule of drafting laid down in the *Attorney-General's References* was clearly regarded as a small price to pay.

1.183   It was said in the *Attorney-General's References,* and repeated in *Bayley and Easterbrook,*[95] that in this respect the same principles apply to theft as to attempted theft. If this were right it would follow that, had Husseyn made off with the holdall without first opening it to see what was inside, he could have been convicted of stealing the bag's unspecified contents but not of stealing the sub-aqua equipment which *was* the bag's contents, because he did not know it was there and could not have intended to keep it. But this would be absurd. Theft, unlike attempted theft, can be committed only in respect of specific property, however unspecifically the charge may be worded. If the defendant has not stolen anything in particular then he has not stolen anything at all. If he has not stolen the equipment which is in the bag then he has not stolen the contents of the bag. A conviction of stealing the contents, specified or not, may be impossible if the contents are not what he wants;[96] but if they are what he wants he can be convicted of stealing them, and it scarcely matters whether they are described in the indictment. It is submitted that the rule against identifying property whose identity was unknown to the defendant can apply only to inchoate offences, and not to theft itself.

Attempted theft

1.184   Section 1(1) of the Criminal Attempts Act 1981 provides:

"If, with intent to commit an offence to which this section applies, a person does an act which is more than merely preparatory to the commission of the offence, he is guilty of attempting to commit the offence."

The Act replaces the common law offence of attempt.[97] The maximum penalty on a conviction of attempt is the same as that for the full offence.[98]

---

94   Wording the charge in this way does not imply that there *were* any contents, and under
      the Criminal Attempts Act 1981 it is immaterial whether there were: *Smith and Smith*
      [1986] Crim.L.R.166. *Cf. infra,* para. 1.188.
95   [1980] Crim.L.R. 503.
96   *Easom* [1971] 2 Q.B. 315; *supra,* para. 1.118.
97   s. 6(1).
98   s. 4(1).

Subject to certain exceptions section 1 applies to any offence which, if it were completed, would be triable in England and Wales as an indictable offence.[99] This obviously includes theft as well as aggravated forms of theft. The meaning of an intent to commit one of these offences has already been considered,[1] and it remains to examine the requirement of "an act which is more than merely preparatory to the commission of the offence". There was formerly a difficulty regarding the availability of a charge of attempt where the commission of the full offence was impossible, but the position is now reasonably clear.

Acts more than merely preparatory

1.185 Attempted theft is typically[2] committed by a person who intends to appropriate property belonging to another but has not reached the point of actually doing so. The question whether he has done so may of course involve a consideration of the meaning of the requirement of appropriation,[3] and the more loosely that requirement is construed the earlier will be the transition from the attempt to the full offence. If, for example, the act of offering another's property for sale without authority is regarded as an appropriation,[4] the theft is complete when the offer is made; if not, it is at most an attempt, and the theft is complete only when the property is removed.

1.186 But the mere fact that a person intends to steal does not necessarily render him guilty even of an attempt. It must be proved that, while he may not have actually appropriated the property, he has at least done an act which is "more than merely preparatory" to an appropriation. He is not guilty if he has decided to steal but has done nothing about it, and he is not guilty if he has taken steps which are no more than preparation for the appropriation itself. A distinction must therefore be drawn between steps which are merely preparatory and steps which are not. A clear example of the former would be the acquisition of safe-cracking equipment; of the latter, the actual opening of the safe. But at common law it proved extremely difficult to determine whether the defendant's preparations had been sufficiently far advanced to qualify as an attempt. A test often referred to was whether the act in question was "immediately and not merely remotely connected" with the commission of the full offence,[5] which confirmed that some acts were sufficiently

---

99   s. 1(4).
1   *Supra*, paras. 1.108 ff., 1.182.
2   It is possible actually to appropriate property and still be guilty only of an attempt, *viz.* where the property is wrongly supposed to belong to another: *infra*, para. 1.189.
3   *Supra*, paras. 1.63 ff.
4   *Supra*, paras. 1.68 ff.
5   *Eagleton* (1855) Dears. 515; *Davey v. Lee* (1967) 51 Cr.App.R. 303.

proximate to the full offence to qualify as attempts while some were not, but offered little assistance in the task of distinguishing between them. The new test, that of whether the act is more than merely preparatory, is scarcely more illuminating. Every step the defendant takes with a view to the intended appropriation is in a sense preparatory; but what *else* can a particular step be, so as to be more than *merely* preparatory?

1.187   In *Widdowson*[6] the Court of Appeal endorsed a suggestion made before the Act by Lord Diplock,[7] *viz.* that the defendant "must have crossed the Rubicon and burnt his boats". Unfortunately this memorable phrase is highly misleading: it implies that, however close the defendant may have come to committing the full offence, he is not guilty of an attempt as long as he can still change his mind and decide not to commit the offence after all. The opening of the safe would not be an attempt to steal the contents because it would still be possible for the defendant to close the safe and go home empty-handed.[8] The Rubicon test might perhaps be defended by pointing out that the safe-cracker has indeed "burnt his boats" in the sense that once he has opened the safe he might as well take the contents: to go on is no more hazardous than to go back. But this is so only on the assumption that the opening of the safe is itself an offence comparable to the full offence of theft. The defendant might well be guilty of, for example, burglary;[9] but his liability for the attempt can hardly hinge on his liability for some other offence. If he *is* guilty of an attempt then to that extent he has of course burnt his boats, but in that sense the test is no test at all. In *Gullefer*[10] the Court of Appeal rejected it, pointing out that it was not incorporated in the wording of the Act. It was suggested instead that the attempt is complete when the merely preparatory acts come to an end and the defendant embarks on "the crime proper". This may not take the matter much further, but it does at least indicate in general terms what other characteristics a preparatory act must have (apart from being preparatory) in order to be more than *merely* preparatory: it must be possible to say that by doing the act the defendant is not just preparing to commit the full offence but is, loosely speaking at any rate, actually committing it. Guidance more specific than this is perhaps unlikely to be forthcoming. It is essentially a question of impression for the jury, subject of course to control by the

---

6   (1986) 82 Cr.App.R. 314.
7   In *D.P.P. v. Stonehouse* [1978] A.C. 55 at p. 68.
8   Similarly in *Boyle and Boyle* (1987) 84 Cr.App.R. 270, where the appellants had damaged a door with intent to enter the building, the Court of Appeal was (with respect) wrong to say that they were guilty of attempted burglary even on the Rubicon test. The fact that they had damaged the door did not commit them to entering the building.
9   *Infra*, paras. 7.02 ff.
10   [1987] Crim.L.R. 195.

judge,[11] and (rightly or wrongly)[12] will tend to boil down to the linguistic question of whether what the defendant did can naturally be described as an "attempt".

Attempting the impossible

1.188   Before the Criminal Attempts Act it had been held by the House of Lords in *Haughton v. Smith*[13] that a person who intended to commit an offence and did his utmost to do so could not be convicted of an attempt if, unbeknown to him, it was in the circumstances impossible for him to succeed in committing the full offence. This rule was taken to its logical conclusion in *Partington v. Williams*,[14] where it was held that a person who tries to steal from a particular receptacle is not guilty of attempted theft if the receptacle is in fact empty. One of the objectives of the Act was to reverse this unfortunate development. Section 1(2) provides:

> "A person may be guilty of attempting to commit an offence to which this section applies even though the facts are such that the commission of the offence is impossible."

Therefore a conviction of attempted theft may now be secured without proof that there was in fact some property there to be stolen.[15]

1.189   The effect of section 1(2) is to confirm that, for example, putting one's hand into someone else's pocket may be "more than merely preparatory" to the offence of stealing from the pocket, and may therefore be an attempt to steal from it, even if that offence cannot be committed because the pocket is empty. An alternative way of framing the defence might be to argue that, if what the pocket contains is something which the defendant does not want and would not keep (*e.g.* fluff), then in trying to appropriate the contents of the pocket he is trying to do something which would not be theft if he did it,[16] and he is therefore not attempting to steal. The argument is fallacious (because a person's intention is what he *thinks* he is going to do, even if in fact he cannot do it), but section 1(3) disposes of it anyway:

> "In any case where:
> (*a*)   apart from this subsection a person's intention would not be regarded as having amounted to an intent to commit an offence; but

---

11   s. 4(3).
12   Probably wrongly, because the word "attempt" forms no part of the definition of the offence: see E. Griew's annotations to the Act in *Current Law Statutes.*
13   [1975] A.C. 476.
14   (1976) 62 Cr.App.R. 220.
15   *Smith and Smith* [1986] Crim.L.R. 166.
16   *Easom* [1971] 2 Q.B. 315; *supra*, para. 1.118.

(*b*) if the facts of the case had been as he believed them to be, his intention would be so regarded, then, for the purposes of subsection (1) above, he shall be regarded as having had an intent to commit that offence."

The effect of these two provisions goes beyond the straightforward case where the defendant's object would be an offence if he achieved it but he cannot achieve it. They also catch the defendant who does exactly what he sets out to do, under the mistaken impression that the facts are such as would render his conduct illegal: for example, the person who takes an umbrella which he believes to belong to someone else but which is in fact his own. In *Anderton v. Ryan*[17] the House of Lords shrank from extending the law to cover such a case, but a year later in *Shivpuri*[18] accepted that this is indeed the effect of the Act. Prosecutions for such conduct are perhaps unlikely to be frequent.

Assault with intent to rob

1.190   Section 8(2) of the Theft Act 1968 provides:

"Any person guilty of . . . an assault with intent to rob . . . shall on conviction on indictment be liable to imprisonment for life."

The House of Lords held in *Courtie*[19] that if an offence carries one penalty when a particular aggravating factor is absent, but a higher penalty when that factor is present, there is not one offence but two. It follows that assault with intent to rob is a separate offence, distinct from that of assault. In any event it will almost invariably amount to attempted robbery, which is also punishable with life imprisonment by virtue of the Criminal Attempts Act 1981.[20]

Burglary with intent to steal

1.191   Under section 9(1)(*a*) of the Theft Act 1968 a person is guilty of burglary if (*inter alia*) he enters a building as a trespasser with intent to steal anything in the building, or enters part of a building as a trespasser with intent to steal anything in that part. This is only one form of burglary and is discussed below together with the other varieties of the offence.[21]

17   [1985] A.C. 560.
18   [1987] A.C. 1.
19   [1984] A.C. 463.
20   s. 4(1).
21   Paras. 7.02 ff.

Going equipped for stealing

1.192   Section 25(1) of the Theft Act 1968 provides:

"A person shall be guilty of an offence if, when not at his place of abode, he has with him any article for use in the course of or in connection with any burglary, theft or cheat."

The offence is punishable on conviction on indictment with three years' imprisonment. Section 25(4) provides that a person may arrest without warrant anyone who is, or whom he with reasonable cause suspects to be, committing the offence; but it is in any event an arrestable offence within the meaning of section 24 of the Police and Criminal Evidence Act 1984.[22]

Possession when not at place of abode

1.193   The offence in fact consists not of *possession* of the offending article but of *having it with* one, which may be slightly narrower in that it implies "a degree of immediate control".[23] On the other hand the defendant probably need not have the article on his person: *e.g.* it would be sufficient if it were in his vehicle nearby. It is not sufficient that he has it with him at his "place of abode"; but his place of abode is the place (*i.e.* the site) where he intends to abide, and does not therefore include a vehicle unless he lives in it *and* it is parked on a site where he intends to abide.[24]

Articles for use in connection with theft

1.194   The article in question may be any kind of article, provided that the defendant has it with him "for use in the course of or in connection with" a theft (or one of the other specified offences). Clearly an article may be used in connection with a theft though not in the course of it, *e.g.* for disposing of the loot. But in either case it must be proved that the defendant had the article with him "for" such use, which means that he must have *intended* that he or someone else should use it for that purpose.[25] If he has not made up his mind to use it (or to let someone else use it), even if an opportunity should present itself, he does not intend to do so and he does not have the article "for" such use.[26]

Proof of intent

1.195   No doubt the best proof of an intention to use an article is the fact that it was used, and a person who uses an article in the course of a

---

22   s. 24(2)(*d*).
23   *Kelt* [1977] 1 W.L.R. 1365, on the same phrase in Firearms Act 1968 s. 18(1).
24   *Bundy* [1977] 1 W.L.R. 914.
25   *Ellames* [1974] 1 W.L.R. 1391.
26   *Hargreaves* [1985] Crim.L.R. 243.

theft or attempted theft may be charged with going equipped—though there is little reason to do so.[27] In other cases the prosecution may derive some slight assistance from section 25(3), which provides:

"Where a person is charged with an offence under this section, proof that he had with him any article made or adapted for use in committing a burglary, theft or cheat shall be evidence that he had it with him for such use."

But this is no more than common sense. Obviously the possession of an article made or adapted for use in committing theft is some evidence of an intention to use it for that purpose. Whether it is *cogent* evidence is another matter, which will of course depend on the circumstances. In any event the scope of the provision is limited. Most of the articles used by thieves in the course of their professional activities are neither made nor adapted for such use, but serve the purpose well enough in their original form. It is not the nature of such articles which suggests an intent to steal, but the circumstances in which the defendant is found in possession of them. And in such a case section 25(3) does not assist.

Vehicle interference

1.196 Section 9(1) of the Criminal Attempts Act 1981 provides:

"A person is guilty of the offence of vehicle interference if he interferes with a motor vehicle[28] or trailer[29] or with anything carried[30] in or on a motor vehicle or trailer with the intention that an offence specified in subsection (2) below shall be committed by himself or some other person."

This offence is punishable on summary conviction with three months' imprisonment or a fine of level 4 on the standard scale or both.[31] A constable may arrest without warrant anyone who is, or whom he with reasonable cause suspects to be, guilty of the offence.[32] The offences specified in section 9(2) are the theft of the motor vehicle or trailer, or part of it, or of anything carried in or on it, and taking it without consent contrary to section 12(1) of the Theft Act 1968;[33] and if it is shown that

27 *Minor v. D.P.P.* (1987) 86 Cr.App.R. 378.
28 *i.e.* a mechanically propelled vehicle intended or adapted for use on roads: s. 9(5), Road Traffic Act 1972 s. 190(1).
29 *i.e.* a vehicle drawn by a motor vehicle: *ibid.*
30 A *person* is not "carried" in or on a vehicle within the meaning of Theft Act 1968 s. 12(1) unless the vehicle is moving (*Miller* [1976] Crim.L.R. 147), but the same can hardly apply here.
31 s. 9(3), Criminal Justice Act 1982 s. 46.
32 s. 9(4).
33 *Infra*, paras. 5.02 ff. S. 9(2) refers, by way of explanation of the reference to s. 12(1) of the Theft Act, to an offence of taking *and driving away*; but this is clearly an oversight, since s. 12(1) (unlike its precursor) does not require the conveyance to be driven away at all.

the defendant intended one of these offences to be committed it is immaterial that it cannot be shown which.[34] Thus, although a person committing the offence may well be guilty of an attempt, it need not be proved whether he was attempting to steal the vehicle or trailer itself, or to steal something carried in or on it, or to take it without the owner's consent but with no intention of permanently depriving him of it. Moreover a person may be convicted of this offence even if his intention was merely to enable another person to commit one of the offences specified, although he could not be convicted of attempting to aid and abet that offence.[35]

ALTERNATIVE VERDICTS

1.197 Under section 6(3) of the Criminal Law Act 1967 a person tried on indictment for one offence may be convicted of another if the allegations in the indictment amount to or include, expressly or by implication, an allegation of that other offence. An allegation of robbery, burglary by stealing or theft with a firearm obviously includes an allegation of theft, and a person tried on indictment for one of those offences may therefore be convicted of theft instead. Moreover an allegation of an offence is to be taken as including an allegation of an attempt to commit that offence.[36] A person indicted for an offence of stealing may therefore be convicted instead of attempting to commit that offence. It was formerly supposed that section 6(3) could only be invoked in order to convict the defendant of an offence whose ingredients were included among those of the offence charged; but in *Wilson*[37] the House of Lords held that this is not so. It seems that an allegation of one offence may by implication include an allegation of another if the commission of the latter offence is one way (albeit not the only way) of committing the former. A person charged on indictment with burglary contrary to section 9(1)(*b*) of the Theft Act 1968, by entering a building as a trespasser and stealing therein, may therefore be convicted of entering as a trespasser with *intent* to steal contrary to section 9(1)(*a*), although it is possible to commit the former without committing the latter.[38] It was held before *Wilson* that a person charged with robbery could not be convicted of assult with intent to rob, because it is theoretically possible to rob without

34 s. 9(2).
35 Criminal Attempts Act 1981 s. 1(4)(*b*).
36 s. 6(4).
37 [1984] A.C. 242.
38 *Whiting* (1987) 85 Cr.App.R. 78.

committing an assault;[39] but virtually all robberies do involve an assault, and the decision is now unlikely to be followed. Perhaps there can be a conviction of going equipped to steal on an indictment for theft. It is likely to be some time before the implications of *Wilson* become clear.

---

39 *Tennant* [1976] Crim.L.R. 133. This is because an attempt to put a person in fear of force, if coupled with a theft, is sufficient for the full offence of robbery even if the intended victim is not put in fear.

CHAPTER 2

Obtaining by Deception

2.01 Where a person obtains property with the consent of the person to whom it belongs, it seems that he is not guilty of theft:[1] but if he procures that consent by improper means he may commit other offences instead. If he procures it by fraud he may be guilty of the offence of obtaining property by deception.[2] Section 15(1) of the Theft Act 1968 provides:

> "A person who by any deception dishonestly obtains property belonging to another, with the intention of permanently depriving the other of it, shall on conviction on indictment be liable to imprisonment for a term not exceeding ten years."

The offence is triable either way.[3] Where it is committed by a body corporate with the consent or connivance of any director,[4] manager, secretary or other similar officer of the body corporate, or any person purporting to act in any such capacity, that person is also guilty of the offence.[5]

PROPERTY

2.02 The partial definition of property set out in section 4(1) of the Theft Act 1968 for the purposes of the offence of theft[6] is equally applicable to that of obtaining property by deception:[7]

> " 'Property' includes money and all other property, real or personal, including things in action and other intangible property."

Therefore the offence can be committed by obtaining anything regarded as property by the general law,[8] whether tangible or otherwise. Land is a form of property which cannot generally be the subject of theft,[9] but this

---

1   *Supra,* paras. 1.73 ff.
2   For a fuller account see *Fraud* chs. 2, 3.
3   Magistrates' Courts Act 1980 s. 17(1), Sch. 1.
4   If the affairs of the body corporate are managed by its members, a member acting in connection with his functions of management is regarded as a director: s. 18(2).
5   s. 18(1)
6   *Supra,* para. 1.02.
7   s. 34(1).
8   For some borderline cases, see *supra,* paras. 1.13 f.
9   s. 4(2); *supra,* para. 1.04.

rule has no application to the deception offence. One does not steal one's neighbour's land by moving the boundary fence without his knowledge, but it may be an offence to deceive him into thinking that the fence is in the wrong place and agreeing to move it.

BELONGING TO ANOTHER

2.03 The property in question must belong to someone other than the defendant at the time when he obtains it. Section 5(1) of the Theft Act 1968, which sets out the most important cases in which property is regarded as belonging to another for the purposes of the offence of theft, is equally applicable to the deception offence:[10]

> "Property shall be regarded as belonging to any person having possession or control of it, or having in it any proprietary right or interest (not being an equitable interest arising only from an agreement to transfer or grant an interest)".

This provision is discussed above.[11] Subsections (2) to (5) of section 5, which in various circumstances deem property to belong to a person who has neither possession nor control of it nor any proprietary interest in it,[12] have no application to the deception offence. Conversely section 4(4), which in effect restricts the circumstances in which wild creatures and their carcases are regarded as belonging to another,[13] does not apply here either.

2.04 It must be emphasised that it is not sufficient that the defendant has obtained property *from* another: it must be property which, at least until the defendant obtained it, *belonged* to that other. This requirement is not satisfied if, the property did not exist before the defendant obtained it. Thus a person who by deception induces a freeholder to grant him a lease is not guilty of obtaining the lease by deception, because the lease does not exist until it is granted, and as soon as it is granted it belongs to the defendant.[14] A charge of obtaining the land itself (in the sense of obtaining possession of it)[15] might be possible, because the land itself does belong to the freeholder: but the question would then arise whether the lessee can be said to intend permanently to deprive the freeholder of it.[16]

---

10   s. 34(1).
11   Para. 1.21 ff.
12   *Supra*, paras. 1.29 ff.
13   *Supra*, para. 1.61.
14   *Chan Wai Lam v. R.* [1981] Crim.L.R. 497 (C.A. of Hong Kong).
15   *Infra*, para. 2.08.
16   *Infra*, para. 2.32.

There would be no difficulty if the lease were already in existence and the defendant obtained an assignment of it.

2.05 Similarly a person who deceives another into drawing a cheque in his favour (as against endorsing an existing cheque in his favour) cannot be charged with obtaining the chose in action represented by the cheque, *viz.* the right to the sum for which the cheque is drawn: that chose in action is indeed property which he has obtained by deception, but it has never belonged to anyone other than the defendant himself. The point was overlooked in *Duru*,[17] and the decision (that in those circumstances the offence is committed) can be justified only on the alternative basis there relied upon, *viz.* that the property obtained is not the chose in action which the cheque represents but the piece of paper of which it physically consists. A charge on this basis might seem unduly technical, and it would normally be more appropriate to charge the offence of procuring the execution of a valuable security by deception.[18] Similar reasoning would apply to a person who by deception (*e.g.* multiple applications) obtains an allotment of company shares direct from the company, *i.e.* not through an issuing house. He obtains the shares by deception, but the shares belong to no-one until they are allotted. Again he could be charged with obtaining paper (*i.e.* share certificates) as against the rights represented by the paper, or with procuring the execution of a valuable security by deception, or even with obtaining services by deception.[19]

OBTAINING

2.06 The first major difference between obtaining by deception and theft is that in the case of the deception offence the property need not be "appropriated" but only "obtained". Section 15(2) provides:

> "For the purposes of this section a person is to be treated as obtaining property if he obtains ownership, possession or control of it, and 'obtain' includes obtaining for another or enabling another to obtain or retain."

Obtaining ownership

2.07 The defendant "obtains" the property if he obtains ownership of it, even without possession or control. It is immaterial that the title he obtains is voidable on the grounds of fraud; but if the effect of the fraud were to render the transaction completely void he would not have

17 [1974] 1 W.L.R. 2.
18 Theft Act 1968 s. 20(2); *Fraud* para. 3.40 ff.
19 Theft Act 1978 s. 1(1); *infra,* para. 2.33.

obtained ownership at all. It is also sufficient if he already has possession or control of the property, and by deception obtains ownership as well.[20]

Obtaining possession or control

2.08 Even if the owner has no intention of parting with the ownership of the property, or if his intention to do so is nullified by the fraud, the defendant obtains the property if he obtains possession or control of it. Thus the offence might be committed if the owner were deceived into thinking that the defendant wished only to borrow the property temporarily whereas in fact he intended to keep it for good.

Obtaining for another

2.09 A person obtains property if he obtains it for another. Thus A may be guilty of the offence if by deception he induces B to confer ownership, possession or control of B's property on C. C need not be a party to the fraud.

Enabling another to obtain

2.10 Nor is it necessary that the defendant should himself obtain the property for another; it is sufficient if he enables another to obtain it for himself. A may be guilty of the offence if by deception he enables C to obtain ownership, possession or control of B's property, either for C himself or for D. Again C need not be a party to the fraud. In *D.P.P. v. Stonehouse*[21] the appellant, a prominent businessman and politician, took elaborate steps to create the impression that he had drowned at sea. He intended that his wife should be deceived into making a claim on his life insurance, and that the insurance company should be deceived into paying her. The House of Lords upheld his conviction of attempting to obtain the insurance money by deception: had his plan succeeded, he would have "obtained" the money by deception, because his deception would have enabled his wife to obtain it.

Enabling another to retain

2.11 Finally the defendant "obtains" property if he merely enables another person to retain property which that other person already has. But this is subject to the proviso that the property obtained must be property belonging to another; and in order to make sense of the section

---

20 *Cf. Collis-Smith* [1971] Crim.L.R. 716.
21 [1978] A.C. 55.

this must be construed as meaning that the property must belong to someone who is neither the defendant nor the person enabled to retain the property. Where a person other than the defendant has sole ownership, possession and control of the property, it is literally property belonging to a person other than the defendant; but it can hardly be said that the defendant is obtaining property belonging to another if he merely enables that person to retain the ownership, possession and control which he already has. In any case the defendant would not intend thereby to deprive that person of the property. Therefore the offence would not be committed if a friend of the defendant had obtained ownership, possession and control[22] of property under a voidable contract,[23] and the defendant ensured by deception that the contract was not rescinded. There would be no-one from whom the property could be obtained, or who could be deprived of it. But if the friend had obtained only possession or control of the property and not the ownership of it, it would be possible to commit the offence by enabling him to retain that possession or control, even without enabling him to obtain ownership as well. The property would "belong" not only to the friend but also to the owner, and by enabling the friend to retain possession or control the defendant would be "obtaining" property belonging to another (*sc.* the owner); and he would no doubt be regarded as intending to "deprive" the owner of the property by ensuring that he did not get it back.[24] Similarly if the friend had obtained ownership under a voidable contract, but not possession or control, it would theoretically be sufficient if the defendant enabled him to retain his ownership by dissuading the former owner from rescinding the contract. But in that case the friend's retention of ownership would doubtless enable him to obtain possession or control as well.

2.12   What section 15(2) does not say is that a person "obtains" property if he enables *himself* to retain property which he already has. Presumably such conduct is not therefore sufficient: it would scarcely fall within the ordinary meaning of the word, and in any event section 15(2) appears to provide an exhaustive definition. Thus there is a curious anomaly. If a person other than the defendant is in possession of property belonging to another, the defendant can commit the offence by enabling that person to retain possession. But if the defendant himself is in possession of the property, it seems that he cannot commit the offence merely by deceiving

---

22   Or, in the case of intangible property, ownership only.
23   For the purposes of the offence of theft it is arguable that property obtained under a contract which is voidable on the grounds of fraud or other mistake continues to belong to the original owner by virtue of Theft Act 1968 s. 5(4): *supra*, paras. 1.56 ff. But s. 5(4) has no application to the offence of obtaining by deception.
24   *Cf. supra*, para. 1.109.

the owner into letting him keep it. In certain circumstances this might however amount to another deception offence, such as obtaining services by deception.[25]

DECEPTION

2.13 The defendant must obtain the property by deception.[26] The requirement of deception replaced the old requirement of a "false pretence",[27] *i.e.* a fraudulent misrepresentation. The Criminal Law Revision Committee proposed the change not only in the interests of simple language but also to effect a change of emphasis.

> "The word 'deception' seems to us . . . to have the advantage of directing attention to the effect that the offender deliberately produced on the mind of the person deceived, whereas 'false pretence' makes one think of what exactly the offender did in order to deceive. 'Deception' seems also more apt in relation to deception by conduct." [28]

It is commonly assumed that the change is of no real significance and that misrepresentation is still an essential element of the offence. It is submitted that this is not necessarily so, and indeed that the passage quoted above demonstrates that it was not intended to be so. A false pretence, or misrepresentation, is something the defendant *does* ("what exactly the offender did in order to deceive"); a deception is the *result* of what he does ("the effect . . . deliberately produced on the mind of the person deceived"), assuming that he is successful. It is now the result which counts, not the way in which it is achieved. If it can be achieved without employing a false pretence (or misrepresentation), then it is possible to commit the offence without doing so. Whether it *is* possible to effect a deception without resorting to a misrepresentation is perhaps debatable; but it is debatable only because a requirement of misrepresentation in the ordinary sense of the word would be inconveniently narrow, and the courts have therefore expanded the concept of fraudulent misrepresentation so far that it includes virtually any attempt to deceive. In *Scott v. Brown, Doering, McNab & Co.*[29] A. L. Smith L.J. said that if a person were induced to buy shares at a price in excess of their true value by the fact that others were buying the shares at inflated prices in order to create a false market, he would have an action against them in the tort of deceit (which requires a fraudulent misrepresentation). Presumably a

25 Theft Act 1978 s. 1(1); *infra*, para. 2.33.
26 For a fuller discussion of the nature of deception, see *Fraud* ch. 2.
27 Larceny Act 1916 s. 32.
28 Cmnd. 2977 para. 87.
29 [1892] 2 Q.B. 724 at p. 734.

purchase of shares is regarded as involving an implied representation by the buyer to the rest of the market, to the effect that he is buying because he thinks the shares are worth the price and not merely in order to create the impression that he thinks so. He may indeed be striving to convey that impression, but it seems artificial to say that he is *representing* it to be the case. In *Stonehouse*,[30] the case of the bogus drowning, the House of Lords was prepared to treat the appellant's conduct as involving a representation to the effect that he was dead. But the idea of a man representing that he is dead, and hoping to be believed, is somewhat bizarre.

2.14 It is submitted that reasoning as artificial as this is no longer necessary, because what is now required is not misrepresentation but deception; and a person is deceived if he is deliberately induced to believe something which is not true.

> "To deceive is, I apprehend, to induce a man to believe that a thing is true which is false, and which the person practising the deceit knows or believes to be false." [31]

Whether the belief is induced by misrepresentation or in some other way would seem to be immaterial. Moreover the absence of a requirement of misrepresentation may perhaps have substantive effects going beyond the mere avoidance of the need for artificial reasoning. It is arguable, for example, that a person who simply fails to disclose information which he has a legal duty to disclose is guilty of deceiving the person to whom he should have disclosed it, whereas he clearly commits no misrepresentation. The question is simply whether non-disclosure can be said to have the effect of inducing, in the person to whom disclosure is not made, a belief that the facts are other than they are; and where there is a duty to disclose,[32] *e.g.* because the defendant is in a fiduciary position,[33] it seems reasonable to suppose that it probably can. In that case the new requirement of deception has opened up new possibilities of which full advantage has yet to be taken.

The proposition believed

2.15 If deception consists in the inducement of a mistaken belief in the mind of the victim, it seems logical to begin the analysis of an alleged

---

30 [1978] A.C. 55.
31 *Re London and Globe Finance Corporation Ltd* [1903] 1 Ch. 728 at p. 732, *per* Buckley J.; approved by Lords Reid and Morris in *D.P.P. v. Ray* [1974] A.C. 370 at pp. 379 and 384.
32 In the absence of such a duty it is submitted that non-disclosure not only does not amount to deception but cannot properly be regarded as dishonest: *infra*, para. 2.35; *cf. supra*, paras. 1.154 ff.
33 This may be the explanation of *Silverman* (1987) 86 Cr.App.R. 213: *infra*, para. 2.16.

deception by determining exactly what the proposition was which the victim was allegedly induced to believe. This proposition need not be one of fact as distinct from one of law,[34] but it must be a proposition capable of truth or falsity at the time when the victim is induced to believe it. A person who obtains goods on credit is promising that he will pay the price, but if he fails to do so it does not follow that he obtained the goods by deception: a promise is not a proposition, and cannot be true or false. Therefore it is incorrect to allege that the defendant committed a deception by falsely representing that he would pay, or that anything else would happen in the future. But this does not mean that persons who break their promises, or make forecasts which turn out to be wrong, are never guilty of deception. Section 15(4) provides that "deception" includes "a deception as to the present intentions of the person using the deception or any other person". Therefore a person who pretends that he intends to do a thing, when in fact he does not, is guilty of deception; and the same must apply (though the Act does not expressly say so) if he pretends that he expects a thing to happen when in fact he does not. Whether he subsequently decides to honour his promise after all, or whether to his surprise his forecast turns out to be right, is not strictly relevant. What matters is his actual state of mind at the time when he made the promise or the forecast, and whether he pretended to intend or expect something which in fact he did not intend or expect.

2.16 Similarly it is not deception to convince another person of something which is no more than a matter of opinion, *e.g.* that goods offered for sale are of high quality in some loose and unverifiable sense:[35] such a belief is neither true nor false. But if there is some accepted scale of quality, by reference to which it can be objectively determined whether the goods match up to their description, the question is no longer one of opinion but one of fact. A similar distinction has to be drawn when the alleged deception relates not to the quality of the goods or services provided but to the price demanded for them. If the defendant asks a price higher than others would ask, but without any deception as to the nature or quality of what he is selling, is he inducing the customer to believe only that the price is a fair one (which is probably a matter of opinion) or that it is reasonably competitive with the prices charged by others (which is probably a matter of fact)? In *Bassett and Jeff*[36] it was regarded as a false pretence to charge an exorbitant sum for work which was unnecessary in the first place, but it is not clear whether it would have

---

34 s. 15(4). Of course it is arguable that the present state of the law is as much a fact as anything else.
35 *Levine and Wood* (1867) 10 Cox 374.
36 (1966) 51 Cr.App.R. 28.

made a difference if the work had been necessary although the price was still excessive. The problem was again evaded in *Silverman*,[37] where it was said that the charging of an excessive price could amount to a deception where there was a situation of "mutual trust" in which the customer depended on the defendant for fair and reasonable conduct. The fact that the defendant is in a position of trust may perhaps turn what would otherwise be mere non-disclosure into deception, but there still has to be a specific and objectively false proposition of fact or law which the victim is induced to believe. If all he is induced to believe is that what he is getting is worth the price asked, and if that is a matter not of fact but of opinion, it is hard to see how the existence of a fiduciary relationship affects the position. It may be that the best solution is to concentrate not on the customer's belief that the price *is* fair or competitive but on his belief that the defendant thinks it is. As in the case of promises and forecasts, it may be that the crucial proposition lies not in what the defendant says but in what his words imply about his state of mind. If he deliberately gives the impression that he thinks his wares are worth the price when in fact he thinks they are not, he is practising a deception as to his own opinion.

Falsity of the proposition

2.17 Obviously there is no deception unless the proposition which the victim is induced to believe is in fact false. Strictly speaking it is for the prosecution to prove that the proposition is false even if, were it true, it would be easy for the defence to prove it;[38] but in the absence of any evidence of its truth relatively slight evidence may be sufficient to establish that it is false.[39] It is not sufficient that the defendant thinks it is false if in fact it is true;[40] but there might then be a deception as to the defendant's own state of mind,[41] and there would seem to be at least an attempt to deceive.[42]

Belief in the proposition

2.18 It is convenient to speak of a requirement that the victim should be induced to "believe" that the proposition in question is true, but this is something of an over-simplification. There certainly must be a state of mind induced in the victim; this would seem to rule out the possibility of

---

37 (1987) 86 Cr.App.R. 213.
38 *Ng* [1958] A.C. 173; *Mandry and Wooster* [1973] 1 W.L.R. 1232.
39 *Mandry and Wooster, supra* n. 38.
40 *Deller* (1952) 36 Cr.App.R. 184.
41 *Cf. supra*, para. 2.15.
42 Criminal Attempts Act 1981 s. 1(1), (2); *Shivpuri* [1987] A.C. 1.

deceiving a machine, such as a computer.[43] And there is certainly no deception (though there may be an attempt) if the intended victim parts with his property in the full knowledge that the proposition is false, while it is certainly sufficient if he is fully convinced that it is true. But between these two extremes the position is less clear. Is there a deception, for example, if the alleged victim is induced to think that the proposition is *probably* true when in fact it is false? It can hardly be a defence that there is some lingering doubt in his mind. On the other hand it would be odd to say that he has been deceived if he is fairly sure, but not entirely certain, that the proposition is false. It might of course be argued that the deception was as to the defendant's own belief in the truth of the proposition in question;[44] but if the alleged victim strongly suspected not only that the proposition was false but also that the defendant knew it was, this approach would not help.

2.19 A further difficulty may arise from the alleged victim's *attitude* towards the truth or falsity of the proposition in question, as distinct from his assessment of the likelihood that it is true. It is clearly unnecessary that he should give the matter any conscious thought: a subconscious assumption will do, provided that it is somehow fostered by the defendant. But it may be that, whether or not it occurs to him to consider the matter, the alleged victim is simply not interested in whether the proposition is true or false. In most such cases it is immaterial whether there is a deception because, even if there is, the defendant will not have obtained the property *by* the deception: he would still have got it even if the victim had known the truth.[45] Sometimes, however, the victim's indifference is less than total: he is not concerned whether the proposition is true or false, provided only that he does not *know* it to be false. This will normally be the attitude of a seller of goods for which the buyer pays with a credit card, or with a cheque backed by a cheque guarantee card. Provided that the conditions set out on the card are satisfied, the seller is assured that he will be able to recover the price of the goods from the issuing bank or credit card company. This is because his acceptance of the card creates a unilateral contract under which the bank or company is obliged to pay him. Therefore the buyer's implied representation that the seller can expect to be paid in due course is in fact true, and involves no deception even if the buyer has no authority to use the card as he does (*e.g.* because it is not his, or because he has exceeded his permitted credit limit). But in *Metropolitan Police Commissioner v. Charles*[46] it was held

43 So held by a trial judge in *Moritz* (unreported, 1981).
44 *Supra,* para. 2.15.
45 *Infra,* para. 2.25.
46 [1977] A.C. 177.

by the House of Lords that a person who draws a cheque and supports it with an apparently valid cheque guarantee card is normally making an additional representation to the effect that he has the bank's authority to use the card so as to guarantee a cheque for that amount; and if in fact he has no such authority he is guilty of deception, although the seller does not care whether he has it or not. The seller is regarded as "believing" that the buyer has the bank's authority to use the card because his indifference to the matter is not entirely unqualified: he does not care whether the buyer has the bank's authority or not, provided he does not actually know that the buyer has no such authority. If he did know this he would not accept the cheque, because he would then be a party to an attempted fraud on the bank and would not be entitled to payment after all. It follows, according to *Charles*, that if the buyer in fact has no authority to use the card then the seller will normally have been deceived into thinking that he has. And in *Lambie*[47] the House confirmed that similar reasoning applies where the buyer uses a credit card without authority.

Inducement of the belief

2.20 Clearly there is no deception unless the victim's mistaken belief is attributable, at least in part, to something which the defendant has done or said. If the intended victim ignores the defendant's efforts to convince him and reaches the desired conclusion in reliance on his own investigations alone, there is no deception but only an attempt.[48] The most obvious way to induce someone to believe a proposition is to state it to him, and it is advisable for the prosecution to rely upon an express statement whenever possible. But there is no need to prove that such a statement is literally false, because there is no need to prove an express statement at all: deception means the inducement of a mistaken belief, and it is possible to create a false impression by means of a statement which is literally true (*e.g.* by virtue of what is left unsaid).

2.21 For the same reason there need not be an express statement, or even any words at all. Section 15(4) makes it clear that a deception may be effected "by words or conduct". Certain common ways of obtaining property will commonly have the effect of creating particular impressions upon the mind of the person from whom the property is obtained. A person who buys goods on credit is normally giving the seller the impression both that he intends to pay for them and that he has at least a reasonable expectation of being in a position to do so.[49] A person who

---

47 [1982] A.C. 449.
48 *Roebuck* (1856) D. & B. 24.
49 *Cf. Harris* (1975) 62 Cr.App.R. 28; *D.P.P. v. Ray* [1974] A.C. 370.

pays for goods by cheque is normally giving the impression that he has an account at the bank on which the cheque is drawn, and that the state of the account is such that in the ordinary course of events the cheque can be expected to be honoured[50] (or, if it is post-dated, that it can be expected to be honoured if presented on or after the prescribed date).[51] Even if it *is* likely to be honoured the payee may still have been deceived into accepting it. It may be that the reason why the cheque will be honoured is one of which he would not approve, *e.g.* the fact that the drawer expects to receive another cheque from the payee by way of partial reimbursement and to ensure that the return cheque is cleared before his own is presented.[52] Or it may be that the cheque will be honoured only because it is supported by a cheque guarantee card, in which case the payee will have been induced to believe that the drawer has the bank's authority to use the card.[53] Similarly where payment is made by credit card the payee will normally have been induced to believe that the customer has the authority of the company issuing the card to use it for a transaction of that amount.[54] This is so even if, as is usually the case, the payee has no interest in the state of the customer's account.

2.22 More surprisingly, it was said in *Williams (Jean-Jacques)*[55] that a schoolboy who knowingly exchanged obsolete foreign banknotes at a bureau de change for sums far in excess of their real value could properly have been convicted of obtaining the money by deception. In effect this means that, where a dealer is known to deal only in goods of a particular type, a person offering him goods is thereby attempting to induce in him the belief that the goods offered are goods of the type in which he deals. It follows that if the person offering the goods knows they are not goods of that type, but the dealer buys them under the impression that they are, the contract is voidable for fraud. How such a rule can be reconciled with the principle of *caveat emptor* is not apparent. It may indeed be that anyone who obtains property from a person whom he knows to be labouring under a material misapprehension can be regarded as obtaining the property by deception. In that case deception is substantially wider than fraudulent misrepresentation.[56]

Deliberate or reckless

2.23 Section 15(4) requires that the deception be "deliberate or reckless". In view of the nature of deception this phrase conceals two

50 *Page* [1971] 2 Q.B. 330.
51 *Gilmartin* [1983] Q.B. 953.
52 *Greenstein* [1975] 1 W.L.R. 1353.
53 *Charles* [1977] A.C. 177; *supra,* para. 2.19.
54 *Lambie* [1982] A.C. 449.
55 [1980] Crim.L.R. 589.
56 *Cf. supra,* para. 2.14.

distinct requirements. Firstly, the defendant must either know that the proposition which the victim believes to be true is in fact false, or at least be reckless as to that possibility; and secondly he must either intend to induce the victim to believe it, or at least be reckless whether he does so. In the case of the former requirement there is authority to the effect that a person is not reckless whether a proposition is false unless he realises that it may be, or does not honestly believe it to be true.[57] It may be arguable that in the light of the House of Lords' redefinition of recklessness in *Caldwell*[58] a person is reckless whether a proposition is false (or whether he induces another person to believe that it is true) if there is an obvious risk that it may be false (or that he may induce the other person to believe it) but he fails to give any thought to that possibility. It is submitted however that if a person does not even appreciate the possibility of misleading another then his conduct may be culpable but it cannot be described as deception. In any event the point is academic: even if such a person were guilty of deception his obtaining of property could hardly be dishonest, because he would not realise that he was doing something which others might regard as dishonest.[59] It is true that it is the obtaining which must be dishonest, not the deception: a person whose recklessness (in the *Caldwell* sense) had misled another, and who subsequently discovered the truth, might take dishonest advantage of the mistake so as to obtain property. But in that case he would probably be committing a deliberate deception by failing to correct the misapprehension he had already brought about.[60]

CAUSATION

2.24 It is not sufficient merely that the defendant practises a deception and obtains property belonging to another. At the very least the deception must precede the obtaining.[61] Even if the deception does come first, it does not follow that the defendant has obtained the property *by* the deception. This requirement has two aspects. Firstly there must in fact have been some causal connection between the deception and the obtaining; secondly that connection must be sufficiently close for it to be said that the latter was achieved by means of the former.

57 *Waterfall* [1970] 1 Q.B. 148; *Royle* [1971] 1 W.L.R. 1764; *Staines* (1974) 60 Cr.App.R. 160; *cf. Derry v. Peek* (1889) 14 App. Cas. 337.
58 [1982] A.C. 341; *infra*, para. 6.23.
59 *Supra*, para. 1.141.
60 *Brownlie v. Campbell* (1880) 5 App. Cas. 925 at p. 950, *per* Lord Blackburn; *cf. D.P.P. v. Ray* [1974] A.C. 370.
61 *Collis-Smith* [1971] Crim.L.R. 716.

Factual causation

2.25 The deception must in fact have had some causal effect in enabling the defendant to obtain the property. If it had no such effect, the full offence is not made out (though there may be an attempt if the defendant intended that to be the effect).[62] This will be the case, for example, if the victim is contractually obliged to hand over the property on payment by cheque: if the defendant knows that the cheque is bad he is guilty of deception in inducing the victim to believe that it is good, but he is not obtaining the property *by* the deception because even if the victim knew that the cheque was bad he would have no alternative but to accept it.[63] At the opposite extreme it is obviously sufficient if the victim would never have allowed the defendant to obtain the property had it not been for the deception. The victim's evidence to this effect is highly desirable but not essential, *e.g.* if he cannot reasonably be expected to have any recollection of the incident.[64] Also sufficient is a deception consisting in the misuse of a credit card or cheque guarantee card:[65] although the person accepting the card will not normally care whether the defendant is entitled to use it, his apathetic assumption that the defendant *is* so entitled is sufficient to amount to a deception. Had he not been deceived in this sense (*i.e.* had he known that the use of the card was unauthorised) he would not have handed over the property, unless of course he would for some reason have been willing to participate in the fraud. In the absence of evidence that he would have been willing to do so it can be assumed that he would not,[66] although the prosecution should doubtless call him unless there is good reason not to. If the defence wish to suggest otherwise they can of course call him themselves.

2.26 Difficulties begin to arise when the deception may have had some effect in inducing the victim to part with the property, but the prosecution are unable to prove that he would definitely not have done so had he not been deceived. There may be various reasons for this. The point on which the victim is deceived may be one of intrinsically limited importance, in which case it may be arguable that he might well have acted as he did even if he had known the truth. Thus it was held in *Laverty*[67] that a person who sells a car after changing the number-plates does not obtain the price by deceiving the purchaser as to the car's original registration number unless there is some evidence that the number was a matter of concern to

62   *Edwards* [1978] Crim.L.R. 49.
63   *Cf. Andrews and Hedges* [1981] Crim.L.R. 106.
64   *Etim v. Hatfield* [1975] Crim.L.R. 234.
65   *Supra*, para. 2.19.
66   *Lambie* [1982] A.C. 449.
67   [1970] 3 All E.R. 432.

the purchaser. But the decision is questionable on the facts, since the effect of the deception was to avoid awkward questions about *why* the number had been changed, which (since the car had in fact been stolen) would have had to be answered untruthfully if the sale were to go through. It must surely be sufficient if the effect of one deception is to avoid the need for another.

2.27 Alternatively it may be that the deception in no way detracts from the value of the proposed transaction to the person deceived, but is in the nature of a fraud on a third party. In that case the question is whether the person deceived would still have parted with the property even if he had known of the fraud, thus making himself a party to it. The issue has arisen in several cases where persons employed to sell their employers' goods to the public (usually British Rail catering staff) have sold their own goods instead, thus defrauding their employers of the profit. In *Rashid*[68] the appeal was allowed on the grounds of a misdirection, but the court was inclined to the view that on a proper direction no jury would have convicted: the customers would be interested only in the quality of the goods and not in who they belonged to. Indeed, British Rail's customers might well *prefer* somebody else's sandwiches to the real thing. In *Doukas*,[69] however, it was held that a jury is entitled to assume that members of the public would not willingly participate in a fraud.

> "Of course each case of this type may produce different results according to the circumstances of the case and according, in particular, to the commodity which is being proffered. But, as we see it, the question has to be asked of the hypothetical customer, 'Why did you buy this wine; or, if you had been told the truth, would you or would you not have bought the commodity?' It is, at least in theory, for the jury in the end to decide that question." [70]

This approach was followed in *Corboz*[71] and approved by the House of Lords in *Cooke*.[72] Where the offence charged is the full offence of obtaining property by deception, the question whether the victim would have parted with the property anyway is certainly one of fact for the jury. Whether the same applies to inchoate offences such as going equipped to obtain property by deception (which was charged in *Rashid, Doukas* and *Corboz*) or conspiracy to do so (which was the point in issue in *Cooke*) is arguably another matter, and is discussed below.[73]

2.28 In any event it is submitted that the problem can be disposed of more simply. Much of the discussion assumes that an obtaining of property is

68 [1977] 1 W.L.R. 298.
69 [1978] 1 W.L.R. 372.
70 At p. 376.
71 [1984] Crim.L.R. 629.
72 [1986] A.C. 909.
73 Para. 2.38.

not achieved *by* deception unless it would not have been achieved *but for* the deception. It is submitted that this assumption is unfounded. A plaintiff seeking damages for a loss which he claims to have suffered as a result of negligent misrepresentation must prove that the misrepresentation caused his loss; but he need not prove that he would not have suffered the loss had he known the truth. It is sufficient if the representation was only one of the factors which he took into account in deciding to alter his position as he did.[74] It need not be the only factor, and it need not be the crucial factor. Similarly, in a deception case the prosecution must prove a causal connection between the deception and the obtaining; but this does not mean they must prove that the defendant would not have obtained the property had the victim known the truth. It means only that the victim's belief in the proposition which the defendant has led him to believe must be one of the factors which he takes into account in deciding whether to let the defendant have the property. If, for example, a British Rail steward sells his own sandwiches to a passenger who thinks they are British Rail sandwiches, there is no need to prove that the passenger would definitely have refused to buy them had he known the truth: it is sufficient if he would have been *less likely* to do so, *i.e.* if his belief that they were genuine was a factor which in some measure contributed towards his decision to buy them. This is a test which should not be too difficult to satisfy.

2.29 It may be objected that the implied representation of authority made by a person using a cheque card or credit card contributes nothing whatever towards the payee's decision to accept such payment, and that the only basis on which the misuse of such cards can amount to obtaining by deception (as we have seen that it can)[75] is that the payee would not accept the card if he knew that the user had no authority to use it. But a person may be influenced by factors of which he is not conscious: if he assumes something to be the case, and would not act as he does if he knew that it were not the case, then in a sense he *is* influenced by the assumption. Alternatively it may be that causation is established if *either* the deception is one of the factors influencing the victim *or* the defendant would not have obtained the property but for the deception.

Operative causation

2.30 On the other hand it cannot necessarily be said that the property is obtained *by* the deception merely because the deception plays some part in the chain of events which culminates in the obtaining of the property.

---

74 *JEB Fasteners Ltd v. Marks Bloom & Co.* [1983] 1 All E.R. 583.
75 *Supra*, para. 2.19.

It is not sufficient that the defendant would not have obtained the property had he not at some stage practised a deception: this may be so only because it was by deception that he obtained the *opportunity* to obtain the property. In that case the deception may in a purely factual sense be one of the causes of the obtaining, but it may not be regarded as a cause for legal purposes. In other words it may be a cause but not an "operative" cause, or a *causa sine qua non* but not a *causa causans*. Thus a man who deceived a woman into accepting him as a lodger, and subsequently induced her to provide him with board as well, did not obtain the board *by* the deception, although had it not been for the deception he would not have been accepted as a lodger in the first place and *a fortiori* would not have been offered board as well.[76] Similarly a person who deceives a bookmaker into accepting a bet, and wins the bet, does not obtain his winnings by the deception but by picking the winner of the race; and this is so even though he could not have won the bet without first placing it, and he could not have placed it without deceiving the bookmaker.[77] It has even been held in an unreported Assizes case that a person who obtains a job by deception does not then obtain the salary by deception but by doing the job.[78]

2.31   In these latter situations the difficulty is largely circumvented by section 16(2)(c) of the Theft Act 1968, under which a person is guilty of obtaining a pecuniary advantage by deception if by deception he dishonestly obtains an opportunity to earn remuneration (or greater remuneration) in an office or employment, or to win money by betting.[79] It does not follow that a person obtaining money in similar circumstances can never be convicted of the more serious offence of obtaining property by deception. In *King and Stockwell* [80] the appellants, masquerading as tree surgeons, had falsely told a widow of 68 that the trees in her garden were dangerous, and offered to remove them for £500. They were convicted of attempting to obtain property by deception, and their appeal was dismissed. Had they removed the trees and collected the money, they would have obtained the money by deceiving the widow and not merely by removing the trees. The only question in such a case is whether the deception is an "operative cause" of the obtaining; and this is a question of fact, to be answered by the jury as a matter of common sense.

76   *Gardner* (1856) D. & B. 40.
77   *Clucas* [1949] 2 K.B. 226.
78   *Lewis,* January 1922; *Russell on Crime* (12th ed., 1964) vol. 2, p. 1186, n. 66.
79   *Fraud* paras. 3.37 ff.
80   [1987] Q.B. 547.

INTENTION PERMANENTLY TO DEPRIVE

2.32 As in the case of theft, the defendant must intend permanently to deprive of the property the person to whom it belongs.[81] A person who obtains property by deception with the intention of subsequently returning it will not normally be guilty of the offence. But here too there may be a constructive intention permanently to deprive where no such intention literally exists: section 6 applies, with the substitution of references to obtaining for those to appropriation, as it applies to theft.[82] Thus it is sufficient if the defendant intends to return the property only on receiving payment for it, or only when all the "goodness" has gone out of it, or only after such a long period as to make the obtaining "equivalent to an outright taking". It might be argued, for example, that if a person obtains a sub-lease of land for a period one day shorter than the unexpired portion of the head lease he is deemed to intend permanently to deprive his lessor of the land.[83]

2.33 Moreover the requirement of an intention permanently to deprive is largely undermined by two of the offences created by the Theft Act 1978. Section 1(1) of that Act provides:

"A person who by any deception dishonestly obtains services from another shall be guilty of an offence."

This offence is triable either way[84] and is punishable on conviction on indictment with five years' imprisonment.[85] It is wider than it seems, because "services" is broadly defined by section 1(2):

"It is an obtaining of services where the other is induced to confer a benefit by doing some act, or causing or permitting some act to be done, on the understanding that the benefit has been or will be paid for."

A person who allows another to obtain property is clearly conferring a benefit on him, either by doing an act or by causing or permitting an act to be done. If it is understood that the property has been or will be paid for, the person obtaining it is obtaining "services" within the meaning of the section. If he also obtains it dishonestly and by deception, he is guilty of the offence. It follows that a person who obtains property by deception, but with no intention of keeping it permanently, is guilty of obtaining not property but services—provided only that he obtains it on the understanding that he, or someone else, has paid for it or will do so. Only where

---

81 *Cf. supra,* paras. 1.108 ff.
82 s. 15(3); *cf. supra,* paras. 1.126 ff.
83 *Cf. Chan Wai Lam v. R.* [1981] Crim.L.R. 497.
84 s. 4(1).
85 s. 4(2)(*a*).

it is intended to be *gratis* will the obtaining of it not amount to an obtaining of "services". Thus it is an offence to deceive another into parting with his property under a contract of hire, even if the hire charge is paid in full, but not simply to borrow it without asking or paying.

2.34 Even if there is no understanding that the benefit has been or will be paid for, the prosecution may be able to fall back on one of the offences created by section 2 of the Theft Act 1978. Section 2(1) provides, in part:

"Subject to subsection (2) below, where a person by any deception —

. . .

    (c)   dishonestly obtains[86] any exemption from or abatement of liability[87] to make a payment;

    he shall be guilty of an offence."

This offence too is triable either way[88] and is punishable on conviction on indictment with five years' imprisonment.[89] It differs from the offences under paragraphs (a) and (b) of section 2(1) (*viz.* securing the remission of a liability and inducing a creditor to wait for or to forgo payment respectively) in that it does not require the liability evaded to be an existing liability. In other words it may consist of a deception practised before any liability is incurred. If a person obtains property without payment, for which payment would normally be required, he is obtaining an "exemption" from liability to make a payment; and if he dishonestly obtains that exemption by deception, *e.g.* by falsely claiming to be entitled to it, he is guilty of the offence. Similarly if the price were reduced, but not waived altogether, he would be obtaining an "abatement" of liability. Indeed, in that case he would be guilty of obtaining services by deception as well, because there would still be an understanding that the property was to be paid for, albeit at a reduced rate. In neither case would it be a defence that he intended to return the property later, though this might conceivably be relevant to the issue of dishonesty. Thus it seems that the existence of an intention permanently to deprive is essential to a conviction only if there is no understanding that the property has been or will be paid for, *and* it cannot be said that by obtaining it for nothing the defendant has obtained an exemption from the price which would otherwise have been charged. In other cases the intention permanently to deprive is in effect no more than an aggravating factor, rendering the defendant liable to a maximum of ten years' imprisonment instead of five.

---

86   This includes obtaining for another or enabling another to obtain: s. 2(4).
87   *i.e.* legally enforceable liability: s. 2(2).
88   s. 4(1).
89   s. 4(2)(*a*).

DISHONESTY

2.35 The obtaining of the property must be dishonest, which means firstly that it must be an act which ordinary people would regard as dishonest and secondly that the defendant must have done it in the realisation that ordinary people would think so.[90] The deception need not itself be dishonest, though of course it will usually be the element of deception which makes it dishonest for the defendant to obtain the property as he does. Section 2(1) of the 1968 Act, which provides that in certain situations an appropriation of property is not dishonest,[91] has no direct application to offences other than theft;[92] but it is submitted that, even without direct statutory authority, the concept of dishonesty can and should be judicially defined at least to the extent of excluding those who obtain property to which they believe themselves legally entitled. We do not need a jury to tell us that it is not dishonest to act under a claim of right. Similarly it is submitted that if there is such a thing as an obtaining by deception which gives rise to no civil liability (which is not impossible if the concept of deception is not to be tied down by such principles as *caveat emptor*)[93] then such an obtaining ought not to be regarded as dishonest, whatever the ordinary layman might think.[94]

JURISDICTION

2.36 The general rule is that the offence is committed where the property is obtained, not where the deception is practised. Therefore there is an offence under English law if the property is obtained in England or Wales although the deception occurs elsewhere,[95] but not *vice versa*.[96] Where property is despatched from one jurisdiction to another it may be debatable whether it is "obtained" in the former or the latter. In *Harden*[97] it was held that cheques sent from Jersey to the appellant in England had been obtained by him in Jersey, because title passed as soon as the cheques were posted; but this was so only because it had been agreed that the posting of the cheques should constitute receipt. In *Tirado*[98] the Court of Appeal held on somewhat similar facts that money sent to England

---

90 *Ghosh* [1982] Q.B. 1053; *supra*, paras. 1.139 ff.
91 *Supra*, para. 1.142.
92 *Woolven* (1983) 77 Cr.App.R. 231.
93 *e.g. Williams (Jean-Jacques)* [1980] Crim.L.R. 589; *supra*, para. 2.22.
94 *Cf. supra*, paras. 1.154 ff.
95 *Ellis* [1899] 1 Q.B. 230.
96 *Harden* [1963] 1 Q.B. 8; *Tirado* (1974) 59 Cr.App.R. 80; *R. v. Governor of Pentonville Prison, ex p. Khubchandani* (1980) 71 Cr.App.R. 241.
97 [1963] 1 Q.B. 8.
98 (1974) 59 Cr.App.R. 80.

from abroad was obtained in England, because in this case there was no such agreement. The situation which arose in *Harden* was regarded as an exception to a general principle that property is not obtained until it is received. Unfortunately the court was not referred to its earlier decision in *Baxter*,[99] where *Harden* was treated as establishing a general rule that money sent by post is obtained where it is posted; but that was clearly a misinterpretation of *Harden* and there can be little doubt that *Tirado* now represents the law. Property is "obtained" when, and where, the defendant obtains possession or control of it,[1] unless by virtue of some agreement he has obtained the ownership of it at some earlier stage.

2.37   When section 1(1)(*d*) of the Nuclear Material (Offences) Act 1983 is brought into force, any act done in relation to or by means of nuclear material, which would have amounted to an offence of obtaining property by deception had it been done within the jurisdiction, will amount to that offence notwithstanding that it is done outside the jurisdiction. The Act is discussed elsewhere.[2]

GOING EQUIPPED

2.38   Under section 25(1) of the Theft Act 1968 it is an offence for a person to have with him, when not at his place of abode, any article for use in the course of or in connection with any burglary, theft or cheat;[3] and "cheat" is somewhat mysteriously defined to mean an offence of obtaining property by deception contrary to section 15(1). An intention to commit some other deception offence, such as those under the Theft Act 1978,[4] will not suffice. Therefore the defendant must have intended not only to obtain property belonging to another but also permanently to deprive that person of it. He must also have intended to obtain the property *by* the proposed deception.[5] This requirement can present difficulty if it is possible that the intended victim might still part with the property even if he were not deceived, because the person intended to suffer loss is not the victim of the deception but a third party—*e.g.* where the intention is to pass off the defendant's own property as his employer's. The authorities suggest that in such a case it is a question of fact for the jury whether the intended victim would co-operate if he were not

99   [1972] Q.B. 1.
1   See s. 15(2): *supra,* para. 2.06.
2   *Supra,* paras. 1.165 ff.
3   *Supra,* para. 1.192.
4   *Supra,* paras. 2.33 f.
5   *Supra,* paras. 2.24 f.

deceived.[6] But this approach, adequate though it may be on a charge of the full offence (with which these authorities were not concerned), presents difficulties in the context of an inchoate offence such as going equipped or conspiracy (with which they were). On a charge of the full offence the question is whether the person actually deceived would have parted with the property had he known the truth. This is a question of fact, and the answer may well depend to some extent on the characteristics of the person in question. On a charge of an inchoate offence, however, where the persons to be deceived are members of the public unknown to the defendant at the time of the alleged offence, the question whether those persons would or would not co-operate if they knew the truth is not a simple question of fact: it depends who those persons turn out to be. They are "hypothetical" customers, not real ones.[7] The question cannot therefore be answered without making certain assumptions about the general public. If the jury take the not unreasonable view that some people might co-operate in the fraud and others might not, they will need some guidance as to the assumptions which they ought to make for the purposes of the case. Moreover it would seem that in principle the issue in such a case ought to be not what would in fact have happened if the customers had known the truth, but what the defendant *thought* would happen. In that case the question is not what assumptions the jury ought to make about the customers but what assumptions the defendant did in fact make. If he claims to share the somewhat cynical view of human nature expressed by the Court of Appeal in *Rashid*,[8] the assertion may be hard to disprove.

6 *Doukas* [1978] 1 W.L.R. 372; *Cooke* [1986] A.C. 909.
7 *Doukas, supra* n. 6, at p. 376. See also *Whiteside and Antoniou* [1989] Crim.L.R. 436; *supra,* para. 2.27.
8 [1977] 1 W.L.R. 298; *supra,* para. 2.27.

CHAPTER 3

Obtaining by Threats

3.01 With certain exceptions,[1] English law does not generally prohibit the making of threats *per se*. What it does sometimes prohibit is the use of threats for the purpose of inducing others to do that which they might not otherwise do; and one of the things which people are commonly threatened into doing is parting with their property. The obtaining of property by threats can amount to theft if the threat is such as to nullify any apparent consent on the part of the victim,[2] and to robbery if it is a threat of immediate force.[3] In this chapter we consider some offences which may be committed by a person who obtains property by threats even if he is not thereby guilty of stealing the property. But in each case the offence consists not in the obtaining of the property but in the making of the threat. In effect these offences are *inchoate* offences against property.

BLACKMAIL

3.02 Section 21(1) of the Theft Act 1968 provides:

"A person is guilty of blackmail if, with a view to gain for himself or another or with intent to cause loss to another, he makes any unwarranted demand with menaces . . ."

Blackmail is triable on indictment only and is punishable with fourteen years' imprisonment.[4]

---

1 *e.g.* threats to murder (Offences against the Person Act 1861 s. 16); threats to destroy or damage property (Criminal Damage Act 1971 s. 2: *infra*, para. 6.08); threats to steal nuclear material (Nuclear Material (Offences) Act 1983 s. 2(3): *cf. supra*, para. 1.166); threats of violence for the purpose of securing entry into premises (Criminal Law Act 1977 s. 6: *infra*, para. 7.55).
2 *Supra*, para. 1.95.
3 *Supra*, para. 1.173.
4 s. 21(3). A person who commits blackmail, and at the time of committing it or being arrested for it has in his possession a firearm or imitation firearm, is guilty of an offence punishable with life imprisonment (14 years in the case of an offence committed before 29 September 1988) unless he shows that he had it in his possession for a lawful object: Firearms Act 1968 s. 17(2), Schs. 1, 6; Criminal Justice Act 1988 s. 44(3), (4); *cf. supra*, para. 1.180.

Menaces

3.03 A requirement of "menaces" is a curious one to find in a statute which strives to use everyday language as far as possible, but the word is borrowed from earlier legislation.[5] The *Oxford English Dictionary* defines "menace" as "a declaration or indication of hostile intention, or of a probable evil or catastrophe; a threat"; and in *Thorne v. Motor Trade Association* it was said that the requirement would be satisfied by "threats of any action detrimental to or unpleasant to the person addressed".[6] Since a proposal to act in a manner *not* detrimental or unpleasant to the person addressed can hardly be described as a threat at all, it would seem to follow that "menaces" means simply "threats". But this went further than was necessary to the decision, and other cases have established that it is not every threat which amounts to a menace. In *Boyle and Merchant*[7] the Court of Criminal Appeal said:

> "If the threat is of such a character that it is not calculated to deprive any person of reasonably sound and ordinarily firm mind of the free and voluntary action of his mind it would not be a menace within the meaning of the section." [8]

This was presumably what the Criminal Law Revision Committee had in mind in preferring "manaces" to the more mundane "threats".

> "We have chosen the word 'menaces' instead of 'threats' because, notwithstanding the wide meaning given to 'menaces' in *Thorne's* case, . . . we regard that word as stronger than 'threats', and the consequent slight restriction of the scope of the offence seems to us right." [9]

If so, the Committee's interpretation was borne out in *Clear*,[10] another case decided under the old law:

> "Words or conduct which would not intimidate or influence anyone to respond to the demand would not be menaces . . . , but threats and conduct of such a nature and extent that the mind of an ordinary person of normal stability and courage might be influenced or made apprehensive so as to accede unwillingly to the demand would be sufficient for a jury's consideration." [11]

3.04 In *Garwood*[12] the Court of Appeal broadly accepted this test (subject to a gloss discussed below) but thought it unnecessary to explain it to a jury.

5 Larceny Act 1916 ss. 29(1)(i), 30.
6 [1937] A.C. 797 at p. 817, *per* Lord Wright.
7 [1914] 3 K.B. 339.
8 At p. 345.
9 Cmnd. 2977 para. 123.
10 [1968] 1 Q.B. 670.
11 At p. 679.
12 [1987] 1 W.L.R. 319.

"In our judgment it is only rarely that a judge will need to enter upon a definition of the word menaces. It is an ordinary word of which the meaning will be clear to any jury." [13]

The only occasions on which the court thought it might be necessary to explain the word were those where the threat's actual effect on the person to whom it is addressed is different from the effect which it would have had on an ordinary person of normal stability.[14] But "menaces" is not a word in everyday use, and if it is left unexplained the jury are likely to assume that it is simply legal jargon for a threat. The reason why it needs no explanation in most cases is that in most cases the threat alleged would amount to menaces on any view. But if there is any doubt whether the action threatened would have been sufficiently damaging for the threat of it to influence an ordinary person of normal stability and courage, the jury should surely be told that this is what is required. In *Harry*[15] the treasurer of a college rag committee had sent letters to 115 local shopkeepers asking them to buy "indemnity posters" which would "protect" them from any "inconvenience" resulting from rag activities. Very few of the shopkeepers complained about the letter, and none of those who complained had paid. The jury were directed to acquit the treasurer of blackmail: in view of the actual effect of the letter on 115 real recipients it could not be said that a hypothetical ordinary person might have been influenced by it. Yet, had the judge ruled that there was sufficient evidence that the letter might have had that effect, according to *Garwood* he would not have been required to direct the jury that they could not convict unless they thought that that fact had been proved beyond reasonable doubt. It is submitted with respect that it is sometimes necessary to define "menaces" to the jury even where there is no suggestion that the threat's effect on an ordinary person would have been any different from its effect on the victim himself.

3.05 The direction in *Garwood* was in precisely the terms laid down in *Clear*, except that the jury were asked whether an ordinary person might have acceded unwillingly to *a* demand rather than *the* demand. The Court of Appeal did not remark upon the difference, but it is not without significance. The point is that it is an over-simplification to ask, as was advocated in *Boyle and Merchant*,[16] whether the threat is "calculated to deprive [a] person of reasonably sound and ordinarily firm mind of the free and voluntary action of his mind". A person who gives in to a threat (at any rate to a threat of something less than physical violence) does not

13 At p. 321.
14 *Infra*, para. 3.09 f.
15 [1974] Crim.L.R. 32.
16 [1914] 3 K.B. 339; *supra*, para. 3.03.

act involuntarily except in a metaphorical sense: it is rather that he has
come to a rational decision to accept the disadvantage involved in
acceding to the demand, in preference to that involved in submitting to
the implementation of the threat. Even in the context of duress, which
can exonerate a defendant compelled to commit a crime by a threat which
might have overborne the will of an ordinary person, the prosecution
cannot succeed merely by proving that the defendant's act was voluntary
in the sense that he intended to act as he did. In *Lynch v. D.P.P. for
Northern Ireland*[17] Lord Edmund-Davies accepted Professor Glanville
Williams's analysis:

> "True duress is not inconsistent with act and will as a matter of legal
> definition, the maxim being *coactus volui*. Fear of violence does not differ in
> kind from fear of economic ills, fear of displeasing others, or any other
> determinant of choice. It would be inconvenient to regard a particular type
> of motive as negativing will." [18]

Lynch was overruled in *Howe*,[19] but this view of the nature of duress was
endorsed.[20]

3.06 Similarly on a charge of blackmail the prosecution need not prove
that an ordinary person would have had no alternative but to comply
with the demand, only that he might in fact have been induced to do so.
This depends whether he would have regarded compliance as a lesser evil
than the implementation of the threat, which in turn depends on the
nature not only of the threat but also of the demand. Under the *Clear*
test both are relevant: the question is whether an ordinary person of
normal stability and courage might have been induced by the threat to
accede unwillingly to the demand which was actually made, not to some
hypothetical demand which was not. The issue in *Harry* was not whether
an ordinary shopkeeper might think it worth submitting to some
unspecified disadvantage in order to avoid the attentions of rowdy
students, but whether he might think it worth paying £1 (the minimum
price of a poster) for that purpose. Such a person might perhaps reason
that if the posters had cost £10 each he would have let the students do
their worst, but that at £1 the offer was a bargain. Indeed it is possible
that some of the shopkeepers who did pay—not necessarily timorous
souls—would not have done so had it not been for the threat implicit in
the letter. The fact that they did not think it worthwhile (or politic) to
complain does not prove otherwise. Had this been proved it is submitted

17 [1975] A.C. 653 at pp. 709 f.
18 *Criminal Law: The General Part* (2nd ed. 1961) p. 751. "The term 'will' is here used to
signify the mental accompaniment of voluntary as opposed to involuntary movement":
ibid., n. 2.
19 [1987] A.C. 417.
20 At pp. 428 and 436, *per* Lord Hailsham L.C. and Lord Bridge respectively.

that the threat would have amounted to menaces, because the demand was so moderate that the threat of even minor inconvenience would have been enough to induce ordinary people to accede to it.

3.07 It may seem paradoxical, or worse, that the more a person demands the less likely he is to be guilty of blackmail. It has indeed been suggested that this cannot be the law, and that we must therefore settle for a rule that a threat which *would* be sufficient if the demand were small is still sufficient even if the demand is large.[21] But such a rule would be unworkable. Virtually any threat will seem compelling if the accompanying demand is sufficiently small. Even if the shopkeepers in *Harry* would not have valued the prospect of a peaceful rag week at as much as £1, they would surely have thought it worth a penny. Everyone attaches *some* value to the avoidance of inconvenience.[22] It does not follow that the offence was in fact committed, because the minimum price was not a penny but £1; still less does it follow that the offence would have been committed had the price been £10 or £100. The scale of the demand must logically be as crucial as the nature of the threat; and this does indeed mean that the same threat may suffice if the demand is for one pound but not if it is for a hundred. Any other rule would be arbitrary. There is nothing wrong in demanding £100 *without* menaces, because if the person addressed prefers to keep his money he is free to do so; and it can hardly make any difference that the demand is accompanied by a threat so feeble that no-one would pay as much as £1 to avert it. A threat which is obviously dwarfed by the demand it is supposed to reinforce is no more effective, and therefore no more culpable, than no threat at all. This does not mean that the would-be blackmailer has an incentive to demand as much as possible. There is no point in demanding more than the victim might conceivably pay. Moreover a demand out of all proportion to the threat reinforcing it can usually be construed as incorporating an implied, more moderate demand with which the victim might actually comply. But if the demand is *solely* for property which no-one would dream of parting with in order to avert the threat which is made, it is submitted that the threat cannot qualify as menaces.

3.08 It should be noted also that the money requested in *Harry* was to go to charity. It may be doubted whether the outcome would have been the same if the money had been going into the students' own pockets. This factor might prevent a demand with menaces from being "unwarranted",[23] but was it relevant to the issue of whether there *were* any

21 Glanville Williams, *Textbook of Criminal Law* (2nd ed.) p. 832.
22 Of course the complainers might have refused to pay as a matter of principle.
23 *Infra*, para. 3.19.

menaces? The problem is a general one: is it sufficient if the threat alone would not induce an ordinary person to comply with the demand, but compliance would bring the victim some other benefit (over and above the avoidance of the threatened sanction) such that the *combination* of benefits on offer is sufficiently attractive to induce him to comply? In principle this factor ought to assist the prosecution, since it effectively reduces the net cost to the victim of complying with the demand, and we have seen that the smaller the demand the more effective is the threat. Suppose that an ordinary shopkeeper would think £1 too much to pay for *either* the satisfaction of the altruistic impulse *or* a trouble-free rag week, but might think it worth paying up if his £1 were buying him both. The threat of trouble would not then be sufficient to induce compliance in itself, but it would help to turn the scale; and this should surely be enough.[24]

3.09   In *Garwood* the Court of Appeal recognised two situations in which it was prepared to countenance an exposition of the concept of menaces to a jury. The first is that in which the threat might have affected the mind of an ordinary person of normal stability, but did not affect the person to whom it was in fact addressed. A threat of this type was said to be sufficient to constitute menaces. This is certainly so if the reason for the threat's lack of impact is the existence of special circumstances of which the defendant is unaware. A threat by a large man to assault a small one would obviously be sufficient even if, unbeknown to the former, the latter were a black belt in karate and relished the challenge. Similarly in *Clear*[25] an employee of a company was held to have exerted menaces on the managing director by threatening to give perjured evidence in forthcoming litigation against the company, apparently unaware that since the company was insured against the liability in question it was a matter of complete indifference to the managing director whether the company won or lost.

> "There may be special circumstances unknown to an accused which would make the threats innocuous and unavailing for the accused's demand, but such circumstances would have no bearing on the accused's state of mind and of his intention."[26]

But if the defendant *knows* of the circumstances in question, and therefore knows that the person threatened will be unimpressed by the threat, he can hardly be guilty of blackmail. This was recognised in *Clear*. Immediately after the passage just quoted the judgment adds:

24   *Cf. Barton v. Armstrong* [1976] A.C. 104.
25   [1968] 1 Q.B. 670.
26   At pp. 679 f.

"If an accused knew that what he threatened would have no effect on the victim it might be different." [27]

It is submitted that it clearly would be different.

3.10 The second of the exceptional situations referred to in *Garwood* is that in which the threat might not have affected the mind of an ordinary person of normal stability, but did affect that of its actual victim. This situation is of some importance because it is precisely the sort of person least likely to stand up to threats who is most likely to be subjected to them. In *Garwood* itself the appellant had threatened a youth with violence unless he fetched some money. He did so, and the appellant demanded that more money be forthcoming in three days' time. The jury sent a note to the recorder asking in effect whether it would be sufficient if the appellant's conduct appeared more menacing to the youth than it would have appeared to someone less timid. The recorder replied in terms which might have been interpreted as meaning that this would indeed suffice. On appeal it was held that the situation envisaged in the jury's note would not amount to menaces unless the defendant were aware of the threat's likely effect on the person actually threatened. Thus the prosecution could not have succeeded in *Harry* merely by proving that one of the shopkeepers to whom the letter was sent happened to be an exceptionally timid person who would certainly have paid £1 to avoid any trouble: they would have had to prove that the defendant *knew* that one of the recipients was exceptionally timid. It might of course be said that by the laws of probability it would be astonishing if a random sample of 115 shopkeepers did *not* include one who was exceptionally timid.

3.11 Section 21(2) provides:

". . . it is . . . immaterial whether the menaces relate to action to be taken by the person making the demand."

It goes without saying that a threat is no less compelling merely because the action threatened is to be taken by a third party.

Demand with menaces

3.12 The requirement of a "demand with menaces" implies that the prosecution must establish two separate and independent ingredients: first the making of a demand, and second the use of menaces as (in the words of the subsection)[28] "a . . . means of reinforcing the demand". But we have seen that whether or not a threat amounts to "menaces" depends to

27   At p. 680.
28   *Infra*, para. 3.19.

some extent on the nature of the demand;[29] and, conversely, the requirement of a "demand" cannot sensibly be defined except in terms of the requirement of menaces. There are two reasons for this. Firstly, for the purposes of the offence of blackmail it is immaterial whether or not a particular proposal qualifies as a demand unless it is reinforced by menaces; therefore it would be pointless to discuss the circumstances in which a proposal *not* so reinforced might nevertheless constitute a demand. Secondly, *any* proposal that another should act (or refrain from acting) in a particular way, however deferential in phrasing and tone, must surely amount to a demand if it *is* accompanied by menaces. It seems to follow that the requirement of a demand adds little. A person makes a "demand with menaces", it is submitted, if he menaces another person and the menaces are expressly or impliedly conditional upon that person's acting (or not acting) in a particular way. For A to tell B that A will do something which B does not want him to do, unless B does something which A wants him to do, must in itself be at least an implied demand that B shall do that thing. Similarly if the menaces are conditional upon some third person's acting (or not acting) in a particular way: if A tells B that he will do something which B does not want him to do, unless C does something which A wants him to do, A is implicitly demanding that B use his best endeavours to induce C to do that thing—unless, of course, A knows that B has no influence over C. And if B's welfare were a matter of concern to C, and it were therefore to be expected that A's threat would be communicated to C, the menaces would amount to an implied demand, addressed to C, that he should do the thing required.

3.13 But one cannot demand in the abstract: there must be something which is demanded, and that thing must be reasonably specific. If the defendant simply threatens the victim and leaves it to him to come up with a proposal sufficiently attractive to dissuade the defendant from carrying out his threat, he is not making a demand because there is nothing in particular which he is demanding. It may be possible to infer that he is demanding money,[30] but there may be no evidence of this. Alternatively it might perhaps be said that what he is demanding is a satisfactory counter-proposal; but the demand must surely relate to the action or inaction required, not merely a proposal to act or to refrain from acting. This seems to be implicit in the reference in section 21(2) to "the act or omission demanded". It might have been preferable if the offence had been defined simply as one of using unwarranted menaces with a view to gain or intent to cause loss. The additional requirement of

---

29 *Supra*, paras. 3.05 ff.
30 *e.g. Collister and Warhurst* (1955) 39 Cr.App.R. 100.

a demand serves little useful purpose, and may have the effect of excluding the more subtle practitioner of the art of blackmail. But if such a person makes his threats by letter he will at least be caught by the new offence of sending a threatening communication.[31]

View to gain or intent to cause loss

3.14 Section 21(2) provides that "The nature of the act or omission demanded is immaterial . . .". But this provision must be read subject to the requirement in section 21(1) that the defendant must make the demand "with a view to gain for himself or another or with intent to cause loss to another". Any demand will do, provided it is made with a view to gain or an intent to cause loss. "Gain" and "loss" are defined by section 34(2), which provides:

> "For purposes of this Act—
> (*a*) 'gain' and 'loss' are to be construed as extending only to gain or loss in money or other property, but as extending to any such gain or loss whether temporary or permanent; and—
>   (i) 'gain' includes a gain by keeping what one has, as well as a gain by getting what one has not; and
>   (ii) 'loss' includes a loss by not getting what one might get, as well as a loss by parting with what one has . . . "

3.15 Thus a demand for some benefit other than property (such as a service) might not suffice, not because it would not be a demand but because it might not be made with a view to gain or an intent to cause loss. If it were so made it would suffice, *e.g.* if it were a demand for the gratuitous provision of a service for which payment would otherwise be required. But a demand for property is sufficient whether or not the defendant intends permanently to deprive the victim of it,[32] and apparently even if his motive in demanding it is not primarily financial. In *Bevans*[33] the appellant had gone to a doctor and threatened to shoot him unless he gave the appellant a morphine injection to ease his osteo-arthritis. He was convicted of blackmail and his appeal was dismissed. The drug which he demanded was property, and a demand for property is by definition a demand made with a view to gain. He might well have been prepared to pay for the drug had it been available on the open market, and his purpose in threatening the doctor was to get hold of it rather than to avoid having to pay for it; but this was immaterial. Presumably he would still have been acting with a view to gain if he had

---

31 Malicious Communications Act 1988 s. 1(1)(*a*)(ii): *infra*, paras. 3.26 ff.
32 *Cf.* theft (*supra*, paras. 1.108 ff) and deception (*supra*, paras. 2.32 ff).
33 (1987) 87 Cr.App.R. 64.

offered to pay, though his willingness to do so might perhaps be relevant to the issue of whether he had reasonable grounds for making the demand.[34]

3.16 Similarly a person who demands money with menaces is doing so with a view to gain even if he is entitled to the money.[35] The acquisition of property is itself a "gain"; there is no need to show that the defendant's financial position would on balance be any the healthier for it. To say that a person is in gainful employment does not imply that his salary is worth more to him than the leisure he forgoes in order to earn it. Even if "gain" did mean "net profit", it is only in the doctrine of consideration that a sum of money is worth no more than a legal claim to the same sum. A bird in the hand is worth two in the bush. If the defendant is legally entitled to what he demands, it follows that he has reasonable grounds for demanding it; and this takes him halfway towards establishing that his demand with menaces is not "unwarranted".[36] But he can still be guilty of blackmail if he knows that the menaces are not a proper way of enforcing his rights.

3.17 It is also sufficient if the defendant acts not with a view to gain but with intent to cause loss. Suppose that he instructs the person menaced to abandon or damage that person's own property. If the menaces were such as to render the victim's compliance with the demand involuntary (which would probably be so only if the threat were one of physical violence, if then) there might be an offence of theft or criminal damage: the victim would be acting not as a free agent but as the defendant's puppet. But the demand would be sufficient for blackmail whether or not the menaces had this effect.

Making a demand

3.18 The requirement that the defendant should "make" a demand is unfortunately somewhat ambiguous. If what is intended to be a demand does not reach its intended victim, has a demand been made or is there only an attempt? In *Treacy v. D.P.P.*[37] a majority of the House of Lords held that a person who sent a blackmailing letter had "made" the demand as soon as he posted the letter. He would therefore still have committed the offence even if the letter had never arrived. Lords Hodson and Guest

---

34 *Infra*, para. 3.20.
35 This appears to have been assumed in *Lawrence and Pomroy* (1971) 57 Cr.App.R. 64; see also *Parkes* [1973] Crim.L.R. 358. The use of threats to extract the payment of debts may also amount to other offences: *infra*, para. 3.31.
36 *Infra*, para. 3.19.
37 [1971] A.C. 587.

pointed out that the posting of the letter would formerly have constituted
the old offence of uttering a writing demanding property with menaces,
and thought it unlikely that Parliament would have intended to narrow
the scope of the offence. Lord Diplock too attached importance to this
consideration, but he also thought it natural to speak of a person
"making" a demand by posting a letter. The latter argument might have
less weight in the case of written communications despatched by private
courier, or in some other manner less irrevocable than the posting of a
letter; the former would have no application to non-written communications such as words spoken into a telephone. Lord Reid, dissenting,
thought that these cases were indistinguishable from the posting of a letter
and that in neither case would a demand have been made unless the
communication were received. The reasoning of the majority fails to make
clear which of Lord Reid's premises was incorrect. It is submitted that in
general a demand which goes astray has not been "made" at all and
amounts to no more than an attempt. This would not be the only context
in which the posting of a letter constituted an exception to a general
requirement of communication.[38]

Unwarranted demand with menaces

3.19 Blackmail, unlike theft and deception, does not require an element
of dishonesty. One effect of the omission is that it may be blackmail to
use menaces for the purpose of enforcing one's legal rights.[39] Nor is it in
itself a defence that ordinary people would think the defendant's conduct
justified.[40] But if ordinary people would think so, it is unlikely that the
defendant himself will disagree; and if he thinks so too then he does have
a defence. Section 21(1), after setting out the elements of the offence, goes
on to provide:

> ". . . and for this purpose a demand with menaces is unwarranted unless the
> person making it does so in the belief—
> (a) that he has reasonable grounds for making the demand; and
> (b) that the use of the menaces is a proper means of reinforcing the
> demand."

In order to escape liability the defendant must have held *both* of the
specified beliefs. But it is for the prosecution to prove that he did not,
once he has raised the issue by adducing evidence that he did.[41] Proof that
it would be unreasonable to believe either or both of these things is not
in itself sufficent:

38 *Cf.* the "postal acceptance" rule in the law of contract: *Henthorn v. Fraser* [1892] 2 Ch.
27.
39 *Supra*, para. 3.16; *cf.* s. 2(1)(*a*), *supra*, para. 1.144.
40 *Cf. supra*, para. 1.141.
41 *Lawrence* (1971) 57 Cr.App.R. 64; *Harvey* (1980) 72 Cr.App.R. 139 at p. 142.

"The subsection is concerned with the belief of the individual defendant in the particular case . . . It matters not what the reasonable man, or any man other than the defendant, would believe save in so far as that may throw light on what the defendant in fact believed." [42]

Belief in reasonable grounds for demand

3.20   A person clearly has reasonable grounds for making a demand if what he demands is legally due to him; therefore he *believes* that he has reasonable grounds if he believes that what he demands is legally due. It is immaterial that he may be mistaken about the facts or even the law, since the belief that there are reasonable grounds for the demand need not itself be based on reasonable grounds. It must also be reasonable to demand something to which one is *morally* entitled; and therefore a person believes that he has reasonable grounds for a demand if he believes that certain circumstances exist *and* (in the eyes of reasonable people, as represented by the jury) he would in fact be morally entitled to what he demands if the circumstances were as he believes them to be.[43] But the wording of the section goes further than this: it is apparently sufficient if the defendant himself thinks he is morally entitled to what he demands, when (even on the defendant's view of the facts) no reasonable person would agree. On a literal reading of the section a person charged with blackmail is entitled to be judged according to his own, perhaps highly eccentric, notions of moral obligation. Such an interpretation can produce strange results. In *Lambert* [44] the evidence was that the defendant had offered to sell to his wife's lover the defendant's "rights" to his wife, and had threatened in the alternative to reveal the affair to the lover's wife and his employer. The jury were directed that the defendant's guilt or innocence depended on his own opinion as to whether he was acting rightly or wrongly.[45] This is even more lenient than a requirement of dishonesty would be: at least in that case the defendant would be unable to rely on his own opinion that his action was right if he knew that most people would think it was wrong.[46] That result has been achieved, in the case of offences of dishonesty, by belatedly narrowing the scope of a defence which was arguably conferred by judicial legislation in the first place.[47] The express wording of the Act is less easily overridden. Where a person thinks that his conduct is justified, but knows that most people

---

42   *Harvey* (1980) 72 Cr.App.R. 139 at p. 141.
43   Unless, perhaps, he unreasonably thinks that he is *not* morally entitled to it. This situation is unlikely to arise and even less likely to be proved.
44   [1972] Crim.L.R. 422.
45   He was acquitted.
46   *Ghosh* [1982] Q.B. 1053; *supra*, para. 1.141.
47   *Supra*, paras. 1.139 ff.

would disagree, it is one thing to say that he is acting "dishonestly"; to say that he does not act "in the belief . . . that he has reasonable grounds" for what he does (because he knows that his grounds are not *objectively* reasonable, although he subjectively thinks that they are) would be quite another.

Belief in propriety of menaces

3.21 Similar difficulties arise in the case of the requirement that the defendant believe the use of the menaces to be a proper means of reinforcing the demand, but it may be that in this case they are somewhat more easily resolved. Again the Act appears to treat the defendant himself as the sole arbiter of what is proper, and again this approach seems unduly lenient; but it was qualified to some extent in *Harvey, Uylett and Plummer*,[48] where the appellants had paid another man over £20,000 for a quantity of cannabis which he failed to supply. The appellants kidnapped his wife and child and threatened to take reprisals against them if he did not return the money. The jury were directed that the making of threats to kill, maim or rape could never be believed to be "proper". The Court of Appeal pointed out that whether or not the defendant believes it is proper to make the threats is a question of fact, but added that he does not believe it is proper to make them if he knows that it would be illegal to carry them out.

> " 'Proper' is . . . plainly a word of wide meaning, certainly wider than (for example) 'lawful'. But the greater includes the less and no act which was not believed to be lawful could be believed to be proper within the meaning of the subsection. Thus no assistance is given to any defendant, even a fanatic or a deranged idealist, who knows or suspects that his threat, or the act threatened, is criminal, but believes it to be justified by his end or his peculiar circumstances. The test is not what he regards as justified, but what he believes to be proper. And where, as here, the threats were to do acts which any sane man knows to be against the laws of every civilised country no jury would hesitate long before dismissing the contention that the defendant genuinely believed the threats to be a proper means of reinforcing even a legitimate demand." [49]

What the court apparently meant (though it said the reverse) is that the category of acts which are *not* proper is wider than, but includes, the category of acts which are not lawful (*i.e.* criminal). A lawful act may or may not be proper, but an unlawful act never is. Similarly a *threat* to do a lawful act may or may not be proper, but a threat to do an unlawful act is not. Therefore a person who threatens to do an act which he *knows*

48   (1980) 72 Cr.App.R. 139.
49   At p. 142.

to be unlawful is making a threat which he knows to be improper. If he has threatened to do an act which would in fact be unlawful, the only question is whether he knew that it would be. And if he claims not to know that killing, maiming and rape are unlawful then he is either lying or mad.

3.22 It is submitted with respect that the court was right to try to inject the concept of propriety with some objective content, but wrong in its choice of criterion. It would be absurd for the defendant's liability to turn solely on his own opinion of his conduct, and absurdity ought to be avoided if possible. The question is whether it *is* possible in view of the wording of the Act, and if so how. The Act postulates a belief that the use of the menaces is "proper". But what determines whether an act *is* proper? Is it entirely a matter of personal judgment, or do objective considerations enter into it? In other words, would it be illogical for a person to say, with reference to a given act, "I personally would regard it as proper, but I know that in fact it is not"? Such a statement would be self-contradictory if for "proper" we were to substitute "justified" (with which the court in *Harvey* contrasted it), or perhaps even "reasonable" (which is what the defendant must believe the *demand* to be), but apparently not if we substituted "honest".[50] Where "proper" fits into this spectrum of objectivity must itself be a matter of opinion, but it would not be obviously wrong to use it as denoting what is deemed acceptable by society as a whole and not merely by the user himself. This was certainly the intention of the Criminal Law Revision Committee, who chose it because it "directs the mind to consideration of what is morally and socially acceptable".[51] What is more questionable is the court's assumption that it is never morally or socially acceptable to commit a criminal offence, or even to threaten to commit one. No-one would seriously suggest that this is literally true. What the court seems to be saying in effect is that a threat is improper if most people would think it so (even if it is a threat to do a lawful act) *or* if it is a threat to commit an offence (even if few people would therefore think it improper). It follows that the defendant cannot believe his use of menaces to be a "proper" means of reinforcing his demand if he knows *either* that what he is threatening would be an offence if he did it *or* that most people would think it improper to threaten to do it. The exclusion of the defence in the former case is necessitated neither by the wording of the Act nor by the absurdity of treating the defendant's own opinion as crucial, and it is submitted with respect that it goes too far.

50   *Ghosh* [1982] Q.B. 1053; *supra*, para. 1.141.
51   Cmnd. 2977 para. 123.

3.23   The analogy with dishonesty can perhaps be pressed further. It was suggested above that implicit in the test of dishonesty is a requirement of unlawfulness as determined by the civil law.[52] Similarly, and for similar reasons, it is submitted that it is inappropriate for the criminal law to stigmatise the making of a threat as blackmail if the person threatened, having parted with his property in order to avert the threat, would have had no redress in civil law. Civil law, like criminal, seldom prohibits threats as such, but it sometimes strikes down transactions *procured* by threats. It therefore serves as a yardstick by which the propriety of a threat may be measured, at any rate where the act demanded is a transfer of property. If such a transfer would be legally unimpeachable it would seem strange that the attempt to procure it should be a criminal offence at all, let alone one as serious as blackmail. If the transaction is not "improper" in the eyes of the civil law then *a fortiori* it should not be criminal. Admittedly section 21(1) appears to rule out any suggestion that the validity of the proposed transaction is in itself a complete defence, by requiring the defendant to *believe* that his use of menaces is proper; but if it *is* objectively proper then it can hardly matter whether he knows it is.[53] Usually, of course, an agreement procured by threats is at least voidable on the grounds of duress, so the question will not arise. But this may not invariably be so. It has been said that, in order to amount to duress, a threat must not only constitute pressure which the law regards as illegitimate: it must also amount to "compulsion" of the victim's will.[54] He must submit to it because that is not just the least unattractive course of action open to him, but the only practicable choice. If the sanction threatened would be unattractive to him but not wholly disastrous, his decision to opt for a marginally preferable alternative would on this view leave him with no legal redress. And in that case it would arguably not be improper to place him in a dilemma which, in law, gives him no ground for complaint.

Jurisdiction

3.24   When a demand with menaces is made by a communication passing (or intended to pass) from one jurisdiction to another, there is room for argument as to whether the offence is committed in the former jurisdiction or the latter or both. In *Treacy v. D.P.P.*[55] a bare majority of the House of Lords held that a demand made in a letter sent from England to

---

52   *Supra*, para. 1.154.
53   *Cf. supra*, para. 1.156 f.
54   *Universe Tankships Inc. of Monrovia v. International Transport Workers' Federation* [1983] A.C. 366 at p. 400, *per* Lord Scarman. The requirement is criticised by Goff and Jones, *The Law of Restitution* (3rd ed.) p. 206.
55   [1971] A.C. 587; *supra*, para. 3.18.

Germany is made in England, because the demand is "made" as soon as the letter is posted. This would seem to imply that a demand sent from Germany to England would *not* be made in England, a conclusion which would be something of a "blackmailer's charter".[56] For the majority, Lord Hodson (with whom Lord Guest agreed) did not accept that this would follow, and suggested that such a case "might involve deciding whether a demand made outside the jurisdiction could be treated as a continuous demand subsisting until the addressee received it".[57] Lord Diplock expounded a general theory of territorial jurisdiction, to the effect that the only case implicitly excluded from an English statutory prohibition is that in which neither the defendant's conduct *nor* its harmful consequences occur within the jurisdiction. This theory has not yet received general acceptance; but it seems unlikely that, having strained the wording of the Act to catch the blackmailer who operates from England on a victim abroad, the courts would find themselves unable to apply it to his counterpart operating from abroad on a victim in England. Probably Lord Hodson's suggestion would be endorsed. The fact that a demand in a letter is "made" where the letter is posted does not necessarily mean that it is not also made where the letter is received.

3.25 When section 1(1)(*d*) of the Nuclear Material (Offences) Act 1983 is brought into force, any act done in relation to or by means of nuclear material, which would have amounted to an offence of blackmail had it been done within the jurisdiction, will amount to that offence notwithstanding that it is done outside the jurisdiction. The Act is discussed elsewhere.[58]

SENDING THREATENING ARTICLES

3.26 Section 1(1) of the Malicious Communications Act 1988 provides in part:

"Any person who sends[59] to another person—
(*a*) a letter or other article which conveys—
. . .
      (ii) a threat . . .
. . .
is guilty of an offence if his purpose, or one of his purposes, in sending it is that it should, so far as falling within paragraph (*a*) . . . above, cause distress or anxiety to the recipient or to any other person to whom he intends that it or its contents or nature should be communicated."

56 *Treacy* [1971] A.C. 537 at p. 550, *per* Lord Reid.
57 At p. 558.
58 Supra, paras. 1.165 f.
59 This includes delivering and causing to be sent or delivered: s. 1(3).

The offence is punishable on summary conviction with a fine of level 4 on the standard scale.[60] Section 1 came into force on 29 September 1988.[61]

3.27   Our concern is with the person who makes a threat with a view to inducing the victim to part with property. A hint that such action on the part of the victim might avert the implementation of the threat will normally amount to a demand, by implication at least, and in that case the person making the threat will be guilty of the more serious offence of blackmail (unless the threat is too trivial to be regarded as "menaces", or the demand and the menaces are not "unwarranted"). But if the defendant is careful not to combine his threat with even an implied demand, he will not be guilty of blackmail. He might however be guilty of the offence under the 1988 Act: if his purpose in making the threat is to induce the victim to buy him off, he can hardly hope to achieve that objective without causing the victim "distress or anxiety".

3.28   Where the threat *is* combined with a demand, but the combination does not amount to blackmail because it is not "unwarranted" within the meaning of section 21(1), the making of the threat is not prohibited by the 1988 Act either. Section 1(2) provides:

> "A person is not guilty of an offence by virtue of subsection (1)(*a*)(ii) above if he shows—
> (*a*)   that the threat was used to reinforce a demand which he believed he had reasonable grounds for making; and
> (*b*)   that he believed that the use of the threat was a proper means of reinforcing the demand."

But it would seem that the 1988 Act, by requiring the defendant to "show" that his state of mind was that described, places on him the legal burden of proving the point and not merely the evidential burden of raising the issue.

DEMANDING PAYMENT FOR UNSOLICITED GOODS

3.29   Section 2(1) of the Unsolicited Goods and Services Act 1971 creates an offence of demanding payment for goods sent to a person without his prior request. It provides, as amended:[62]

> "A person who, not having reasonable cause to believe there is a right to payment, in the course of any trade or business makes a demand for

---

60   s. 1(4).
61   s. 3(2).
62   Criminal Justice Act 1982 ss. 38, 46.

payment, or asserts a present or prospective right to payment,[63] for what he knows are unsolicited goods[64] sent[65] (after the commencement of this Act) to another person with a view to his acquiring[66] them, shall be guilty of an offence and on summary conviction shall be liable to a fine not exceeding level 4 on the standard scale."

Section 2(2) creates a more serious offence of employing threats for the purpose of obtaining such payment. As amended,[67] it provides:

"A person who, not having reasonable cause to believe there is a right to payment, in the course of any trade or business and with a view to obtaining any payment for what he knows are unsolicited goods sent as aforesaid—
(*a*) threatens to bring any legal proceedings; or
(*b*) places or causes to be placed the name of any person on a list of defaulters or debtors or threatens to do so; or
(*c*) invokes or causes to be invoked any other collection procedure or threatens to do so,
shall be guilty of an offence and shall be liable on summary conviction to a fine not exceeding level 5 on the standard scale."

3.30 Neither offence is committed by a person who demands payment otherwise than in the course of a trade or business, or who demands it in the reasonable belief that he is entitled to it. Presumably the reasonable man is taken to know the rule that silence on the part of a person to whom an offer is made cannot bind him to acceptance of the offer.[68] But if a recipient of unsolicited goods agrees to acquire them he may thereby undertake a liability to pay for them, and in that event these provisions will no longer apply. The extraction of payment by improper methods may however amount to the offence next to be considered.

HARASSMENT OF DEBTORS

3.31 Section 40(1) of the Administration of Justice Act 1970 provides in part:

"A person commits an offence if, with the object of coercing another person to pay money claimed from the other as a debt due under a contract, he—
(*a*) harasses the other with demands for payment which, in respect of their frequency or the manner or occasion of making any such demand, or

---

63   An invoice or similar document stating the amount of any payment is regarded as asserting a right to the payment unless it complies with the requirements of the Unsolicited Goods and Services (Invoices etc.) Regulations 1975, S.I. 1975 No. 732: s. 6(2), substituted by Unsolicited Goods and Services (Amendment) Act 1975 s. 2(2).
64   *i.e.* goods sent without any prior request made by the person to whom they are sent, or on his behalf: s. 6(1).
65   Including goods delivered: s. 6(1).
66   Including hiring them: s. 6(1).
67   Criminal Justice Act 1982 ss. 38, 46.
68   *Felthouse v. Bindley* (1863) New Rep. 401.

155

of any threat or publicity by which any demand is accompanied, are calculated to subject him or members of his family or household to alarm, distress or humiliation;

(*b*) falsely represents, in relation to the money claimed, that criminal proceedings lie for failure to pay it;

(*c*) falsely represents himself to be authorised in some official capacity to claim or enforce payment; or

(*d*) utters a document falsely represented by him to have some official character or purporting to have some official character which he knows it has not."

These offences are punishable on summary conviction with a fine of not more than level 5 on the standard scale.[69] A demand for payment is probably "calculated" to cause alarm, distress or humiliation within the meaning of section 40(1)(*a*) if it is *likely* (though not intended) to do so, and to that extent the offence may be one of strict liability. But section 40(3) provides:

"Subsection (1)(*a*) above does not apply to anything done by a person which is reasonable (and otherwise permissible in law) for the purpose—

(*a*) of securing the discharge of an obligation due, or believed by him to be due, to himself or to persons for whom he acts, or protecting himself or them for future loss; or

(*b*) of the enforcement of any liability by legal process."

Thus it is only demands for payment amounting to *unreasonable* harassment which are caught by this offence. It may however be committed by a person who concerts with others in the taking of such action, whether or not his own course of conduct by itself amounts to harassment.[70]

69 s. 40(4); Criminal Justice Act 1982 ss. 38, 46.
70 s. 40(2).

CHAPTER 4

Goods Obtained by Stealing, Deception or Blackmail

4.01 Certain provisions in the Theft Act 1968 refer to goods which are "stolen"—a term which for these purposes includes goods obtained by most (but not all) of the offences discussed in chapters 1 to 3. Section 22 creates an offence of "handling" such goods; section 28 empowers a court upon conviction to make certain orders by way of restitution in respect of them. Neither provision extends to all forms of property: both are confined to "goods". But the distinction is of limited importance, because section 34(2)(*b*) provides that for the purposes of the Act

" 'goods', except in so far as the context otherwise requires, includes money and every other description of property except land, and includes things severed from the land by stealing."

"Property" includes things in action and other forms of intangible property;[1] though not normally regarded as goods,[2] these things are therefore "goods" for the purposes of the Act and can be the subject not only of theft and obtaining by deception but also of handling[3] and of restitution orders. Things severed from land are goods for this purpose but land itself (although it can in certain circumstances be stolen)[4] is not.

HANDLING STOLEN GOODS

4.02 Section 22(1) of the Theft Act 1968 provides:

"A person handles stolen goods if (otherwise than in the course of the stealing) knowing or believing them to be stolen goods he dishonestly receives the goods, or dishonestly undertakes or assists in their retention, removal, disposal or realisation by or for the benefit of another person, or if he arranges to do so."

The offence is triable either way[5] but is punishable on conviction on indictment with 14 years' imprisonment[6]—*i.e.* it is potentially a more serious offence than theft itself.

1 s. 4(1).
2 e.g. Sale of Goods Act 1979 s. 61.
3 *Attorney-General's Reference (No. 4 of 1979)* [1981] 1 W.L.R. 667.
4 s. 4(2)(*a*); *supra*, para. 1.05.
5 Magistrates' Courts Act 1980 s. 17(1), Sch. 1.
6 Theft Act 1968 s. 22(2).

156

Stolen goods

4.03 The offence of handling stolen goods can be committed only in respect of goods which are "stolen" goods within the meaning of the Act: the phrase "knowing or believing them to be stolen goods" does not mean that it is sufficient if the defendant believes the goods to be stolen when in fact they are not.[7] Goods may be stolen goods as a result either of themselves being obtained by "stealing" (which in this context has an extended meaning) or by being the proceeds of goods which have been so obtained.

"Stealing"

4.04 Section 1(1) of the Theft Act 1968 provides in effect that to "steal" is to commit the offence of theft, and it might therefore be supposed that the term "stolen goods" would refer simply to goods which have been the subject of that offence. But whereas it is true that all goods obtained by theft thereby become stolen goods, the term extends also to goods obtained in other ways. Section 24(4) provides:

"For purposes of the provisions of this Act relating to goods which have been stolen . . . goods obtained in England or Wales or elsewhere either by blackmail or in the circumstances described in section 15(1) of this Act shall be regarded as stolen; and 'steal', 'theft' and 'thief' shall be construed accordingly."

The offence created by section 15(1) is that of obtaining property by deception.[8] Thus goods become stolen if a person other than the person to whom they belong[9]

(a) dishonestly appropriates them, intending permanently to deprive that person of them, or
(b) dishonestly obtains them by deception, intending permanently to deprive that person of them, or
(c) obtains them by making an unwarranted demand with menaces,[10]

assuming in each case that no general defence operates to shield him from criminal liability.[11] It follows that the owner's consent to the obtaining,

---

7 *Haughton v. Smith* [1975] A.C. 476. For what it does mean, see *infra*, paras 4.50 ff. A person who wrongly believes goods to be stolen may be guilty of attempting to handle them: *Shivpuri* [1987] A.C. 1; *infra*, para. 4.36.
8 *Supra*, Ch. 2.
9 In case (c) (blackmail) the goods need not have belonged to anyone else at all: if A blackmails B into creating a chose of action in A's favour it will therefore be stolen goods although it has never belonged to anyone but A.
10 But there is a potential difficulty if the title to goods so obtained is not necessarily voidable: *infra*, para. 4.28.
11 *Cf. Walters v. Lunt* [1951] 2 All E.R. 645.

although it may mean that the obtaining is not "stealing" within the meaning of section 1(1),[12] does not necessarily prevent the goods from being "stolen" goods for the purposes of section 22(1): they may well be stolen if the owner's consent is procured by deception or threats. Indeed, goods obtained by blackmail are stolen goods even if the person obtaining them does so with the intention of subsequently returning them. Where the owner does not consent at all, however, or his consent is procured by deception rather than threats, the goods do not become stolen goods unless there is an intention permanently to deprive him of them. Thus a conveyance taken without the owner's consent, contrary to section 12(1),[13] does not thereby become stolen unless the taking amounts also to theft; nor does an article which is removed, contrary to section 11(1), from a building where it is kept for public display.[14] Similarly a person who obtains goods by deception, but with no intention permanently to deprive, may thereby commit an offence of obtaining either "services" or an exemption from liability;[15] but the goods do not thereby become stolen goods.

Goods stolen outside the jurisdiction
4.05 Section 24(1) provides:

"The provisions of this Act relating to goods which have been stolen shall apply whether the stealing occurred in England or Wales or elsewhere, and whether it occurred before or after the commencement of this Act, provided that the stealing (if not an offence under this Act) amounted to an offence where and at the time when the goods were stolen; and references to stolen goods shall be construed accordingly."

Thus there is no requirement that the goods be obtained within the jurisdiction, and therefore no requirement that the obtaining be an offence under English law. Goods obtained abroad can be handled in England or Wales, provided that the obtaining

(a) would have amounted to "stealing" (*i.e.* an offence of theft, blackmail or obtaining property by deception)[16] had it occurred in England or Wales, *and*
(b) did in fact amount to an offence (not necessarily a precise equivalent of the English offence relied upon) under the law then in force in the place where it occurred.

12 *Supra,* paras 1.73 ff.
13 *Infra,* paras 5.02 ff.
14 *Infra,* paras 5.31 ff.
15 Theft Act 1978 s. 1(1), s. 2(1)(*c*); *supra,* paras 2.33 f.
16 The extended meaning given to the word "steal" by s. 24(4), *supra,* applies to the rest of s. 24.

Proceeds of stolen goods

4.06 Goods which have not themselves been obtained by theft, deception or blackmail may nevertheless be deemed to be stolen goods if they are the proceeds of goods so obtained. Section 24(2) provides that, for purposes of the provisions of the Act relating to goods which have been stolen,

". . . reference to stolen goods shall include, in addition to the goods originally stolen and parts of them (whether in their original state or not), –
(*a*) any other goods which directly or indirectly represent or have at any time represented the stolen goods in the hands of the thief as being the proceeds of any disposal or realisation of the whole or part of the goods stolen or of goods so representing the stolen goods; and
(*b*) any other goods which directly or indirectly represent or have at any time represented the stolen goods in the hands of a handler of the stolen goods or any part of them as being the proceeds of any disposal or realisation of the whole or part of the stolen goods handled by him or of goods so representing them."

Proceeds in the hands of the thief
4.07 For the purposes of section 24(2) a "thief" is a person who obtains goods by theft, deception or blackmail.[17] If such a person disposes of or realises any of the goods so obtained, the effect of section 24(2)(*a*) is that the proceeds in his hands are themselves stolen goods. This does not mean that he is guilty of handling them by receiving them,[18] since the goods must be stolen at the time of the conduct relied upon: it is not sufficient that they become stolen goods as a *result* of that conduct. But a person who knowingly received the proceeds from the thief would be guilty of handling them. If, moreover, the thief does dispose of or realise the proceeds, not only do they continue to be stolen goods even after he has parted with them[19] but the proceeds in his hands of *that* disposal or realisation are also stolen goods; and so on. Similarly, it would seem, if the disposal or realisation is effected by someone else but the proceeds subsequently come into the hands of the thief. Suppose A steals a car and sells it to B, who does not know of the theft. The proceeds in A's hands are now stolen. Suppose further that B resells the car to C. The proceeds of the resale are not stolen in B's hands,[20] but would be if by a subsequent transaction they came into A's. It might perhaps be argued that they would then be in the hands of the thief *qua* proceeds not of the disposal or realisation (by B) of the goods stolen but of the subsequent transaction whereby they came to A: if the draftsman had meant to include not only

17   s. 24(4), *supra*, para. 4.04.
18   Nor by disposing of the goods originally stolen: *infra*, para. 4.74.
19   Subject to s. 24(3), *infra*, para. 4.20.
20   They would be if B were guilty of handling the car: *infra*, para. 4.09.

proceeds coming into the hands of the thief *through* a disposal or realisation of the goods stolen but also the proceeds of a prior disposal or realisation by someone else, he would have written not "which . . . represent . . . the stolen goods in the hands of the thief *as being*[21] the proceeds of any disposal or realisation" but ". . . *and are* the proceeds [*etc.*]". But the choice of phrase can be explained on the alternative ground that it does not *add* to the requirement that the goods should "represent . . . the stolen goods": it serves rather to spell out what that requirement means. Moreover the law would be open to abuse if the thief could arrange for another person to dispose of the goods stolen and return the proceeds to the thief, secure in the knowledge that the proceeds would not be deemed stolen unless guilty knowledge could be proved on the part of the intermediary.

4.08   But there is a further difficulty: the goods which find their way back to the thief may be the proceeds not of the goods originally stolen, but of goods which were themselves the proceeds of a prior disposal or realisation of those goods. Suppose, in the example above, B uses the money he receives from C to buy a van, which he then resells (or gives) to A. Is the van now stolen goods? If the phrase "as being the proceeds . . ." is interpreted as suggested above, the van does "indirectly represent . . . the stolen goods in the hands of the thief as being the proceeds of [a] disposal or realisation of . . . goods . . . representing the stolen goods" (*viz.* the price B received for the car). But is it the proceeds of a disposal or realisation of goods "so" representing those goods? Does the qualification "so" mean only that the goods whose proceeds are in question must themselves have "represented the stolen goods . . . as being the proceeds of [a] disposal or realisation of . . . the goods stolen"? If so then the van is stolen, because it is the proceeds of the proceeds of the car, and it is now in the hands of the thief. Or does the "so" mean in addition that those goods must have represented the stolen goods *in the hands of the thief?* In that case the van is not stolen, because it is the proceeds of goods which, although they were the proceeds of the stolen car, have not themselves been in the hands of the man who stole it. The latter construction seems more natural: since the words "represent . . . the stolen goods" are qualified not only by "as being the proceeds of . . . the stolen goods" but also by "in the hands of the thief", the structure of the sentence suggests no reason why "so" should refer to one but not the other. On the other hand it can hardly be right that the proceeds of one disposal or realisation become stolen goods on their return to the thief, but not the proceeds of two. The policy underlying section 24(2)

21   Emphasis supplied.

would seem to require that goods can "so" represent the stolen goods without doing so "in the hands of the thief".

Proceeds in the hands of a handler
4.09   Under section 24(2)(*b*) the proceeds of a disposal or realisation of goods obtained by theft, deception or blackmail (or of a succession of such disposals or realisations) are similarly deemed to be stolen if they come into the hands of "a handler of the stolen goods or any part of them". A "handler" of stolen goods is a person who commits the offence of handling in respect of those goods. A person who deals with stolen goods, but neither knows nor believes that they are stolen, is not a handler. If, therefore, B knowingly receives a car stolen by A and sells it to C, the proceeds will themselves be stolen goods even if they never come into the hands of A; but if B acted innocently they would not, because, though still representing the goods originally stolen, the proceeds would have represented them in the hands neither of the thief nor of a handler.

4.10   The position is less clear if the goods received and disposed of by the handler are not the goods originally stolen but the proceeds of those goods, proceeds which are deemed to be stolen by virtue of section 24(2)(*a*): *e.g.* if A himself sells the car which he has stolen and pays the proceeds to B, who knows that they are the proceeds of stolen goods but uses them to buy a van. The van is the proceeds of a disposal or realisation of the stolen goods handled by B; it has not been in the hands of the thief, but it is in the hands of a handler. It might be argued that this is not enough, since goods are not caught by section 24(2)(*b*) unless they have been in the hands not just of a handler but of a handler of "the stolen goods or any part of them". Arguably that expression includes only a handler of the goods originally stolen, and not a handler of the proceeds of those goods. Throughout the subsection a distinction is maintained between "the goods originally stolen" (also referred to, doubtless for the sake of brevity, as "the goods stolen" or "the stolen goods") and "any other goods which . . . represent . . . the stolen goods". Had the draftsman intended to include a handler of the latter as well as the former he would surely have said so. It seems, moreover, that if he did mean to exclude a handler of proceeds he was attempting to carry out the intentions of the Criminal Law Revision Committee:

> "In our opinion the offence [of handling] should apply to any goods which represent, or have represented, the original stolen goods either in the hands of the thief or in the hands of a handler *of the original stolen goods* as being the proceeds of the original stolen goods or of goods so representing them." [22]

---

22   Cmnd. 2977 para. 138 (emphasis supplied).

4.11   It does not follow that that objective has been achieved. Section 24(2) says that the goods there described are deemed not just to *be* stolen goods but to be *included* in any reference to stolen goods. When section 22(1) says that a person "handles stolen goods if . . . he dishonestly receives the goods . . .", by virtue of section 24(2) the reference to "the goods" includes certain proceeds of the goods originally stolen; it seems, therefore, that a person who dishonestly receives such proceeds, knowing or believing them to be stolen, is handling not just the proceeds but the goods originally stolen. When B receives the proceeds of the sale of the car stolen by A, he is handling the car. The definition in section 22(1) of what is meant by a handler of stolen goods must in turn apply to the words "a handler of the stolen goods" in section 24(2)(*b*); therefore B falls within those words although he has had no dealings with the stolen car itself. Therefore the van which he buys with the proceeds is goods which "represent . . . the stolen goods in the hands of a handler of the stolen goods", and is itself stolen.

4.12   It may be objected that, since this interpretation of section 24(2)(*b*) depends for its validity on the fiction that a handler of the proceeds of stolen goods is a handler of the stolen goods themselves, it would be circular to invoke it for the purpose of bringing that fiction into play in the first place. In that case it would follow that paragraph (*b*) applies to proceeds in the hands of a person who has handled the goods originally stolen *either* literally *or* by dealing with proceeds which have been in the hands of the thief and are therefore deemed to be included among the goods originally stolen by virtue of paragraph (*a*), but *not* by dealing with proceeds which have been in the hands only of a handler and are therefore deemed to be included among the goods originally stolen by virtue only of paragraph (*b*) itself. Suppose A steals a car and sells it to B, who knows that it is stolen. B falls within the terms of section 22(1), without the assistance of section 24(2): he has literally handled the car. B now resells it to C. The proceeds are stolen goods by virtue of section 24(2)(*b*): they are the proceeds of a disposal or realisation of the stolen car and they are in the hands of a person who literally handled it. B uses them to buy a van from D, who knows that they are the proceeds of stolen goods. D is therefore a handler. He uses the proceeds to buy a truck. Is the truck now stolen goods by virtue of section 24(2)(*b*)? It represents the stolen car in D's hands as being the proceeds of a disposal or realisation of goods representing it, but is D "a handler of the stolen goods" as section 24(2)(*b*) requires? Only if he is deemed to have handled not just the proceeds of the car but the car itself, which can be done only by first reading section 22(1) in the light of section 24(2)(*b*). Arguably it is impermissible for paragraph (*b*) thus to pull itself up by its own bootstraps. Whether it is strictly illogical is debatable; but again the policy of catching *all* the proceeds of stolen goods in the hands of thieves or handlers would militate against such a conclusion. It is submitted that the process of extending section 22(1) by reference to section 24(2), and *vice versa*, can if necessary be continued *ad infinitum*.

Stolen money and bank accounts
4.13 Where the stolen goods are simply exchanged for other goods (including money) there is no difficulty in regarding the goods so obtained as the proceeds of the stolen goods; but in other situations the position may be less clear. A difficult problem can arise where stolen money (*i.e.* money which has either itself been stolen or is the proceeds of goods which have) is paid into a bank account, and money is then withdrawn from the account or cheques drawn upon it. Are such cheques or monies themselves the proceeds of stolen goods?

4.14 *Accounts containing only stolen money.* Sometimes the position is clear. If the stolen money is used to open a new account, or is paid into an existing account so as to clear an overdraft, the whole of the resulting credit balance (a form of intangible property belonging to the account-holder)[23] will "represent . . . the stolen [money] . . . as being the proceeds of [a] disposal or realisation" of it. Provided that the account-holder is either the thief or a handler of the stolen goods, the credit balance will therefore itself be stolen goods.[24] Any money which the account-holder then withdraws, and anything bought by him with any such money, will also represent the stolen goods and will itself be deemed to be stolen. Similarly if the account were overdrawn up to or beyond an agreed limit, and the effect of the influx of stolen money were to reduce the overdraft below that limit, the account-holder would thereby acquire a right to increase it again: this right too would be a form of intangible property[25] derived from the stolen money and (if the account-holder is the thief or a handler) would therefore be stolen goods. So would any withdrawals thus rendered possible.

4.15 In *Attorney-General's Reference (No. 4 of 1979)*[26] the Court of Appeal said that the same would apply where, instead of himself withdrawing money from the account, the account-holder draws a cheque in favour of another person.

23 *Supra*, para. 1.12.
24 "Goods" includes intangible property: *supra*, para. 4.01.
25 *Kohn* (1979) 69 Cr.App.R. 395.
26 [1981] 1 W.L.R. 667.

"We have no doubt that when such a cheque is paid, so that part of such a balance in the thief's account is transferred to the credit of the receiver's account, the receiver has received stolen goods because he has received a thing in action which '. . . directly represent[s] . . . the stolen goods in the hands of the thief as being the proceeds of . . . realisation of the . . . goods stolen . . .' The same conclusion follows where the receiver directly cashes the cheque drawn on the thief's account and receives money from the paying bank." [27]

These two situations are arguably distinguishable. Cash obtained directly from the thief's bank is clearly the proceeds of his bank balance, whether it is withdrawn by the thief himself or by another person who cashes one of the thief's cheques. If the payee of the cheque pays it into his own bank account, however, it is only in a loose sense that part of the thief's credit balance is "transferred" to the account of the payee: the payee acquires fresh rights against his own bank, but there is no assignment of the drawer's rights against his.[28] The property acquired by the payee is property quite distinct from that previously owned by the thief, not the same property in different hands. But this argument is perhaps unduly technical: the acquisition of the one credit balance corresponds directly to the loss of the other, and it is natural to describe the one as the "proceeds" of the other.

4.16   A further question is whether a cheque is itself stolen goods if the account on which it is drawn contains only stolen money. This question did in fact arise on the facts of *Attorney-General's Reference (No. 4 of 1979)*, though it was not the point referred to the Court of Appeal:

"The allegation in this case was that the defendant received stolen goods when she received the thief's cheque. [Counsel for the defendant], in the course of argument, was disposed to accept a suggestion from a member of the court that a cheque drawn by the thief, directed to her bank, and intended to enable the defendant to obtain transfer of part of the thief's credit balance, or cash, might not itself be stolen goods within the meaning of section 24(2)(*a*). The point is not necessary for decision on the point of law referred to us and it has not been fully argued. It appears to us that there is much to be said in favour of the proposition that receipt of such a cheque, drawn in circumstances wherein it is plain that it must serve to transfer the proceeds of stolen goods, would constitute receiving stolen goods on the ground that such a cheque would directly or indirectly represent the stolen goods within section 24(2)(*a*)." [29]

It is submitted with respect that the view provisionally expressed in this passage is incorrect. The *proceeds* of a cleared cheque can be regarded as

27   At p. 675.
28   Bills of Exchange Act 1882 s. 53; *Schroeder v. Central Bank of London* (1876) 34 L.T. 735.
29   At pp 675 f.

the proceeds of the account on which it is drawn, because it is only by debiting that account that the proceeds can be obtained. The cheque itself is another matter: it is an item of property in its own right, and does not depend for its existence on the funds in the drawer's account. If it is honoured, the account will be debited, but that does not make it the proceeds of the account. It is submitted that a cheque may be stolen goods if it has itself been obtained by theft, deception or blackmail, or by way of payment for goods so obtained or for the proceeds of such goods, but not merely because it is drawn on an account which contains only stolen money.

4.17 *Accounts containing stolen and innocent money.* A more difficult problem arises if the credit which represents stolen money paid into the account becomes mixed with other credits which do not. This may be the case either because the account was already in credit when the stolen money was paid in, or because more (and non-stolen) money is paid in later. In either case it may be arguable that money subsequently taken out of the account is the proceeds not of the stolen credit but of the innocent one, and is therefore not stolen. Similarly if the account was overdrawn when the stolen money was paid in, but only to a point falling short of an agreed overdraft limit, it may be arguable that subsequent withdrawals represent the account-holder's original right to further credit and not the additional rights derived from the stolen money. In the *Attorney-General's Reference* the Court of Appeal stated that the difficulty in such a case is one of proof and not of principle.

> "The mere fact that stolen cheques have been paid into a mixed account will often render more difficult proof that at least part of what was received by a defendant from that account represented the stolen goods in the hands of the thief as being the proceeds of the goods stolen. It does not preclude such proof." [30]

4.18 Whether it is easy, hard or impossible to prove the point will depend on the circumstances. If the innocent credits (whether created before or after the stolen one, or both) are insufficient to cover the amount of the withdrawal, it follows that the money withdrawn must be at least in part (which is all that is required) the proceeds of the stolen credit. But if the innocent credits total such an amount that they *could* cover the withdrawal, it is hard to see how the prosecution might prove that they did not in fact cover it. The issue for the court in the *Attorney-General's Reference* was whether this can be inferred if it is proved to have been the intention of the parties. It was held that the point could not be established solely by reference to the admitted intentions of the alleged

[30] At p. 676.

receiver, but the court left open the possibility of relying on the intentions of the account-holder himself:

> "It may perhaps be that a payment can be proved to have been a payment of money representing stolen goods, even where there was enough honest money in the account to cover the payment, if there is proof direct or by way of necessary inference of the intention of the paying thief to pay out the stolen money. That problem can be decided when it arises." [31]

4.19   The difficulty in relying on the account-holder's intention to pay out stolen rather than honest money, even if it can be proved, is that any such intention is essentially meaningless unless it affects proprietary rights. It would be effective only if the account-holder (who is *ex hypothesi* either the thief or a handler of the goods stolen) had the power to divide up the mixed fund in his hands and to determine which of the portions thus divided is to belong to the original owner; but he appears to have no such power. The principle applied by the civil law is that withdrawals from such a fund are deemed to be withdrawals of the account-holder's own money unless there is not enough of his own money to cover them.[32] The adoption of this rule by the criminal law would have the advantage of certainty. As the law apparently stands, the whole of a partially stolen fund can be distributed without the prosecution ever being able to prove that it is any particular payment which is stolen rather than one or more of the others. Under the civil law rule, the payment deemed to be stolen might not be the one on which the prosecution would choose to rely; but it would be better than nothing.

Goods ceasing to be stolen

4.20   Once stolen (or deemed to be stolen), goods do not remain stolen for ever after. Section 24(3) provides:

> ". . . no goods shall be regarded as having continued to be stolen goods after they have been restored to the person from whom they were stolen or to other lawful possession or custody, or after that person and any other person claiming through him have otherwise ceased as regards those goods to have any right to restitution in respect of the theft."

It will be convenient to consider first the effect of this provision on the goods originally stolen, then its possible application where the proceeds of those goods are themselves deemed to be stolen under section 24(2), and finally the question whether its application to the goods originally stolen affects their proceeds and *vice versa*.

---

31   *Ibid.*
32   *Re Hallett's Estate* (1879) 13 Ch.D. 696.

Goods originally stolen

4.21 *Restoration to lawful possession or custody.* Goods obtained by theft, deception or blackmail cease to be stolen goods once they are restored to "lawful possession or custody" (the terms seem virtually interchangeable and "possession" will here be used to include both), and cannot thereafter be handled—unless, of course, they are stolen again. The provision that they cease to be stolen "after they have been restored to the person from whom they were stolen" seems not to be a genuine alternative to the rule just stated, but simply to declare in effect that for the purposes of that rule the possession of the person from whom the goods were stolen (hereinafter referred to as the "owner") is always "lawful". Therefore the goods may continue to be stolen even if the owner comes into contact with them after the theft, *e.g.* by marking them for the purpose of identification, provided that he does not take them into his possession.[33] The possession of a person other than the owner will clearly be lawful for this purpose if that person is authorised by the owner to take possession of the goods, and probably also if he has no authority to take possession but does so in good faith on the owner's behalf. Certainly the possession of a police officer acting in the execution of his duty is lawful whether he has the owner's authority or not.[34]

4.22 Since the taking of stolen goods into lawful possession precludes any subsequent handling of those goods, the precise meaning of "possession" (or, if there is any difference, "custody") may be crucial. If, for example, a police officer keeps stolen goods under observation with a view to apprehending their intended recipient, a person subsequently receiving them will be guilty of handling[35] only if the officer's conduct did not amount to a taking of possession.[36] In *Attorney-General's Reference (No. 1 of 1974)*,[37] where the officer had immobilised a car containing such goods and waited to interview the driver, the Court of Appeal regarded the distinction between possession and mere observation as essentially one of intention.

> "If the police officer seeing these goods in the back of the car had made up his mind that he would take them into custody, that he would reduce them into his possession or control, take charge of them so that they could not be removed and so that he would have the disposal of them, then it would be a perfectly proper conclusion to say that he had taken possession of the

---

33 *Greater London Metropolitan Police Commissioner v. Streeter* (1980) 71 Cr.App.R. 113. On the question of what amounts to a taking of possession see *infra,* para. 4.22.
34 This was assumed in *Attorney-General's Reference (No. 1 of 1974)* [1974] Q.B. 744.
35 As against attempted handling: *infra,* para. 4.36.
36 Unless it could be shown that the receiver had *arranged* to receive the goods before the officer took possession.
37 [1974] Q.B. 744.

goods. On the other hand, if the truth of the matter is that he was of an entirely open mind at that stage as to whether the goods were to be seized or not and was of an entirely open mind as to whether he should take possession of them or not, but merely stood by so that when the driver of the car appeared he could ask certain questions of that driver as to the nature of the goods and why they were there, then there is no reason whatever to suggest that he had taken the goods into his possession or control." [38]

In principle the officer will intend to take possession if he has made up his mind to do so in the event of certain conditions being fulfilled, *e.g.* should the driver offer no explanation.[39] But the passage quoted may perhaps imply that he does not take possession unless he has decided to take charge of the goods in any event, come what may.

4.23 *Loss of right to restitution.* Even if the goods stolen do not find their way back to lawful possession or custody, they will cease to be stolen goods if the owner (and any person claiming through him, *e.g.* an insurer) ceases "as regards those goods to have any right to restitution in respect of the theft". The exact meaning of the "right to restitution" in this context depends on the nature of the "theft", *i.e.* on whether it was literally an offence of theft or one of deception or blackmail.

4.24 If the goods were obtained without even an apparent consent on the part of the owner, so that the obtaining was literally an offence of theft contrary to section 1(1) of the Act, the owner will have a cause of action in the tort of conversion. This action will lie not only against the thief himself but also against any person subsequently acquiring the goods, unless the circumstances of the acquisition are such as to bring it within one of the exceptions to the rule *nemo dat quod non habet:* only in this latter case will the acquirer obtain a title which will afford him a defence to an action by the original owner. The fact that the owner has a cause of action in respect of goods stolen from him does not mean that he is entitled to recover the goods themselves: under section 3 of the Torts (Interference with Goods) Act 1977 the court may either order the defendant to return the goods claimed or offer him the option of paying damages based on their value instead. But the owner clearly has a "right to restitution" if he has a right to one or the other of those remedies. The phrase cannot be confined to a right to the return of the goods themselves, because the owner is never entitled to that remedy as of right, and a criminal court can hardly speculate whether a civil court would exercise its discretion to grant it.

38 At p. 753.
39 *Cf. Attorney-General's References (Nos. 1 and 2 of 1979)* [1980] Q.B. 180; *supra,* para. 1.123.

4.25 The goods continue to be stolen only as long as the owner has a right to restitution which subsists both "as regards those goods" and "in respect of the theft". A right to the restitution of the goods (or of their value) which arose out of some other transaction altogether would obviously not suffice, because it would not be a right to restitution "in respect of the theft". The phrase "as regards those goods", on the other hand, if it is not redundant, means that goods may cease to be stolen although the owner still has a right to restitution in respect of the theft, if he no longer has such a right as regards *those goods* (*sc.* the goods whose continuing stolenness is in issue). Presumably the situation here envisaged is that in which the owner still has a claim against the thief for damages in respect of the theft, but has no claim against the person currently in possession of the goods because that person acquired them in circumstances falling within one of the exceptions to the *nemo dat* rule and thus conferring on him a title superior to that of the original owner himself. A right to restitution "as regards" particular goods must mean a *title* to those goods which confers on its holder a cause of action against a person currently withholding them from him, not just a right to compensation in respect of past conversions such as the original theft.

4.26 A possible objection to this construction is that the owner's title to the goods cannot be described as a right to restitution "in respect of the theft". Perhaps the objection can be met as follows. A right to restitution as regards particular goods is a subsisting title to those goods, superior to that of their current possessor. But a right to restitution as regards goods which have been stolen is not a right "in respect of the theft" unless the possessor's title is inferior *because* he either is the thief or derives his title from the thief, and not for some other reason independent of the theft. If A steals goods belonging to B and sells them to C in circumstances falling outside the exceptions to the *nemo dat* rule, B has a better title than C because C's title is no better than A's: therefore B has a right to restitution which is not only a right as regards the goods but also a right in respect of the theft, and the goods are still stolen goods. If B then agrees to pay C a proportion of their value by way of settlement of C's *bona fide* claim to them, but C in breach of the agreement refuses to deliver them up, B still has a right to restitution as regards the goods; but that right is now derived from the agreement rather than the theft. Therefore it is no longer a right to restitution in respect of the theft, and the goods are no longer stolen goods.

4.27 Where the owner agrees to part with the ownership or possession of the goods, but his consent is procured by deception and the obtaining is therefore an offence contrary to section 15(1), slightly different considerations apply. The owner has no cause of action against the person in possession of the goods[40] unless and until he rescinds the agreement under which they were obtained, which he is entitled to do on the grounds of fraud.[41] The "right to restitution" of goods so obtained cannot mean simply a better title than that of the current possessor, as it seems to in the case where the owner does not consent at all, because until he rescinds the agreement the owner has no such right. Goods cease to be stolen goods when the owner ceases to have a right to restitution as regards those goods; if, as section 24(4) provides, goods obtained by deception are stolen goods, it follows that the victim of such a deception must initially have a right to restitution. Presumably that right consists in his *potential* claim to the goods, *i.e.* his right to rescind the agreement so that any title conferred by it reverts to him. The goods will therefore cease to be stolen goods if for any reason his right to rescind is barred, *e.g.* if a third party purchases the goods in good faith without notice of the fraud[42] or if the owner chooses to affirm the agreement after discovering the truth. Delay in rescinding, after discovery of the truth, is not a bar in itself but only evidence of affirmation;[43] delay in *discovering* the truth, which can bar rescission in the case of innocent misrepresentation,[44] apparently has no such effect in the case of fraud.[45]

4.28   Where the goods are obtained by blackmail, and the menaces do not nullify the owner's consent to the obtaining altogether[46] but do amount to duress so as to vitiate that consent, the owner's "right to restitution" must again consist in his right to rescind the transaction so that title to the goods will revert to him.[47] It is arguable that any transaction procured by blackmail must by definition be voidable, because if the menaces employed by the defendant were not sufficiently compelling as to render voidable the transaction thereby procured then the combination of those menaces with the demand for that transaction would in principle not be "unwarranted" as section 21(1) requires; but this reasoning admittedly derives little support from the wording of the

---

40   He does of course have a right to recover damages from the deceiver for the tort of deceit, but that is not a right to restitution *as regards the goods: supra*, para. 4.25.
41   s. 2(2) of the Misrepresentation Act 1967, which empowers the court to reject a claim for rescission and award damages in lieu, does not apply to fraudulent misrepresentation. Even if the concept of deception (unlike that of misrepresentation) includes the breach of a duty of disclosure (see *Fraud* para. 2.10), such a breach will also justify rescission.
42   Sale of Goods Act 1979 s. 23.
43   *Clough v. L.N.W. Railway* (1871) L.R. 7 Ex. 26 at p. 35.
44   *Leaf v. International Galleries* [1950] 2 K.B. 86.
45   *Armstrong v. Jackson* [1917] 2 K.B. 822.
46   A threat of personal violence would doubtless have this effect.
47   The victim may have a cause of action against the blackmailer in tort, but this is not a right to restitution *as regards the goods: supra*, para. 4.25.

subsection itself.[48] If, then, it is possible for a transaction to be procured by blackmail without being thereby rendered voidable, a person from whom goods are obtained under such a transaction will have no right to restitution as regards those goods. He might perhaps have a claim in restitution against the blackmailer on the grounds of the latter's crime, but if such a claim were purely personal (as distinct from a right to avoid the transaction altogether and recover the goods), it would not be a right to restitution as regards the goods obtained.[49] In that case there is a conflict between subsections (3) and (4) of section 24: the latter says that goods obtained by blackmail are stolen goods, while the former says that goods as regards which the owner has ceased to have any right to restitution are not stolen goods. The conflict could be resolved by construing section 24(3) literally, so as to apply only where the owner has *ceased* to have a right to restitution and not where he had no such right in the first place, but this seems too artificial. The difficulty perhaps suggests that the procuring of an unimpeachable transaction, even by threats, is not blackmail after all.

Proceeds of stolen goods

4.29 *Restoration to lawful possession or custody.* Where the goods originally stolen have been disposed of or realised, the proceeds may also be stolen goods.[50] Section 24(3) does not spell out exactly how, if at all, it affects such proceeds. In the first place, do they cease to be stolen goods if they find their way back to the owner or to the police? It cannot be said that they have literally been "restored to the person from whom they were stolen", because they were not themselves stolen from anyone; but we have seen that proceeds caught by section 24(2) are apparently deemed not just to be stolen goods but to be included among the goods originally stolen.[51] Presumably, therefore, they cease to be stolen if they are "restored" to the person from whom they are deemed to have been stolen. Moreover section 24(3) also applies if stolen goods are restored "to other lawful possession or custody", which clearly includes both police custody and that of the owner himself.

4.30 *Loss of right to restitution.* The victim of theft, deception or blackmail[52] has a right to restitution not only as regards the goods originally obtained from him but also as regards the proceeds of any disposal or realisation of those goods, because he is entitled (if necessary

48   *Supra,* para. 3.23.
49   *Supra,* para. 4.25.
50   *Supra,* paras 4.06 ff.
51   *Supra,* para. 4.11.
52   Subject to the problem discussed at para. 4.28, *supra.*

after rescinding any transaction under which the goods were obtained from him) to "trace" his property into its proceeds and claim the proceeds instead. But he will lose his right to do this if the proceeds are disposed of in circumstances falling within one of the exceptions to the *nemo dat* rule, including a disposal by a person with a voidable title to a *bona fide* purchaser for value. In that event the proceeds will cease to be stolen, because the owner will have ceased to have any right to restitution as regards those proceeds.

Relationship between goods originally stolen and proceeds

4.31 *Goods originally stolen ceasing to be stolen.* Where the goods originally stolen cease to be stolen by virtue of section 24(3), the question may arise whether any proceeds of those goods, themselves deemed to be stolen under section 24(2), automatically cease to be stolen too. The answer would seem to depend on which limb of section 24(3) has come into play in respect of the goods originally stolen. If they have ceased to be stolen because they have been restored to the possession or custody of the person from whom they were stolen, the proceeds must also cease to be stolen, because the owner cannot claim the proceeds once he has recovered the goods themselves: he has ceased to have any right to restitution as regards the proceeds, and they therefore fall within the second limb of section 24(3). This might not be so if the goods originally stolen had been restored to *other* lawful possession or custody, such as that of a police officer. Nor would it be so merely because the owner had lost his right to restitution as regards those goods, because they had been disposed of in circumstances falling within one of the exceptions to the *nemo dat* rule: this would not prevent him from claiming the proceeds of that or some previous disposal, and there seems no reason why such proceeds once caught by section 24(2) should not continue to be stolen.

4.32 *Proceeds ceasing to be stolen.* Similarly it is clear that the goods originally stolen can continue to be stolen even after section 24(3) has converted some or all of their proceeds into non-stolen goods. Whether they do continue to be stolen will depend on the circumstances. Stolen goods clearly do not cease to be stolen merely because the owner loses his right to claim their proceeds; but if he *recovers* the proceeds this might have the effect of satisfying his claim to the goods themselves, in which case he would no longer have a right to restitution as regards those goods and they would therefore cease to be stolen. But this could only be so if the proceeds recovered represented at least the value which the goods would have had if legitimately offered on the open market.

Proof that goods are stolen

4.33   The prosecution must be prepared to prove that the goods alleged to have been handled were in fact stolen. They need not identify the thief, or even the owner: sometimes the circumstances of the defendant's acquisition of the goods will leave no room for doubt. But the point must be established by admissible evidence. An informal admission by the defendant that the goods were stolen may be admissible to prove that he *believed* that they were; or it may be admissible to prove the facts observed by him (*e.g.* the suspicious behaviour of the person from whom he obtained the goods)[53] on which that belief was based, and from which the jury may be invited to draw the same conclusion as he did; but if it is based on matters reported to him by others, those reports will be admissible only on the issue of belief and not on that of whether the belief was correct.[54] Similarly if the defendant receives money which he regards as being the proceeds of stolen goods and therefore as itself being stolen money, his intention is relevant to the issues of knowledge and of dishonesty but not to that of whether the money actually *is* the proceeds of stolen goods.[55]

4.34   Where it is relevant to an issue in the proceedings whether a person other than the defendant has committed an offence, and that person has been convicted of that offence by or before a court in the United Kingdom or by a Service court elsewhere, the fact of the conviction is admissible as evidence that he did commit the offence;[56] and on proof of the conviction he is taken to have done so unless the contrary is proved.[57] A "conviction" for this purpose includes not only a finding of guilt but also a guilty plea, whether or not (in either case) sentence has been passed.[58] The prosecution may therefore be able to prove that the goods were stolen at some stage by proving the conviction of the alleged thief. But the defendant can still attempt to prove that the alleged thief was wrongly convicted, or that the goods had ceased to be stolen goods before the defendant had any dealings with them.

4.35   Section 27(4) of the Theft Act 1968, which allows the admission in evidence of a statutory declaration by any person that he despatched or failed to receive any goods or postal packet, or that any goods or postal packet when despatched or received by him were in a particular state or

53   *Korniak* (1983) 76 Cr.App.R. 145.
54   *Hulbert* (1979) 69 Cr.App.R. 243.
55   *Attorney-General's Reference (No. 4 of 1979)* [1981] 1 W.L.R. 667; *cf. supra,* paras 4.17 ff.
56   Police and Criminal Evidence Act 1984 s. 74(1).
57   *Ibid.,* s. 74(2).
58   *Golder* [1987] Q.B. 920.

condition,[59] applies to proceedings for handling goods stolen in the course of transmission (whether by post or otherwise) as well as proceedings for the theft itself.

Goods wrongly believed to be stolen

4.36   If it cannot be proved that the goods in question were at the relevant time stolen goods within the meaning of the Act, the defendant cannot be convicted of the full offence of handling stolen goods; but there is a catch. If it can at least be proved that at that time he *believed* that the goods were stolen, he may instead be convicted of an attempt. This is the effect of section 1(2) and (3) of the Criminal Attempts Act 1981, which provide in effect that it is not a defence to a charge of attempt that the commission of the full offence was in the circumstances impossible.[60] The House of Lords initially held in *Anderton v. Ryan*[61] that this did not render the appellant guilty of attempting to handle stolen goods where she had received goods which were not stolen under the impression that they were; but in *Shivpuri*[62] it was held that the appellant had attempted to smuggle prohibited drugs by importing a substance which he wrongly believed to be a prohibited drug, and *Anderton v. Ryan* was overruled. A person who deals in one of the ways specified by section 22(1) with goods which he believes to be stolen is guilty of handling if he is right, and of attempted handling if he is wrong. It should however be noted that *Shivpuri* relieves the prosecution only of the burden of proving that the goods were in fact stolen, not of proving that the defendant believed that they were. Attempt involves an intention to commit the full offence; therefore the belief required for the full offence is equally required for the attempt. This point is considered further in the context of the mental element required for the full offence.[63]

Forms of handling

4.37   "Handling" is only a convenient label for the offence, and section 22(1) covers a wider range of activities than that term might suggest: it extends not only to a person who "receives" the goods but also to one who "undertakes or assists in their retention, removal, disposal or realisation by or for the benefit of another person, or . . . arranges to do so". In *Bloxham*[64] Lord Bridge said it was "well settled" that receiving and the other forms of handling represented two (but only two) distinct

59   *Supra,* para. 1.168.
60   *Supra,* paras 1.188 f.
61   [1985] A.C. 560.
62   [1987] A.C. 1.
63   *Infra,* para. 4.57.
64   [1983] 1 A.C. 109.

offences. This is not strictly correct: there is only one offence.[65] What is well settled is that the indictment should specify whether the defendant is alleged to have handled the goods by receiving them or by dealing with them in one of the other ways referred to in section 22(1).[66] If in doubt, the prosecution should include alternative counts.[67] For most practical purposes it is as if the subsection did indeed create two offences, and prosecutors might be well advised to think of it in those terms. But a count which alleges both receiving and some or all of the other forms of the offence is not bad for duplicity. The offence can take the following forms:

(a) receiving the goods;
(b) undertaking their retention, removal, disposal or realisation for the benefit of another person;
(c) assisting in their retention, removal, disposal or realisation by another person; or
(d) arranging to do (a), (b) or (c).

Receiving

4.38 The word "receives" is not defined and, subject to one qualification, presumably means the same as it did in the superseded offence of receiving stolen property.[68] If so, to receive goods is to take possession of them.[69] Physical handling is not in itself sufficient,[70] and the retention of exclusive possession by one person is incompatible with the taking of possession by another;[71] but a sharing of possession is enough. Moreover possession may be constructive as well as actual. Possession by the defendant's servant or agent is sufficient if authorised or ratified by the defendant. Each taking of possession is a separate offence, so that a count alleging the receipt of different items on different occasions is bad for duplicity.[72] The possible qualification referred to above is that it is now possible to handle *intangible* property:[73] if receiving always involves a taking of physical possession, intangible property cannot be received and can be handled only in other ways. Arguably a person who acquires

---

65 *Griffiths v. Freeman* [1970] 1 W.L.R. 659.
66 *Willis and Syme* [1972] 1 W.L.R. 1605.
67 *Nicklin* [1977] 1 W.L.R. 403.
68 Larceny Act 1916 s. 33(1).
69 *Berger* (1915) 11 Cr.App.R. 72. *Cf.* s. 27(3), *infra,* para. 4.62, which refers to the possession of stolen goods where, in view of the similarity to s. 22(1), one might expect a reference to receiving instead.
70 *Hobson v. Impett* (1957) 41 Cr.App.R. 138.
71 *Wiley* (1850) 2 Den. 37.
72 *Smythe* (1980) 72 Cr.App.R. 8. It may however be possible to charge one count covering a period of time: *ibid.* at p. 13.
73 *Supra,* para. 4.01.

ownership of a chose in action thereby "receives" it; but in that case it would presumably be receiving to acquire ownership (without possession) of tangible property too, which seems not to be the case. There is no reason why every form of the offence should be available in respect of every kind of property. Intangible property cannot be "removed" either.

Undertaking retention, removal, disposal or realisation for the benefit of another

4.39   The other ways in which goods can be "handled" constitute an extension of the old offence and have presented some difficulties of interpretation. Read literally, the clause "or . . . undertakes or assists in their retention, removal, disposal or realisation by or for the benefit of another person" appears to envisage a bewildering variety of activities: *e.g.*

(a) undertaking the retention of the goods by another person;
(b) undertaking the retention of the goods for the benefit of another person;
(c) assisting in the retention of the goods by another person;
(d) assisting in the retention of the goods for the benefit of another person;

and so on, with similar possibilities in respect of the removal, disposal and realisation of the goods. In *Bloxham*,[74] however, the House of Lords confined the clause to a narrower range of permutations than this literal analysis would suggest.

> "The . . . words contemplate four activities (retention, removal, disposal, realisation). The offence can be committed in relation to any one of these activities in one or other of two ways. First, the offender may himself undertake the activity *for the benefit of* another person. Secondly, the activity may be undertaken *by* another person and the offender may assist him." [75]

In other words, of the possibilities above only (b) and (c) represent genuine alternatives; (a) and (d) do not, and may be disregarded.

4.40   This passage also throws light on the significance of the word "undertakes". That word is unfortunately ambiguous: one can undertake a task either by doing it (or, perhaps, starting or trying to do it) or by promising to do it. The latter construction would leave little or no scope to the words "or if he arranges to do so". Lord Bridge appears to prefer the former, because (unlike section 22(1) itself) he refers to an offender

---

74   [1983] 1 A.C. 109.
75   At p. 113, *per* Lord Bridge, with whom the remainder of their Lordships agreed.

assisting in the undertaking of an activity by another person. One can assist a person to do something, but hardly assist him to promise to do it. To undertake the retention of goods must therefore mean simply to retain them; to undertake their removal is to remove them; and so on. This appears to have been the intention of the Criminal Law Revision Committee:

> "The reference to undertaking these activities will include a person who acts on his own in order to help the thief . . ." [76]

The obvious objection to this view is that no self-respecting draftsman would write "undertakes . . . their retention" if he meant "retains them". If it were intended to mean what his Lordship apparently understands it to mean, the subsection might be expected to read as follows:

> "A person handles stolen goods if . . . he dishonestly receives the goods, or dishonestly retains, removes, disposes of or realises them for the benefit of another person,[77] or dishonestly assists in their retention, removal, disposal or realisation by another person,[78] or if he arranges to do so."

But the draftsman presumably thought it worth putting up with the clumsy phrase "undertakes or assists in their retention . . ." for the sake of condensing two clauses into one. It would not be the only point in the Act at which clarity was sacrificed to brevity.

4.41 It follows that a person who knowingly retains stolen goods, or removes, disposes of or realises them, is thereby guilty of handling if (but only if) he does so for the benefit of another person. A person who purchases stolen goods in good faith is not guilty of handling by receiving, because he neither knows nor believes that the goods are stolen; if he then discovers that they are stolen but nevertheless decides to keep them, he is "undertaking their retention" but he is not doing so for the benefit of another person, and is therefore still not guilty of handling them. It would be surprising if he were, since he is expressly exempted from liability for theft.[79]

4.42 Similarly it is not handling simply to dispose of goods which one knows to be stolen. In *Bloxham*[80] the appellant had innocently bought a stolen car and sold it when he found out that it was stolen. It was argued

76   Cmnd. 2977 para. 128.
77   "On behalf of another person" might be clearer still: *cf. infra,* para. 4.43.
78   Or "assists another person to retain, remove, dispose of or realise them". Simply "assists another person to do so" will not do because if the retaining (*etc.*) is done *by* another person it need not also be done *for the benefit of* another person. Perhaps "assists another person to do so (whether or not for the benefit of any person)".
79   s. 3(2); *supra,* para. 1.105.
80   [1983] 1 A.C. 109.

that he had thereby undertaken the disposal or realisation of the car for the benefit of another person, *viz.* the purchaser. The House of Lords allowed his appeal on the grounds that the sale was not something done for the purchaser's benefit, either within the natural meaning of those words taken in isolation or in the context of section 22(1). Lord Bridge, having distinguished (in the passage quoted above) between undertaking an activity for the benefit of another person and assisting in the undertaking of that activity *by* another person, went on:

> "... if the analysis holds good, it must follow, I think, that the category of other persons contemplated by the subsection is subject to the same limitations in whichever way the offence is committed. Accordingly, a purchaser, as such, of stolen goods, cannot, in my opinion, be 'another person' within the subsection, since his act of purchase could not sensibly be described as a disposal or realisation of the stolen goods *by* him. Equally, therefore, even if the sale to him could be described as a disposal or realisation for his benefit, the transaction is not, in my view, within the ambit of the subsection." [81]

4.43 An act may of course be done "for the benefit of" a person other than the person by whom it is done: those words are not redundant. What his Lordship appears to mean is that a transaction undertaken by one person cannot be undertaken for the benefit of another (within the meaning of the subsection) unless it might, in different circumstances, have been undertaken by that other person himself. A sale of goods to a particular person could in no circumstances be a sale undertaken by that person himself, and therefore cannot be a disposal or realisation for his benefit. A person in possession of goods, on the other hand, is in a position to sell them himself; if instead he procures another person to sell them on his behalf, the sale is not undertaken *by* him but it is undertaken for his benefit. It may indeed be that this is the *only* situation in which a disposal or realisation (as distinct from a retention or removal) is undertaken by one person for the benefit of another. Lord Bridge had earlier said, when discussing the ordinary meaning of the phrase without reference to its context:

> "It is only when [a person] is selling as agent for a third party ... that it would be entirely natural to describe the sale as a disposal or realisation for the benefit of another person." [82]

4.44 It should not however be assumed that a person who has innocently bought stolen goods can always sell them with impunity. What *Bloxham* decides is that he is not handling the goods by undertaking their disposal or realisation for the benefit of the purchaser. But if he induces

81   At p. 114.
82   At p. 113.

the purchaser to believe that the goods are his to sell, he will be obtaining the price by deception.[83] If the purchaser knows or believes that the goods are stolen, the purchaser will himself be guilty of handling by receiving them; and in that case the seller (if he knows that the purchaser knows)[84] might perhaps be guilty of aiding and abetting the purchaser's offence. In *Bloxham*[85] Lord Bridge recognised that this might "conceivably" be so, and it was apparently so under the old law.[86] It might however be argued that since the wording of section 22(1) (as construed in *Bloxham*) exempts the seller from liability as principal offender, it cannot have been intended that he should be liable as an accessory instead. There is some authority for the view that, where a bilateral transaction is expressly forbidden for one of the parties but not for the other, Parliament may be taken to have intended to exempt the latter party altogether.[87]

Assisting in retention, removal, disposal or realisation by another

4.45 Stolen goods which are retained, removed, disposed of or realised by one person may be handled by another person who (otherwise than in the course of the stealing)[88] assists him. The retention, removal, disposal or realisation need not itself amount to handling on the part of the person undertaking it, because he may not be acting for the benefit of anyone else; he may not even know or believe that the goods are stolen. But his assistant, if *he* knows or believes that the goods are stolen, is guilty as a principal offender. It seems, moreover, that the "assistant" is guilty even if his efforts turn out to be no help at all. In *Kanwar*[89] a woman who had told the police that certain goods belonged to her, when they had in fact been stolen by her husband, was held not just to have attempted to assist in his retention of the goods but to have actually assisted. This was so although the police were not deceived, and her husband was not in fact enabled to retain the goods for a moment longer than he otherwise would have. It has even been said that assistance is not confined to help but includes ("amongst other things") encouragement.[90] It is submitted with respect that this goes too far. If the draftsman had meant to include a person who "abets, counsels or procures" as well as one who "aids" he would doubtless have said so. At any rate it seems that mere presence at

---

83 *Supra*, ch. 2.
84 If the purchaser knew but the seller thought he did not, the seller would probably be *attempting* to obtain by deception.
85 [1983] 1 A.C. 109 at p. 115.
86 *Carter Patersons & Pickfords Carriers Ltd v. Wessel* [1947] K.B. 849.
87 e.g. *Whitehouse* [1977] Q.B. 868; *contra, Sockett* (1908) 1 Cr.App.R. 101. See G. Williams, *Textbook of Criminal Law* (2nd ed.) pp 364 ff.
88 *Infra*, para. 4.72.
89 [1982] 1 W.L.R. 845.
90 *Coleman* [1986] Crim.L.R. 56.

a disposal of the goods, not amounting to help or even encouragement, is not enough:[91] the defendant must assist *in* the proceedings, not just *at* them.

Assisting in removal, disposal or realisation

4.46 The notion of assistance in the removal of the goods is self-explanatory. Assistance in their disposal or realisation may take such obvious forms as introducing a buyer, effecting delivery or collecting the price, but not merely accepting the benefit of the proceeds.[92] On the other hand the proceeds may themselves be stolen goods,[93] in which case a person who knowingly takes possession of them will be guilty of handling by receiving. A buyer of stolen goods is receiving them if he takes possession of them, but is presumably assisting in their realisation by the seller even if he does not. The seller could not realise them without the assistance of a buyer. It has even been held that the buyer *undertakes* their realisation *for the benefit of* the seller,[94] but in the light of *Bloxham*[95] this must be wrong. The buyer does not undertake the realisation of the goods at all,[96] let alone for the benefit of the seller.

Assisting in retention

4.47 As in the case of disposal or realisation, one does not assist in the retention of stolen goods merely by accepting the benefit of them. In *Sanders*[97] the appellant was held not to have assisted in the retention of a fan heater and a battery charger by using them, even if in doing so he took them into his possession or control (though in that case he would be receiving them). The use of goods is facilitated by their retention, not *vice versa*.

> "It must be proved that in some way the accused was assisting in the retention of the goods by concealing them, or making them more difficult to identify, or by holding them pending their ultimate disposal, or by some other act that was part of the chain of the dishonest handling." [98]

Assistance in the retention of stolen goods "by holding them pending their ultimate disposal" can in some cases be effected with little or no positive action on the part of the defendant. In *Brown*[99] the police had gone to the appellant's flat and asked him whether he knew anything

---

91   *Harris*, 1 July 1986, Criminal Appeal Office transcript no. 7011/C/85.
92   *Coleman* [1986] Crim.L.R. 56.
93   *Supra*, paras 4.06 ff.
94   *Deakin* [1972] 1 W.L.R. 1618.
95   [1983] 1 A.C. 109; *supra*, para. 4.42.
96   *Ibid*. at p. 114, *per* Lord Bridge.
97   (1982) 75 Cr.App.R. 84.
98   At pp 86 f.
99   [1970] 1 Q.B. 105.

about the theft of certain food and cigarettes. He replied that he did not, and made no attempt to prevent the police from searching the flat. It subsequently transpired that the stolen goods had been hidden in the flat, with the appellant's knowledge, by the thief. As in *Kanwar*, the appellant had not just omitted to disclose the truth but had told a lie (*viz.* that he knew nothing of the theft), and was presumably assisting in the thief's retention of the goods by virtue of that fact alone; but the jury were directed that the mere failure to reveal the stolen goods might in itself amount to assisting in their retention. This was held to be a misdirection. There is no duty to assist the police in their enquiries, whether or not they ask for such assistance, and failing to do so (as distinct from telling them lies) is not the same as assisting the culprit. But the court applied the proviso: the appellant's silence, though not in itself an act of assistance, was strong evidence that he was "assisting in their retention by housing the goods and providing accommodation for them, by permitting them to remain there".[1]

4.48   This last phrase is ambiguous. It is clearly sufficient if the defendant gives permission (express or implied) for the goods to remain on his premises, and this is so whether such permission is granted before or after the goods arrive. What is less clear is whether he can be said to assist in their retention merely by acquiescing in their presence when he finds them already there. The reference in *Brown* to "housing the goods and providing accommodation for them" would seem to imply that he can, and was so interpreted in *Pitchley*;[2] but its application to the facts of that case was misconceived. The appellant (according to his own evidence) had been asked by his son to look after some money and paid it into his post office savings account. Only later did he find out that the money had been stolen, and having found out he did nothing about it. This conduct, it was held, amounted to handling, in that the appellant was "permitting the money to remain under his control in his savings bank book".[3] It is not clear whether this was regarded as a retention by the appellant for the benefit of his son, or as assistance by him in a retention by his son. The reliance on *Brown* suggests the latter, but the two cases are distinguishable. Pitchley did not permit his son to keep the stolen banknotes under the mattress, or for that matter "in his savings bank book": he exchanged them for a chose in action consisting in an increase in the credit balance of his savings account. Not only was this chose in action not "retained" by the son, it was not even stolen goods: though it was the proceeds of the stolen money, it had not been in the hands of the

1   At p. 108.
2   (1972) 57 Cr.App.R. 30.
3   At p. 36.

thief or of a handler.[4] The son, in whose hands the proceeds of the stolen money *would* have been stolen, had no interest in the appellant's bank balance: had he acquired the money honestly he might have retained an equitable interest in it, but "he who comes to equity must come with clean hands". The only person other than the appellant who may have had an interest in his bank balance was the victim of the theft. The decision is, with respect, clearly wrong; but, this difficulty aside, the reasoning suggests that one can assist in the retention of stolen goods merely by acquiescing in their presence on one's premises or otherwise under one's control.

Arranging to receive, undertake or assist

4.49 Finally the section catches a person who does not in fact receive the goods or play any part in their retention, removal, disposal or realisation, but merely "arranges to do so". In the light of *Bloxham*[5] this means that one can handle stolen goods by

(a) arranging to receive them;
(b) arranging to undertake their retention, removal, disposal or realisation for the benefit of another person; or
(c) arranging to assist in their retention, removal, disposal or realisation by another person.

An agreement to do any of these things may of course be a conspiracy to handle stolen goods,[6] but only if at least two of the parties to the agreement know that the goods are stolen.[7] It is possible to handle stolen goods by arranging to do one of the things mentioned above even if the person with whom the arrangement is made does not know that the goods are stolen. It may even be possible to make such "arrangements" by unilateral action rather than agreement, *e.g.* by making preparations for the reception of the goods; but this construction would probably go too far. The word "arranges" must surely refer to arrangements by way of agreements with other people. And in one respect conspiracy is wider than this form of handling: goods cannot be handled until they are stolen. An arrangement to receive the proceeds of a theft which has not yet been committed is not itself a handling of those proceeds, though it may be a conspiracy to handle them.[8]

---

4 *Supra,* paras 4.06 ff.
5 [1983] 1 A.C. 109; *supra,* para. 4.39.
6 Criminal Law Act 1977 s. 1(1).
7 *Ibid.,* s. 1(2). This provision literally applies only to conspiracies to commit offences of strict liability, but must apply *a fortiori* to other conspiracies too.
8 *Park* (1987) 87 Cr.App.R. 164.

Knowledge or belief

4.50 The defendant need not know what the stolen goods are,[9] nor precisely how they came to be stolen goods (*i.e.* whether they were obtained by theft, deception or blackmail); but he must either know or believe that they *are* stolen goods. This obviously does not mean that he must be familiar with section 24 of the Theft Act:[10] it is sufficient that he knows the goods to have been obtained by blackmail, for example, or to be the proceeds of stolen goods in the hands of the thief, even if he might be surprised to learn that such goods are in law regarded as stolen goods. In other words, a person knows or believes stolen goods to be stolen if he knows or believes the facts which in law render them stolen.[11]

Belief falling short of knowledge

4.51 What the Act fails to make clear, however, is the nature of the distinction it draws between knowledge and belief. When does a person believe goods to be stolen without knowing them to be stolen? The obvious answer is "when they are *not* stolen"; but that possibility is irrelevant for present purposes because the full offence[12] cannot be committed at all unless the goods *are* stolen.[13] If the words "or believing" add anything they must refer to a person who believes that the goods in question are stolen, and is correct in that belief, but does not *know* that they are stolen. The Criminal Law Revision Committee's example of such a person was the man who, asking no questions, buys goods at a ridiculously low price from a stranger in a pub;[14] but if this man's state of mind is more than mere suspicion (which, however strong, is not in itself sufficient)[15] it is not clear how it falls short of knowledge. For some time the Court of Appeal declined to clarify the point, and recommended trial judges to follow its example,[16] but in *Hall (Edward)* [17] it finally ventured an explanation.

> "A man may be said to know that goods are stolen when he is told by someone with first hand knowledge (someone such as the thief or the burglar) that such is the case. Belief, of course, is something short of knowledge. It may be said to be the state of mind of a person who says to himself: 'I cannot say I know for certain that these goods are stolen, but

9 *McCullum* (1973) 57 Cr.App.R. 645.
10 *Supra*, paras. 4.04 ff.
11 Or, presumably (and provided always that the goods are in fact stolen), if he believes a proposition of fact to be true which is not true but which would render the goods stolen if it were: *infra*, para. 4.54.
12 As distinct from an attempt: *supra*, para. 4.36.
13 *Haughton v. Smith* [1975] A.C. 476.
14 Cmnd. 2977 para. 134.
15 *Grainge* [1974] 1 W.L.R. 619; *Moys* (1984) 79 Cr.App.R. 72.
16 *e.g. Reader* (1977) 66 Cr.App.R. 33.
17 (1985) 81 Cr.App.R. 260.

there can be no other reasonable conclusion in the light of all the circumstances, in the light of all that I have heard and seen.' Either of those two states of mind is enough to satisfy the words of the statute. The second is enough (that is, belief) even if the defendant says to himself 'Despite all that I have seen and all that I have heard, I refuse to believe what my brain tells me is obvious'. What is not enough, of course, is mere suspicion. 'I suspect that these goods may be stolen, but it may be on the other hand that they are not'." [18]

Whether a direction along these lines is called for depends how the case for the Crown is conducted.[19] There is no need to give the full direction in every case where the issue of belief arises, but in some cases, and especially where suspicion has been referred to, it will be prudent to do so.[20] And in such a case there may be room for argument as to exactly what the *Hall* direction means, and precisely what function (if any) it envisages for the words "or believing".

Grounds for certainty

4.52 One interpretation of the guidance given in *Hall* is that the defendant must always be certain in his own mind that the goods are stolen. On this view the only difference between knowledge and belief is that that certainty will be based on first-hand information in the one case and on circumstantial evidence in the other. It has been objected that such an interpretation would be at odds with the wording of section 22(1) itself, which, it is said, "implies a distinction between two states of mind, not between two modes of arriving at the same state of mind".[21] But all that section 22(1) implies is that knowledge and belief are *somehow* different, not that they are necessarily different states of mind. The difference may indeed lie in the route rather than the destination. Even if a person is certain that a given proposition is true, and he is right, it does not follow that he knows that proposition to be true. Whether his certainty amounts to knowledge depends to some extent on his reasons for being certain. If he is convinced that a particular car is stolen, and he is right, but his only reason for thinking so is the fact that it has been resprayed, we might say that he *believes* the car is stolen but surely not that he *knows* it is: and this is because the reasoning does not justify the conclusion. A car which has been resprayed is doubtless more likely to have been stolen (other things being equal) than one which has not, but many cars are resprayed which have not been stolen. To regard a respray as conclusive evidence of theft is irrational; and it would be odd to describe irrational certainty (even if it happens to be correct) as knowledge. It is therefore arguable

18 At p. 264.
19 *Harris* (1987) 84 Cr.App.R. 75.
20 *Toor* (1986) 85 Cr.App.R. 116.
21 J. C. Smith [1987] Crim.L.R. at p. 123.

that certainty is a necessary element of both knowledge and belief, and that the distinction between them turns solely on the *grounds* for such certainty. On this view a person *knows* that stolen goods are stolen if he is certain that they are stolen because he has reliable first-hand information to that effect, and he *believes* that they are stolen if he is certain that they are stolen because there is circumstantial evidence to that effect.

4.53 A further objection to this view is that a person whose certainty is based on inadequate grounds not only does not *know* the truth: he does not even *believe* it within the meaning of section 22(1) as interpreted in *Hall*. A person who is certain of something does of course believe it in the ordinary meaning of the word, whether his grounds for doing so are compelling or non-existent. But the *Hall* direction implies that even belief must be based on a solid evidential foundation, in which case irrational certainty is not enough. If this is right then the distinction suggested in the previous paragraph is reduced to one between certainty based on first-hand information and certainty based on *overwhelming* circumstantial evidence. These two cases may be thought too similar to justify distinguishing between them. If (it may be said) the goods are in fact stolen, and the defendant is certain that they are, and there is ample (albeit circumstantial) evidence to justify his certainty, he does not just believe that they are: he knows it. Section 22(1) refers to knowledge and belief as alternatives. It cannot therefore be right to define belief so narrowly that any belief which is correct (as for the purposes of section 22(1) it must be) amounts to knowledge.

4.54 It is submitted however that this objection too is not conclusive. Certainty that goods are stolen is not invariably the same as knowledge that they are, even if they are indeed stolen and even if there is good reason to suppose that they are. This is because, as we have seen, a person knows that goods are stolen (within the meaning of section 22(1)) if he knows *facts* which in law render them stolen, whether or not he also knows that this is the legal effect of those facts.[22] If he is certain of facts which, were they true, would in law render the goods stolen, and his certainty is entirely justified by apparently conclusive evidence of those facts, but the evidence happens to be misleading and the facts are not as he supposes them to be, he obviously does not *know* the facts to be as he supposes (because one cannot know that which is not true): he only believes it. Suppose, for example, there is a wealth of circumstantial evidence that the goods have been obtained by deception, and the

---

22 *Supra*, para. 4.50.

defendant therefore concludes that that is indeed how they were obtained. Had they been obtained by deception they would be stolen goods. He therefore believes them to be stolen for the purposes of section 22(1), even if he does not know that goods obtained by deception are in law regarded as stolen goods, because he believes that certain facts exist which (if they did exist) would in law have that effect. But suppose now that this apparently overwhelming evidence is in fact misleading, and the goods have not been obtained by deception after all. The defendant does not *know* them to have been obtained by deception, because they have not. Nor, it is submitted, does he know them to be stolen goods—*even if in fact they are, e.g.* because they were obtained by blackmail. In that case it might be argued that he believes the goods to be stolen, that he has good reason so to believe, that he is in fact right, and that he therefore knows them to be stolen. But it is only in an elliptical sense that he "believes them to be stolen". What he believes is a proposition of fact, *viz.* that they were obtained by deception, and in believing that proposition he is wrong. He does not become right merely because, unbeknown to him, the legal effect of the true facts is the same as that of the facts which he wrongly supposes to exist. Since he is still wrong, his state of mind cannot properly be described as knowledge. It follows that even if "belief" is interpreted as certainty justified by overwhelming circumstantial evidence, a person who justifiably and correctly believes certain goods to be stolen does not necessarily *know* that they are; and even on this narrow construction the words "or believing" are therefore not wholly redundant.

Degrees of certainty

4.55 An alternative, and wider, view of the concept of belief espoused in *Hall* is that it does not require complete certainty at all. On this view the reason why first-hand information confers knowledge, while circumstantial evidence gives rise only to belief, is that they are not just different routes to absolute certainty but justify different *degrees* of certainty. One can be *absolutely* certain that an event has happened if one sees it happen, or (perhaps) if one is told that it happened by an unimpeachable witness who did see it. One can be *nearly* certain that it happened if there is overwhelming circumstantial evidence to that effect. Absolute certainty, based on first-hand information, is knowledge; near-certainty, based on overwhelming circumstantial evidence, is not knowledge but belief. This interpretation would make the offence easier to prove, but at the cost of blurring its boundary to the point of invisibility. At what point does near-certainty (which on this view is sufficient) fade into strong suspicion (which is not)? It has been held insufficient that the defendant thinks the goods are more likely to be stolen than not.[23] What then is the judge to say if the jury ask whether it is sufficient that the defendant thought there was a 75% chance of the goods being stolen? Or a 90% chance? A possible solution would be to kill two birds with one stone by making use of a concept which has to be explained to the jury anyway, namely that of proof beyond a reasonable doubt. The prosecution must prove to the jury, beyond a reasonable doubt, that the goods were in fact stolen; perhaps they must also prove that that fact was clear to *the defendant* beyond a reasonable doubt. But ultimately it must, on this view, be a question of degree.

Wilful blindness
4.56 It is clearly wrong to direct the jury that it is sufficient if the defendant suspected the goods were stolen but deliberately "shut his eyes" to the circumstances; but it is permissible to direct them that such "wilful blindness" is evidence from which they may infer knowledge or belief.[24] Whether this approach is helpful or misleading depends exactly what wilful blindness is understood to mean. If it is just a loaded synonym for "suspicion", it is not clear how a state of mind which is not sufficient can be evidence of a different state of mind which is. Since suspicion alone is not belief, there must be some additional element which converts it into belief, and of which (on this view) it is evidence; but the nature of this extra ingredient remains obscure. If, on the other hand, the essence of wilful blindness is the failure to ask obvious questions about the provenance of the goods, it is perhaps not unreasonable to regard it as evidence of knowledge or belief. In *Bellenie*[25] it was said that if the jury think the defendant's eyes were blind they must go on to consider whether this was the result of his knowledge or belief that the goods were stolen, or merely of gullibility, stupidity or inattention. This implies that a person may refrain from asking questions precisely *because* he already knows or believes the truth and prefers not to have it spelt out to him, and that a failure to ask the questions which any reasonable person would ask is therefore evidence that the defendant did know or believe it. Whether it is cogent evidence of that fact is another matter. It might equally be said that a person who refrains from asking obvious questions may do so because he *suspects* that the goods may be stolen (which would not suffice) and prefers not to convert that suspicion into knowledge or belief (which would). If that were the explanation for the defendant's lack of curiosity, it is submitted that he could not properly be convicted.

23 *Reader* (1977) 66 Cr.App.R. 33.
24 *Griffiths* (1974) 60 Cr.App.R. 14; *Lincoln* [1980] Crim.L.R. 575.
25 [1980] Crim.L.R. 437.

Belief and attempted handling

4.57 These problems are compounded when the charge is one of attempted handling rather than the full offence. In this case it is immaterial whether the goods in question actually are stolen[26] —indeed it may be precisely because they are *not* stolen that the charge is only one of attempt. The issue is whether the defendant intended to handle stolen goods;[27] the problem is whether such an intent involves certainty that the goods are stolen, or whether something less than certainty will suffice. This depends to some extent on what is meant by knowledge and belief in the context of the full offence. If that offence requires absolute certainty that the goods are stolen (based on first-hand information in the case of knowledge and on circumstantial evidence, overwhelming or otherwise, in the case of belief),[28] then clearly nothing less than absolute certainty can suffice for an attempt, because an intent to commit an offence requires at least the state of mind required for that offence. But in the case of the full offence it is arguable that the defendant's certainty must be not only correct but also based on reasonable grounds.[29] If so, intent would to that extent be wider than belief, because a defendant who is sure that the goods are stolen *intends* to handle stolen goods even if he has no good reason to think so—and even if he is wrong.

4.58 If, on the other hand, the "belief" which is sufficient for the full offence is something less than certainty, the question arises whether it is equally sufficient for the attempt. That possibility is not precluded by the rule that an attempt requires at least the *mens rea* of the full offence; but it is arguably precluded by the requirement of an intent to handle *stolen* goods. Does a person have such an intention if he is fairly sure, but not absolutely certain, that the goods in question are stolen? This is only one instance of a more general problem which is discussed elsewhere.[30] But if certainty is not required for the full offence it seems unlikely that it would be required for the attempt.

Proof of knowledge or belief

Matters known to the defendant

4.59 The simplest way of proving that the defendant knew or believed the goods to be stolen is to prove that he witnessed the theft or other obtaining. Alternatively it may be proved that he was aware of matters from which the inference that the goods had been stolen was irresistible. These matters may be no more than circumstantial evidence (*e.g.* the

---

26   *Shivpuri* [1987] A.C. 1.
27   Criminal Attempts Act 1981 s. 1(1).
28   *Supra*, para. 4.52.
29   *Supra*, para. 4.53.
30   *Infra*, para. 7.31.

supplier's anxiety to dispose of the goods, even at an undervalue) or they may amount to first-hand information (*e.g.* the supplier's admission to the defendant that he had stolen them).[31] But information conveyed to the defendant by others would not be admissible on the issue of whether they *were* stolen, only on that of whether he knew or believed that they were.[32]

Recent possession

4.60 It has long been established that a person's possession of goods which have recently been stolen is in itself evidence that he either stole the goods or received them knowing them to be stolen;[33] and now that the offence can be committed in ways other than receiving,[34] the same inference may be drawn against a person who deals with recently stolen goods in one of those other ways.[35] The inference is not inevitable, even if the defendant offers no explanation or no credible one, and particularly if he has not taken possession of the goods. The burden of proof remains on the prosecution throughout. If, therefore, the defendant offers a reasonable explanation, he cannot be convicted unless the court is satisfied that his explanation is untrue.[36] But he cannot safely remain silent. This principle is commonly referred to as "the doctrine of recent possession", although the name has been criticised.

"The so called doctrine of recent possession is misnamed. It has nothing to do with goods recently possessed. It concerns possession of goods recently stolen. It is not even a doctrine. It is in fact no more than an inference which a jury may, or may not, think it right to draw about the state of mind of a defendant who is dealing in goods stolen not long beforehand. It is based on common sense."[37]

The "so called doctrine" is indeed a matter of common sense rather than a rule of law: it is

". . . only a particular aspect of the general proposition that where suspicious circumstances appear to demand an explanation, and no explanation or an entirely incredible explanation is given, the lack of explanation may warrant an inference of guilty knowledge in the defendant."[38]

But the term "recent possession" is accurate as far as it goes: the word "recent" here refers not to an event which has not long since occurred, but to a state of affairs which has not been long in existence. If the

31 *Hall* (1985) 81 Cr.App.R. 260; *supra,* para. 4.51.
32 *Supra,* para. 4.33.
33 *Langmead* (1864) Le. & Ca. 427. For the difficulties involved in determining which, see *infra,* paras 4.79 ff.
34 *Supra,* paras 4.37 ff.
35 *Ball* [1983] 1 W.L.R. 801, not following a dictum in *Sloggett* [1972] 1 Q.B. 430.
36 *Aves* [1950] 2 All E.R. 330.
37 *Ball* [1983] 1 W.L.R. 801 at p. 805.
38 *Raviraj* (1986) 85 Cr.App.R. 93 at p. 103.

defendant is in possession of goods which have recently been stolen, then (unless of course he was in possession of them before they were stolen) his possession must itself be recent. The real objection to the term, since the extension of the offence to dealings other than receiving, is that it refers only to *possession*.

4.61 Since it is only in the case of goods recently stolen that guilty knowledge can be inferred from the mere fact of the defendant's dealings with them, the principle cannot be relied upon in the absence of any satisfactory evidence as to the period elapsing between the theft and the finding of the goods in his possession or the other dealings relied upon.[39] Precisely how short the period must be will depend to some extent on the nature of the goods: the more frequently such goods can be expected to pass from hand to hand in the ordinary course of events, the sooner it becomes impossible to infer guilty knowledge on the part of a person dealing with them. Banknotes change hands more often than cars do.

Theft or dealings with stolen goods on another occasion
4.62 Section 27(3) of the Theft Act 1968, a modified version of section 43(1) of the Larceny Act 1916, creates two striking exceptions to the general principle against the admissibility of the defendant's conduct on other occasions. It provides:

"Where a person is being proceeded against for handling stolen goods (but not for any offence other than handling stolen goods), then at any stage of the proceedings, if evidence has been given of his having or arranging to have in his possession the goods the subject of the charge, or of his undertaking or assisting in, or arranging to undertake or assist in, their retention, removal, disposal or realisation, the following evidence shall be admissible for the purpose of proving that he knew or believed the goods to be stolen goods:
(*a*) evidence that he has had in his possession, or has undertaken or assisted in the retention, removal, disposal or realisation of, stolen goods from any theft taking place not earlier than twelve months before the offence charged; and
(*b*) (provided that seven days' notice in writing has been given to him of the intention to prove the conviction) evidence that he has within the five years preceding the date of the offence charged been convicted of theft or of handling stolen goods."

4.63 These provisions apply only where the defendant is charged with no offence other than handling, and only for the purpose of proving that he knew or believed the goods to be stolen. The prosecution may invoke it once they have adduced evidence of possession or of one of the other

---

39 *Thompson* 28 October 1986, Criminal Appeal Office transcript no. 1469/D/86. The point was conceded in *Simmons* [1986] Crim.L.R. 397.

forms of handling, but if the defendant denies that he had any dealings with the goods at all then section 27(3) does not help to prove that he did. If there are a number of handling counts in an indictment, and knowledge is in issue on some but not others, the judge must exercise very great care before allowing evidence of other dealings or convictions to be given; and if he does allow it he must then take equal care to ensure that the jury realise the evidence goes only to the issue of knowledge or belief.[40] Even so, this is a remarkable exception to the rule against evidence going only to criminal disposition,[41] and where the subsection allows such evidence there remains a general discretion to exclude it.[42] Indeed, the Court of Appeal appears almost to regard evidence of previous convictions as *prima facie* inadmissible subject to the judge's discretion to admit it, rather than *vice versa:*

> "We think it right to say that it must not be regarded as a matter of course that judges will allow in handling cases the prosecution to adduce evidence of previous convictions for handling merely because the obvious and only issue in the case is guilty knowledge. That we are sure was never the intention of Parliament. What this section really does, is to give to the court a discretion to admit that evidence whenever the demands of justice seem to warrant it. In deciding whether or not to exercise that power a judge must obviously have regard to the fairness with which the trial is conducted, both in regard to the prosecution and the defence." [43]

This passage relates only to evidence of previous convictions under paragraph (*b*), but, although paragraph (*a*) is in one respect less oppressive (in being confined to dealings with goods stolen since a date twelve months before the offence charged, rather than within the preceding five years), it is submitted that similar considerations must apply. Paragraph (*b*) does at least have the safeguard that the defendant's conduct on the earlier occasion has already been proved to have been an offence.

4.64 *Dealings with stolen goods.* Subject to the considerations referred to above, section 27(3)(*a*) permits the adducing of evidence that the defendant has

(a) had stolen goods in his possession, or
(b) undertaken their retention, removal, disposal or realisation, or
(c) assisted in their retention, removal, disposal or realisation.

---

40 *Wilkins* (1975) 60 Cr.App.R. 300.
41 See R. Munday, "Handling the Evidential Exception" [1988] Crim.L.R. 345.
42 *List* [1966] 1 W.L.R. 9; *Herron* [1967] 1 Q.B. 107; *Knott* [1973] Crim.L.R. 36; *Perry* [1984] Crim.L.R. 680; and see now Police and Criminal Evidence Act 1984 s. 78(1).
43 *Rasini* 13 March 1986, The Times 20 March 1986, Criminal Appeal Office transcript no. 1136/B/85 at p. 5.

The acts which may be proved obviously correspond closely to the different forms of handling,[44] the fact of possession being by definition proof of a prior receiving; but paragraph (*a*) differs from paragraph (*b*) in that the defendant need not have been convicted in respect of the conduct relied upon. Therefore it can be invoked where he is found in possession of two stolen articles and charged with handling them both: possession of each article may be evidence of guilty knowledge regarding the other.[45] Moreover the prosecution may rely upon the defendant's conduct on an occasion in respect of which he is not charged without first having to prove that he was guilty on that occasion. They need not prove that a retention, removal, disposal or realisation of stolen goods by him was undertaken for the benefit of another person;[46] they may rely upon acts done by him "in the course of the stealing";[47] they need not even show that on the other occasion he acted dishonestly, or that he knew or believed that the other goods were stolen (though if he clearly did *not* know or believe this, his conduct can scarcely have any bearing on the issue of his knowledge or belief on the occasion charged).

4.65 On the other hand paragraph (*a*) apparently does not apply to evidence of a mere *arrangement* to do one of the acts listed, even if it can be proved that the arrangement amounted to handling[48] and even if the defendant is charged accordingly. Moreover it only permits evidence that he did act in one of the ways specified, not evidence of the circumstances[49]—although in the absence of such evidence it is hard to see how the mere fact of his conduct might help to prove guilty knowledge on the occasion charged. Nor does paragraph (*a*) allow the admission of statements made by the defendant by way of explanation of his conduct on the other occasion; but if there is any doubt as to whether he was in possession of the other goods, *e.g.* because they were found at a residence which he shared with others, such a statement may be admitted for the purpose of proving that he was.[50] And it can hardly be proved that he was in possession of stolen goods without at least mentioning what sort of goods they were.[51]

4.66 The goods with which the defendant is alleged to have dealt, on an occasion other than that in respect of which he is charged, must have been

44 *Supra,* paras 4.37 ff.
45 *Simmons* [1986] Crim.L.R. 397.
46 *Cf. supra,* para. 4.43.
47 *Cf. infra,* para. 4.72.
48 *Cf. supra,* para. 4.49.
49 *Bradley* (1979) 70 Cr.App.R. 200.
50 *Wood* [1987] 1 W.L.R. 779.
51 *Fowler* (1987) 86 Cr.App.R. 219.

"stolen" (which includes being obtained by deception or blackmail)[52] not earlier than twelve months before the occasion in respect of which he is charged. It is not sufficient that his dealing with the other goods took place within that period if the theft of those goods did not. But the twelve months are reckoned from the date of the alleged offence, *e.g.* not the date when the goods were found in the defendant's possession but the date when he received them. It is immaterial whether the dealings relied upon took place before or after the date of the offence charged; indeed it is immaterial that the goods dealt with were not even stolen until after that date, because the theft will still have taken place "not earlier than twelve months before" it.[53]

4.67 Some illustrations may be of assistance. Let us assume in each case that the defendant is charged with receiving, in January 1989, a car which was stolen in October 1988.

(1) In March 1988 he was found in possession of a van which had been stolen in February. His possession of the van is admissible evidence on the charge of receiving the car.

(2) The van was not stolen until April 1989 and the defendant received it in May. His possession of the van in May is admissible on the charge of receiving the car in January.

(3) The van was stolen in December 1987 but was not received by the defendant until September 1988. His possession of it is inadmissible, because the *theft* of the van took place more than twelve months before the alleged *receiving* of the car: it is immaterial that the car was *stolen* less than twelve months after the van was, and it is immaterial that the defendant did not *receive* the van until less than twelve months before receiving the car. If it were not clear exactly when he received the car, the prosecution might attempt to date the receiving as early as possible (*e.g.* November 1988) so as to bring the theft of the van within the critical period; but if the defendant denied having received the car within twelve months of the theft of the van, the prosecution would have to prove that he had.

(4) In each of cases (1) to (3) above the defendant is charged with receiving the van as well as the car. His possession of the van is still admissible on the charge relating to the car in cases (1) and (2) and is still inadmissible in case (3). But in all three cases his possession of the car is admissible on the charge relating to the van.

4.68 *Previous convictions.* Subject to the requirement of seven days' notice in writing, section 27(3)(*b*) allows the prosecution to adduce

52 s. 24(4); *supra,* para. 4.04.
53 *Davis* [1972] Crim.L.R. 431.

evidence that within the five years preceding the date of the alleged offence
the defendant was convicted of theft (which here too appears to include
obtaining property by deception or blackmail)[54] or handling. Paragraph
(*b*) is somewhat unfortunately worded in that it envisages the proof of a
previous conviction for the purpose of proving guilty knowledge on the
occasion charged, without indicating how the former might be relevant
to the latter. The mere fact of being convicted of an offence of dishonesty
is hardly likely to improve a person's capacity for detecting whether goods
are stolen. Presumably the intention is that the conviction should be
treated as evidence that the defendant did in fact commit the offence of
which he was convicted, which (as under paragraph (*a*), but more
compellingly in that it shows dishonesty on the previous occasion) may
in turn tend to suggest guilty knowledge on the occasion charged. In that
case the paragraph must be read as rendering admissible not only the fact
of the conviction itself but also the fact of the defendant's guilt; and it
must also be read as creating an exception to the common law rule that
a criminal conviction is not evidence of the defendant's guilt for the
purpose of subsequent proceedings.[55] This latter rule has since been
modified by section 74(3) of the Police and Criminal Evidence Act 1984,
but only where the evidence of the commission of the offence is relevant
to a matter in issue in subsequent proceedings "for a reason other than a
tendency to show in the accused a disposition to commit the kind of
offence with which he is charged". Section 27(3)(*b*) of the Theft Act
appears to permit proof of a previous offence for no purpose other than
a tendency to show a disposition to commit offences of dishonesty; and
in that case it must be read as permitting (but not requiring) the fact of
guilt to be inferred from the fact of conviction, independently of the 1984
Act.

4.69   The proof of a previous conviction for an offence of dishonesty,
while more cogent than the proof of dealings which may or may not have
been innocent, is by the same token potentially more prejudicial. If,
therefore, it is likely to be of no more than minimal assistance to the jury
in determining the only issue on which it is admissible (*viz.* that of guilty
knowledge or belief), the judge should exercise his discretion to exclude
it.[56] Moreover it was said in *Fowler*[57] that paragraph (*b*) must be construed
literally and favourably towards the defendant: it allows the prosecution
to relate the fact that he was convicted of handling stolen goods, and

---

54   s. 24(4); *supra,* para. 4.04. The precursor of s. 27(3)(*b*), s. 43(1)(*b*) of the Larceny Act
1916, permitted evidence of a conviction of any offence involving fraud or dishonesty.
55   *Hollington v. F. Hewthorn & Co. Ltd* [1943] K.B. 587.
56   *Herron* [1967] 1 Q.B. 107; *Perry* [1984] Crim.L.R. 680.
57   (1987) 86 Cr.App.R. 219.

where and when, but no more. They may not introduce details of the circumstances, or even the description of the goods as set out in the particulars of offence in the relevant indictment, unless of course the similarity is so striking as to render the commission of the other offence admissible at common law. But if the jury are allowed to know nothing of the background to the earlier conviction they can only assume, from the bare fact of the conviction, that the defendant must have been guilty—which even section 74(3) of the Police and Criminal Evidence Act does not require them to do if there is evidence that he may not have been. Perhaps, then, the *defence* are entitled to adduce evidence of the circumstances of the offence relied upon by the prosecution, with a view to showing either that the defendant was wrongly convicted on the earlier occasion or that the circumstances were so dissimilar to those of the offence now charged that no adverse inferences can fairly be drawn.

Dishonesty

4.70 Dishonesty *vis-à-vis* the owner of the goods is not essential, though its presence or absence may be an important factor.[58] Handling (unlike theft, it is submitted)[59] need not involve an infringement of the owner's rights, because it is in the nature of an offence against the public interest: the availability of willing handlers encourages theft. The definition of dishonesty laid down in *Ghosh*,[60] in terms of generally accepted standards of behaviour, may therefore be more appropriate here than it is in the case of theft. But, as in that case, there is no need to give the full *Ghosh* direction if the defendant has failed to raise the issue of whether he knew that anyone else would regard his conduct as dishonest.[61] And there is no need to direct the jury on the need for dishonesty at all if the only issue is whether he knew or believed that the goods were stolen. If he claims that he did not and the jury conclude that he did, a finding of dishonesty is inevitable.[62]

Handling and theft

4.71 A source of some difficulty is the relationship between the offences of handling and theft. There are two distinct issues. The first is the degree of overlap between the two offences; the second the practical problem of determining whether a particular defendant is a thief or a handler. The two issues are however related in that the answer to the first yields a convenient solution to the second.

---

58 *Roberts* (1985) 84 Cr.App.R. 117.
59 *Cf. supra*, paras 1.68 ff, 1.154 ff.
60 [1982] Q.B. 1053; *supra*, para. 1.141.
61 *Roberts* (1985) 84 Cr.App.R. 117.
62 *Page* 14 May 1984, Criminal Appeal Office transcript no. 6030/B/83.

Overlap

The thief as handler

4.72 The problem of the overlap between the two offences can be approached by asking first whether a person who is clearly guilty of theft can also be charged with handling, and secondly *vice versa*. The answer to the first question is that a thief can sometimes be guilty of handling the goods which he steals, but that the possibility is largely theoretical. The theft itself is not handling for the obvious reason that the goods are not stolen goods until they have been stolen. Even if there is a dishonest appropriation before the thief takes the goods into his possession, so that he receives goods which have already been stolen, he will be guilty of handling only if he receives them "otherwise than in the course of the stealing". If a pickpocket takes a wallet and immediately passes it to an accomplice to avoid detection, the accomplice is receiving stolen goods; but he is receiving them in the course of the stealing, and is therefore not a handler but only a thief. In one sense the wallet has already been stolen, because by taking it the pickpocket committed the full offence of theft; but in another sense it is still being stolen, because the stealing is not an isolated act but a co-ordinated operation. Goods cannot be handled until, in this latter sense, the stealing is over.

4.73 Unfortunately the Act offers no guidance as to how long the stealing lasts. If the accomplice passes the wallet on to a third member of the gang after putting a safe distance between himself and the victim, is this too a receiving in the course of the stealing? The problem is similar to that raised by the requirement in the definition of robbery that the defendant use or threaten force "immediately before or at the time of" stealing.[63] That expression has been broadly construed: a thief who uses force in order to make his getaway does so "at the time of" stealing.[64] In the context of handling, however, where it is of course the defence who must contend that the stealing was still going on at the material time, the process of stealing appears to be somewhat briefer. In *Pitham and Hehl* [65] a man had taken the appellants to another man's house and proceeded to "sell" them the furniture—which they knew he had no right to do. It was held that he had stolen the furniture and they had handled it. Once he had offered it to them the appropriation was complete,[66] and from that point on "there was no question of these two appellants taking part . . . in dealing with the goods 'in the course of the stealing' ".[67] An objection to this view is that it would render those words redundant, because any

---

63 *Supra*, paras. 1.175 ff.
64 *Hale* (1978) 68 Cr.App.R. 415.
65 (1977) 65 Cr.App.R. 45.
66 On this point the decision is criticised *supra*, para. 1.70.
67 At p. 49.

dealing with goods which have already been stolen would by definition be "otherwise than in the course of the stealing". Moreover it perhaps goes further than was necessary, since (although the facts are not entirely clear) it seems that the offer may have been made on one occasion and accepted on another. Had it been accepted immediately (and assuming that it was indeed an appropriation), it is submitted with respect that the acceptance would clearly have been "in the course of the stealing" within the meaning of the Act. If it were not, it is hard to see what would be.

4.74 The removal and retention of stolen goods by the thief himself do not amount to handling because, even if they are done "otherwise than in the course of the stealing", they are not done "for the benefit of another person"; nor, for the same reason, do a disposal or realisation by the thief,[68] though he might perhaps be an accessory to a receiving from him. If he procured another person to dispose of the goods on his behalf, he might be an accessory to an offence by that person of undertaking the disposal or realisation of the goods for the benefit of another person (*sc.* the thief); indeed he might be handling the goods himself by *assisting* in their disposal or realisation by another person, if an agent can be said to have his principal's assistance in selling the principal's goods.

> "If the defendant's handling of the goods occurs only in the course of the stealing, he cannot be found guilty of handling by receiving . . . But, if he handles them later, *i.e.* after the stealing, he commits an offence under [section 22(1)]. It is, therefore, perfectly possible for a man to be guilty of stealing and receiving the same goods." [69]

But in none of the examples above would a handling charge be particularly appropriate. Thieves are not exempt from the law of handling, but where the thief has done no more than arrange for the disposal of the goods which he has stolen it is surely preferable simply to charge him with the theft. That is not to say that there may not be exceptional circumstances where the possibility of a handling charge might be useful. An example might be the case where the thief cannot be charged with the theft because it was committed outside the jurisdiction.

The handler as thief
4.75 Nearly all handlers are also guilty of theft, because the concept of an appropriation is wide enough to include nearly all the forms of handling, and in the context of handling the element of dishonesty almost inevitably involves an intention permanently to deprive. In *Stapylton v. O'Callaghan*[70] the respondent had been found in possession of another man's driving licence, but the magistrate felt unable to convict him of

68 *Bloxham* [1983] 1 A.C. 109; *supra*, para. 4.42.
69 *Dolan* (1976) 62 Cr.App.R. 36 at p. 39.
70 [1973] 2 All E.R. 782.

theft because it was possible that the licence had been stolen by a third person and that the respondent had obtain it from him. The Divisional Court remitted the case with a direction to convict:

". . . the magistrate has found that the respondent dishonestly possessed himself of the licence and intended to keep it. That seems clearly to me to be a dishonest appropriation of property belonging to another with the intention of permanently depriving the other of it. At that point one may stop, as it were, and draw a line and say the offence of theft is complete." [71]

Similarly a person who dishonestly undertakes the retention, removal, disposal or realisation of stolen goods for the benefit of another person will normally be stealing them. All these acts are appropriations of the goods. But assisting another person to do them might not be an appropriation in itself, though it would presumably make the assistant an accessory to a theft by the other person if that person did them dishonestly. And merely arranging to do one of these things could hardly be an appropriation in even the broadest sense of the word.

4.76 Probably the most important case of a handler who may not be guilty of theft, however, is the one who handles goods obtained by deception or blackmail rather than theft. A person obtaining goods in either of these ways may well acquire a good title to them, albeit a voidable one (and in the case of blackmail perhaps not even that).[72] Goods in the possession of a person with a voidable title to them probably belong to no-one but him.[73] Receiving the goods, or doing anything else with them, with that person's consent cannot therefore be theft.

Alternative verdicts
4.77 Under section 6(3) of the Criminal Law Act 1967, as interpreted by the House of Lords in *Wilson*,[74] a person tried on indictment for one offence may be convicted of another if the allegation of the former offence "includes" an allegation of the latter, albeit only in the sense that the commission of the latter is one way of committing the former. But it is unlikely that a conviction of handling is possible on a count of theft. In *Woods*[75] the Court of Appeal had no hesitation in finding that an allegation of larceny did not include, either expressly or by implication, one of receiving. The court was reinforced in its view by the provisions of section 22(1) of the recently-enacted Theft Act, in which the words "otherwise than in the course of the stealing" were regarded as particularly significant. If the court thought this meant that the new

71 At p. 784.
72 *Supra*, para. 3.23.
73 *Supra*, para. 1.58.
74 [1984] A.C. 242.
75 [1969] 1 Q.B. 447.

offence of handling would not also amount to theft, it was mistaken.[76] Handling can and usually does constitute theft, and in a sense is therefore one way of committing theft. But it is quite distinct from the typical case of theft, and it is submitted that an allegation of theft cannot fairly be regarded as including one of handling. Even if it can, a conviction of handling would be consistent with an acquittal of theft only if the handling proved were of the comparatively unusual type which does not amount to theft as well.

4.78   The words "otherwise than in the course of the stealing", relied upon in *Woods* as confirming that theft does not include handling, in a sense establish the converse. But for those words, theft would be a way of committing handling; because of them, it is not. A person charged only with handling cannot therefore be convicted of theft.

Thief or receiver?

4.79   A difficult problem can arise where the defendant is found in possession of goods which have recently been stolen. The difficulty arises from the orthodox view that such possession may prove him guilty of either theft or handling,[77] but will generally be inconclusive as to which. The indictment can of course include counts of both offences in the alternative; but in order to secure a conviction of either offence the prosecution must prove the defendant guilty of that one, not just that he must be guilty of one or the other.[78] Sometimes the circumstances will not be entirely equivocal. In *Langmead*[79] Pollock C.B. said that if the whole of the case against the defendant were his possession of the stolen goods, it would point to his being the thief rather than a receiver. This might no doubt be so if the interval between the theft of the goods and their discovery in the defendant's possession were so short that there was scarcely time for them to change hands. If the interval is somewhat longer, it may still be more likely that the defendant stole them himself, or conversely the circumstances may suggest that he is more likely to be a receiver; but proof on the balance of probabilities is not enough, even if the less likely alternative would itself amount to another offence.[80] The difficulty is that the two possibilities are mutually exclusive—*i.e.* they are not just *treated* as alternatives (in the sense that the prosecution do not ask for a conviction on both) but actually represent alternative views of the facts, both of which cannot be correct. The prosecution cannot therefore prove one without disproving the other.

---

76   *Supra*, para. 4.75.
77   *Supra*, para. 4.60.
78   *Attorney-General of Hong Kong v. Yip Kai Foon* [1988] A.C. 642.
79   (1864) Le. & Ca. 427 at p. 439.
80   *Attorney-General of Hong Kong v. Yip Kai Foon* [1988] A.C. 642.

4.80 In *Plain*[81] it was recognised that the prosecution evidence would seldom rule out either possibility.

> ". . . it should be made perfectly clear that where there are alternative charges of larceny and receiving against the same man in respect of the same property, the proper course in almost every case will be to allow both charges to proceed and be decided ultimately by the jury. Only in very rare cases would it be right to accede to a submission that there was no evidence on the larceny count or, on the other hand, no evidence upon the receiving count at the end of the prosecution case which justified that charge going to the jury." [82]

But there is a difficulty here. If the charges are true alternatives, in the sense of representing mutually inconsistent allegations, the jury cannot find the defendant guilty of one unless they are satisfied that he is innocent of the other. The House of Lords has said that there may nevertheless be a case to answer on each of two such alternatives,[83] but it is hard to see how this can really be so. The same evidence can scarcely justify the jury in finding that either of two mutually inconsistent propositions is proved beyond reasonable doubt. Yet the courts have found not one way out of the dilemma but two. One solution is theoretically defensible but somewhat artificial, the other theoretically dubious but thoroughly pragmatic. The first enables the defendant to be convicted of theft although there is no evidence that he is the thief and not a receiver; the second enables him to be convicted of handling although there is no evidence that he is a receiver and not the thief.

Theft at a time unknown

4.81 We have seen that the great majority of handlers are also guilty of theft,[84] and this certainly includes a receiver of goods which he knows to have been stolen. It follows that if the defendant is clearly guilty either of stealing the goods in the first place or of dishonestly receiving them later, he must be guilty of theft, because that offence (unlike handling) is broad enough to cover either of those acts. Thus in *Devall*[85] the appellants had been indicted on alternative counts of theft and handling, and the theft counts were left to the jury on the alternative basis of a "second appropriation"—*i.e.* a receiving. The Court of Appeal quashed the convictions on other grounds but refused to criticise this ruling, although it was thought desirable that in such a case a separate count should be laid giving particulars of the facts relied upon. The court seems to have envisaged not two but three alternative counts—one of stealing the goods in the first place, one of handling them by receiving them, and one of

81   [1967] 1 W.L.R. 565.
82   At p. 567.
83   *Bellman* [1989] 2 W.L.R. 37.
84   *Supra*, para. 4.75.
85   [1984] Crim.L.R. 428.

stealing them by receiving them. But this course would defeat the object of the exercise. The object of the course taken by the trial judge was to enable the jury to convict of *something* even if they were not sure whether the defendants were the original thieves or receivers. The Court of Appeal's suggestion would rule out this possibility, because the jury could not convict of the original stealing unless they were sure that the defendant had not stolen by receiving instead, and *vice versa*. In any event there is no reason why a count of theft should have to be precise as to the occasion or even the manner of the alleged appropriation: these would seem to be immaterial averments. If the defendant is found in possession of the goods on a day subsequent to that of the original theft, he can simply be charged with stealing them at some time between those two days.

4.82 The learned editor of *Archbold*[86] objects that the approach endorsed in *Devall* is inconsistent with the Court of Appeal's decision in *Brown (Kevin)*.[87] It was there held that where the defendant is alleged to have committed an offence by doing two or more different things, each of them in itself sufficient for the offence, he may not be convicted of it if some jurors think that he did one of those things and the rest think that he did another: subject to the rules regarding majority verdicts, the jury as a whole must be agreed on *one* thing which they are all sure that he did. There is a distinction between a tribunal of fact[88] which is collectively sure that a defendant is guilty of either one offence or another, but is not sure which, and one whose members disagree, some of them being sure that he is guilty of one offence and some that he is guilty of the other. Strictly speaking *Devall* is concerned with the former situation and *Brown* with the latter. But there is no suggestion in *Devall* that it would be wrong for the jury to convict if half its members were sure that the defendant was the original thief and half that he was a receiver. In the light of the direction there approved, the foreman of a jury thus divided could hardly be blamed for pointing out to his fellows that there is no need to waste their breath debating the point, since they have been told that in either case they can convict of theft. At first sight that would appear to be precisely the reasoning forbidden by *Brown*.

4.83 The Court of Appeal has expressed the opinion that this argument exaggerates the significance of *Brown* and that there is no inconsistency;[89]

---

86 43rd ed., paras. 18–5 f.
87 (1983) 79 Cr.App.R. 115.
88 *Brown* may be equally applicable, *mutatis mutandis*, to magistrates. Where the prosecution make two distinct allegations, can a bench of three convict if one member thinks that one allegation is proved, a second that the other is, and the third that neither is?
89 *More* [1986] Crim.L.R. 552 (*sub nom. Moore*). The House of Lords declined to decide the point on the grounds that it was irrelevant to the appeal: [1987] 1 W.L.R. 1578.

but the distinction is, with respect, not adequately explained. Professor J. C. Smith, however, has pointed out a real difference. *Brown* itself was a case where the prosecution alleged a number of different acts, each of which would amount to the offence charged. There was no need for the prosecution to prove all of them, but it alleged that all of them had in fact been done. The Court of Appeal's decision was that it was insufficient if some jurors were sure only that one of those acts had been done, while others were sure only that a different act had been done. In the *Devall* situation, on the other hand, each juror will typically be sure that the defendant is *either* the original thief *or* a receiver.

> "The jurors are all presumably satisfied that the property was stolen by someone on occasion (a) and that the defendant was soon afterwards found in possession of it. They are all satisfied as to the same primary facts. The whole jury has dismissed any innocent explanation of the incriminating circumstances the defendant may have offered and is satisfied that he acted dishonestly in the matter. It seems to follow that the jurors who are satisfied beyond reasonable doubt that he stole on occasion (a) are also satisfied that, *if they are wrong about that*, he stole on occasion (b); and *vice versa*. The whole jury is satisfied that he stole the property in question either on occasion (a) or on occasion (b)." [90]

4.84 This will nearly always be so, but it is conceivable that it might not be. Suppose the defendant has testified that he bought the goods and that he had no idea that they might be stolen. The jury is divided as to how much, if any, of this is true. One juror is sure that the defendant is telling the truth when he says he bought the goods, but that he is lying when he says he did not know they were stolen. This juror is satisfied that the defendant stole on occasion (b). But he may not be satisfied that, if he is wrong about that, the defendant must have stolen on occasion (a). He may be utterly convinced that the defendant did not obtain the goods on occasion (a) at all, but on occasion (b). If told that his analysis was wrong, he might concede that in that case the defendant must have been telling the truth and that he did not steal the goods at any stage. Another juror might be sure that the defendant did not buy the goods at all, without also being sure that if he did buy them then he must have known that they were stolen. Both jurors are sure that the defendant stole on one of the two occasions; neither is sure that if it was not the one then it must have been the other. If *Devall* can be reconciled with *Brown* only in the way suggested by Professor Smith, the jury ought in principle to be directed not to convict unless each juror is sure (a) that the defendant stole on one of the two occasions (though he need not be sure which), *and* (b) that if it was not the occasion which that juror thinks it was then it must have

90   "Satisfying the Jury", [1988] Crim.L.R. 335 at p. 343.

been the other. It cannot be sufficient if some jurors are adamant that it was not the first occasion, and the rest that it was not the second. A jury cannot properly convict if half of its members think that the other half must be wrong.

4.85 The device approved in *Devall* is in any event open to criticism on the grounds of its artificiality. In *Cash*[91] a differently constituted Court of Appeal, presided over by Lord Lane C.J., referred without enthusiasm to the possibility of inviting a jury to convict of theft even if they think that the defendant may be a handler.

> "We do not believe that this tortuous process, leading in some cases to such an artificial verdict could have been the intention of Parliament." [92]

But in *Shelton*[93] another trial judge adopted the *Devall* solution and invited the jury to convict the defendant of theft on the basis of a "second appropriation", and yet another division of the Court of Appeal upheld his ruling (except that he should have discharged the jury from giving a verdict on the alternative count of handling, instead of directing them to acquit). Indeed, the court incorporated the *Devall* solution into a set of guidelines for such cases:

> ". . . for the guidance of judges and counsel we make the following comments. First that the long-established practice of charging theft and handling as alternatives should continue whenever there is a real possibility, not a fanciful one, that at trial the evidence might support one rather than the other. Secondly, that there is a danger that juries may be confused by reference to second or later appropriations since the issue in every case is whether the defendant has in fact appropriated property belonging to another. If he has done so, it is irrelevant how he came to make the appropriation provided it was in the course of theft. Thirdly, that a jury should be told that a handler can be a thief, but he cannot be convicted of being both a thief and a handler. Fourthly, that handling is the more serious offence, carrying a heavier penalty because those who knowingly have dealings with thieves encourage stealing. Fifthly, in the unlikely event of the jury not agreeing amongst themselves whether theft or handling has been proved, they should be discharged. Finally, and perhaps most importantly, both judges and counsel when directing and addressing juries should avoid intellectual subtleties which some jurors may have difficulty in grasping: the golden rule should be 'Keep it short and simple'." [94]

4.86 It is submitted with respect that jurors are indeed likely to be confused by references to a receiving as a second appropriation, and that that is a very good reason for not inviting them to treat receiving as theft.

91 [1985] Q.B. 801.
92 At p. 806.
93 (1986) 83 Cr.App.R. 379.
94 At pp 384 f.

It is no use simply asking them whether they are sure that the defendant appropriated the property without explaining which of the acts alleged against him, if proved, would amount to an appropriation; but the explanation would be likely to confuse them. Moreover, many non-lawyers are (rightly or wrongly) confident that they know the difference between stealing and receiving without having it spelt out to them. Such people may feel not just confused but baffled at being told that the latter equals the former. Handling may be technically the more serious offence in that it carries a heavier maximum penalty, but many jurors will know that a casual (*i.e.* non-professional) receiver is likely to be treated more leniently than a thief. They may therefore feel uneasy at being asked to say that they are sure the defendant is a thief when they think he is probably only a receiver.

Possession as evidence of receiving only
4.87   The second, more pragmatic, solution to the problem involves simply assuming that the defendant is not the thief unless there is positive evidence (over and above the mere fact of recent possession) that he is. In *Griffiths*[95] the appellant had been convicted of handling a pair of stolen candlesticks. On appeal it was argued that the jury should have been directed not to convict him of handling unless they were sure that he had received the candlesticks "otherwise than in the course of the stealing", *i.e.* that he was not the thief. The argument was rejected.

> "There was no issue as to whether the receipt of the candlesticks was otherwise than in the course of the stealing. In a case in which there is, on the evidence, an issue as to whether the receipt of stolen goods was in the course of the stealing or otherwise a direction would be necessary. To give such a direction in this case, in which there was no issue to which counsel's submission could relate, would have been both confusing and wrong."[96]

This reasoning was amplified and followed in *Cash*:[97]

> "There was no issue as to whether the receipt of the stolen goods was in the course of the stealing. It was not suggested to or by any witness that the appellant was the thief or that the property came into his possession in the course of the stealing; there was no evidence that the appellant was the burglar. Furthermore, when he went into the dock, there was a presumption that he was innocent of any charge of burglary as well as of handling. There was no evidence to displace that presumption so far as burglary was concerned. The presumption was displaced by evidence so far as dishonest handling was concerned. If, therefore, there was no evidence that the appellant was the burglar or had taken part in the burglary, the jury, as a matter of logic and common sense, were entitled to find that his handling,

95   (1974) 60 Cr.App.R. 14.
96   At p. 16.
97   [1985] Q.B. 801.

which was not in dispute, was a handling otherwise than in the course of the stealing." [98]

And both *Griffiths* and *Cash* were approved and applied by the Privy Council in *Attorney-General of Hong Kong v. Yip Kai Foon*.[99]

4.88   The approach adopted in *Cash* may well be "common sense" but it is hardly "logic". Although it is an essential element of the offence of handling that the defendant's act should be done "otherwise than in the course of the stealing", the prosecution apparently need not prove that element, and the jury need not be directed on it, unless there is evidence which raises the issue. Evidence of recent possession does not raise the issue, because it is arbitrarily deemed to be evidence only of receiving and not of the original theft. Thus *Cash* implicitly rejects the dictum in *Plain*[1] to the effect that, in a recent possession case where both theft and handling are charged, there will normally be a case to answer on both: on the contrary, it now seems that there will normally be no case to answer on the theft charge.[2] The only exception recognised is the case where the defendant is found in possession so soon after the theft that the "inevitable inference" is that he is the thief, in which case it would presumably be the handling charge on which there was no case to answer. This leaves no role for the device of alternative counts except where the prosecution are not sure whether the lapse of time was so brief as to bring that exception into play. In general it may now be said that a person found in possession of recently stolen goods can be convicted on the basis that he received the goods after the original theft, but not (in the absence of further evidence to that effect) on the basis that he committed the original theft himself; and his conviction on the former basis can, on an appropriate direction, be one of either handling or theft.

Multiple handlers

Joinder of defendants
4.89   Section 27(1) of the Theft Act 1968 provides:

> "Any number of persons may be charged in one indictment, with reference to the same theft, with having at different times or at the same time handled all or any of the stolen goods, and the persons so charged may be tried together."

Thus two or more handlers may be indicted and tried together even if they have nothing in common beyond the allegation that they have all

---

98   At p. 805.
99   [1988] 2 W.L.R. 326.
  1   [1967] 1 W.L.R. 565; *supra*, para. 4.80.
  2   See also *Greaves*, The Times 11 July 1987.

handled proceeds of the same theft. This is so even if, as has been suggested,[3] rule 9 of the Indictment Rules 1971 (which permits the joinder of offences in the same indictment where those charges are founded on the same facts, or form or are part of a series of offences of the same or a similar character) has no application to the joinder of charges against different defendants.

Conviction on indictment for joint handling
4.90   Section 27(2) goes on:

> "On the trial of two or more persons indicted for jointly handling any stolen goods the jury may find any of the accused guilty if the jury are satisfied that he handled all or any of the stolen goods, whether or not he did so jointly with the other accused or any of them."

This provision would seem to have been rendered redundant by the House of Lords' decision in *D.P.P. v. Merriman*[4] that a person indicted for any joint offence may be convicted of committing it on his own.

Analogous offences
Acquisition or disposal of military stores
4.91   It is convenient to mention here two offences with an obvious affinity to that of handling stolen goods. Section 195(1) of the Army Act 1955 provides, as amended:[5]

> "Any person who, whether within or without Her Majesty's dominions, acquires any military stores or solicits or procures any person to dispose of any military stores, or acts for any person in the disposing of any military stores, shall be guilty of an offence against this section unless he proves either
> (a)   that he did not know, and could not reasonably be expected to know, that the chattels in question were military stores, or
> (b)   that those chattels had (by the transaction with which he is charged or some earlier transaction) been disposed of by order or with the consent of the Defence Council or of some person or authority who had, or whom he had reasonable cause to believe to have, power to give the order or consent, or
> (c)   that those chattels had become the property of an officer who had retired or ceased to be an officer, or of a warrant officer, non-commissioned officer or soldier who had been discharged, or of the personal representatives of a person who had died."

The offence is triable either way and is punishable on conviction on indictment with two years' imprisonment or a fine or both.[6] "Military

---

3   *Tizard* [1962] 2 Q.B. 608; *Assim* [1966] 2 Q.B. 249.
4   [1973] A.C. 584.
5   Defence (Transfer of Functions) (No. 1) Order 1964 (No. 488) Art. 2, Sch. 1.
6   s. 195(2). On summary conviction the offence carries three months' imprisonment or a fine of the prescribed sum or both: *ibid.*

stores" includes any chattel of any description belonging to Her Majesty which has been issued for use for military purposes or is held in store for the purpose of being so issued when required, and any chattel which formerly fell within that description.[7] A person "acquires" military stores if he buys them, takes them in exchange or in pawn or otherwise receives them, whether the receiving would otherwise be unlawful (*e.g.* as amounting to handling) or not;[8] and he "disposes" of them if he sells them, gives them in exchange, pledges them or otherwise hands them over, whether the handing over would otherwise be unlawful (*e.g.* as theft) or not.[9]

4.92 Similar offences are created in respect of the acquisition and disposal of air force stores and naval property, by section 195 of the Air Force Act 1955 and section 98 of the Naval Discipline Act 1957 respectively, with the substitution in the former case of "airman" for "soldier" and in the latter of "rating" for "warrant officer, non-commissioned officer or soldier".

Handling salmon

4.93 Section 32(1) of the Salmon Act 1986 provides:

". . . a person shall be guilty of an offence if, at a time when he believes or it would be reasonable for him to suspect that a relevant offence has at any time been committed in relation to any salmon,[10] he receives the salmon, or undertakes or assists in its retention, removal or disposal by or for the benefit of another person, or if he arranges to do so."

The offence is punishable on conviction on indictment with two years' imprisonment or a fine or both, and on summary conviction with three months' imprisonment or a fine of the statutory maximum or both.[11] A "relevant offence" is one which is committed by taking, killing or landing the salmon in England, Wales or Scotland,[12] or in the course of the commission of which the salmon is so taken, killed or landed.[13] It need not be an offence of unlawfully taking or destroying fish contrary to Schedule 1 of the Theft Act 1968,[14] but may be an offence under the Salmon and Freshwater Fisheries Act 1975 (*e.g.* of fishing by improper

---

7   s. 195(5).
8   s. 195(5).
9   s. 195(5).
10 "Salmon" means all migratory fish of the species *Salmo salar* and *Salmo trutta* and commonly known as salmon and sea trout respectively, or any part of any such fish: s. 40(1).
11 s. 32(5).
12 It may be an offence under Scots law: s. 32(7).
13 s. 32(2).
14 *Infra,* para. 7.88.

methods,[15] or out of season,[16] or without a licence).[17] The prosecution need not prove that a relevant offence had in fact been committed in relation to the salmon in question, but it is a defence to show that no such offence had been committed.[18] Conduct which itself constitutes a relevant offence does not amount to this offence as well.[19] It is a defence that the defendant was acting in good faith for purposes connected with the prevention or detection of crime or the investigation or treatment of disease.[20]

4.94   The parallels with the offence of handling stolen goods are obvious.[21] The ways in which the offence can be committed are virtually the same.[22] The main difference (apart from the reversal of the burden of proof on the issue of whether a relevant offence has in fact been committed) is that the defendant need not know or believe that a relevant offence has been committed in relation to the salmon: even suspicion (which is insufficient on a charge of handling) is not required here. It is sufficient if it would be *reasonable* for the defendant to suspect it. The test is purely objective. Moreover it is immaterial that the grounds for suspicion (or actual belief, if it exists) do not relate specifically to a particular offence that has been committed, nor exclusively to relevant offences.[23] All that is required is reasonable grounds for suspicion that (whatever else may have been done with it) someone, somewhere (in England, Wales or Scotland), has committed a relevant offence in relation to the salmon.

RESTITUTION ORDERS

4.95   Section 28(1) of the Theft Act 1968[24] confers upon criminal courts certain powers to order the restoration of (or restitution in respect of) goods which have been stolen. For this purpose goods are "stolen" in the

---

15   Part I of the 1975 Act.
16   ss. 19–21.
17   s. 27.
18   s. 32(3).
19   s. 32(4). *Cf.* the words "otherwise than in the course of the stealing" in Theft Act 1968 s. 22(1), *supra,* para. 4.72.
20   s. 32(4).
21   For a comparison see W. Howarth, "Handling Stolen Goods and Handling Salmon" [1987] Crim.L.R. 460.
22   There is no mention of undertaking or assisting in the *realisation* of the salmon, but even in the context of handling stolen goods it is not clear what "realisation" adds to "disposal".
23   s. 32(3).
24   As substituted by the Criminal Justice Act 1972 s. 64(1), Sch. 5.

circumstances set out in subsections (1) and (4) of section 24[25]—*i.e.* whether they are obtained in England and Wales or elsewhere (provided that the obtaining is an offence in the country where it occurs), and whether they are literally stolen or are obtained by deception contrary to section 15(1)[26] or by blackmail.[27] The court's powers are exercisable if

(a) a person is convicted of any offence with reference to the theft[28] (whether or not the stealing is the gist of his offence), or
(b) a person is convicted of any other offence but an offence with reference to the theft is taken into consideration in determining his sentence.

The court which may exercise these powers is the court by or before which that person is convicted (except that where he is committed for sentence the power to make an order passes to the Crown Court),[29] and they may be exercised whether or not the passing of sentence is in other respects deferred.[30] But they may not be exercised unless in the opinion of the court the relevant facts sufficiently appear from evidence given at the trial[31] or from the available documents,[32] together with admissions made by or on behalf of any person in connection with any proposed exercise of the powers.[33] This means that they should be invoked only where there is no substantial doubt as to the parties' respective entitlements: if there is any real dispute, the appropriate forum for resolving it is a civil court.[34] Where an order is made against the person convicted, he may appeal,

---

25 s. 28(6). For s. 24(1) and (4) see *supra*, paras 4.04 f. s. 24(2), which deems certain proceeds of stolen goods to be stolen goods (*supra*, para. 4.06), has no direct application, but it is expressly provided that a restitution order may be made in respect of such goods against the person convicted: s. 28(1)(*b*), *infra*, para. 4.98. Similarly there is no need to incorporate the rule in s. 24(3), that goods cease to be stolen goods when the person from whom they were stolen ceases to have any right to restitution in respect of the theft (*supra*, para. 4.23), because the court's powers to order restitution can be exercised only in favour of persons currently entitled to recover the goods in question.
26 *Supra*, ch. 2.
27 *Supra*, paras 3.02 ff.
28 The "theft" includes an obtaining by blackmail or deception where appropriate: ss. 24(4), 28(6). Presumably the handling of goods so obtained would be an offence "with reference to" the theft: it is not clear what else would.
29 Criminal Justice Act 1967 s. 56(5); *R. v. Blackpool JJ., ex p. Charlson and Gregory* [1972] 1 W.L.R. 1456. Unless the court directs otherwise an order is automatically suspended until the expiry of the prescribed period for the giving of notice of appeal, or until the determination of any appeal: Criminal Appeal Act 1968 s. 30(1) (applied by Theft Act 1968 s. 28(5)), Criminal Justice Act 1972 s. 6(5).
30 Criminal Law Act 1977 s. 65(4), Sch. 12.
31 *i.e.* evidence adduced before sentence is passed: *Church* (1970) 55 Cr.App.R. 65.
32 *i.e.* any written statements or admissions which were made for use, and would have been admissible, as evidence at the trial, the depositions taken at any committal proceedings and any written statements or admissions used as evidence in those proceedings: s. 28(4).
33 s. 28(4).
34 *Stamp v. United Dominions Trust (Commercial) Ltd* [1967] 1 Q.B. 418; *Ferguson* [1970] 1 W.L.R. 1246.

whether the conviction is summary[35] or on indictment;[36] where it is made against another person who has possession or control of the goods stolen, it seems that he can challenge it only if it is made by a magistrates' court, and then only by way of case stated on a point of law or jurisdiction.[37]

The goods stolen

4.96   The court may order anyone having possession or control of the goods stolen to restore them to any person entitled to recover them from him.[38] Clearly a person may be "entitled to recover" goods from another for this purpose if he has a better title to them than that other, although he might not be able to recover the goods themselves but only their value.[39] The order may be made against *anyone* with possession or control, not just the person convicted. An order against a third party might be a source of injustice if he acquired the goods innocently and for value; it is therefore provided that if such an order is made and it appears to the court that the person convicted has sold the goods to a person acting in good faith, or has borrowed money on the security of them from a person so acting, the court may order that there shall be paid to the purchaser or lender, out of any money of the person convicted which was taken out of his possession on his apprehension,[40] a sum not exceeding the amount paid for the purchase by the purchaser[41] or (as the case may be) the amount owed to the lender in respect of the loan.[42]

Other goods

4.97   Where it is impossible or inappropriate to order the restoration of the goods originally stolen, the court may award the victim (or other person now entitled to those goods) some other property in lieu. Such an order, unlike one in respect of the stolen goods themselves, may be made only against the person convicted. It may be made in respect of goods which are the *proceeds* of the stolen goods, or in respect of *money* taken out of that person's possession on his apprehension, or both (*e.g.* where the proceeds in the hands of the person convicted fall short of the full value of the goods stolen).[43]

---

35   Magistrates' Courts Act 1980 s. 108. He might also appeal by way of case stated.
36   *Parker* [1970] 1 W.L.R. 1003.
37   Magistrates' Courts Act 1980 s. 111.
38   s. 28(1)(*a*).
39   *Cf.* the (presumably synonymous) "right to restitution" as regards stolen goods, referred to in s. 24(3): *supra,* para. 4.24.
40   For this phrase see *infra,* para. 4.99.
41   *Not* the value of the goods: the purchaser may be compensated for his actual loss but not (by this route, at any rate) for any loss of bargain.
42   s. 28(3).
43   s. 28(2). The person in whose favour the orders are made may not of course recover *more* than the value of the goods stolen.

Proceeds of the goods stolen

4.98   On the application of a person entitled to recover from the person convicted any other goods directly or indirectly representing the goods stolen (as being the proceeds of any disposal or realisation of the whole or part of them or of goods so representing them),[44] the court may order those other goods to be delivered or transferred to the applicant.[45] This power may be exercised only in respect of proceeds which are currently in the hands of the person convicted[46] and which the applicant is entitled to recover from him: it does not extend to an order for the sale of goods so that the proceeds may be divided among two or more claimants.[47]

Money to the value of the goods stolen

4.99   Alternatively (or in addition) the court may order that a sum not exceeding the value of the goods stolen[48] shall be paid to any person who would be entitled to recover the goods themselves if they were in the possession of the person convicted. The money out of which such a payment may be ordered to be made need not be the proceeds of the goods stolen, but it must have been "taken out of [the] possession [of the person convicted] on his apprehension".[49] This requirement may be satisfied if the money in question is found in a place where the person apprehended has control over it (*e.g.* his home or a safe deposit box),[50] and even if it is not seized until some time *after* his apprehension,[51] but not if he still has it (or has recovered it)[52] at the time of his conviction.

---

44   *Cf.* s. 24(2): *supra*, para. 4.06.
45   s. 28(1)(*b*).
46   It may be possible to restrain him from disposing of such proceeds, *e.g.* the credit balance of a bank account, by means of an injunction under s. 37(1) of the Supreme Court Act 1981 (*Chief Constable of Kent v. V.* [1983] Q.B. 34) or a restraint or charging order under ss. 76–79 of the Criminal Justice Act 1988.
47   *Thibeault* (1982) 76 Cr.App.R. 201.
48   Where the defendant is convicted of handling only some of the goods stolen, the court should not order the payment of the value of all the goods stolen (whether or not such an order would be literally authorised by the Act) but only that of the goods which he is proved to have handled: *Parker* [1970] 1 W.L.R. 1003.
49   s. 28(1)(*c*). No application need be made: Criminal Justice Act 1972 s. 6(3).
50   *Ferguson* [1970] 1 W.L.R. 1246. In *Parker* [1970] 1 W.L.R. 1003 the question was left open whether money found in the appellant's wallet, in a garden whither he had fled from the police and where he was arrested, had been taken out of his possession.
51   *Ferguson* [1970] 1 W.L.R. 1246.
52   It may not be retained by the police solely with a view to enabling a restitution order to be made: *Malone v. Commissioner of Police of the Metropolis* [1980] Q.B. 49, approved by Donaldson and Slade JJ. (but doubted by Lord Denning M.R.) in *Chief Constable of Kent v. V.* [1983] Q.B. 34.

CHAPTER 5

Taking Without Stealing

CONVEYANCES

5.01 The taking of certain types of property without authority may constitute an offence even if it does not amount to theft, for example because there is no intention permanently to deprive the owner. The most important example of such property is what is referred to in the Theft Act 1968 as a "conveyance". Section 12(1) of that Act creates two offences, one of taking a conveyance without lawful authority and one of driving or allowing oneself to be carried in or on a conveyance taken without such authority. Until 12 October 1988 both offences were triable either way and were punishable on conviction on indictment with three years' imprisonment;[1] since that date they are summary only, punishable with six months' imprisonment or a fine not exceeding level 5 on the standard scale or both.[2] But where a person is committed for trial on another charge, the indictment may include a count of an offence under section 12(1) if that charge is founded on the same facts or evidence as a count charging an indictable offence or is part of a series of offences of the same or a similar character[3] as an indictable offence which is also charged, provided (in either case) that the facts or evidence relating to the offence under section 12(1) were disclosed in an examination or deposition taken before a justice in the presence of the defendant.[4] The Crown Court cannot then impose a greater penalty than could have been imposed on summary conviction.[5] A person indicted for theft may be convicted of an offence under section 12(1) instead,[6] but in the case of an offence committed on or after 12 October 1988 will be liable only to the same penalties as on summary conviction.[7] A charge of attempting to commit the offences will no longer be possible.[8]

---

1 s. 12(2).
2 Criminal Justice Act 1988 s. 37(1)(*a*).
3 For the interpretation of this phrase see *infra,* para. 6.56 ff.
4 Criminal Justice Act 1988 s. 40(1).
5 Criminal Justice Act 1988 s. 40(2).
6 Theft Act 1968 s. 12(4).
7 Criminal Justice Act 1988 s. 37(1)(*b*).
8 Criminal Attempts Act 1981 s.1(4).

212

Taking a conveyance without authority

5.02 Section 12(1) provides, in part:

". . . a person shall be guilty of an offence if, without having the consent of the owner or other lawful authority, he takes any conveyance for his own or another's use . . ."

Conveyances

5.03 Section 12(7)(*a*) provides that for the purposes of the section

" 'conveyance' means any conveyance constructed or adapted for the carriage of a person or persons whether by land, water or air, except that it does not include a conveyance constructed or adapted for use only under the control of a person not carried in or on it, and 'drive' shall be construed accordingly . . ."

Thus the offence is not confined to motor vehicles but extends to any device constructed for the purpose of personal transport, powered by any means or none, and even to an article not originally constructed for that purpose but adapted for it (*e.g.* a box converted into a go-kart). But it does not extend to an article which, though *capable* of being used for the carriage of a person (and perhaps actually so used by the defendant), is neither constructed nor adapted for that purpose (*e.g.* a supermarket trolley). The definition refers only to a *conveyance* constructed or adapted for that purpose, so that an article so constructed or adapted presumably is not a conveyance within the meaning of the section unless it is also a conveyance in the ordinary sense of the word; but it is hard to imagine what might fail to qualify on this ground alone. A horse is neither "constructed" for the carriage of a person (except perhaps by nature, which is not what is meant) nor "adapted" for that purpose, even if saddled.[9] The unauthorised riding of horses or other animals appears not to amount to any offence unless an intention permanently to deprive can be established.

Devices controlled by persons not carried in or on them
5.04 The definition of a conveyance is effectively subject to two exceptions. The first is that a device constructed or adapted for use only under the control of a person not carried in or on it is not a conveyance within the meaning of the section, even if it otherwise qualifies as a conveyance by virtue of being constructed or adapted for the carriage of a person. An example would be a device for the transport of a child under the control of an adult, such as a pushchair. The Criminal Law Revision Committee's explanation for this exception was that "the essence of the

9 *Neal v. Gribble* [1978] R.T.R. 409.

offence is stealing a ride" [10]—as against borrowing the wherewithal to provide someone *else* with a ride. But if the person carried has any degree of control over the conveyance, however slight, it is not constructed or adapted for use *only* under the control of the person not carried, and the exception will not apply.

Pedal cycles

5.05 Pedal cycles, though technically conveyances within the meaning of the section, are the only type of conveyance in respect of which the offences under section 12(1) cannot be committed. Section 12(5) provides, as amended:[11]

> "Subsection (1) above shall not apply in relation to pedal cycles; but, subject to subsection (6) below,[12] a person who, without having the consent of the owner or other lawful authority, takes a pedal cycle for his own or another's use, or rides a pedal cycle knowing it to have been taken without such authority, shall on summary conviction be liable to a fine of level 3 on the standard scale."

This act of legislative discrimination against cyclists, by comparison with the owners of canoes, hang-gliders and skateboards, was justified by the Criminal Law Revision Committee with the assertion that "For taking pedal cycles a penalty of three years' imprisonment seems too high".[13] On the other hand the Committee acknowledged that "using other people's bicycles without leave has become a serious nuisance in many places, involving great inconvenience and even hardship to the owners";[14] and now that the offences under section 12(1) are no longer indictable there is surely a case for repealing the exception. The unauthorised taking of a bicycle is admittedly more likely to involve an intention permanently to deprive (and therefore to constitute theft) than is the taking of a motor vehicle, which if abandoned may be traced to its owner by its registration number; but the exception applies only to pedal cycles, not to all conveyances other than motor vehicles. The Theft Act does not define the expression "pedal cycle". The Road Traffic Act 1972 defines a "cycle" as "a bicycle, tricycle, or cycle having four or more wheels, not being in any case a motor vehicle",[15] and a "motor vehicle" as "a mechanically propelled vehicle intended or adapted for use on roads";[16] but certain electrically assisted pedal cycles are deemed not to be motor vehicles[17] and may therefore qualify as pedal cycles for the purposes of the Theft Act.

10   Cmnd. 2977 para. 84.
11   Criminal Justice Act 1982 ss. 38, 46.
12   *Infra,* para. 5.18 f.
13   Cmnd. 2977, para. 84.
14   *Ibid.,* para. 83.
15   s. 196(1).
16   s. 190(1).
17   s. 193(1)(*c*); Electrically Assisted Pedal Cycles Regulations 1983, S.I. 1983 No. 1168.

Taking

5.06 The defendant must "take" the conveyance. This means that he must deliberately[18] move it from the place where it is. In *Bogacki*[19] the appellant had boarded a bus and tried without success to start the engine. The jury were directed that if he had taken possession of the bus then he had taken the bus. The Court of Appeal disagreed:

> ". . . before a man can be convicted of the completed offence under section 12(1) it must be shown that he took the vehicle, that is to say, that there was an unauthorised taking possession or control of the vehicle by him adverse to the rights of the true owner or person otherwise entitled to such possession or control, coupled with some movement, however small . . . of that vehicle following such unauthorised taking." [20]

The appellant was therefore guilty only of attempting to take the bus.[21] Similarly a person who is a passenger in or on a conveyance does not thereby "take" it,[22] though he does allow himself to be carried in or on it.[23] The requirement of a taking of control seems to add little or nothing: even if it were possible to move a conveyance without taking control of it, this would hardly satisfy the requirement next to be considered.

Taking for one's own or another's use

5.07 The defendant must not only take the conveyance but must take it "for his own or another's use". In the great majority of cases he will in fact have used it, by riding in or on it while taking it, and this is clearly enough to constitute the offence. In *Bow*[24] a poacher had found his own vehicle blocked in by that of a gamekeeper. He therefore moved the gamekeeper's vehicle out of the way by getting into it, releasing the handbrake and coasting downhill. He was held to have taken the vehicle for his own use because he had in fact used it as a conveyance by riding in it: the fact that his motive was to move the vehicle rather than himself was immaterial.

5.08 The judgment in *Bow* includes dicta to the effect that the words "takes . . . for his own . . . use" simply mean "takes and uses". This construction would accord with the Criminal Law Revision Committee's view of the offence as essentially one of "stealing a ride", but it is

---

18 Not accidentally: *Blayney v. Knight* (1975) 60 Cr.App.R. 269.
19 [1973] Q.B. 832.
20 At p. 837.
21 That was in fact what he had been charged with, but the judge apparently overlooked this.
22 *Chief Constable of Avon and Somerset Constabulary v. Jest* [1986] R.T.R. 372.
23 *Infra*, paras. 5.20 ff.
24 [1977] R.T.R. 6.

apparently too narrow. The alternative of taking the conveyance for *another's* use clearly envisages a taking by the defendant with a view to the *future* use of the conveyance by another; this suggests that a taking for one's own use can include (although it is not confined to) a taking with a view to future use by oneself. And in that case there is no requirement that the conveyance should actually *be* used at all, only that if it is not actually used it should at least be moved with a view to its being *subsequently* used. Indeed the reason why the requirement is satisfied where the defendant has in fact used the conveyance in the course of taking it may be simply that this is the best possible evidence of an intention to use it.[25] This reasoning is borne out by other cases. In *Pearce*[26] a conviction was upheld where the appellant had put a rubber dinghy on a trailer and driven off with it. He had not in fact used it as a conveyance, as he would have done if he had removed it by paddling it down river; it must therefore have been assumed that he had taken it for the purpose of using it as a conveyance later[27]—an assumption which, in the absence of any suggestion that he might have had some more esoteric purpose in mind, seems reasonable enough. Similarly in *Marchant and McCallister*[28] the appellants had pushed a car a few feet from where it was parked. Their convictions of attempting to take the car for their own use were upheld on the grounds that their intention had clearly been to use the car as a conveyance after they had moved it.

5.09 If the defendant neither rides in or on the conveyance while moving it, nor takes it for the purpose of riding in or on it later or of enabling another person to do so, the offence is not made out. In *Stokes*[29] the appellant and two friends, by way of a practical joke, had moved an acquaintance's car round the corner from where it was parked so that the owner would think it had been stolen. It was disputed whether any of the three had been inside the car while it was moved, and the significance of the point was not emphasised to the jury. The conviction was quashed. The jokers had not moved the car for the purpose of driving it later; if none of them had in fact driven it, or even ridden in it while the others pushed it, they would not have taken it for their own or another's use.[30]

---

25 S. White, "Taking the Joy out of Joy-riding" [1980] Crim.L.R. 609, argues that the requirement is purely one of *mens rea,* and defends the corollary (rejected in *MacPherson* [1973] R.T.R. 157) that the offence requires a specific intent which can be negatived by proof of intoxication.
26 [1973] Crim.L.R. 321.
27 In *Marchant and McCallister, infra,* the court stated at p. 364 that this had been Pearce's purpose. The grounds for the assertion are not clear.
28 (1984) 80 Cr.App.R. 361.
29 [1982] R.T.R. 59.
30 The point was conceded in *Dunn and Derby* [1984] Crim.L.R. 367.

Lawful authority

5.10   There are three ways in which the question of lawful authority may arise: the offence is not committed if the defendant does in fact have lawful authority for the taking, nor if he *believes* that he has it, nor if he believes that he *would* have it if the owner knew of the circumstances.

Actual authority

5.11   The defendant must take the conveyance "without having the consent of the owner or other lawful authority". The consent of a person in possession of the conveyance under a hiring or hire-purchase agreement is deemed to be that of the owner.[31] Moreover the owner's consent appears to be a defence even if he has no immediate right to possession of the conveyance: it would not seem legitimate to construe the word "owner" as if it referred to the person to whom the property "belongs" for the purposes of the offences which utilise that concept,[32] nor to add a gloss that the owner's consent is no defence unless it amounts to lawful authority. It follows that if the defendant is himself the owner he cannot commit the offence by taking the conveyance from a bailee without the latter's consent.[33] If the owner has in fact consented to the taking it cannot amount to the full offence, whether or not the defendant knows that he has; even if the defendant thinks that the owner has not consented when he has, he cannot now be guilty of an attempt.[34] The fact that the owner would have consented had he been asked is not in itself a defence,[35] although it would be a defence if the defendant knew this were the case.[36] The owner's consent is merely the chief example of lawful authority to take a conveyance: it goes without saying that any legal right to remove the conveyance without such consent, whether derived from legislation or from common law, will rule out criminal liability.

5.12   *Authority obtained by fraud.* It might be supposed that only a consent given in full knowledge of the circumstances would be a defence, but this is not so. Even a consent procured by fraud will suffice. In *Peart*[37] the appellant had obtained the loan of a van by telling its owner that he urgently needed to get to Alnwick. This was a lie: he actually wanted to get to Burnley, but knew that the owner would not let him take the van

---

31   s. 12(7)(*b*).
32   *e.g.* theft: *supra*, paras. 1.17 ff.
33   *Cf. Turner (No. 2)* [1971] 1 W.L.R. 901; *supra*, para. 1.56.
34   Criminal Attempts Act 1981 s. 1(4).
35   *Ambler* [1979] R.T.R. 217.
36   *Infra*, para. 5.19.
37   [1970] 2 Q.B. 672.

that far. It was held that the fraud did not invalidate the owner's consent to the taking. The court expressly reserved the question of whether this might be the effect of a deception as to some more fundamental matter such as the defendant's identity,[38] but inclined to the view that it would not. In *Whittaker v. Campbell*[39] the appellant had obtained the hire of a van by producing a driving licence belonging to one Dunn and giving that name as his own. On his appeal against a conviction of taking the van without consent, the Crown Court took the view that the owner of the van had consented to its being taken by Dunn and not by the appellant. The Divisional Court indicated that, had it been necessary to decide the point, it would have regarded the owner as having consented to the van's being taken by the person physically present, albeit under the mistaken impression that that person was called Dunn and held a driving licence;[40] but it was not necessary to decide it, because on neither view would there have been a taking without consent.

> ". . . it does not appear sensible to us that, in cases of fraud, the commission of the offence should depend not upon the simple question whether possession of the vehicle had been obtained by fraud, but upon the intricate question whether the effect of the fraud had been such that it precluded the existence of objective agreement to part with possession of the car, as might for example be the case where the owner was only willing to part with possession to a third party, and the accused fraudulently induced him to do so by impersonating that third party.
> We find it very difficult to accept that the commission of an offence under this subsection should depend upon the drawing of such a line which, having regard to the mischief to which this subsection is directed, appears to us to be irrelevant." [41]

5.13 The court's anxiety to preserve the criminal law from the horrors of the civil law of mistake is perhaps understandable, but the subtle distinctions of the civil law serve only to reflect the infinite variety of life. The criminal law cannot discard them without fettering its own flexibility. It now seems that these distinctions need not be drawn for the purposes of a charge under section 12(1), whether or not it would be difficult to draw them. If, for example, the defendant obtains the owner's consent by impersonating someone well known to the owner, the civil law would certainly regard the consent as being granted to that person and not to the defendant;[42] but according to *Whittaker v. Campbell* it is indeed

38 It is perhaps curious that it was thought unnecessary to decide the point: the appellant had also pretended to be the father of a young man known to the van's owner, and the owner had told the police that he would not have let the appellant take the van if he had known that this was untrue.
39 [1984] Q.B. 318.
40 This would probably be the position in civil law: *cf. Lewis v. Averay* [1972] 1 Q.B. 198.
41 At p. 329.
42 *Cf. Cundy v. Lindsay* (1878) 3 App.Cas. 459, where the person impersonated was known to the victim only by reputation; *a fortiori* if he is known personally.

granted to the defendant. The owner may consent to the conveyance's being used for one *purpose* and not for another, and its use for the latter purpose will then be a taking without his consent;[43] yet when established legal principles state that he has consented to its being taken by one *person* and not by another, the criminal law may nonetheless deem a taking by the latter to be a taking with the owner's consent. Simplicity is a virtue, but this is surely too high a price to pay. On the facts of *Whittaker v. Campbell* itself there would seem to have been an offence of obtaining services by deception;[44] but this charge would not be available if (as in *Peart*)[45] the conveyance were borrowed rather than hired, because there would then be no understanding that the benefit thereby conferred had been or would be paid for.[46]

5.14 *Authority obtained by threats.* Consistency would require that if fraud cannot nullify the owner's consent, nor can threats; but even in *Whittaker v. Campbell* the court hesitated to go that far.

> "Now it may be that, if the owner is induced by force to part with possession of his vehicle, the offence is committed, because a sensible distinction may be drawn between consent on the one hand and submission to force on the other. This is a point which, however, we do not have to decide." [47]

But threats, like deceptions, come in different varieties, and a threat of force is merely an example drawn from one end of the spectrum. If a deception as to the defendant's own identity does not invalidate the owner's consent it seems unlikely that a threat of a purely economic sanction would do so. The appropriate charge in such a case would be one of blackmail.[48] The criminal law can and must distinguish between those threats which invalidate consent and those which do not; but this makes it all the harder to see why it cannot do the same for different types of fraud. Perhaps the explanation is that in the context of fraud no rough and ready criterion presents itself, whereas it would be easy enough (if something of an over-simplification) simply to differentiate between threats of force and threats of other sanctions.

---

43 *Infra*, para. 5.15.
44 Theft Act 1978 s. 1(1); *supra*, para. 2.33.
45 [1970] 2 Q.B. 672; *supra*, para. 5.12. Peart initially paid the owner £2 for the loan of the van, but somewhat ungraciously took it back on discovering (before driving away) that the van had a defective exhaust. It is hard to understand why his failure to pay should exempt him from liability: surely it made his conduct more culpable than Whittaker's, not less?
46 Theft Act 1978 s. 1(2).
47 [1984] Q.B. 318 at p. 328. *Cf. Hogdon* [1962] Crim.L.R. 563.
48 *Supra*, paras. 3.02 ff.

5.15 *Authority exceeded.* An authority conferred upon the defendant will not assist him if it relates only to a taking other than that relied upon by the prosecution. The fact that he has the owner's consent to use the conveyance for a particular purpose does not give him *carte blanche* to use it in any way he may choose. In *Phipps and McGill*[49] one of the appellants had borrowed a car to go to Victoria Station, the owner having agreed to this on condition that the car was returned the same evening. The appellants did not return it but drove it to Hastings on the following day. The Court of Appeal rejected as "impossible" the submission that once a person has the owner's permission to use a conveyance for some limited purpose he cannot thereafter be guilty of taking it without the owner's consent, however far he may take it and however much the owner might object. That case was decided under the old law, but was followed in *McKnight v. Davies.*[50] The appellant in the latter case was a lorry-driver and was required to return his lorry to his employer's depot after completing the day's deliveries. Unfortunately he drove it into a low bridge on the way. By way of reaction to this traumatic experience he drove to a public house for a drink, gave three men a lift home, drove to another public house for another drink, parked the lorry near his own home overnight, and finally returned it to the depot early in the morning. The Divisional Court regarded *Phipps and McGill* as disposing of the argument that his initially lawful possession was a complete defence, but expressly rejected the converse view that the slightest deviation from the appointed route would suffice.

> "Not every brief, unauthorised diversion from his proper route by an employed driver in the course of his working day will necessarily involve a 'taking' of the vehicle for his own use. If, however, as in . . . *Wibberley*[51] he returns to the vehicle after he has parked it for the night and drives it off on an unauthorised errand, he is clearly guilty of the offence. Similarly, if in the course of his working day, or otherwise while his authority to use the vehicle is unexpired, he appropriates it to his own use in a manner which repudiates the rights of the true owner, and shows that he has assumed control of the vehicle for his own purposes, he can properly be regarded as having taken the vehicle within section 12."[52]

The appellant had done so, not when he set off for the first public house, but when he left it.

5.16 It has been suggested that these authorities produce anomalous

49 (1970) 54 Cr.App.R. 301.
50 [1974] R.T.R. 4.
51 [1966] 2 Q.B. 214.
52 At p. 8.

results when combined with those which decide that a consent procured by fraud is a good defence.[53]

> "It seems that the man who is honest at the outset but goes beyond the bounds of the authority given to him is liable to be convicted, but the expert confidence trickster who obtains the owner's consent to the taking by fraud cannot be convicted thereafter, whatever he does with the vehicle . . ." [54]

It is submitted with respect that this view exaggerates the scope of the immunity conferred by a consent fraudulently obtained. If the owner consents to the use made of the conveyance, it is immaterial that his consent was obtained by a deception as to the defendant's attributes or even his identity; but if the fraud relates to the *purpose* for which the conveyance is required, the effect may well be that the owner consents only to its use for the purpose which the defendant claims to intend and not to that which he does in fact intend. If the defendant then uses it as he in fact intended all along, he will be doing so without any authority at all.

5.17 This reasoning is not inconsistent with *Peart*.[55] All that that case decided was that the appellant had not taken the van without the owner's consent merely because he had told the owner that he wanted to go to Alnwick when in fact he meant to go to Burnley. It is true that he not only *intended* to drive the van to Burnley, but did in fact do so. Had it been held that even this unauthorised journey could not render him guilty of a taking without consent, the decision would indeed have been inconsistent with a rule that the offence may be committed by making an unauthorised journey instead of (or as well as) the authorised one. But it was not so held. The case had been presented on the basis that the appellant had taken the van without consent by initially taking possession of it and driving it away.

> "It is to be observed that this was the sole issue in effect left to the jury. There was no issue left to them as to whether in this particular case there could have been a fresh taking within the meaning of the Act of this particular van at some time after it was originally driven away . . . The consent which has to be considered is thus a consent at that time to taking possession of the van with licence to drive and use it." [56]

Had the appellant been convicted on the basis that he had taken the van to Burnley when he was authorised only to take it to Alnwick, the conviction would presumably have been upheld. This view has been challenged on the grounds that the appellant made only one journey and,

---

53 *Supra,* paras. 5.12 f.
54 J. Dine, *Cases and Materials on the Theft Acts* (1985) p. 104.
55 [1970] 2 Q.B. 672; *supra,* para. 5.12.
56 At p. 675.

if he did not take the van without consent when he *started* that journey, "it is difficult to see at what point a new 'taking' (without consent) could be identified".[57] This is true, but hardly conclusive. Even if the appellant's route to Burnley did not take him towards Alnwick at all, however briefly, it could still not be said that his initial departure was unauthorised; but his arrival in Burnley certainly was. Since the prosecution could prove that he had exceeded his authority *somewhere* between the two, it would have been unreasonable to expect them to pin-point exactly where.

Belief in actual authority
5.18   The offence does not require dishonesty, but a person who takes a conveyance without authority is not guilty if he thinks he does have authority. Section 12(6) provides, in part:

> "A person does not commit an offence under this section by anything done in the belief that he has lawful authority to do it . . ."

The defendant may believe that he has the owner's consent even if he knows that he has no licence or insurance.[58] There is no requirement that the belief should be a reasonable one;[59] but the less reasonable it would be, the less likely it is that the defendant really held it. The curious case of *Jaggard v. Dickinson*[60] decides that for the purposes of the corresponding provision of the Criminal Damage Act 1971 even a belief attributable to self-induced intoxication will suffice—a surprisingly lenient decision, but there is no obvious way of distinguishing that provision from this one. The question nearly arose in *Gannon*,[61] where the appellant had emerged from a party in an advanced state of intoxication and attempted to drive home in someone else's car. Afterwards he could remember nothing about the incident but suggested that he must have mistaken the car for his own, having forgotten that he had wisely left his own car at home. This explanation was not entirely implausible, since both cars were white Cortinas and he was apparently able to start the one which was not his with his own key. The jury were nevertheless directed that such a mistake would afford no defence if it were due to intoxication. On appeal the defence relied on *Jaggard v. Dickinson;* but the Court of Appeal thought it unnecessary to decide the point, because it had been up to the defendant to raise the issue of whether he had believed that he had the owner's consent (or, which comes to the same thing, that he *was* the owner). Since he could not remember what had happened, he had been unable to give any evidence which might raise the issue. It is perhaps

57   E. Griew, *The Theft Acts 1968 and 1978* (5th ed., 1986) p. 115 n. 57.
58   *Clotworthy* [1981] R.T.R. 83.
59   A dictum in *Clotworthy, supra,* implying otherwise is clearly wrong.
60   [1981] Q.B. 527; *infra,* para. 6.41.
61   [1988] R.T.R. 49.

surprising that the evidence of the similarity between the two cars was regarded as being insufficient for this purpose.

Belief that owner would consent

5.19 Section 12(6) also provides:

"A person does not commit an offence under this section by anything done in the belief . . . that he would have the owner's consent if the owner knew of his doing it and the circumstances of it."

This provision corresponds to section 2(1)(*b*) which provides that an appropriation of property in similar circumstances is not dishonest.[62] Again the belief need not be reasonable.

Driving and being carried in a conveyance taken without authority

5.20 Section 12(1) also creates a secondary offence which can be committed only in respect of a conveyance already taken without authority. It provides, in part:

". . . a person shall be guilty of an offence if, without having the consent of the owner or other lawful authority, he . . . , knowing that any conveyance has been taken without such authority, drives it or allows himself to be carried in or on it."

Driving and being carried

5.21 The defendant must either "drive" the conveyance or allow himself to be carried in or on it. There is fortunately no need to investigate the case law on the meaning of the word "drive" for the purposes of the road traffic legislation, for two reasons. Firstly, section 12(7)(*a*) provides that for the purposes of the section the word "drive" is to be construed in accordance with the definition of "conveyance" there set out. That definition begins by including all conveyances constructed or adapted for the carriage of persons by land, water or air, and then excludes conveyances constructed or adapted for use only under the control of persons not carried in or on them.[63] This seems to imply not only that a conveyance may be "driven" within the meaning of the section although it is not the sort of conveyance in respect of which that verb would normally be used (such as a boat or an aircraft) but also that it is driven if it is used for the carriage of a person under the control of that person. Indeed, since the primary offence of "taking" the conveyance need not involve taking it out of the possession of the owner but may be committed

---

62 *Supra*, para. 1.145.
63 *Supra*, paras. 5.03 f.

by any unauthorised use,[64] it would seem that a person who commits the secondary offence by driving the conveyance must necessarily be guilty of taking it as well. Driving a conveyance previously taken *with* authority can amount to a taking; it would be strange if driving one taken *without* authority could not.

5.22   The second reason for shirking a detailed discussion of the meaning of the word "drive" is that any use of a conveyance which might conceivably amount to driving it must surely involve allowing oneself to be carried in or on it, which is not in itself a taking of the conveyance[65] but is sufficient for the secondary offence. Any person who is voluntarily in or on a conveyance while it moves is allowing himself to be carried. If he discovers that the conveyance has been taken without authority when he is already being carried in or on it, he presumably commits the offence if he fails to alight from it at the earliest practicable opportunity.[66] But the conveyance must actually move while he is in or on it and after he discovers that it has been taken without authority: "allowing" oneself to be carried means being carried with one's consent, not just giving one's consent to being carried at some later stage. Boarding a vehicle for the purpose of being given a lift is not therefore sufficient.[67] Nor is embarking on a boat: to be "carried" is to be transported from one point to another, not just kept from sinking.[68]

Lawful authority

5.23   In the context of this offence the issue of lawful authority arises in two ways: firstly in respect of the original taking, and secondly in respect of the defendant's own act of driving or allowing himself to be carried.

Authority for taking
5.24   The requirement that the defendant must know that the conveyance has been taken without the consent of the owner or other lawful authority obviously implies that it must in fact have been so taken. There must therefore be admissible evidence of the taking. What the defendant may have been told by the taker or anyone else is inadmissible.[69] The fact that he thought the conveyance had been taken without authority might formerly have been enough for an attempt, but such a charge is no

---

64   *Supra*, para. 5.15.
65   *Chief Constable of Avon and Somerset Constabulary v. Jest* [1986] R.T.R. 372.
66   Cf. *Boldizsar v. Knight* [1980] Crim.L.R. 653, where the defendant pleaded guilty in these circumstances.
67   *Diggin* [1981] R.T.R. 83.
68   *Miller* [1976] Crim.L.R. 147.
69   e.g. *Francis* [1982] Crim.L.R. 694.

longer available.[70] It is obviously no defence that the taking was not just unauthorised but actually amounted to theft.[71] On the other hand it apparently need not even have been an offence under section 12(1); unless such a requirement can be implied, it would be no defence that (for example) the taker thought he had lawful authority for the taking. If the defendant knows that this was not the case, it hardly matters that the taker thought it was. Similarly it would presumably be sufficient if the defendant himself took the conveyance in the mistaken belief that he had lawful authority to do so and continued to drive it, or allowed himself to be carried in or on it, after discovering that he had no such authority.

5.25 *Knowledge that conveyance taken without authority.* The defendant must *know* that the conveyance has been taken without the consent of the owner or other lawful authority. This requirement may be compared with the requirement in the offence of handling stolen goods that the defendant must *know or believe* the goods to be stolen goods.[72] In that context it has been held that one does not *know* goods to be stolen unless one has first-hand information to that effect.[73] Perhaps, then one does not know a conveyance to have been taken without authority unless one is told so by someone who witnessed the taking, such as the taker himself, and circumstantial evidence (which, if sufficiently convincing, might justify "belief") would not suffice. *A fortiori* mere suspicion is not enough.

Authority to drive or be carried
5.26 *Actual authority.* In selecting the excerpt from section 12(1) presented above as the definition of the secondary offence[74] it has been assumed that the qualification "without having the consent of the owner or other lawful authority" applies to that offence as well as to the principal offence of taking the conveyance. The correctness of this assumption might be thought self-evident were it not for the fact that existing texts make no mention of any such requirement.[75] It is submitted that it is not only the original taking of the conveyance which must be done without the consent of the owner or other lawful authority, but also the defendant's driving of it or being carried in or on it. It would of course be highly exceptional for the point to arise, but even in highly exceptional

---

70 Criminal Attempts Act 1981 s. 1(4).
71 *Tolley v. Giddings* [1964] 2 Q.B. 354.
72 *Supra*, paras. 4.50 ff.
73 *Hall* (1985) 81 Cr.App.R. 260; *supra*, para. 4.51.
74 *Supra*, para. 5.20.
75 J. C. Smith, *The Law of Theft* (5th ed., 1984) paras. 290 ff.; E. Griew, *The Theft Acts 1968 and 1978* (5th ed., 1986) paras. 5–20 ff. *Archbold* (43rd ed., 1988) gives a model indictment at para. 20–301 which does not allege that the defendant's act was itself unauthorised. *Cf. infra*, p. 359.

cases it ought to be possible to state the facts which the prosecution must prove. Briefly, the reasons for the interpretation here proposed are threefold. Firstly, to convict a person of the offence when his use of the conveyance is in fact authorised would be absurd. This could only occur if he did not realise that his use was authorised, because if he did he would have the defence conferred by section 12(6), *viz.* that he believed (rightly) that he had lawful authority to do what he did. But section 12(6) is itself a second reason for supposing that the requirement applies. It can hardly be a defence that the defendant *thought* his actions were authorised but not that (albeit unbeknown to him) they actually were. The third reason is that the wording of section 12(1) is quite unambiguous. In full, it reads:

"Subject to subsections (5) and (6) below, a person shall be guilty of an offence if, without having the consent of the owner or other lawful authority, he takes any conveyance for his own or another's use or, knowing that any conveyance has been taken without such authority, drives it or allows himself to be carried in or on it."

The subject of the verbs "drives" and "allows" is the word "he" in the phrase "he takes any conveyance"; and *that* phrase is indisputably qualified by the words "without having the consent of the owner or other lawful authority". Therefore those words must also qualify the phrase "he . . . drives it . . .". It would have been otherwise if the subsection had read ". . . or if, knowing that any conveyance has been taken without such authority, he drives it . . ."; but it does not.

5.27   *Belief in actual authority or that owner would consent.* Section 12(6) applies to all of the offences created by section 12. It is therefore a defence to a charge of the secondary offence that, at the time when he drove the conveyance or allowed himself to be carried in or on it, the defendant believed that he had lawful authority to do so or that he would have had the owner's consent if the owner had known of his doing so and of the circumstances. It may be necessary for the bench to consider this defence as well as the issue of whether the defendant knew that the conveyance had been taken without authority.[76]

Possession of firearm

5.28   Under section 17(2) of the Firearms Act 1968, an offence punishable with life imprisonment[77] is committed by a person who commits an

76 *Briggs* [1987] Crim.L.R. 708.
77 Criminal Justice Act 1988 s. 44(3). For offences committed before s. 44 came into force on 29 September 1988 (by virtue of s. 171(6)) the maximum remains at 14 years: s. 44(4).

offence under section 12(1) of the Theft Act 1968 and at that time, or at the time of being arrested for that offence, has in his possession a firearm or imitation firearm, unless he shows that he had it in his possession for a lawful object. This offence is discussed elsewhere.[78]

Intent to take a conveyance

Going equipped

5.29 The offence of going equipped to steal, discussed in connection with theft,[79] applies also to a person who (when not at his place of abode) has with him any article for use in the course of or in connection with an offence under section 12(1).[80]

Vehicle interference

5.30 A person commits the summary offence of vehicle interference, also discussed in connection with theft,[81] if he interferes with a motor vehicle or trailer, or with anything carried in or on it, with the intention that an offence under section 12(1) of the Theft Act 1968 shall be committed by himself or some other person.[82] This offence is a useful alternative to a charge of attempting to steal the vehicle, particularly since the defendant is equally guilty whether he intends to take the vehicle itself or only to steal from it.[83]

ARTICLES ON PUBLIC DISPLAY

5.31 Another offence of taking property without necessarily intending permanently to deprive its owner of it is created by section 11 of the Theft Act 1968. Section 11(1) provides, in part:

> "Subject to subsections (2) and (3) below, where the public have access to a building in order to view the building or part of it, or a collection or part of a collection housed in it, any person who without lawful authority removes from the building or its grounds the whole or part of any article displayed or kept for display to the public in the building or that part of it or in its grounds shall be guilty of an offence . . ."

The offence is triable either way and is punishable on conviction on

---

78 *Supra*, para. 1.180.
79 *Supra*, paras. 1.192 ff.
80 Theft Act 1968 s. 25(5).
81 *Supra*, para. 1.196.
82 Criminal Attempts Act 1981 s. 9(1), (2)(c).
83 *Ibid.*, s. 9(2).

indictment with five years' imprisonment.[84] It apparently owes its existence to a total of three such cases which had come to the attention of the Criminal Law Revision Committee, at least one of which probably amounted to theft anyway because the person who took the article demanded a ransom for its return.[85] Whether this represented a social menace necessitating the creation of a special offence may perhaps be doubted. Moreover the definition of the offence is far from simple, and in some respects positively irrational. We must first consider what *premises* fall within the protection conferred by section 11, and then what *articles* on such premises do so.

Premises protected

Buildings and grounds

5.32 The only premises capable of being protected by the offence are buildings and the grounds of buildings. The word "building" is not defined; but it is perhaps unlikely that the public would be interested in entering a structure other than a building for the purpose of viewing it, or that anyone would house a collection in such a structure.[86] Such authority as exists on what constitutes a building for the purposes of the offence of burglary[87] is doubtless equally relevant here. But in this context, unlike that of burglary, there is no statutory extension of the term to include an inhabited vehicle or vessel: the offence is confined to buildings in the ordinary meaning of the word. The reference to the *grounds* of a building is remarkably vague. *Prima facie* it would seem to include any land adjacent to the building which is owned or occupied by the same person or persons as the building itself; but there is plenty of room for argument.

Public access to the building

5.33 Neither a building nor its grounds are protected by the section unless the public have access to the building (not just the grounds). Clearly this requirement may be satisfied even if the public are admitted to the building only on payment of a fee or subject to other conditions (*e.g.* not in parties exceeding a certain size, or, in the case of children, only when accompanied by an adult). Probably it could be satisfied even if a minority of the public (*e.g.* children under a certain age) were excluded

---

84 s. 11(4).
85 *Cf. supra*, para. 1.131.
86 But it has been pointed out that a structure without a roof is a borderline case and that the ruins of a building are arguably not themselves a building: E. J. Griew, *The Theft Acts 1968 and 1978* (5th ed.) para. 5-04.
87 *Infra*, para. 7.03.

altogether. But if access were restricted to those possessing some special qualification such as membership of an association, it might not be true to say that the *public* has access (unless, perhaps, that qualification were freely and immediately available to anyone willing to pay for it). Section 11(2) provides in part:

> "It is immaterial for purposes of subsection (1) above, that the public's access to a building is limited to a particular period or particular occasion . . ."

The building is still a building to which the public have access even if they have access to it only some of the time. But in certain circumstances the offence cannot be committed on a day when the public do not have access at all.[88]

Access in order to view

5.34 A building and its grounds are not necessarily protected even if the public do have access to the building. The public must have access "in order to view" one of the following:

    (a) the building, or
    (b) part of the building, or
    (c) a collection housed in the building, or
    (d) part of a collection housed in the building.

Neither the building nor the grounds are protected if the public have access to the building only for some purpose other than that of viewing the building or its contents (*e.g.* to have tea or to use the lavatories).

5.35 This requirement is ambiguous: to say that "the public have access in order to view" the building or its contents may mean either that that is the public's purpose in entering or that it is the occupier's purpose in letting them in. Obviously it is immaterial that some members of the public may come in for other reasons, *e.g.* to get out of the rain. But is it sufficient that the public (or some of them) come in to see the building and its contents, if that is no part of the occupier's purpose in allowing them access? A trial judge has ruled that it is not. In *Barr*[89] the defendant removed a cross and ewer from a church.[90] The vicar gave evidence that the church was open to the public purely for devotional purposes, and not to enable them to admire its architecture or the aesthetic qualities of the objects on display. The judge's ruling was that the public did not have access in order to view the church or its contents because it was the vicar's

---

88   *Infra*, para. 5.43.
89   [1978] Crim.L.R. 244.
90   He placed them next to his friend who was asleep in the churchyard. On waking to find himself in a churchyard surrounded by these articles the friend thought he must be dead.

purpose that was crucial, not the public's. It is submitted with respect that the ruling was correct. The section refers to the public *having access* in order to view, not to their *entering* in order to do so. If the vicar had granted permission for the public to enter, but no-one ever did, it could still be said that the public *had* access (though they did not use it). In other words "access" seems to mean no more than permission to enter (or the availability of permission to those complying with any necessary conditions, such as the payment of an admission fee), coupled no doubt with the provision of some means of ingress; and in that case access can exist only for the purpose for which such permission is granted. It is clearly sufficient if the viewing of the building and its contents is *one* of the purposes for which permission is granted, and to this extent an occupier hoping to be protected by the section would be well advised to keep an open mind; but it is submitted that this cannot be regarded as one of *his* purposes merely because he knows it will be the purpose of some of those who enter.

Collections
5.36   Even if the building itself is of no conceivable interest, it is sufficient if the public have access to it in order to view a collection or part of a collection housed in it. A single article obviously could not be a "collection" in itself (though it might be part of a collection, the rest of which was housed elsewhere).[91] It would be somewhat strained to describe even two or three articles as a collection, though this might depend whether they were disparate articles, or a matching set, or separate parts of a single work of art. If the article or articles on display amount neither to a collection nor to part of a collection, the section does not apply unless the public have access in order to view the building as well.

5.37   The phrase "part of a collection housed in it" does not make it clear whether it is the whole collection which must be housed in the building (though the public may have access in order to view only part of it) or merely the part which the public have access in order to view; but the latter must surely be intended. It would be remarkable if the section had no application where a collection is divided between two buildings, both open to the public, on the grounds that the collection as a whole is housed in neither. Similarly it must be sufficient if part of the collection is housed inside the building and part in the building's grounds, and the public have access to the building in order to view the part housed in the building. This interpretation is supported to some extent by the fact that the offence may consist in the removal of an article displayed in

91   *Cf. infra*, para. 5.37.

the grounds and not in the building; but this reasoning is not conclusive because there is no requirement that the article removed should itself be part of a collection at all.

5.38   *Temporary collections.* Section 11(1) provides:

> "For this purpose 'collection' includes a collection got together for a temporary purpose . . ."

But if the article removed forms part of a temporary collection, and is not on loan for exhibition with a permanent one, the offence is not committed unless the article is removed on a day when the public have access.[92]

5.39   *Collections made or exhibited for commercial purposes.* Section 11(1) continues:

> ". . . but references in this section to a collection do not apply to a collection made or exhibited for the purpose of effecting sales or other commercial dealings."

Collections made or exhibited for such purposes are not collections within the meaning of the section; therefore it does not apply if the public have access to the building solely in order to view such a collection. But it is not in itself a defence that the article *removed* is displayed for a commercial purpose, because that article need not be part of a collection at all: it need only be displayed or kept for display. Thus it would be sufficient if the public had access to the building in order to view the building itself, and the defendant removed one of a range of souvenirs displayed for sale. It would make no difference that the public had access in order to view the articles displayed for sale as well as the building, even (it would seem) if the viewing of the building were wholly secondary to the occupier's primary purpose of selling the souvenirs: provided that *one* of the objects of the public's access is to enable them to view the building, articles on display are protected by the section whether they are part of a collection or not.

5.40   A collection is not necessarily "made or exhibited for the purpose of effecting sales" merely because some or all of the articles comprised in it are available for purchase. The sale of such articles may be the purpose neither of those who have put the collection together nor of those who exhibit it, even if it is the purpose of the owners who allow their property to be exhibited. If, however, the exhibitors' purpose is partly to bring the articles exhibited to the attention of a wider audience but partly also to

---

92   s. 11(2); *infra,* para. 5.43.

sell them or arrange other commercial dealings, it would seem that the collection would not be a "collection" within the meaning of the section: a collection is excluded if it is made or exhibited for one of those purposes. It is not included merely because it has some other purpose as well.

Articles protected

5.41 Articles on protected premises are themselves protected if they are displayed or kept for display to the public either

(a) in the building to which the public have access (except that if the public have access in order to view only part of the building it is only articles displayed or kept for display in that part which are protected), or
(b) in the building's grounds.

An article is presumably "displayed" if it not only *can* be seen but is placed on view in order that it may be. But it need not actually *be* displayed at all: it is sufficient if it is *kept* for display, *e.g.* in a store-room awaiting a suitable opportunity to display it.

Removal

5.42 In order to commit the offence the defendant must remove a protected article, or part of such an article, from the building or its grounds. It is not enough that he moves it from one part of the building to another (even if the public have access to the former but not the latter), nor from one part of the grounds to another—though if his intention is to remove it from the building or the grounds altogether this may amount to an attempt. It is sufficient if he removes it from the building into the grounds,[93] or (unless, perhaps, the building can be regarded as *part* of the grounds) *vice versa*.

Day of removal

5.43 In general there is no restriction on the time at which the article must be removed; but in one case there is an exception. Section 11(2) provides, in part:

". . . where anything removed from a building or its grounds is there otherwise than as forming part of, or being on loan for exhibition with, a collection intended for permanent exhibition to the public, the person removing it does not thereby commit an offence under this section unless he removes it on a day when the public have access to the building as mentioned in subsection (1) above."

93 *Cf. Barr* [1978] Crim.L.R. 244, *supra*, para. 5.35.

Thus the article must be removed on a day when the public have access *unless* it forms part of, or is on loan for exhibition with, a collection intended for permanent exhibition to the public (in which case the day on which the article is removed is immaterial). In *Durkin*[94] the appellant had removed a painting from a municipal art gallery on a Sunday. The gallery was closed on Sundays. Therefore the offence was not committed unless the collection housed in the gallery was a collection intended for permanent exhibition. The defence argued that it was not so intended and that the restriction on the day of the removal therefore applied, because the individual pictures comprised in the collection were not permanently exhibited: each of them was periodically relegated to a store-room for some weeks or months before being put back on display. The Court of Appeal rejected the argument. A collection is "intended for permanent exhibition" if it is intended to be permanently *available* for exhibition. It is not necessary that every article in the collection should itself be, or even be intended to be, permanently exhibited. The restriction applies only where the whole collection is a temporary one, or where the article removed is not part of (or on loan for exhibition with) a collection at all.

5.44 Where the restriction does apply, the article must be removed on a day when the public not only have access to the building but have access for the purposes set out in section 11(1) (*i.e.* in order to view the building or part of it, or a collection or part of a collection housed in it). But, provided that the article is removed on such a day, there is no requirement that it be removed *at a time* when the public have access. In *Durkin* the appellant had removed the painting at 1.30 a.m. on Sunday; had he done so at 11.30 p.m. on Saturday the problem would not have arisen, because Saturday was a day on which the public had access to the gallery (albeit not at 11.30 p.m.). The words "on a day when the public have access" can hardly be read as an ellipsis for "on a day on which and at a time when the public have access".

Lawful authority

5.45 Obviously the offence is not committed if the defendant does in fact have lawful authority to remove the article in question. Moreover section 11(3) provides:

> "A person does not commit an offence under this section if he believes that he has lawful authority for the removal of the thing in question or that he would have it if the person entitled to give it knew of the removal and the circumstances of it."

It is immaterial whether he has reasonable grounds for such a belief.

94   [1973] Q.B. 786.

MAKING OFF WITHOUT PAYMENT

5.46   The Theft Act 1978 creates an offence which is not strictly an offence of *taking* property but which will often consist in a failure to pay for property already taken. Where one person obtains property from another, and has no intention of paying for it, he will probably be guilty of obtaining it by deception[95] if he knows that the other person expects him to pay; but it may be impossible to prove that at the time when he obtained the property he had already decided not to pay.[96] Alternatively he may have helped himself to the property, in which case there may at that moment have been no-one there to be deceived. He may therefore be guilty of theft; but again this may require proof that he never intended to pay. If he first takes the property innocently and then dishonestly decides to leave without paying for it, his departure will not be an appropriation of property belonging to another if by taking the property he has obtained not only possession and control of it but also title.[97] Thus a person who fills his petrol tank at a self-service garage and drives off without paying may be guilty neither of obtaining the petrol by deception nor of stealing it.[98] Of course it is not illegal merely to fail to pay one's debts. But a buyer who is not intended to receive credit in any real sense may nevertheless be allowed, for one reason or another (*e.g.* because by the time the price can be determined it will be too late to get the goods back), to obtain ownership and control of the goods before he is required to pay for them. He is however expected to pay as soon as is reasonably practicable, and in any event before he leaves the premises. In this situation a failure to pay the price is arguably almost tantamount to theft.

5.47   Section 3(1) of the 1978 Act therefore provides:

> "Subject to subsection (3) below, a person who, knowing that payment on the spot for any goods supplied or service done is required or expected from him, dishonestly makes off without having paid as required or expected and with intent to avoid payment of the amount due shall be guilty of an offence."

The offence is triable either way[99] and is punishable on conviction on indictment with two years' imprisonment.[1] Any person may arrest without warrant anyone who is, or whom he with reasonable cause suspects to be, committing or attempting to commit the offence.[2] The

---

95   Theft Act 1968 s. 15(1); *supra,* ch. 2.
96   *Cf. D.P.P. v. Ray* [1974] A.C. 370.
97   *Supra,* para. 1.18.
98   *Cf. Edwards v. Ddin* [1976] 3 All E.R. 705.
99   s. 3(1).
 1   s. 4(2)(*b*).
 2   s. 3(4).

power of arrest does not extend to someone who has finished making off,[3] but clearly the defendant may be still in the act of making off for some time after leaving the premises where he should have paid.

Goods supplied or service done

Goods supplied

5.48 The payment which the defendant intends to avoid must be due in respect either of goods which have been supplied or of a service which has been done. "Goods" includes money and every other description of property except land.[4] Goods are clearly "supplied" if possession or control of them, with or without ownership,[5] is conferred by the person to whom they belong. It is probably also sufficient if the defendant helps himself to them, as in the case of petrol: it might be said that the word "supplied" implies some positive act on the part of the supplier, but there is surely no difference in principle between putting the petrol in a customer's tank and putting it in a pump from which the customer is invited to serve himself. If this case were not covered, the section would largely have failed in its purpose. The goods need not be supplied to the defendant himself, provided it is he who undertakes to pay for them: it would be sufficient, for example, if he ordered food or drink for a companion.

Service done

5.49 It is also sufficient (though this would not be in any sense an offence against property) if a service is done, either for the defendant or for someone else at his request. "Service" is not defined, and it is arguable that a service can be "done" only by positive action and not by merely permitting the defendant or another to act. Section 1(2) provides that there may be an obtaining of services where a person is induced to confer a benefit by (*inter alia*) permitting an act to be done, but this applies only to the offence of obtaining services by deception contrary to section 1(1).[6] In any event it is possible that a service might be "obtained" without being "done".

Payment on the spot required or expected

Payment

5.50 The defendant must be required or expected to *pay* for the goods

---

3 *Cf. Drameh* [1983] Crim.L.R. 322.
4 s. 5(2); Theft Act 1968 s. 34(2)(*b*).
5 But if ownership is retained, a charge of theft may be possible.
6 *Supra*, para. 2.33.

or the service. Clearly this does not mean that the section applies only where cheques and credit cards are not acceptable: the use of a credit card is a form of payment, not a postponement of payment, because its effect is to replace the supplier's claim against the customer with a claim against the company issuing the card.[7] No doubt the same applies to payment by cheque supported by a cheque guarantee card. The position might be more doubtful if the supplier held himself out as being willing to accept cheques not so supported. It has been said that the tender of a cheque operates as conditional payment of a debt,[8] but for practical purposes the acceptance of an unsupported cheque is closer to the granting of credit than to exacting payment in any real sense. Of course it gives the supplier the right to sue on the cheque rather than on the original contract, but this is unlikely to improve his position much. Anyway the question would only arise in the unlikely event of customers being neither required nor even *expected* to use a cheque card.

On the spot

5.51 It must also be required or expected that the defendant shall pay *on the spot*. This is a remarkably loose expression to find in a penal provision. Presumably it is not to be understood literally: a person is not expected to pay "on the spot" if he is expected to come back to the same place and pay the bill next week.[9] It must be required or expected that he will pay before he leaves the place where the goods are supplied or the service done. If the goods are supplied, or the service done, in a vehicle or vessel (*e.g.* a meal in a riverboat restaurant, or a journey in a cab), it may be necessary that he be required or expected to pay before he disembarks or alights from the vehicle or vessel, or at any rate before he walks away from it; but this would probably exclude those who bilk cab-drivers, because it is common enough for a passenger to fetch the wherewithal to pay the fare from inside his house or other destination.[10]

Required or expected

5.52 At first sight section 3(1) appears to say that the defendant need not be *required* to pay on the spot or even to pay at all, provided that he is at least *expected* to do so. But his departure without paying cannot be dishonest (as the section requires), let alone dishonest to the point of criminality, if he is not legally required to pay. One is expected to tip a waiter, but failure to do so is not yet a criminal offence. Moreover a closer

---

7   *Re Charge Card Services Ltd* [1988] 3 W.L.R. 764.
8   *D. & C. Builders v. Rees* [1966] 2 Q.B. 617 at p. 628, *per* Winn L.J. *Cf. Hammond* [1982] Crim.L.R. 611.
9   But it is sufficient if he is required or expected to pay at the time of collecting goods on which work has been done or in respect of which service has been provided: s. 3(2).
10   *Cf. Drameh* [1983] Crim.L.R. 322.

reading reveals that the offence is committed only if the defendant intends to avoid payment of "the amount due", which implies that some amount must actually *be* due and not just expected. In *Troughton v. Metropolitan Police*[11] a cab-driver was taking the appellant in the general direction of the appellant's home when he stopped to obtain clearer directions. When these directions were not forthcoming (the appellant being the worse for drink) the driver took him to a police station. It was held that the appellant could not have committed the offence because he had not been taken home and was therefore not liable for the fare.

5.53 This interpretation is also supported to some extent by section 3(3), which provides:

> "Subsection (1) above shall not apply where the supply of the goods or the doing of the service is contrary to law, or where the service done is such that payment is not legally enforceable."

This appears to imply that the offence *can* be committed where goods are supplied (as distinct from a service being done) in such circumstances that, although the supply is not actually illegal, payment is nevertheless not legally enforceable. The example has been put of a minor who buys goods other than necessaries and makes off without paying for them.[12] This, it is said, would amount to the offence, although it would not be sufficient if the minor had obtained non-necessary *services*. Such a distinction would be hard to justify. Moreover the minor could not be making off with intent to avoid payment of the amount due if no amount *were* legally due.[13] An alternative possibility is that section 3(3) is not intended to differentiate between goods and services at all. On this view the object of the subsection is simply to ensure that only the evasion of legally enforceable liabilities falls within section 3(1).[14] The clearest case where payment for goods or services is not legally enforceable is that in which the very nature of the goods supplied or the services done is such as to make it illegal to supply or do them (as the case may be). Such goods and services are therefore expressly excluded. Obvious examples are prohibited drugs and organised child prostitution respectively. There are also services of a nature so contrary to public policy that, although guilty of no offence in providing them, the provider is not legally entitled to payment. An example of this category is the adult prostitute. But it is hard to think of a type of *goods* of such an intrinsically undesirable

---

11 [1987] Crim.L.R. 138.
12 J. C. Smith, *The Law of Theft* (5th ed.) para. 246.
13 The effect of the repeal of the Infants' Relief Act 1874 by the Minors' Contracts Act 1987 is that such a contract would now be void at common law: *Williams v. Moor* (1843) 11 M. & W. 256.
14 *Cf.* s. 2(2).

character that the supply of them, though not illegal, would be contrary to public policy. Perhaps the draftsman assumed that the supply of goods (unlike the doing of services) required exclusion only when contrary to law, overlooking the possibility that payment for goods (like payment for services) may be irrecoverable because of the characteristics of the person supplied with them rather than those of the goods themselves.

5.54 Similarly it is submitted that a person cannot commit the offence if he refuses to pay the bill in full or at all because the goods or the services are unsatisfactory, and that this is so not just because his conduct is not dishonest but because the amount claimed (though it may be "expected") is not legally due. It must of course be conceded that the words "required or expected", which occur twice in section 3(1), cannot be read as meaning simply "required". Clearly a person may be expected to pay on the spot although he is not required to do so. It does not follow that he need not be required to pay at all. He may be required to pay eventually, and expected (though not strictly required) to pay on the spot. Even in that case it is perhaps debatable whether he ought to be guilty of an offence, let alone an offence of dishonesty, in failing to do what he has no obligation to do; but he cannot be guilty unless he *intends* to avoid doing what he *is* obliged to do, *viz.* to pay the bill eventually.[15] Thus the alternative "or expected" does imply that the offence can be committed by a person who has not yet defaulted on his legal obligations, but not that it can be committed by a person who has no intention of ever doing so. It is submitted that the latter conclusion would be contrary not only to principle but also to the wording of the section, which requires an intent to avoid payment of the amount due.

Failure to pay as required or expected

5.55 The defendant must make off "without having paid as required or expected". If he has not tendered any form of payment or purported payment at all this requirement is obviously satisfied. Nor, presumably, has he "paid" if he has tendered something intrinsically worthless such as counterfeit money. If he has tendered an apparently valid credit card, on the other hand, or a cheque supported by an apparently valid cheque guarantee card, he has clearly "paid" because he has conferred on the supplier an unimpeachable right to payment by the issuing company or bank. It does not follow that he has paid "as required or expected". If he has no right to use the credit card or cheque card (*e.g.* because it is stolen, or because he has already exceeded his credit limit or any existing overdraft facility) he is deceiving the supplier by using it;[16] and deception

15 *Allen* [1985] A.C. 1029; *infra*, para. 5.57.
16 *Charles* [1977] A.C. 177; *Lambie* [1982] A.C. 449; *supra*, para. 2.19.

is scarcely what the supplier requires or expects. He requires (or, perhaps, expects) that if the customer exercises his option to pay by credit card or guaranteed cheque he must use a credit card or cheque card which he is entitled to use. If he tenders a cheque which he knows to be bad, because there are insufficient funds in the account and the cheque is *not* supported by a cheque card, it is doubtful whether he can be said to have "paid" at all (let alone as required or expected).[17] But these questions may in any case be academic: it is suggested below that a person who has *apparently* paid as required or expected cannot properly be described as "making off". If this is accepted then it becomes immaterial whether or not he has paid as required or expected.

Making off

5.56 Having failed to pay as required or expected, the defendant must "make off" (*sc.* from the spot where payment is required or expected).[18] It has been said that in most cases the expression "makes off" does not require elaboration;[19] but in some cases it does, because its precise scope is debatable. The doubtful case is that of the defendant who, before leaving, tenders something which purports to be payment but which is in fact valueless, such as counterfeit banknotes or a bad cheque. Whether or not these devices amount to "payment",[20] it is submitted that a person who has employed one of them does not then "make off"; he does not need to. The expression "makes off" is a graphic one which would hardly have been used in preference to a more conventional phrase such as "leaves" or "goes away" unless it carried some additional nuance of meaning; and it is submitted that the extra implication which it carries is one of guilty haste. A customer makes off without paying if he has to leave in a hurry, because the supplier knows that he has not been paid and may therefore try to prevent the customer from leaving. If the customer has deceived the supplier into thinking that he *has* been paid when in fact he has not, the customer can leave at his leisure and has no need to "make off". To make off, it is submitted, is to depart without the supplier's consent.[21] Where his consent is procured by deception, the appropriate

17 *Cf. supra*, para. 5.50.
18 *Brooks and Brooks* (1982) 76 Cr.App.R. 66, approving a ruling in *McDavitt* [1981] Crim.L.R. 843. Normally the "spot" in question will be the premises where the goods are supplied or the service done. In that case a person who has not left the premises cannot be guilty of the full offence, though he may of course be guilty of an attempt.
19 *Brooks* (1982) 76 Cr.App.R. 66.
20 *Supra*, para. 5.55.
21 See F. Bennion, [1980] Crim.L.R. 670. J. C. Smith objects at [1982] Crim.L.R. 612 that this would not catch the person who tells a cab-driver that he is going indoors to get the fare, and disappears; Bennion's reply, at [1983] Crim.L.R. 205, is that the supplier does not consent to the customer's departure merely by consenting to his fetching the means of payment.

charge is one of inducing a creditor by deception to wait for or forgo payment of an existing liability.[22] A creditor who accepts a cheque by way of conditional satisfaction is deemed to be waiting for payment.[23] That offence requires an intent to make *permanent* default; but, as we shall now see, that does not make it any narrower than the offence of making off without payment.

Intent to avoid payment

5.57 The offence requires two mental elements, in addition to that involved in the concept of dishonesty. First the defendant must know, at the time when he makes off, that payment on the spot is required or expected from him; and secondly he must intend to avoid payment of the amount due. The first of these requirements is self-explanatory: obviously there is no offence if the defendant thinks that the goods or services have been supplied *gratis*, or that someone else is responsible for the bill,[24] or that he is permitted to defer payment until later. The second requirement is more ambiguous. Does a person intend to avoid payment of the amount due if he intends to avoid payment on the spot as required or expected, but does intend to pay eventually? In *Allen (Christopher)*[25] the House of Lords held that he does not. The reasons advanced were, firstly, that the requirement of an intent to avoid payment would otherwise be redundant, because a person who knows that payment on the spot is required or expected and who dishonestly makes off without payment must necessarily intend to avoid payment for the time being at least; and secondly, that if Parliament had meant to require only an intent to avoid payment *as required or expected* (*i.e.* on the spot) it would have said so. The latter reason is of doubtful cogency, since Parliament could equally have made it clear that an intent to make *permanent* default was required (as indeed it did in section 2(1)(*b*) of the same Act, which creates the offence of inducing a creditor by deception to wait for or forgo payment); but the former seems convincing enough. The effect of the decision is that there is no purpose in charging the offence under section 3(1), and undertaking the burden of showing that the defendant "made off" and that he had not paid as required or expected, where he has tendered some form of payment or purported payment which has induced the supplier to let him go. In such a case the appropriate charge is one under section 2(1)(*b*). That offence requires an intent to make permanent default; but so, it transpires, does section 3(1).

22   Theft Act 1978 s. 2(1)(*b*).
23   s. 2(3).
24   *Cf. Brooks* (1982) 76 Cr.App.R. 66.
25   [1985] A.C. 1029.

Dishonesty

5.58 The defendant's conduct in making off with intent to avoid payment of the amount due must also be dishonest, which means that it must be conduct which ordinary people would regard as dishonest and that he must have known that they would so regard it.[26] Since the intent to avoid payment is not established if he intends to pay eventually,[27] it would be exceptional for the requirement of dishonesty to prove crucial.

POSTAL PACKETS

5.59 Section 53 of the Post Office Act 1953 provides, as amended:[28]

> "If any person unlawfully takes away or opens a mail bag[29] sent by any ship,[30] vehicle[31] or aircraft employed by or under the Post Office for the transmission of postal packets[32] under contract, or unlawfully takes a postal packet in course of transmission by post out of a mail bag so sent, he shall be guilty of [an offence] and be liable to imprisonment for a term not exceeding five years."

The offence is triable either way.[33] A postal packet is in course of transmission by post from the time of its being delivered to any post office[34] to the time of its being delivered to the addressee. For this purpose it is delivered to a post office if it is delivered to a letter carrier or other person authorised to receive postal packets of that description for the post, or to an officer of the Post Office to be dealt with in the course of his duty; and it is delivered to the addressee if it is delivered at the premises to which it is addressed or redirected (except for a post office from which it is to be collected), to any box or receptacle to which the occupier of those premises has agreed that postal packets addressed to persons at those premises may be delivered, or to the addressee's servant or agent or to some other person considered to be authorised to receive

---

26 *Ghosh* [1982] Q.B. 1053; *supra,* para. 1.141.
27 *Supra,* para. 5.57.
28 Theft Act 1968 s. 33(1), Sch. 2 Part I.
29 Including any form of container or covering in which postal packets in course of transmission by post are conveyed, whether or not it contains any such packets: s. 87(1).
30 Including any boat or vessel whatsoever: s. 87(1).
31 Including a railway vehicle: s. 87(1).
32 A postal packet is a letter, postcard, reply postcard, newspaper, printed packet, sample packet, parcel or other packet or article transmissible by post, including a telegram: s. 87(1).
33 Magistrates' Courts Act 1980 s. 17(1), Sch. 1.
34 "Post office" includes any house, building, room, vehicle or place used for the purposes of the Post Office, and any post office letter box, which in turn includes any pillar box, wall box, or other box or receptacle provided by the permission or under the authority of the Post Office for the purpose of receiving postal packets, or any class of postal packets, for transmission by or under the authority of the Post Office: s. 87(1) as amended by Post Office Act 1969 s. 76, Sch. 4.

it.[35] Evidence that an article is in the course of transmission by post, or has been accepted on behalf of the Post Office for transmission by post, is sufficient evidence that the article is a postal packet.[36] Section 27(4) of the Theft Act 1968 provides for the admission of statutory declarations as to the despatch, receipt or non-receipt of postal packets; and a statutory declaration made by any person that a vessel, vehicle or aircraft was at any time employed by or under the Post Office for the transmission of postal packets under contract is admissible as evidence of the facts stated, subject to the conditions set out in section 27(4)(*a*) and (*b*) of the Theft Act 1968.[37]

5.60 Section 55 of the Post Office Act 1953 provides, as amended:[38]

"Any person who fraudulently retains, or wilfully secretes or keeps, or detains, or who, when required by a person engaged in the business of the Post Office, neglects or refuses to deliver up—
(*a*) any postal packet which is in course of transmission by post and which ought to have been delivered to any other person; or
(*b*) any postal packet in course of transmission by post or any mail bag which has been found by him or by any other person,
shall be guilty of [an offence] and be liable to a fine and to imprisonment for a term not exceeding two years."

The offence is triable either way.[39] If a postal packet in course of transmission by post is secreted by a person engaged in the business of the Post Office,[40] he commits a separate offence under section 57 which is also triable either way but on conviction on indictment carries seven years' imprisonment. Both offences are covered by the provisions already referred to[41] in respect of the proof that an article is a postal packet, and proof of its despatch and receipt or non-receipt.

ELECTRICITY

5.61 Electricity is not property and cannot therefore be stolen;[42] but the dishonest use of it is an offence. Section 13 of the Theft Act 1968 provides:

"A person who dishonestly uses without due authority, or dishonestly causes to be wasted or diverted, any electricity shall on conviction on indictment be liable to imprisonment for a term not exceeding five years."

---

35 s. 87(2) as amended by British Telecommunications Act 1981 s. 77.
36 s. 72(1) as amended by Post Office Act 1969 s. 76, Sch. 4.
37 s. 72(3), added by Theft Act 1968 s. 33(1) and Sch. 2 Part I. For s. 27(4) see *supra*, para. 1.168.
38 Post Office Act 1969 s. 76, Sch. 4; Theft Act 1968 s. 33(1), Sch. 2 Part I para. 6.
39 Magistrates' Courts Act 1980 s. 17(1), Sch. 1.
40 Post Office Act 1969 s. 76, Sch. 4.
41 *Supra,* para. 5.59.
42 *Low v. Blease* [1975] Crim.L.R. 513.

The offence is triable either way.[43] It is capable of being applied not only to the by-passing of an electricity meter in order to avoid payment but also to the dishonest use of electrical equipment belonging to another, where the essence of the dishonesty lies in the use of the equipment rather than of the electricity. An example is the unauthorised use of computer time. Such use cannot be charged as theft of the time used (because the use of property is not itself property) nor of the computer itself (because there is no intention permanently to deprive). It may involve conspiracy to defraud, but only if two or more persons are implicated. Abstracting electricity is hardly an appropriate charge, but it is better than nothing.

43 Magistrates' Courts Act 1980 s. 17(1), Sch. 1.

CHAPTER 6

Damage

6.01 Offences of damage to property are chiefly the province of the Criminal Damage Act 1971. The causing of explosions is governed in addition by the Explosive Substances Act 1883, and there are a number of offences of damaging or endangering particular types of property.

DAMAGING PROPERTY BELONGING TO ANOTHER

6.02 Section 1(1) of the Criminal Damage Act 1971 provides:

"A person who without lawful excuse destroys or damages any property belonging to another intending to destroy or damage any such property or being reckless as to whether any such property would be destroyed or damaged shall be guilty of an offence."

Unless charged as arson,[1] the offence is punishable on conviction on indictment with ten years' imprisonment; but, although technically triable either way, in cases of comparatively minor damage it is effectively a summary offence only.[2] Proceedings for damaging property belonging to the defendant's spouse must be instituted by or with the consent of the Director of Public Prosecutions.[3]

Property

6.03 Section 10(1) provides:

"In this Act 'property' means property of a tangible nature, whether real or personal, including money . . ."

Intangible property is "property" for the purposes of the Theft Act[4] but not for those of the Criminal Damage Act. Therefore a person who "destroys" a chose in action belonging to another, *e.g.* by emptying

---

1 Which is punishable with imprisonment for life: *infra,* para. 6.63.
2 *Infra,* paras. 6.51 ff.
3 Theft Act 1968 s. 30(4). This requirement does not apply where the spouses are jointly charged or where by judicial decree or order (wherever made) they are at the time of the offence under no obligation to cohabit. The consent of a Crown Prosecutor is treated as that of the Director: Prosecution of Offences Act 1985 s. 1(7).
4 *Supra,* para. 1.12.

another's bank account, may be guilty of theft but not of criminal damage. But any form of tangible property can be the subject of the offence, including land and buildings. The only exceptions are mushrooms and other fungi growing wild on any land, and the flowers, fruit and foliage of any plant, shrub or tree which is growing wild on any land (but not the plant, shrub or tree itself);[5] the picking of these things on another person's land does not constitute theft unless done for reward or for sale or other commercial purpose,[6] and it would be anomalous if destroying or damaging them did amount to an offence. These actions could scarcely be undertaken for a commercial purpose except insofar as damage is incidental to picking, and in that case the appropriate charge (if any) is one of theft.

6.04 Similarly, wild creatures and their carcases can be the subject of criminal damage only in those circumstances where they can be stolen (*viz.* where a creature has been tamed or is ordinarily kept in captivity, or where the creature or its carcase has been reduced into possession which has not been lost or abandoned or is in the course of being reduced into possession).[7] Oddly, the restriction takes a different form: whereas the Theft Act treats wild creatures as property which can be stolen only in certain circumstances, the Criminal Damage Act does not regard wild creatures falling outside those circumstances as being property at all. The difference seems to have no practical significance.

Belonging to another

6.05 Section 10 of the Criminal Damage Act goes on:

"(2) Property shall be treated for the purposes of this Act as belonging to any person:
(*a*) having the custody or control of it;
(*b*) having in it any proprietary right or interest (not being an equitable interest arising only from an agreement to transfer or grant an interest); or
(*c*) having a charge on it.

(3) Where property is subject to a trust, the persons to whom it belongs shall be so treated as including any person having a right to enforce the trust.
(4) Property of a corporation sole shall be so treated as belonging to the corporation notwithstanding a vacancy in the corporation."

These provisions are closely modelled on those of section 5 of the Theft Act 1968, which sets out the circumstances in which property belongs to

5   s. 10(1)(*b*).
6   Theft Act 1968 s. 4(3); *supra,* para. 1.10.
7   s. 10(1)(*a*); *cf. supra,* para. 1.61.

another for the purposes of the offence of theft, and reference should be made to the discussion of those provisions.[8] There are minor differences. "Possession or control" has become "custody or control", which might conceivably exclude a person with constructive possession but neither custody nor control. It is expressly provided that property belongs to a person who has a charge on it, but it seems inconceivable that a charge might be held not to constitute a proprietary right or interest. The only difference of real substance is that there is no equivalent of section 5(3) of the Theft Act (which deems property and its proceeds to belong to a person from whom or on whose account it is received in such circumstances that the receiver is under an obligation to him to retain and deal with the property or its proceeds in a particular way)[9] or of section 5(4) (which deems them to belong to a person entitled to restoration where the property is obtained by mistake).[10] Although such cases are doubtless unlikely to arise, it is hard to see why it should be an offence to keep property in these circumstances but not to damage it.[11]

Destruction or damage

Destruction

6.06 To destroy property is to cause it to cease to exist. There may be scope for argument as to whether property is destroyed if it continues to exist in a radically different form, *e.g.* if it is rendered permanently useless,[12] but such argument would be academic since any borderline case must at least constitute damage.[13] Even if the charge alleges only destruction it is submitted that proof of damage will suffice, on the ground that the greater includes the less. In this chapter "damage" includes destruction unless the context otherwise requires.

Damage

6.07 The important question is, what sort of dealings with property amount to "damaging" it? As usual the courts have tended to treat the interpretation of this "ordinary English word" as a question of fact for the jury or the magistrates,[14] confining themselves to decisions that particular actions can or (occasionally) cannot be sufficient.

---

8 *Supra,* paras. 1.20 ff.
9 *Supra,* para. 1.30.
10 *Supra,* para. 1.40.
11 Deliberate *destruction* of the property might be charged as theft, since it necessarily involves an intention permanently to deprive.
12 *Cf. supra,* para. 1.128.
13 The measure of the "value involved" for the purpose of mode of trial proceedings depends whether the defendant is alleged to have destroyed the property or merely damaged it, but if the damage is irreparable there is no difference. Damage which can be repaired is obviously not destruction.
14 *e.g. Roe v. Kingerlee* [1986] Crim.L.R. 735.

Functional

6.08 A functional object may be damaged by an act which impairs its function, even if the difference is otherwise imperceptible. In *Cox v. Riley*[15] the plastic circuit card of a computerised saw was held to have been damaged when the appellant erased its programs so that the saw could only be used manually. Presumably the outcome would have been the same if he had erased only *some* of the programs so that the card still worked, though not so well. In either case its physical characteristics would have been altered so as to make it less useful. This reasoning has been criticised on the grounds that the circuit card was only "an empty receptacle for the receipt of programs" and that the court was treating the combination of card and programs as something more than the mere sum of its parts.[16] But if a receptacle will not work properly unless it is full, to empty it is to damage it. A person who poured the acid out of a battery could surely be charged with damaging the battery as well as stealing the acid.

6.09 It is more doubtful whether property can be said to be damaged merely because some external factor renders it temporarily unusable or less easy to use. In *Henderson v. Battley*[17] the Court of Appeal held that a cleared building site was damaged when rubbish was dumped on it, because its usefulness was impaired and work and expenditure were required to restore it to its former state. But if a car had been parked on the site and the presence of the rubbish had prevented it from being driven away, no-one would say that the car had been damaged: work and expenditure might be necessary to render it usable, but there would be no effect on the car itself. It is not simply a matter of whether or not there is physical contact between the property and the obstruction. Immobilising a car with a wheel clamp would hardly be sufficient either, because the removal of the obstruction requires neither work nor expenditure but only the use of the key. Perhaps an obstruction impeding the normal use of property constitutes damage only if it is placed *upon* the property (not just nearby) *and* requires work or expenditure for its removal.

Aesthetic

6.10 Objects with no function other than the purely aesthetic can obviously be damaged by being rendered less aesthetically pleasing; indeed, *any* unauthorised alteration will probably suffice, since the culprit can hardly be allowed to claim that his efforts have made the object more attractive than before. Objects which are primarily functional can

---

15 (1986) 83 Cr.App.R. 54.
16 M. Wasik, "Criminal Damage and the Computerised Saw" (1986) 136 N.L.J. 763.
17 Unreported, 29 November 1984; applied in *Cox v. Riley, supra.*

similarly be damaged by making them less appealing to the eye or the other senses, even if their primary functions are in no way impaired. The application of dirt or other extraneous matter may be enough, but it is a question of degree: a raincoat is not necessarily damaged by being spat on if it will be as good as new once the spit is wiped off.[18] A wall or other surface may be damaged by the addition of graffiti or other adornments, even if they are comparatively easy to remove.[19] But the *removal* of graffiti, even if done without authority, might constitute an improvement rather than damage.[20]

Intention or recklessness

6.11 A person who damages property belonging to another does not commit the offence under section 1(1) unless he *either* intends to damage property belonging to another *or* is reckless whether any such property is damaged. In general there is no pressing need to distinguish the two alternatives, because a case falling just short of intention will almost always amount to recklessness anyway. But this is not invariably true, because recklessness technically involves an element which intention does not.[21] Of rather more practical importance is the fact that an indictment will sometimes include two counts of criminal damage, one alleging intention and the other recklessness: indeed the Court of Appeal has recommended this practice, on the grounds that it simplifies the issues for the jury and assists the judge in the event of a conviction.[22] Moreover there are some offences, such as attempts, for which intention is essential and recklessness will not suffice at all.[23] We must therefore examine what is involved not only in the requirement of recklessness whether property belonging to another is damaged, which usually represents the minimum *mens rea* for the full offence, but also in that of intention.

Intention

6.12 An intention to damage property belonging to another consists of two elements: first an intention to damage *some* property, and second a degree of awareness that the property thus damaged may be property belonging to another.

Intention to damage some property
6.13 *Purpose.* There are essentially two distinct situations in which a

---

18 *A. (a juvenile)* [1978] Crim.L.R. 689.
19 *Roe v. Kingerlee* [1986] Crim.L.R. 735 (mud); *Hardman v. Chief Constable of Avon and Somerset Constabulary* [1986] Crim.L.R. 330 (soluble whitewash).
20 *Cf. Fancy* [1980] Crim.L.R. 171.
21 *viz.* the requirement that the risk taken be unjustifiable: *infra*, para. 6.36.
22 *Hardie* [1985] 1 W.L.R. 64.
23 *Infra*, paras. 6.75 ff.

person may be regarded as intending to bring about a particular consequence, such as damage to property. So much has been written in recent years about one of these situations that the other tends to be forgotten, which is unfortunate since it is by far the more common of the two. Borderline cases inevitably attract more attention than straightforward ones. It must therefore be emphasised that the paradigm of an intent to bring a consequence about is the case of a person who acts as he does for that very purpose. He thinks (or knows) that his act may have the effect of bringing that consequence about, and the possibility of its having that effect is the reason (or at any rate *a* reason) why he does it. Obviously he intends to bring about the consequence in question, and it is immaterial how likely or unlikely it may be (or he may suppose it to be) that he will succeed. If he throws a stone at a window because he wants to break it then he intends to break it, even if he knows that his aim is poor and the glass is strong and the odds are stacked against him. It might perhaps be otherwise if he knows that the desired result cannot possibly ensue unless his act is combined with other causes over which he has no control, so that,

". . . if it is achieved, [his] volition will have been no more than a minor agency collaborating with, or not thwarted by, the factors which predominately determine its occurrence." [24]

But it is hard to imagine how in the context of property damage such a situation might arise.

6.14 *Foresight of virtual certainty.* The controversial case is that in which it is not the defendant's purpose to bring the consequence about, but he knows that his actions are very likely to have that effect. In *Hyam v. D.P.P.* [25] it was held by the House of Lords that a person who knows that his actions involve a high probability of death or grievous bodily harm has the "malice aforethought" required for the offence of murder. It was never clear whether this meant that foresight of a high probability amounted to intention or that something less than intention was sufficient for murder, but the question became academic when the House effectively overruled *Hyam* in *Moloney*. [26] It was there held not only that murder does require intention, but that foreseeing a consequence as highly probable does not amount to intending it. On the other hand the House stopped short of saying that a person never intends a consequence unless it is his purpose to bring it about. He may be found to have intended it if he foresaw it as sufficiently likely; but foresight is not itself a form of intention, only evidence of it. Lord Bridge said in *Moloney*:

24 *Cunliffe v. Goodman* [1950] 2 K.B. 237 at p. 253, *per* Asquith L.J.
25 [1975] A.C. 55.
26 [1985] A.C. 905.

"In the rare cases in which it is necessary to direct a jury by reference to foresight of consequences, I do not believe it is necessary for the judge to do more than invite the jury to consider two questions. First, was death or really serious injury in a murder case (or whatever relevant consequence must be proved to have been intended in any other case) a natural consequence of the defendant's voluntary act? Secondly, did the defendant foresee that consequence as being a natural consequence of his act? The jury should then be told that if they answer yes to both questions it is a proper inference for them to draw that he intended that consequence." [27]

6.15 Unfortunately these guidelines were ambiguous in that his Lordship was using the word "natural" in a special sense which he had defined earlier in his speech:

"In the old presumption that a man intends the natural and probable consequences of his acts the important word is 'natural'. This word conveys the idea that in the ordinary course of events a certain act will lead to a certain consequence unless something unexpected supervenes to prevent it. One might almost say that, if a consequence is natural, it is really otiose to speak of it as also being probable." [28]

The absence of any such definition from the guidelines themselves was a possible source of misunderstanding, since a jury might think that a particular consequence of the defendant's acts was a "natural" consequence merely because it followed directly from those acts without any intervening cause. In *Hancock and Shankland* [29] the House accepted that in this respect the *Moloney* guidelines were misleading.

"They require a reference to probability. They also require an explanation that the greater the probability of a consequence the more likely it is that the consequence was foreseen and that if that consequence was foreseen the greater the probability is that that consequence was also intended." [30]

But the House reaffirmed that foresight is not itself a form of intention, only evidence from which intention may or may not be inferred.

6.16 In *Nedrick* [31] the Court of Appeal attempted to "crystallise" the effect of these decisions. It was suggested that, in the unusual case where it may not have been the defendant's purpose to bring about the consequence constituting the offence, the jury may first be reminded that one can intend a result without desiring it – in other words, without its being one's purpose in acting as one does. The reference to probability suggested in *Hancock* was then incorporated into the two questions

27 At p. 929.
28 *Ibid.*
29 [1986] A.C. 455.
30 At p. 473, *per* Lord Scarman, with whom the remainder of their Lordships agreed.
31 [1986] 1 W.L.R. 1025.

proposed in *Moloney*. *Nedrick* itself, like *Moloney* and *Hancock*, was a murder case, but the reasoning is equally applicable to a requirement of an intention to damage property or to bring about any other consequence. (*Moloney* made it clear that "intention" means the same in murder as it does elsewhere in the criminal law.) In *Nedrick* it was said:

> "When determining whether the defendant had the necessary intent, it may . . . be helpful for a jury to ask themselves two questions. (1) How probable was the consequence which resulted from the defendant's voluntary act? (2) Did he foresee that consequence?
>
> If he did not appreciate that [the consequence] was likely to result from his act, he cannot have intended to bring it about. If he did, but thought that the risk . . . was only slight, then it may be easy for the jury to conclude that he did not intend to bring about that result. On the other hand, if the jury are satisfied that at the material time the defendant recognised that [the consequence] would be virtually certain (barring some unforeseen intervention) to result from his voluntary act, then that is a fact from which they may find it easy to infer that he intended [it], even though he may not have had any desire to achieve that result." [32]

This passage is clearly based on the "sliding scale" idea implicit in Lord Scarman's remarks in *Hancock*: the more likely the defendant thought the consequence was, the more likely it is that he intended it. But this appears to have been little more than lip-service, because the judgment goes on:

> ". . . the jury should be directed that they are not entitled to infer the necessary intention, unless they feel sure that [the consequence] was a virtual certainty (barring some unforeseen intervention) as a result of the defendant's actions and that the defendant appreciated that such was the case." [33]

These guidelines, it must again be emphasised, apply only where it may not have been the defendant's purpose to bring about the consequence in question. But the second passage quoted appears to rule out an inference of intention where the consequence was *not* his purpose and where he may have thought the likelihood of its resulting fell somewhere short of a "virtual certainty". This would seem to leave no room for a "sliding scale".

6.17   Even where the defendant does foresee that the consequence is virtually certain to result from his act, it is a misdirection to suggest that this in itself amounts to intention: *Moloney, Hancock* and *Nedrick* all agree that such foresight is no more than evidence from which intention can be inferred.[34] How the jury are to decide whether or not to draw that inference remains obscure. Apparently there is a form of intention (other than purpose) of which foresight of virtual certainty is evidence; but

---

32   At p. 1028.
33   *Ibid.*
34   See also *Farrier*, The Independent 1 February 1988.

nowhere is it explained what this form of intention is. Presumably juries are expected to decide for themselves whether foresight of virtual certainty is what they understand by the word "intention". It is submitted with respect that it is the role of the judge to *tell* them what it means. If it is legitimate to treat foresight of virtual certainty as intention when the jury think fit, it is hard to see why it should not always be treated as intention whatever the jury may think.

Intention to damage property belonging to another

6.18 Clearly a person does not intend to damage property belonging to another if the only property he intends to damage is property which as far as he knows belongs to him alone.[35] On the other hand it is sufficient if he intends to damage *some* property which he knows to belong to another, and succeeds in damaging some *other* property belonging to that or some third person. The wording of the section ("intending to . . . damage any such property", *i.e.* any property belonging to another, not necessarily the property in fact damaged) allows for the operation of the doctrine of transferred malice. It is debatable whether a person intends to damage property belonging to another, as distinct from being reckless whether he does so, if he intends to damage property but is not sure whether it belongs to another—in other words, where he is reckless (in the traditional sense) whether it does. This is an example of a more general problem which is discussed elsewhere.[36] It is thought that this state of mind is probably sufficient, if only on the ground that it is an intention to damage property belonging to another *if* the property damaged should turn out to belong to another. Intention may be conditional without thereby ceasing to be intention.[37] It does not follow that a person has an intention to damage property belonging to another merely because he intends to damage some property and there is an obvious risk that the property may belong to another, if he is unaware of that risk—even if he is unaware of it because he has given no thought to that possibility. This would be recklessness within the meaning of the Act[38] but it is not an *intention* to damage property belonging to another, because it is impossible to intend a consequence without foreseeing it.

Recklessness

6.19 As in the case of intention, the requirement "being reckless as to whether any . . . property [belonging to another] would be . . . damaged"

35 *Cf. Smith* [1974] Q.B. 354; *infra,* para. 6.35.
36 *Infra,* para. 7.31. See also *Millard and Vernon* [1987] Crim.L.R. 393.
37 *Supra,* para. 1.117.
38 *Infra,* para. 6.35.

can be subdivided into two: it involves an element of awareness (or culpable unawareness, or sometimes even blameless unawareness) firstly of the possibility that *some* property may be damaged, and secondly of the possibility that the property thus damaged may be property which belongs to another. But it also includes a third element which has no counterpart in the concept of intention, *viz.* the lack of objective justification for the risk created.

Risk of damage to some property
6.20   Even where a person's conduct in fact creates a risk that some property may be damaged, he is not reckless as to that possibility unless the circumstances giving rise to the risk are at least reasonably apparent. If an article appears to be of solid construction, for example, it is not reckless to handle it in a manner which would not damage it if it were as solid as it appears. The traditional view is that a person is not reckless with regard to a risk of damage unless he actually appreciates that that risk exists; but the scope of the concept of recklessness has now been expanded, so that it is sufficient if the risk is an obvious one and the defendant fails to consider the possibility that any such risk may exist.

6.21   *Risk recognised.* It is long-established usage that a person is "reckless" whether his conduct results in a particular consequence, *e.g.* damage to property, if he recognises the possibility that it may do so but presses on regardless. In *Commissioner of Police of the Metropolis v. Caldwell,*[39] however, the House of Lords not only held that awareness of the risk is not essential where the risk is an obvious one[40] but also appeared to think that awareness is not even *sufficient—i.e.* that the risk must always be an obvious one, whether the defendant is aware of it or not. It is highly unlikely that this is what was meant. A possible explanation is that a risk is "obvious" for this purpose if it would be regarded as such by a reasonable person in possession of all the facts known to the defendant himself. A risk of which the defendant is actually aware is therefore by definition an obvious risk. If he happens to know that a certain article is particularly fragile, then as far as he is concerned any rough handling of it will involve an obvious risk of damage, and it is immaterial that the risk might not be obvious to anyone who did *not* know that the article was fragile. An alternative explanation is that the reasoning in *Caldwell* was concerned primarily with the defendant who does *not* recognise the risk, and that anything said about the liability of a defendant who does recognise it must be read in that context. In other words, the point may have been overlooked.

39   [1982] A.C. 341.
40   *Infra,* para. 6.23.

6.22 *Risk obvious but possibility not considered.* Traditionally, recklessness meant deliberate risk-taking: actual awareness of the risk was essential. In its extreme form this "subjective" view would exonerate even a person whose inability to foresee the consequences of his conduct is itself attributable to his own conduct, *e.g.* where he is too drunk. But in *D.P.P. v. Majewski*[41] it was held that such a person may be regarded as having acted recklessly with regard to a consequence which he would have foreseen had he been sober. On the one hand this decision was hard to reconcile with the subjective view of recklessness then prevalent; but on the other it did nothing to solve the problem of the person whose judgment is impaired by other factors, such as rage or excitement. In *Parker*,[42] frustrated at his inability to make a telephone call from a public kiosk, the appellant had slammed the handset down so hard that it broke. He denied having realised that this might happen. His appeal was dismissed on the grounds that if he had not realised the risk he must have been "deliberately closing his mind to the obvious", which was just as bad. The court's reluctance to accept the defence was understandable, but its reasoning left much to be desired: the idea of deliberately closing one's mind to a possibility of which one is *ex hypothesi* unaware would seem to be a contradiction in terms. In *Stephenson*[43] the Court of Appeal reaffirmed the subjective view, conceding only that if the defendant does appreciate the risk then it is immaterial that bad temper may have caused him to disregard it or deprived him of his self-control. If his temper prevented him from appreciating the risk at all then he was not reckless.

6.23 In *Commissioner of Police of the Metropolis v. Caldwell*[44] the House of Lords found a clearer way of avoiding this conclusion than that resorted to in *Parker*. The respondent had set fire to a hotel, and was charged with the offence of damaging property being reckless whether the life of another would be thereby endangered.[45] He claimed to have been so drunk that the possibility of there being people in the hotel whose lives might be endangered if it were set on fire was one which had not crossed his mind. The appeal might have been disposed of on the ground that according to *Majewski* a person acts recklessly with regard to a particular consequence of his actions if his failure to foresee it is due to intoxication, and that this is so whether the consequence in question is part of the definition of the offence (*e.g.* the damaging of property) or not (*e.g.* the endangering of life). Instead, the House extended the concept of reckless-

41 [1977] A.C. 443.
42 [1977] 1 W.L.R. 600.
43 [1979] Q.B. 695.
44 [1982] A.C. 341.
45 Criminal Damage Act 1971 s. 1(2); *infra,* paras. 6.66 ff.

ness (at any rate for the purposes of the Criminal Damage Act) in such a way as to render the *Majewski* rule largely redundant. This was achieved by construing the word "reckless" in accordance with what the House conceived to be its ordinary meaning.

> " 'Reckless' as used in the new statutory definition of the *mens rea* of these offences is an ordinary English word. It had not by 1971 become a term of legal art with some more limited esoteric meaning than that which it bore in ordinary speech—a meaning which surely includes not only deciding to ignore a risk of harmful consequences resulting from one's acts that one has recognised as existing, but also failing to give any thought to whether or not there is any such risk in circumstances where, if any thought were given to the matter, it would be obvious that there was." [46]

Speaking for the majority of the House, Lord Diplock went on to redefine the statutory requirement of recklessness.

> "In my opinion, a person charged with an offence under section 1(1) of the 1971 Act is 'reckless as to whether any such property would be destroyed or damaged' if (1) he does an act which in fact creates an obvious risk that property will be destroyed or damaged and (2) when he does the act he either has not given any thought to the possibility of there being any such risk or has recognised that there was some risk involved and has nonetheless gone on to do it." [47]

Thus a person damages property recklessly if the risk of damage is obvious but he is so drunk that he fails to give any thought to the possibility of such a risk. His intoxication is not directly relevant: it is his failure to think which is reckless. And it makes no difference if that failure is attributable to rage, excitement or some other factor which temporarily impairs his ability to foresee the consequences of his acts. *Parker* and *Stephenson* were overruled.

6.24 But in its anxiety to catch not only the Caldwells of this world but also the Parkers, the House expressed itself in terms wide enough to catch defendants who are comparable to neither. In the first place Lord Diplock's definition would seem to include a person who fails to consider the likely consequences of his actions because, though not drunk or angry or otherwise excited, he is too busy thinking about something else. If an absent-minded academic puts his wife's white blouse in the washing machine with a red shirt, too preoccupied with his thoughts to realise that the dye may run, he is creating an obvious risk of damage without giving any thought to the possibility of there being any risk. According to *Caldwell* he is therefore guilty of criminal damage if the blouse comes out pink. It may be doubted whether this is a sensible conclusion or whether

46   At pp. 353 f., *per* Lord Diplock.
47   At p. 354.

it was seriously intended, but Lord Diplock suggested no way of avoiding it. Indeed, once the net is widened so as to catch those whose lack of foresight is attributable not to alcohol or other drugs but simply to their mood, it is hard to see how rage or excitement can sensibly be differentiated from preoccupation with other matters. It might be said that Parker was preoccupied with his inability to make a telephone call.

6.25 It can at least be said of the absent-minded academic that if only he did stop to think about the possible consequences of his actions he would recognise the risk: if he fails to recognise it, it is only because he does *not* stop to think. Although on this occasion he has failed to make the connection, his act is the sort of act which in general he knows to involve a risk of damage. Lord Diplock thought that a person is "reckless" within the ordinary meaning of the word if he fails to give any thought to a risk which *would* be obvious (*sc.*, presumably, to him) if he *did* give any thought to the matter. But the definition finally proposed refers simply to "an act which in fact creates an obvious risk". In the light of his Lordship's reliance on what he asserted to be the word's ordinary meaning, it seems reasonable to suppose that by "an obvious risk" he meant a risk which would have been immediately recognised *by the defendant* had he stopped to think. His Lordship's reasoning does not suggest that a defendant can be reckless in creating a risk which might be obvious to someone else but is not obvious to the defendant himself, and would not be obvious to him even if he thought about it. In *Stephenson*,[48] for example, the appellant was a tramp who had intended to spend the night in a hollow in the side of a haystack and had lit a fire to keep himself warm. Any normal person would have readily appreciated that there was an obvious risk of the haystack itself catching fire, as in fact it did; but there was evidence that the appellant suffered from schizophrenia and might not have had the same ability to appreciate such risks as would a normal person.[49] In Lord Diplock's view the Court of Appeal had been wrong to hold that Stephenson was not reckless unless he was actually aware of the risk at the time of his act, and it was sufficient if he *would* have been aware of the risk had he stopped to think; but it was not suggested that he might still have been reckless even if he would *not* have recognised the risk had he stopped to think, merely because someone else in his position would certainly have done so.

6.26 But if it was Lord Diplock's intention to exclude such a case, the terms of his proposed model direction fail to make it clear; and in *Elliott*

48 [1979] Q.B. 695; *supra*, para. 6.22.
49 It does not appear to have been suggested that this amounted to a plea of insanity.

v. C. (a minor) [50] the Divisional Court held that no such qualification could be implied. The respondent, an educationally subnormal girl of 14, entered a garden shed at 5 a.m. after being out all night, poured white spirit on the floor and threw lighted matches on it, thus setting fire to the shed. The magistrates found that at the time of starting the fire she had given no thought to the possibility of there being a risk that the shed and its contents would be destroyed[51] by her actions, but that, in view of her age and understanding, her lack of experience of inflammable spirit and the fact that she must have been exhausted at the time, the risk would not have been obvious to her or appreciated by her even if she *had* given any thought to the matter. They thought it implicit in the reasoning in *Caldwell* that a person in this position was not reckless, and dismissed the information.

6.27   The Divisional Court disagreed, and held that for the purposes of the *Caldwell* test a risk may be "obvious", and a person may therefore be reckless in failing to address his mind to it, even if he would not have appreciated the risk had he given the matter any thought. The two members of the court reached this conclusion by rather different routes. Robert Goff L.J. did so with reluctance, partly on the grounds that the model direction makes no mention of any such qualification, but primarily on the basis of a passage earlier in Lord Diplock's speech which cited Professor Kenny's well-known definition of "malice", approved by the Court of Criminal Appeal in *Cunningham*:[52]

> "In any statutory definition of a crime, malice must be taken . . . as requiring either (1) an actual intention to do the particular kind of harm that in fact was done; or (2) recklessness as to whether such harm should occur or not (*i.e.*, the accused has foreseen that the particular kind of harm might be done and yet has gone on to take the risk of it)." [53]

Lord Diplock argued that the subjective meaning here attached to the word "recklessness" was of no relevance to the matter in hand.

> "My Lords, in this passage Professor Kenny was engaged in defining for the benefit of students the meaning of 'malice' as a term of art in criminal law. To do so he used ordinary English words in their popular meaning. Among the words he used was 'recklessness', the noun derived from the adjective 'reckless', of which the popular or dictionary meaning is: careless, regardless, or heedless, of the possible harmful consequences of one's acts. It presupposes that if thought were given to the matter by the doer before the act was done, it would have been apparent to him that there was a real risk

---

50   [1983] 1 W.L.R. 939.
51   There was no express finding as to whether she had considered the possibility that the shed or its contents might be *damaged*.
52   [1957] 2 Q.B. 396.
53   *Outlines of Criminal Law* (1st ed., 1902).

of its having the relevant harmful consequences; but, granted this, recklessness covers a whole range of states of mind from failing to give any thought
at all to whether or not there is any risk of those harmful consequences, to
recognising the existence of the risk and nevertheless deciding to ignore it.
Conscious of this imprecision in the popular meaning of recklessness as
descriptive of a state of mind, Professor Kenny, in the passage quoted, was,
as it seems to me, at pains to indicate by the words in brackets the particular
species within the genus reckless states of mind that constituted 'malice' in
criminal law. This parenthetical restriction on the natural meaning of
recklessness was necessary to an explanation of the meaning of the adverb
'maliciously' when used as a term of art in the description of an offence under
the Malicious Damage Act 1861 (which was the matter in point in . . .
Cunningham); but it was not directed to and consequently has no bearing on
the meaning of the adjective 'reckless' in section 1 of the Criminal Damage
Act 1971. To use it for that purpose can, in my view, only be misleading." [54]

6.28 In *Elliott v. C.* Robert Goff L.J. thought this passage fatal to the
respondent's argument.

". . . when considering . . . Professor Kenny's definition of recklessness
(which he rejected as being too narrow), Lord Diplock expressly adverted to
the fact that that definition presupposed that 'if thought were given to the
matter by the doer before the act was done, it would have been apparent *to
him*[55] that there was a real risk of its having the relevant harmful
consequences . . .'. It seems to me that, having expressly considered that
element in Professor Kenny's test, and having (as I think) plainly decided to
omit it from his own formulation of the concept of recklessness, it would not
now be legitimate for an inferior court, in a case under this particular
subsection, to impose a qualification which had so been rejected by Lord
Diplock himself." [56]

With great respect, this is a serious misrepresentation of what Lord
Diplock said. He did *not* say that *Kenny's* definition of recklessness
presupposed that, if thought were given to the matter by the doer, the
risk would have been apparent to him: on the contrary, Kenny's definition
implies that the doer *has* given thought to the matter and the risk *is*
apparent to him. What Lord Diplock said, by way of qualification to the
main thrust of his argument, was that this requirement was presupposed
by the "popular or dictionary meaning" of the word "reckless", which
(even with this qualification) was wider than Kenny's definition, and
which his Lordship proceeded to attribute to the word for the purposes
of the Criminal Damage Act. The qualification is part of the test he
accepted, not of the one he rejected. Even Glidewell J., the other member
of the court which decided *Elliott v. C.,* conceded that the passage in
question, among others in Lord Diplock's speech, suggested that he was

54 [1982] A.C. 341 at p. 351.
55 Robert Goff L.J.'s emphasis.
56 [1983] 1 W.L.R. 939 at pp. 949 f.

using the phrase "an obvious risk" to mean "a risk which was obvious to the particular defendant".[57] It is submitted with respect that this misunderstanding undermines the whole of Robert Goff L.J.'s judgment. Admittedly he went on:

> ". . . I wish to add that, for my part, I doubt whether this qualification can be justified in any event. Where there is no thought of the consequences, any further inquiry necessary for the purposes of establishing guilt should *prima facie* be directed to the question why such thought was not given, rather than to the purely hypothetical question of what the particular person would have appreciated had he directed his mind to the matter." [58]

This is a real difficulty. But in view of his Lordship's reluctance to depart from Lord Diplock's reasoning, he might have been willing to accept the qualification had he not been under the misapprehension that Lord Diplock had rejected it.

6.29   Glidewell J. reached the same conclusion *via* different reasoning. He thought that the magistrates' interpretation of *Caldwell* was inconsistent with the actual decision, *viz.* that a person is reckless if he fails to foresee the obvious consequences of his actions because he is too drunk. *Caldwell* makes no attempt to distinguish between a person who would appreciate the risk if he thought about it, but fails to think about it because he is drunk, and one who is too drunk to appreciate the risk even if he did think about it. In Glidewell J.'s opinion it followed, despite the passages in Lord Diplock's speech suggesting otherwise, that the phrase "an obvious risk" in the model direction meant a risk obvious to a reasonably prudent person, not necessarily to the defendant himself. It is submitted with respect that this does not follow. Even before *Caldwell* the courts had evolved special rules for the intoxicated defendant so as to withhold from him the defence that he did not foresee the consequences of his actions.[59] This principle might have been developed by holding that a risk is "obvious" if the defendant would have appreciated it had he stopped to think *and* had he been sober (if he was not).

6.30   But Glidewell J. found confirmation for his interpretation of *Caldwell* in Lord Diplock's speeches in two subsequent decisions. In *Lawrence*,[60] where the *Caldwell* test of recklessness was applied to the offences of reckless driving and causing death by reckless driving, his Lordship had said:

> "One does not speak of a person acting 'recklessly', even though he has given

57   At pp. 945 f.
58   At p. 950.
59   *Majewski* [1977] A.C. 443; *supra*, para. 6.22.
60   [1982] A.C. 510.

no thought at all to the consequences of his act, unless the act is one that presents a real risk of harmful consequences which anyone acting with reasonable prudence would recognise and give heed to." [61]

Later he went on:

"Recklessness on the part of the doer of an act does presuppose that there is something in the circumstances that would have drawn the attention of an ordinary prudent individual to the possibility that his act was capable of causing the kind of serious harmful consequences that the section which creates the offence was intended to prevent, and that the risk of those harmful consequences occurring was not so slight that an ordinary prudent individual would feel justified in treating them as negligible. It is only when this is so that the doer of the act is acting 'recklessly' if before doing the act, he either fails to give any thought to the possibility of there being any such risk or, having recognised that there was such risk, he nevertheless goes on to do it." [62]

And in *Miller*[63] he said:

". . . where the state of mind relied upon is 'being reckless', the risk created by the physical act of the accused that property belonging to another would be damaged must be one that would be obvious to anyone who had given his mind to it at whatever is the relevant time . . ." [64]

But the thrust of all these passages is that, even where the defendant does not consider the possibility of there being a risk, he is *not* reckless *unless* it can at least be said that an ordinary prudent individual in his position would have considered it and recognised the risk. It does not follow (although the second sentence of the second passage does admittedly imply that this is also true) that he *is* reckless if an ordinary prudent individual *would* have done so, even if the defendant himself could not. If this is what Lord Diplock meant, he chose a curiously roundabout way of saying it.

6.31   Nevertheless the House of Lords refused leave to appeal.[65] This fact was regarded as significant in *R. (Stephen Malcolm)*,[66] where the Court of Appeal rejected an ingenious attempt to circumvent *Elliott v. C.* The appellant, a boy of 15, had thrown petrol bombs at a girl's bedroom window. He claimed that he had intended only to frighten her and had not realised that if a bomb had gone through the window it might have killed her. The prosecution argued that even so he had been reckless whether his actions endangered her life[67] because the risk that they might

61 At p. 525.
62 At p. 526.
63 [1983] 2 A.C. 161; *infra*, para. 6.39.
64 At p. 177.
65 [1983] 1 W.L.R. 951.
66 (1984) 79 Cr.App.R. 334.
67 Criminal Damage Act 1971 s. 1(2); *infra*, paras. 6.66 ff.

do so was obvious. Counsel for the appellant suggested that, for the purpose of deciding whether the risk would have been obvious to "an ordinary person" in the defendant's position, this hypothetical person must be invested with such of the characteristics of the defendant as might be relevant to the defendant's own ability to foresee the risk. One such characteristic would be his age: thus the question would be whether the risk would have been obvious, not to a normal adult, but to a normal child of 15. Such an approach would have been analogous to that adopted in *D.P.P. v. Camplin*[68] for the purpose of determining, where provocation is relied upon as a defence to a charge of murder, whether a reasonable person might have reacted as the defendant did; but it was held to be ruled out by *Elliott v. C.*

6.32 The present position is highly unsatisfactory. It is hardly to be supposed that a blind person will be held reckless for inadvertently creating a risk which would have been obvious to a person with the power of sight; yet a child of 14 is apparently reckless if he thoughtlessly creates a risk which, although it would have been obvious to an adult, the child himself is unable to appreciate. Presumably the courts will have to evolve one list of abnormalities which are relevant and another of those which are not. It might perhaps be said that where the appreciation of risks is concerned there is more difference between a blind person and a sighted one than between a 14-year-old and an adult;[69] but this must depend on the circumstances. The effect of the rule is perhaps somewhat mitigated by the test laid down in *Sangha*,[70] *viz.* whether an ordinary prudent bystander would have "perceived an obvious risk". This may imply that it is not enough that such a bystander would upon reflection have recognised that there was a risk, but that it must be a risk which he would have regarded as so obvious that he would not even have had to think about it. If this is the case then the rule in *Elliott v. C.* catches only the defendant whose understanding is so limited that, however long and hard he may think about it, he cannot appreciate the risk he is creating even if it is so obvious that an ordinary person would not only be able to appreciate it if he tried but would do so without having to try. But this is small comfort to the defendant whose understanding *is* so limited.

6.33 *Possibility considered but risk not recognised.* Had the courts interpreted *Caldwell* on the basis that a risk is not "obvious" unless the defendant himself would have recognised it if he had given any thought

---

68 [1978] A.C. 705.
69 A child of under 14 could not be guilty unless he knew that his act was seriously wrong: *J.M. (a minor) v. Runeckles* (1984) 79 Cr.App.R. 255.
70 [1988] 1 W.L.R. 519; *infra*, para. 6.71.

to the matter, the two alternatives of recognising the risk and failing to think would have covered the whole of the ground. A person who failed to recognise a risk which was obvious in that sense, and who therefore eluded one prong of Lord Diplock's fork, must by definition have failed to do so because he had failed to think, in which case he would be impaled upon the other. But the rule that a risk may be "obvious" even if the defendant is incapable of recognising it, while extending the category of obvious risks, has the corollary that it is not necessarily reckless to create such a risk. If a person does consider the possibility that there may be a risk, but still fails to recognise the risk he is creating although an ordinary prudent bystander would have thought it was obvious, he is not reckless (unless he fails to recognise it because he is intoxicated).[71] Thus a person creating a risk which he could not have recognised anyway will be reckless if he has not considered the possibility of such a risk (whether or not he is *capable* of considering it) but not if he has. The respondent in *Elliott v. C.*[72] was reckless because, it was found, she had given no thougt to the possibility that the shed and its contents might be destroyed by her actions. Even if she had, she might still not have recognised the risk; but in that case she would not have been reckless. The distinction has little to commend it and is unlikely to have been envisaged in *Caldwell*, but any rule which mitigates the rigour of *Elliott v. C.* can only be welcomed.

6.34 Since a person is not reckless if he has considered the possibility of a risk but failed to recognise a risk which is obvious, it follows that he is also not reckless if, having recognised that there *would* be a risk if he failed to take suitable precautions, he has taken such precautions as he thinks necessary to eliminate the risk. In that case he has considered the possibility of a risk, and at the time in question he does not recognise that any risk exists. In *Chief Constable of Avon and Somerset v. Shimmen*,[73] the respondent had broken a shop window with his foot while demonstrating to his friends his skill in Korean self-defence. The point of the demonstration was to miss the window by as small a margin as possible, but he stated in evidence that he "thought he had eliminated as much risk as possible by missing by two inches instead of two millimetres". The case was remitted to the justices with a direction to convict.[74] But it was also said that he would still have been reckless even if he had taken precautions which he wrongly thought adequate to eliminate the risk altogether. This latter statement was *obiter* and it is submitted with respect that it must be wrong. On this hypothesis the respondent would neither have failed to

71 *Majewski* [1977] A.C. 443; *supra*, para. 6.22.
72 [1983] 1 W.L.R. 939; *supra*, paras. 6.26 ff.
73 (1987) 84 Cr.App.R. 7.
74 See further *infra*, para. 6.36.

give any thought to the possibility of the risk nor have recognised its existence at the time when he did the damage, which is the only time which is relevant. The fact that he knew there *would* have been a risk if he had *not* taken any precautions is entirely beside the point. Possibly the court was led astray by the suggestion that he was not reckless if he had taken such precautions as he thought would render the risk *negligible*, without eliminating it altogether. If the risk which remained had been so small as to be objectively justifiable, it would not have been reckless of him to take that risk;[75] but his action had so little social value that it could not justify the taking of any risk at all, and it was immaterial whether he personally thought it could.

Risk that property damaged may belong to another
6.35 Recklessness whether one damages property belonging to another, like intent to do so, necessarily involves a degree of fault with regard not only to the possibility of damage but also to the possibility that the property damaged may belong to another. In the case of intention, as we have seen,[76] it is not clear whether the defendant must know that the property he intends to damage does belong to another, or whether it is sufficient if he is aware that it may. In the case of recklessness it clearly *is* sufficient if he is aware that the property endangered may belong to another, and presumably also if he has given no thought to that possibility where the risk is obvious. If a person decides to damage property, considers the possibility that the property damaged may be property belonging to another, rejects it, and proceeds to carry out his intentions, he does not intend to damage property belonging to another and he is not even reckless whether he does so. In *Smith (David Raymond)*[77] the appellant damaged certain roofing material, wall panels and floorboards which he had previously installed in the flat of which he was the tenant. Being part of the building, these items became the property of the landlord; but the appellant, not being a lawyer, thought that they still belonged to him. It was held that he had not even been reckless whether he damaged property belonging to another. It was immaterial whether or not his mistake was a justifiable one for a layman to make. Since *Caldwell* this decision must presumably be qualified to some extent: if it would have been obvious to an ordinary person (*i.e.* not a lawyer) that the items *might* have become the property of the landlord, and the appellant failed to consider that possibility, he would have been reckless. It does not follow that he would be guilty of the offence. It might be said that he thought he had the consent of the person entitled to give

75 *Infra,* para. 6.36.
76 *Supra,* para. 6.18.
77 [1974] Q.B. 354.

such consent (*i.e.*, as he thought, himself), in which case he would have a lawful excuse under section 5(2)(*a*).[78]

Risk unjustified

6.36 Even if a person knows that his conduct may result in property being damaged, and he knows that that property may belong to another, he is not acting recklessly unless a third requirement is satisfied: *viz.* that the risk involved in his conduct should be higher than is in the circumstances objectively justifiable. The judgment thus required is essentially the same as that involved in a finding of negligence. The degree of risk involved (*i.e.* the seriousness of the damage which may result, discounted by the likelihood that it will not) must be weighed against any social value which the conduct in question may have. The greater the probability of damage to another's property, and the more serious any such damage is likely to be, the harder it will be to justify the taking of such a risk; but the possibility of such justification should not be overlooked. It often is, for two reasons. Firstly the outcome of an exercise in cost-benefit analysis would usually be a foregone conclusion, because most defendants' behaviour has no such utility as might justify the taking of any risk at all. In *Chief Constable of Avon and Somerset v. Shimmen*,[79] for example, where the respondent was held to have acted recklessly in breaking a shop window while demonstrating his skill in martial arts, it was no defence that he had tried to reduce the risk to a minimum. Even if he thought he had minimised it as far as possible (*sc.* by increasing the margin of error as far as he could without making the feat too easy and thereby defeating the object of the exercise), he had not eliminated it altogether and he knew that he had not. It was immaterial that he thought he had reduced the risk to a minimum because there was no social value in taking any risk at all.

6.37 The second reason why the element of unjustifiable risk is sometimes overlooked is that even if there are circumstances justifying the taking of the risk it will usually be possible to regard them as giving rise to a general defence (such as self-defence[80] or the arrest of offenders),[81] or to a "lawful excuse",[82] rather than as negating the basic requirement of recklessness. In most cases either approach will yield the same result, but it should not be supposed that they are entirely interchangeable. In the first place it is conceivable that the distinction might have implications for the burden of proof. The definitional elements of an offence must

78 In *Smith* this argument was rejected; *sed quaere. Cf. infra*, para. 6.44.
79 (1987) 84 Cr.App.R. 7; *supra*, para. 6.34.
80 *e.g. Sears v. Broome* [1986] Crim.L.R. 461.
81 *Cf. Renouf* [1986] W.L.R. 522 (reckless driving).
82 *Infra*, paras 6.40 ff.

generally be proved in any event, whereas there is no need to disprove a defence unless the defendant raises the issue. But it is hard to imagine a submission of no case succeeding on the grounds that there is no evidence that the defendant was not justified in taking the risk which he took. More significantly, there may be good reasons for endangering property belonging to another which do not fit into any recognised general defence or excuse. If such a risk materialises, the person responsible for creating it is not guilty of the offence of criminal damage; and this is so not because he was justified in acting recklessly but because he did not act recklessly at all.[83] It is not necessarily negligent to play cricket on a pitch within striking distance of a greenhouse, because if the risk to the greenhouse is sufficiently small it may be outweighed by the social value of cricket.[84] If so, it follows that a batsman who does succeed in damaging the greenhouse is not guilty of doing so recklessly, even if he knows very well that a ball hit hard enough in the right direction will have that effect. It follows (quite apart from the rule that a person may be reckless without actually foreseeing the risk at all)[85] that recklessness, like dishonesty,[86] is not purely a requirement of *mens rea*: it is partly a subjective requirement but partly also an objective one. It also follows that intention is a genuine alternative to recklessness and not just an aggravated form of it. The prosecution may seek to prove either that the defendant intended to damage property belonging to another, or that he only created a risk of such damage; but if they content themselves with the latter course they undertake the additional burden of showing (at any rate if the issue is raised) that the risk he created was an unjustifiable one.

6.38   It should be noted however that the analogy with dishonesty is not a perfect one. A person's conduct is not dishonest unless he realises that ordinary people would think it was,[87] whereas he may be reckless in taking a risk which a reasonable person would think unjustifiable even if he himself does not think it is unjustifiable and does not realise that anyone else might think so. His assessment of the *extent* of the risk is material; his judgment that it is legitimate for him to take it is not.

Supervening intention or recklessness

6.39   Criminal damage is no exception to the general principle that *mens*

---

83 Driving which would otherwise be reckless can be justified only by circumstances amounting to a defence of necessity, narrowly defined (*Conway* [1988] 3 W.L.R. 1238; *cf. Martin* [1989] 1 All E.R. 652); but a careful driver is not reckless just because he knows that he might conceivably run someone over. Even the risk of personal injury, if it is small enough, is outweighed by the social value of mobility.
84 *Cf. Bolton v. Stone* [1951] A.C. 850.
85 *Supra*, paras. 6.22 ff.
86 *Supra*, paras. 1.138 ff.
87 *Ghosh* [1982] Q.B. 1053; *supra*, para. 1.141.

rea must be present at the time of the *actus reus*. Obviously the offence is not committed by a person who damages another's property by accident and without recklessness, even if he is delighted to see what he has done. But if he has a chance to avert the consequences of his actions, and deliberately or recklessly fails to do so, he may be held responsible for those consequences. In *Miller*[88] the appellant awoke from sleep to find that his lighted cigarette had set fire to the mattress on which he was lying, whereupon he simply moved into another room and went back to sleep. The fire caused damage to the house (which, needless to say, was not the appellant's) and he was convicted of arson. He appealed on the ground that although he had started the fire, and even if in failing to put it out or to call the fire brigade he had intended that the house should be damaged or had been reckless whether it would be, the *actus reus* of the offence and the *mens rea* did not coincide. When he started the fire he was not acting intentionally or recklessly,[89] and what he did intentionally or recklessly did not contribute to the damage. One does not cause damage merely by not taking steps to prevent it; had the fire been started by someone else, the appellant would therefore have committed no offence in failing to put it out. But the fact that he had started it himself made all the difference. The Court of Appeal dismissed his appeal on the ground that it was his *continuing* conduct which caused the damage, including both his initial carelessness and his subsequent failure to remedy the situation, and it was therefore sufficient that *some* of that conduct was intentional or reckless in respect of the consequences which ensued. The House of Lords did not disagree with this approach but preferred to say (because it was thought easier to explain to a jury) that when a person has unknowingly set in train events which create a risk of damage to another's property, and he subsequently discovers what he has done, he incurs a responsibility to try to prevent that damage. If he fails to do so and damage ensues, he is guilty of causing the damage intentionally if he fails to prevent it because he wants it to occur (or perhaps if he knows that it almost certainly will), and of causing it recklessly if he fails to prevent it although he is aware of the risk *or* if the risk is obvious but he gives no thought to the possibility of there being any such risk.

Lawful excuse

Statutory excuses

6.40   The offence is not committed if the defendant has a "lawful excuse" for damaging the property in question. Section 5(2) provides:

---

88   [1983] 2 A.C. 161.
89   It was not contended at the trial, though it might have been, that to fall asleep on a mattress in someone else's house without putting one's cigarette out is itself a reckless thing to do.

"A person charged with an offence [under section 1(1)] shall, whether or not he would be treated for the purposes of this Act as having a lawful excuse apart from this subsection, be treated for those purposes as having a lawful excuse:

(*a*) if at the time of the act or acts alleged to constitute the offence he believed that the person or persons whom he believed to be entitled to consent to the destruction of or damage to the property in question had so consented, or would have so consented to it if he or they had known of the destruction or damage and its circumstances; or

(*b*) if he destroyed or damaged . . . the property in question . . . in order to protect property belonging to himself or another or a right or interest in property[90] which was or which he believed to be vested in himself or another, and at the time of the act or acts alleged to constitute the offence he believed:

   (i) that the property, right or interest was in immediate need of protection; and

   (ii) that the means of protection adopted . . . were . . . reasonable having regard to all the circumstances."

For the avoidance of doubt it is expressly provided that "it is immaterial whether a belief is justified or not if it is honestly held".[91] But the notion of a belief which is *not* honestly held is a contradiction in terms: if a person does not honestly believe something he does not believe it at all. The words "if it is honestly held" are therefore redundant.[92] The point of the provision is that the test is a purely subjective one. If the defendant holds one of the beliefs described (plus the intention described in paragraph (*b*) if the belief held is the one there described) he has a lawful excuse, even if his belief is totally unfounded and no reasonable person in his position would have held it. But the fact that no reasonable person would have held it may of course cast doubt on the defendant's assertion that he did.

6.41 The subjective nature of the defence under section 5(2) was carried to surprising lengths in *Jaggard v. Dickinson*.[93] The appellant had been drinking and engaged a taxi to take her to the house of one Heyfron. Her relationship with Heyfron was such that she had his consent to treat his property as if it were hers. Unfortunately the taxi took her to the wrong address, but she thought that the house was Heyfron's and broke a window in order to get in. Clearly she intended to damage property belonging to another, but she thought that the person whom she believed to be entitled to consent to the damage (*viz.* Heyfron) either had consented or would have done so if he had known the circumstances. The

90 Including any right or privilege in or over land, whether created by grant, licence or otherwise: s. 5(4).
91 s. 5(3).
92 But for another interpretation see *infra*, para. 6.43.
93 [1981] Q.B. 527.

magistrates held that she could not rely on this belief because if she had
not been drunk she would have realised the mistake. The Divisional Court
disagreed. It was true that if she had been too drunk to realise that she
was damaging property at all, she would have had no defence;[94] but that
principle had no application to the statutory defence under section 5(2).
The subsection could not be read as if it excluded a belief attributable to
intoxication, particularly since it was expressly provided that even an
unjustifiable belief would suffice.

Belief that owner consents or would have consented
6.42 Section 5(2)(*a*) bears some resemblance to the provisions of the
Theft Act 1968 which state that certain states of mind are deemed not to
be dishonest.[95] In that case there is no express provision that it is a defence
if the defendant thinks the owner *has* consented (though this may be
implied);[96] on the other hand it is a defence if he thinks he *would* have
had the consent of the person to whom the property belongs, had that
person known the circumstances,[97] whereas under the Criminal Damage
Act he must believe that he has (or would have had) the consent of the
person whom he believes to be *entitled* to consent. A person may be
entitled to consent to the damaging of property which does not belong to
him, *e.g.* if he has the authority of the person to whom it does belong. In
Denton[98] it was argued that, conversely, the person to whom it belongs is
not necessarily entitled to consent to its being damaged. The appellant
had set fire to some machinery in the cotton mill where he worked. He
claimed that his employer had asked him to do so in order to enable the
employer to make a fraudulent insurance claim. The judge ruled that the
employer could not be "entitled" to consent to his property being
damaged for a fraudulent purpose. On appeal it was pointed out that a
person commits no offence under the Act by damaging his own property,
however dishonest his motives, and that it can hardly therefore be an
offence for another person to do the job on the owner's instructions. If
the appellant had done the damage in the belief that he had the consent
of the person entitled to consent, he had a defence. Indeed it was said
that he would have had a lawful excuse even without resort to section
5(2)(*a*).

6.43 It was conceded in *Denton* that, fraudulent motives aside, the
appellant's employer was indeed entitled to consent to the property being

94 *Majewski* [1977] A.C. 443; *supra*, para. 6.22.
95 s. 2(1); *supra*, paras. 1.142 ff.
96 *Supra*, para. 1.151.
97 Theft Act 1968 s. 2(1)(*b*); *supra*, para. 1.145.
98 [1981] 1 W.L.R. 1446.

damaged. But he was not in fact the owner of the property: it belonged to two companies. Presumably his position in those companies was such that his consent was their consent. In *Appleyard*[99] the point was not conceded and proved crucial. The appellant had set fire to a store belonging to a company of which he was the managing director. It was held that he was not entitled to consent to the damage. Clearly the concession in *Denton* was no authority on the point, but the court appears to have regarded it as unarguable. This, with respect, is not so. For many purposes the managing director of a company is its *alter ego* and his acts are those of the company. Whether a particular act of his in relation to the company's property is an act done by the company, or (which in this case amounts to the same thing) an act consented to by the company, depends whether it is a valid exercise of the powers vested in him. The fact that he is acting fraudulently, or even that he is defrauding the company itself, does not necessarily mean that his act is not a valid exercise of his powers.[1] Even if he is not in fact entitled to consent to the damage, on a literal reading of section 5(2)(a) he has a defence if he thinks he is. But where his motives are fraudulent the courts might be inclined towards a less literal interpretation than that adopted in *Jaggard v. Dickinson*. The problem is similar to that of theft from a company by a controller of the company,[2] and in that context it has been held that a person does not "believe" that he would have the owner's consent if the owner knew the circumstances unless his belief is an honest one.[3] An extension of this view to the Criminal Damage Act might perhaps be supported by reference to section 5(3), which implies that to afford a defence under section 5 a belief must be "honestly held"; but this surely means only that the defendant must in fact have held it.

6.44 It is debatable whether section 5(2)(a) can apply where the defendant thinks that the property in question belongs to him alone. In *Smith (David Raymond)*[4] the Court of Appeal expressed the view that it could not. To say that the defendant thinks he has the consent of the person entitled to give consent, when he thinks that he *is* that person, "would be to strain the language of the section to an unwarranted degree".[5] But the court was encouraged in this view by the fact that it found such an interpretation unnecessary: a person who intends to damage property which he believes to be his own neither intends to damage, nor is reckless whether he damages, property *belonging to*

99 (1985) 81 Cr.App.R. 319.
1 *Supra*, para. 1.92.
2 *Supra*, para. 1.93; Fraud, paras. 4.26 ff.
3 *Attorney-General's Reference (No. 2 of 1982)* [1984] Q.B. 624; *supra*, para. 1.94.
4 [1974] Q.B. 354.
5 At p. 359.

another.[6] Since this decision the concept of recklessness has been widened
so as to embrace the person who fails to consider an obvious risk,[7]
whereas section 5(2) has been applied to the letter.[8] If an ordinary person
would perceive an obvious risk that the property in question may belong
to another, but the defendant fails to consider that possibility and
assumes that it is his, he apparently *is* reckless whether he damages
property belonging to another; and in that case he might well wish to fall
back on section 5(2)(*a*). Strained though it may sound, he does believe
that the person entitled to consent to the damage (whom incidentally he
believes to be himself) consents to it.

Protection of property
6.45   A person may sometimes be justified in destroying or damaging
property belonging to another even if he knows that the owner would not
consent. It might, for example, be necessary to damage property in order
to save life. The Act does not provide for this possibility, no doubt
because it goes without saying that people are more important than
property and that it may be legitimate to sacrifice the latter for the sake
of the former. What is less self-evident, and is therefore made clear in the
Act, is that it may also be legitimate to sacrifice property (even other
people's property) for the sake of *other* property. Section 5(2)(*b*) provides
a defence if three requirements are satisfied:

(a) the defendant must have damaged the property in question in order
to protect property belonging to himself or another (or a right or
interest in property which was, or which he believed to be, vested
in himself or another);
(b) he must have believed that that property (or right or interest) was
in immediate need of protection; and
(c) he must have believed that the means of protection adopted were
reasonable in the circumstances.

6.46   A person is probably acting in order to "protect" property if his
intention is to preserve it from destruction, damage, loss (permanent or
temporary), immobilisation (*e.g.* of one car by the improper parking of
another), fright or discomfort (in the case of animals) or trespass. But it
seems that the damage must be intended to result *directly* in the protection
of other property. In *Hunt*[9] the appellant was held not to have acted "in
order to protect property" when he started a small fire in an old people's
home in order to demonstrate the inadequacy of the fire alarm. Similarly

6   *Supra,* para. 6.35.
7   *Caldwell* [1982] A.C. 341; *supra,* para. 6.23.
8   *Jaggard v. Dickinson* [1981] Q.B. 527.
9   (1977) 66 Cr.App.R. 105.

it has twice been held that a person who cuts the fence of an American
military base, in the hope that this may result in the removal of nuclear
weapons and a consequential reduction in the risk of nuclear attack on
the base, is not acting in order to protect the neighbouring property which
would also be destroyed in the event of such attack.[10] The objective is
"too remote" from the act intended to achieve it. The logic of this may,
with respect, be doubted. If A tries to induce B to act in a certain way,
because he thinks that if B does act in that way the effect will be to reduce
the danger to A's property (or C's), it can hardly be denied that A is
acting in order to protect the property in question. Anyway there is no
need to deny it, because the defendant must not only act *in order* to
protect other property but must also believe that the latter property is in
immediate need of protection. This belief need not be justified;[11] but
section 5(2)(*b*) has no application if the defendant knows that there is no
immediate risk requiring immediate action.[12] Even if he will sooner or
later have to damage property belonging to another, he must postpone
the prophylaxis until the last possible moment. Where the evil to be
averted has already begun, however, this requirement must inevitably be
satisfied. If the property to be damaged is itself damaging the property to
be protected, the latter is in immediate need of protection against further
damage; if a car is unlawfully parked, the land is in immediate need of
protection against further trespass.

6.47 Whether immediate action is reasonable in such a case is another
matter. The heart of the defence is the requirement that the defendant
must believe it is reasonable in the circumstances for him to damage the
property as he does. Again his belief need not be justified.[13] It does not
follow that the reasonableness or otherwise of his conduct is entirely a
matter for his own unfettered whim. Just as a person cannot claim to be
acting honestly if he knows that ordinary people would think his conduct
dishonest, whether or not he personally agrees,[14] so it is arguable that he
cannot claim to believe that he is acting reasonably if he knows that
ordinary people would regard his conduct as wholly unreasonable. But it
is doubtful whether such a rule can be extracted from the wording of the
Act. Moreover the defence clearly would be available to a defendant so
eccentric that he did not even realise how unreasonable most people
would think his conduct.

10   *Ashford and Smith* [1988] Crim.L.R. 682; *Hill and Hall* [1989] Crim.L.R. 136.
11   s. 5(3).
12   *Hill and Hall, supra* n. 10.
13   s. 5(3).
14   *Ghosh* [1982] Q.B. 1053; *supra,* para. 1.141. *Cf.* also the requirement in the offence of
     blackmail that the demand with menaces be "unwarranted"; *supra,* paras. 3.19 ff.

General defences

6.48 It is clear from the wording of section 5(2) that it does not purport to give an exhaustive account of the circumstances in which one person has a lawful excuse for damaging another's property: it merely extends the defence of lawful excuse to include certain cases which might be thought not to afford a defence under the general principles of criminal law (though they generally will). Circumstances which do give rise to one of the recognised general defences will *a fortiori* amount to a lawful excuse. A person may damage property belonging to another if this is reasonably necessary to protect himself or another person,[15] or to prevent crime or arrest an offender,[16] and for this purpose steps are reasonable if they would have been reasonable had the circumstances been as the defendant believed them to be:[17] as under section 5(2), even an unreasonable mistake may be a defence. But where section 5(2) does not apply it seems that the test of whether the defendant's *conduct* is reasonable (or would have been reasonable in the circumstances which he believed to exist) is an objective one. His own opinion that he is acting reasonably is immaterial, whether or not he thinks that others might agree. It is also arguable that if he damages property in order to protect other property, and it is reasonable for him to do so, he has a defence whether or not the latter property was in *immediate* need of protection as section 5(2) requires.

Other excuses

6.49 Nor should it be assumed that a lawful excuse must be either one of those described in section 5(2) or a recognised general defence. Where the defendant does not *intend* to damage property belonging to another, he must be proved to have done so recklessly; and we have seen that he does not act recklessly unless his act involves a risk of damage which is in the circumstances unreasonable.[18] Even if he does intend to damage the property, there may be circumstances which justify him in doing so. Such circumstances will not negative the element of intention, as they would that of recklessness, but may nevertheless amount to a lawful excuse. There may be statutory authority for the damage.[19] Alternatively it may be permissible as a matter of common law. An occupier of land,

---

15 *Cf. Sears v. Broome* [1986] Crim.L.R. 461.
16 Criminal Law Act 1967 s. 3 provides that the use of *force* in such circumstances is lawful: *a fortiori* property damage must be.
17 *Beckford* [1988] A.C. 130.
18 *Supra*, para. 6.36.
19 *e.g.* s. 9(3) of the Animals Act 1971 permits the killing of a dog which is worrying livestock. It refers only to civil liability, but if there is a defence to a civil action there must *a fortiori* be a lawful excuse for the purposes of the criminal law.

for example, may be entitled to use his land in a manner which he knows will have the effect of damaging a neighbouring occupier's property, provided that his user is objectively reasonable and the damage is due to the abnormal susceptibility of the property damaged.[20] If he is not liable for the damage in tort he must surely have a lawful excuse for the purposes of the criminal law.

6.50 Again, it would seem to accord with the spirit of the Act that there should be a defence if the defendant does not in fact have a legal right to damage the property, but thinks (reasonably or otherwise) that he does. This was the position under the old law,[21] and in *Smith (David Raymond)*[22] the Court of Appeal apparently thought it must still be so. On the other hand the Theft Act 1968 makes express provision for this situation,[23] whereas the Criminal Damage Act does not.

Mode of trial

6.51 Criminal damage is triable either way, but is subject to a special procedure for determining the mode of trial. The object is to preclude the possibility of a charge being committed for trial where the cost of repair or replacement of the property damaged is comparatively small. Even so the offence remains technically triable either way: it would seem, for example, that the defence are still entitled to advance disclosure. The special procedure applies to the offences listed in Schedule 2 to the Magistrates' Courts Act 1980, referred to as "scheduled offences". These offences include not only the actual damaging of property (other than arson)[24] but also aiding, abetting, counselling or procuring such an offence, attempting to commit such an offence and inciting another to do so.

6.52 In the case of a scheduled offence section 22(1) of the Magistrates' Courts Act 1980 requires the magistrates, before embarking on mode of trial proceedings, to consider whether the "value involved" appears to exceed the "relevant sum" (currently £2000).[25] The value involved is what the property damaged would probably have cost to buy in the open market at the time of the alleged offence, unless the damage was

---

20   *Robinson v. Kilvert* (1889) 41 Ch.D. 88.
21   *Twose* (1879) 14 Cox 327.
22   [1974] Q.B. 354.
23   s. 2(1)(*a*); *supra*, para. 1.144.
24   For arson see *infra*, para. 6.63.
25   Criminal Justice Act 1988 s. 38(1). In the case of offences committed before s. 38 came into force (on 12 October 1988) it is £400: Criminal Justice Act 1988 s. 38(2); S.I. 1984 No. 447, Art. 2(1), Sch. 1.

immediately after that time capable of repair, in which case the value involved is *either* what would probably then have been the market price for the repair of the damage *or* what the property would probably have cost to buy in the open market at the time of the alleged offence, whichever is the less.[26] Where the damage is irreparable the value involved is the value of the property itself, not just the difference between its value before and after the damage: for this purpose irreparable damage is tantamount to destruction. In the case of an attempt the value involved is the value involved in the offence alleged to have been attempted; in the case of incitement, the value involved in the offence alleged to have been incited.[27] In assessing the value involved the magistrates must have regard to any representations made by the prosecutor or the defendant.[28] "Representations" can include submissions, assertions or the production of documents, but are something less than evidence; therefore the magistrates are not required to hear evidence, though they have a discretion to do so.[29] There is no appeal against their decision.[30]

6.53 If it appears clear that the value involved does not exceed the relevant sum, mode of trial proceedings are concluded and the charge must be tried summarily.[31] In this case the court cannot impose a sentence of more than three months' imprisonment or a fine[32] of more than £1000,[33] nor can it commit the defendant for sentence.[34] If it appears clear that the value involved does exceed the relevant sum, mode of trial proceedings continue in the normal way.[35] If for any reason it is not clear whether the value involved does or does not exceed the relevant sum, the court must cause the charge to be written down (if this has not already been done) and read to the defendant and must offer him the option of summary trial, explaining the penalties to which he will be liable if he exercises his option and is convicted (*viz.* the same as if the value involved had been less than the relevant sum).[36] If he does not opt for summary trial at this stage, mode of trial proceedings continue as if the value involved had clearly exceeded the relevant sum.[37] The effect is that if the court is unable

26 Magistrates' Courts Act 1980 s. 22(10), Sch. 2.
27 Sch. 2.
28 Including a person charged jointly with him who is under 17 and therefore has no right to trial on indictment anyway: s. 22(9).
29 *R. v. Canterbury and St Augustine's JJ., ex p. Klisiak* [1982] Q.B. 398.
30 s. 22(8).
31 s. 22(2).
32 "Fine" includes a pecuniary penalty but not a pecuniary forfeiture or pecuniary compensation: s. 33(2).
33 S.I. 1984 No. 447, Art. 2(1), Sch. 1.
34 s. 33.
35 s. 22(3).
36 s. 22(4), (5).
37 s. 22(6)(*b*).

to determine whether the offence charged should be dealt with as a summary offence or as one triable either way, the defendant is invited to decide for himself.

Two or more offences

Offences charged together

6.54   In general the special procedure is applicable to any scheduled offence, even if the defendant is also charged with other indictable offences and is committed for trial on those other charges. If the value involved in the scheduled offence does not exceed the relevant sum, the general rule is that that charge cannot be committed for trial with the others.[38] But the combination of two or more charges sometimes results in a relaxation of the general rule, thus permitting a scheduled offence to be committed for trial although the value involved would be insufficient if the offence were charged on its own. Section 22(7) of the Magistrates' Courts Act 1980 provides, in part:

> "Subsection (1) above shall not apply where the offence charged—
> (a)   is one of two or more offences with which the accused is charged on the same occasion and which appear to the court to constitute or form part of a series of two or more offences of the same or a similar character . . ."

If section 22(1) does not apply to an offence, it follows that that offence is exempted from the general rule that a scheduled offence cannot be committed for trial unless the value involved exceeds the relevant sum. Subject to a further provision shortly to be considered, the effect of section 22(7)(a) is therefore that a charge of a scheduled offence *can* be committed for trial, irrespective of the value involved, if that offence and at least one other offence charged on the same occasion constitute or form part of a series of offences of the same or a similar character.[39] This was formerly so not only where the value involved in the scheduled offence itself did not exceed the relevant sum, but also where a series of two or more scheduled offences were charged together and even the *aggregate* value involved in those offences did not exceed it. This latter rule is now reversed (except where any of the charges relates to acts done before 12 October 1988)[40] by the Criminal Justice Act 1988, which adds a new subsection (11) to section 22 of the Magistrates' Courts Act 1980.[41] Section 22(11) now reads (in part):

---

38   s. 22(2). But it may now be possible to include the charge in the indictment by virtue of s. 40(1) of the Criminal Justice Act 1988: *infra*, para. 6.62.
39   *R. v. St Helens Magistrates' Court, ex p. McClorie* (1984) 78 Cr.App.R. 1.
40   Criminal Justice Act 1988 s. 38(4); Criminal Justice Act 1988 (Commencement No. 2 Order) 1988, S.I. 1988 no. 1676.
41   Criminal Justice Act 1988 s. 38(3).

"Where—
(a)   the accused is charged on the same occasion with two or more scheduled
        offences and it appears to the court that they constitute or form part of
        a series of two or more offences of the same or a similar character . . .
this section shall have effect as if any reference in it to the value involved
were a reference to the aggregate of the values involved."

6.55   Thus if two or more *scheduled* offences are charged on the same
occasion, none of them individually involving a value of more than the
relevant sum, and they appear to constitute or form part of a series of
offences of the same or a similar character, they can no longer be
committed for trial unless the *aggregate* of the values involved does exceed
the relevant sum. A person charged with a series of such offences still has
the right to elect where a person charged with only one such offence would
not, but only where the values involved do exceed the relevant sum if
they are added together. Section 22(7)(a) continues to apply, subject
to the other requirements of that provision, where only one of the
charges relates to a scheduled offence: there is no room for the
compromise adopted by section 22(11)(a), because if there is only one
scheduled offence there is nothing to aggregate. Both provisions apply
only if the offences charged on the same occasion appear to "constitute
or form part of a series of two or more offences of the same or a similar
character". That phrase therefore requires examination.

Series of offences
6.56   Section 22(7)(a) exempts a charge of a scheduled offence from the
general rule only if that offence and at least one other offence charged on
the same occasion constitute or form part of a *series* of offences. Similarly
section 22(11)(a) reapplies the general rule (with the modification that it
is sufficient if the *aggregate* of the values involved exceeds the relevant
sum) not just where two or more scheduled offences are charged on the
same occasion, but only where they constitute or form part of a series. It
may therefore be crucial whether a particular clutch of offences can be
described as a series. In *Re Prescott*[42] the defendant obstructed a police
officer and in so doing damaged the officer's trousers. It was held that the
two offences were not only dissimilar but were not even a series, because
they were committed simultaneously: a series of events must "follow one
another in temporal succession".[43] Even two offences which are similar
and *not* simultaneous can fail to constitute a series. In *Braden*[44] the
appellant had been arrested for damaging cars and was charged in

42   (1979) 70 Cr.App.R. 244n; applied, *obiter*, in *Considine* (1979) 70 Cr.App.R. 239.
43   At p. 246, *per* Ormrod L.J. Eveleigh L.J. declined to decide this point but Browne L.J.
        agreed with Ormrod L.J.
44   (1987) 87 Cr.App.R. 289.

addition with damaging the door of a police cell. The latter charge was held not to form part of a series of offences, because it was "too remote in time and place" from the others. Apparently a number of offences do not qualify as a series unless they are committed in the same vicinity; but would it not be sufficient if the defendant's reckless driving left a trail of destruction over a distance of many miles? The length of time separating the offences is clearly relevant, but it might cut both ways. Offences committed several hours apart are apparently not a series; on the other hand it would be absurd to differentiate between a pair of offences committed simultaneously and a pair committed two seconds apart. A workable rule might be that two or more offences form a series if they are committed in the course of incidents which are closely related but separate, and not (as in *Re Prescott*) in the course of the same incident.

Same or similar character
6.57   For the general rule to be excluded by section 22(7)(*a*), or partially reapplied by section 22(11)(*a*), the series of offences comprised by or including the offences charged must be offences "of the same or a similar character". It would seem self-evident that if two or more offences are both or all scheduled offences they must necessarily be offences of at least "similar" character, and probably "the same". Admittedly section 22(11)(*a*) requires *both* that the offences charged on the same occasion should be scheduled offences *and* that they should constitute or form part of a series of two or more offences of the same or a similar character. But this does not imply that some scheduled offences are dissimilar to others. Two scheduled offences committed simultaneously would not constitute a series of offences.[45] If the culprit then committed another, non-scheduled offence, the three offences might then constitute a series, and in that case the two scheduled offences would form *part* of a series; but section 22(11)(*a*) would not apply unless the third offence were of the same or a similar character to the first two, because only then would the first two form part of a series of offences "of the same or a similar character". Thus the presence of that additional requirement does not imply that it is not automatically satisfied by the scheduled offences themselves: it is submitted that it is.

6.58   At the other extreme, two offences are not of a similar character if one is a scheduled offence and the other is not an offence against property at all, such as assault, obstructing a police officer or an offence against public order.[46] But it may be that even an offence against property is not

---

45 *Supra*, para. 6.56.
46 *Re Prescott* (1979) 70 Cr.App.R. 244n; *R. v. Hatfield JJ., ex p. Castle* (1980) 71 Cr.App.R. 287; *R. v. Tottenham JJ., ex p. Tibble* (1981) 73 Cr.App.R. 55, overruling *R. v. Leicester JJ., ex p. Lord* [1980] Crim.L.R. 581.

of a similar character to a scheduled offence unless it too involves property damage. In *Considine*[47] the Court of Appeal rejected the suggestion that a charge of criminal damage could be committed for trial if combined with one of burglary:

"Burglary often involves criminal damage, but criminal damage, as such, is not an offence of the same or a similar character to burglary." [48]

But this statement was *obiter*, the appeal being dismissed on other grounds. It may still be arguable that any offence against property is of a similar character to a scheduled offence. Moreover the burglary in *Considine* was apparently committed with intent to steal. Had it been burglary with intent to do unlawful damage, the position would surely have been different. But the offence other than the scheduled offence must at least be indictable:[49] otherwise the effect of section 22(7)(*a*) would be that an offence of minor damage, triable only summarily if charged on its own, could be committed for trial if charged together with a similar but purely summary offence.

Incitement

6.59 Section 22(7) goes on:

"Subsection (1) above shall not apply where the offence charged—
. . .
(*b*) consists in the incitement to commit two or more scheduled offences."

Therefore a person charged with inciting the commission of two offences of criminal damage to a total value of £10 on 1 October 1988 could be committed for trial. But if the incitement is alleged to have occurred on or after 12 October 1988, the new section 22(11) applies:[50]

"Where—
. . .
(*b*) the offence charged consists in incitement to commit two or more scheduled offences,
this section shall have effect as if any reference in it to the value involved were a reference to the aggregate of the values involved."

Thus a charge of incitement to commit several offences of criminal damage must now be tried summarily unless the total value which would have been involved in the offences incited exceeds the relevant sum.

The prosecutor's options

6.60 Since an assessment of the value involved at less than the relevant

47 (1979) 70 Cr.App.R. 239.
48 At p. 243.
49 *ex p. Castle, supra.*
50 Criminal Justice Act 1988 s. 38(3), (4).

sum deprives the defendant of his right to trial on indictment, the prosecutor wishing to be sure of summary trial has an incentive to allege damage of less than that sum even if he could prove more. He cannot have his cake and eat it: if a continuous spree of vandalism can be charged as one offence involving more than the relevant sum there is no point in charging it as several offences each involving less, because the value involved in each offence will then be deemed to be the aggregate of the values involved.[51] To ensure summary trial he should allege damage to a total value not exceeding the relevant sum; and he may do this by not alleging all the damage which he is in a position to prove. In *R. v. Canterbury and St Augustine's JJ., ex p. Klisiak*[52] the defendant was initially charged with damaging various items to a total value of £414.05. The relevant sum was then £200. The defendant elected to be tried on indictment and the case was adjourned to enable the prosecution to serve witness statements, but they offered no evidence; instead they brought another charge referring to some but not all of the same items, to a total value of only £154.89. The magistrates assessed the value involved at less than the relevant sum and proposed to deal with the case summarily. The defendant's application for judicial review was dismissed: the course taken by the prosecution, though obviously a device to deprive the defendant of his right to trial on indictment, was not an abuse of the process of the court. *A fortiori* it is legitimate, and indeed preferable to the course taken in *Klisiak*, for the prosecutor to be sparing with his allegations at the outset:

> "Providing that the offences are not grave ones and that the powers of the justices *vis-à-vis* sentence are appropriate, there is no reason why the prosecuting authority should not charge an offence which is not the gravest possible allegation on the facts . . . [If] in reality the offence is nothing more than can properly be dealt with summarily by the justices, then it is proper so to charge it, despite the fact that the defendant may thereby lose his right to trial by jury . . ." [53]

Thus it would seem that the only case where it is improper to allege less damage than can in fact be proved is where the actual damage is so great that, were it all alleged, the magistrates would decline jurisdiction. It is unlikely that in such a case the prosecution would wish to ensure summary trial anyway, or that the defendant would object if they did.

6.61   A variation of this tactic may be adopted where the total damage exceeds the relevant sum but a number of defendants are alleged to have

---

51 s. 22(11)(*a*); *supra*, para. 6.54.
52 [1982] Q.B. 398.
53 *Klisiak, supra*, at p. 415.

contributed to it. In *R. v. Salisbury Magistrates' Court, ex p. Mastin* [54] some thirty people had driven vehicles round a bean field and destroyed the entire crop, valued at £5800. Had the prosecution alleged (as they might well have done) that the defendants had been acting in concert, each defendant might have been charged with all the damage; but in that case they could have elected trial on indictment. The prosecution chose instead to allege against each defendant only the minimum damage which he personally could be proved to have caused. This was calculated by measuring the distance between the boundary of the field and the point where each vehicle had come to rest, and assuming that it had taken the shortest route between those points. The result was that the value involved in each case varied between £16 and £117. The Divisional Court refused an application by one of the defendants for certiorari and for a declaration either that the value involved in his case exceeded the relevant sum or that it was unclear whether or not it did so. The prosecution were under no obligation to charge the applicant with the damage done by the other defendants, even if there were evidence that he and the others were parties to a common purpose. Nor were they obliged to charge him with having personally caused damage in excess of the relevant sum if they preferred to charge him with less, particularly since a more ambitious allegation might have been harder to prove. But it was suggested that if the prosecution specifically allege a limited amount of damage it may be desirable to specify the value involved in the charge.

6.62 Conversely, a count of criminal damage which could not be committed for trial in its own right, because the value involved does not exceed the relevant sum, may be added to an indictment after committal on another charge—provided that it is founded on the same facts or evidence as a count charging an indictable offence, or is part of a series of offences of the same or a similar character as an indictable offence which is also charged,[55] and provided also (in either case) that the facts or evidence relating to the offence are disclosed in an examination or deposition taken before a justice in the presence of the defendant.[56] In the event of conviction on a count included by virtue of this rule the powers of the Crown Court are limited to those which the magistrates would have had on summary conviction.[57]

54 (1986) 84 Cr.App.R. 248.
55 *Cf. supra*, paras 6.56 ff.
56 Criminal Justice Act 1988 s. 40(1). This provision extends also to such purely summary offences as taking a conveyance (*supra*, para. 5.02). In its application to scheduled offences involving less than the relevant sum it was anticipated by *Considine* (1979) 70 Cr.App.R. 239.
57 s. 40(2).

Aggravated Offences

Arson

6.63 The common law offence of arson was abolished by section 11(1) of the Criminal Damage Act 1971, but section 1(3) provides:

> "An offence committed under this section by destroying or damaging property by fire shall be charged as arson."

It is perhaps curious that one particular way of damaging property should continue to be singled out for special treatment. Moreover the subsection appears to be mandatory: *any* offence under section 1(1), if committed by means of fire, is arson and must be charged as such. Arson is punishable on conviction on indictment with life imprisonment.[58] It is triable either way[59] unless it also constitutes the more serious offence under section 1(2),[60] but it is not subject to the rules excluding trial on indictment where the value involved is comparatively small.[61] In principle, of course, a person ought to be guilty of arson only if he *intends* the property to be damaged by fire and not in some other way, or is reckless whether it is so damaged; but if this were the draftsman's meaning it would have been easy to spell it out.

Possession of a firearm

6.64 A person who commits an offence under section 1(1) of the Criminal Damage Act, and at the time either of committing or of being arrested for that offence has in his possession a firearm or imitation firearm,[62] is guilty of a further offence unless he shows that he had it in his possession for a lawful object.[63] This offence is punishable on conviction on indictment with life imprisonment.[64]

Nuclear material

6.65 When section 1(1)(*b*) of the Nuclear Material (Offences) Act 1983 is brought into force, any act done in relation to or by means of nuclear material, which would have amounted to an offence under section 1 of

---

58 s. 4(1).
59 Magistrates' Courts Act 1980 s. 17(1) and Sch. 1.
60 *Infra*, paras 6.66 ff.
61 Magistrates' Courts Act 1980 Sch. 2; *supra*, para. 6.51 ff.
62 See *supra*, para. 1.180.
63 Firearms Act 1968 s. 17(2), Sch. 1.
64 Firearms Act 1968 Sch. 6 Pt I as amended by Criminal Justice Act 1988 s. 44(3). In the case of offences committed before s. 44 came into force on 29 September 1988 (s. 171(6)) the maximum remains at 14 years: s. 44(4).

the Criminal Damage Act 1971 had it been done within the jurisdiction, will amount to that offence notwithstanding that it is done outside the jurisdiction. The Act is discussed elsewhere.[65]

DAMAGING PROPERTY WITH DISREGARD FOR DANGER TO LIFE

6.66 Section 1(2) of the Criminal Damage Act 1971 creates an offence which in practice is usually a more serious version of the offence under section 1(1), but which is technically not an aggravated form of that offence because its requirements are in one respect easier to satisfy. It provides:

> "A person who without lawful excuse destroys or damages any property, whether belonging to himself or another—
> (a) intending to destroy or damage any property or being reckless as to whether any property would be destroyed or damaged; and
> (b) intending by the destruction or damage to endanger the life of another or being reckless as to whether the life of another would be thereby endangered;
> shall be guilty of an offence."

The offence is punishable on conviction on indictment with life imprisonment.[66]

Damage to any property

6.67 The definition of the offence requires that the defendant damage some property, but not necessarily property belonging to another. In general it is not an offence under the Act to damage one's own property, for whatever reason,[67] but there is an exception for the person who does so with intent to endanger another's life or being reckless whether another's life is endangered. Thus the offence might be committed by sawing through the rungs of one's own ladder before lending it to someone else. The existence of such an exception to the general rule is hard to justify. An act done with intent to endanger life may admittedly fall short of attempted murder: an intent to endanger life need not be an intent to kill, and even an act done with intent to kill may be "merely preparatory" to the killing.[68] But if there is any need for a broader offence of doing an act with intent to endanger life, or being reckless whether life

65 *Supra*, para. 1.165 f.
66 s. 4(1).
67 *Denton* [1981] 1 W.L.R. 1446; *supra*, para. 6.42.
68 *Cf.* Criminal Attempts Act 1981 s. 1(1).

is endangered, the offence ought not to be confined to acts of damage to property. Endangering another's life by damaging one's own property is hardly more culpable than doing so in any other way. Moreover the appropriate vehicle for the creation of such an offence would be a statute concerned with offences against the person. As it is, the offence under section 1(2) does involve an element of property damage; but the absence of any requirement that the property belong to another means that it is not in any real sense an offence *against* property at all.

6.68 It should also be noted that although section 1(2) appears to envisage a person committing the offence by damaging his own property, being reckless whether such property is damaged, the notion of being reckless whether one's own property is damaged is a contradiction in terms. Recklessness involves the taking of an unjustifiable risk;[69] since one is entitled to damage one's own property on purpose, *a fortiori* one is entitled to risk doing so by accident. Therefore the endangering of one's own property cannot in itself be unjustifiable, and to call it reckless makes no more sense than to call it negligent.[70] It can be reckless in the ordinary sense only to the extent that it endangers others or their property. Where the property damaged is the defendant's own, therefore, the requirement of recklessness whether property is damaged presumably means only that he must have recognised the risk of damage to some property, or failed to give any thought to the possibility of such a risk although it was obvious, and not that the risk must also have been unjustifiable. Even where property belonging to another is concerned, a requirement of unjustifiable risk to property would seem superfluous when combined with one of unjustifiable risk to life.

Intention or recklessness as to danger to life

Intention

6.69 The defendant must either intend to endanger the life of another by the damage or be reckless whether he does so. An intention to endanger life is an intention to create a risk of death. The risk need not be great. To expose another to even a small risk of death is to endanger his life—subject to *de minimis*, no doubt, but in matters of life and death that principle will exclude only the most negligible risks. A person intends to create a risk of death if that is his purpose in acting as he does. Obviously this includes a person whose purpose is not just to create a risk

69 *Supra*, para. 6.36.
70 "Contributory negligence" is not strictly speaking a form of negligence at all, since negligence involves the creation of a risk to the person or property of someone other than the negligent party. One owes a duty of care to one's neighbour but not to oneself.

of death but to kill. A person who does not act as he does in order to create a risk of death, but who knows that his conduct is virtually certain to create such a risk, does not *necessarily* intend to endanger life; but a jury is entitled to infer that that is his intention.[71] It is immaterial whether there is in fact any risk to life, provided that the defendant thinks there is.

Recklessness

6.70 The notion of recklessness whether life is endangered is an unnecessarily complicated one. A danger to life is a risk of death. A person is therefore reckless whether he endangers life if he is reckless whether he creates a risk of death. But to be reckless whether one does a thing is to risk doing that thing; to be reckless whether one endangers life is therefore to risk creating a risk of death. But a risk of a risk of death is simply a risk of death. Suppose a person knows that if he does x there is a 50% chance that it will result in y, and that if y does result there is a 50% chance that it will in turn result in z. Clearly he knows that x involves a 25% risk of z. If that risk is unjustifiable, but he does x nonetheless, he is not just reckless whether he creates a *risk* of z: he is reckless whether z actually occurs. Recklessness whether one endangers life is recklessness whether one causes death. Indeed, to the extent that recklessness involves a subjective appreciation of the risk involved, it adds nothing in this context. A person who does something which he knows to involve a risk of death is not just *reckless* whether he endangers life: he *intends* to do so, because he knows that the endangering of life will inevitably result. Only in its extended sense is recklessness a genuine alternative to intention, *i.e.* where the possibility of there being a risk is obvious but the defendant has given no thought to it.[72]

6.71 Recklessness whether life is endangered, then, is simply recklessness whether one causes death. But there is a further difficulty: can a person be reckless whether he causes death if there is in fact no possibility of death resulting from his conduct? Where a person has recklessly damaged property belonging to another contrary to section 1(1), the question does not arise: obviously there must in fact have been a possibility of damage because damage has in fact resulted. But the offence under section 1(2) does not require that death should actually be caused,[73] only that the defendant should be reckless whether he endangers life—*i.e.* that he

71 *Supra*, paras 6.14 ff.
72 *Supra*, paras 6.22 ff.
73 Nor does it expressly require that life should in fact be endangered, though this is arguably implicit in the requirement of recklessness: it depends what one means by danger. If there was a risk of death in *Sangha* (*infra*), presumably there was also a danger to life.

should risk causing death. To say that by doing a certain act a person risked causing a certain consequence, which did not however occur, is ambiguous. On the one hand it may mean that the act might have resulted in that consequence if the chain of events subsequent to the act had developed in a different way. Alternatively it may mean that the act might have so resulted had it been done in different circumstances—with the implication that the doer, at least, did not realise that the circumstances actually obtaining were such as to rule out any possibility of his act having that effect. Clearly the former case may involve recklessness; but so, it seems, may the latter. In *Sangha*[74] the appellant had started a fire in a flat. The occupants were out, and because of the construction of the building it was impossible for the fire to spread to the other flats. It was held that these facts did not preclude a finding of recklessness whether life was endangered. Such recklessness may exist even if there are special circumstances, unknown to the defendant, which rule out any possibility of death resulting from his act. It is sufficient if the ordinary prudent bystander, without the benefit of hindsight, would have "perceived an obvious risk" of danger to life. Whether this is understood to mean that there must in fact have been a risk which such a bystander would have thought obvious, or that there need not in fact have been a risk at all as long as the bystander would have thought it obvious that there was, is perhaps a matter of taste. The point is that the former interpretation is accurate only on the basis that a "risk" of death includes the case where death cannot in fact result but it appears that it can.

Causation

6.72   The defendant must intend to endanger life, or be reckless whether he does so, by damaging the property—not just by doing the act which causes the damage. In *Steer*[75] the respondent had rung the doorbell of a bungalow and induced the occupants to look out of their bedroom window. He then fired a rifle at the window, not intending to endanger their lives but clearly reckless whether he did so. The House of Lords held that although he had intentionally damaged the window and had also been reckless whether he endangered the lives of the occupants, he had not been reckless whether he endangered their lives *by* damaging the window. The danger was that one of them might have been killed by a bullet, not by flying glass. The gravity of the defendant's conduct might adequately have been marked by charging him with damaging property belonging to another while in possession of a firearm.[76]

---

74   [1988] 1 W.L.R. 519.
75   [1988] A.C. 111.
76   *Supra*, para. 6.64.

Lawful excuse

6.73 Like section 1(1), section 1(2) requires that the defendant's act be done without lawful excuse. But a lawful excuse for damaging another's property is not necessarily a lawful excuse for endangering another's life, and the statutory excuses under section 5(2) do not apply.[77] Just as it is no defence that the property damaged belongs to the defendant himself, so it is immaterial that he has (or thinks he has, or thinks he would have) the consent of the person to whom it does belong. Nor can he rely on the *statutory* defence that he is acting reasonably in order to protect property other than that damaged. But according to general principles it would be a lawful excuse if he were acting reasonably in defence of himself, or of another person; and it is possible that even the defence of property might be sufficient excuse. Of course it would hardly ever be reasonable deliberately to kill a person for the sake of property alone (though even this is not totally inconceivable, *e.g.* if the alternative were the destruction of St Paul's Cathedral), but the offence requires only recklessness. It might well be reasonable to create some small risk to life in order to avert the certain destruction of irreplaceable property. But if the risk is a reasonable one it is not reckless to take it,[78] and there is no need for a lawful excuse at all.

Aggravated offences

6.74 All the aggravated forms of the offence under section 1(1) are equally applicable to the more serious offence under section 1(2). By virtue of section 1(3) an offence under section 1(2) which is committed by damaging property by fire must be charged as arson; but the maximum sentence is life imprisonment anyway, whether the damage is done by fire or not. The offences in relation to firearms[79] and nuclear material[80] also apply.

INTENT TO DAMAGE PROPERTY

Attempts

Attempting to damage property belonging to another

6.75 A person is guilty of attempting to commit the offence under section 1(1) if he intends to damage property belonging to another

77 s. 5(1).
78 *Supra,* para. 6.36.
79 Firearms Act 1968 s. 17(2); *supra,* paras 1.180, 6.64.
80 Nuclear Material (Offences) Act 1983 s. 1(1)(*b*); *supra,* paras 1.165 f, 6.65.

without lawful excuse, and he does an act which is more than merely preparatory to the commission of the offence.[81] He intends to damage property if it is his purpose to bring that consequence about, and he may also be inferred to have intended it if he knows that it is virtually certain to result from his act.[82] It is not enough that he is reckless whether property is damaged;[83] but it is debatable whether he must be sure that the property he intends to damage is property belonging to another, or whether it is sufficient that he thinks it may be.[84] It need not in fact belong to another at all, as long as he thinks that it does.[85]

Attempting to damage property with disregard for danger to life

6.76 Similarly an attempt to commit the offence under section 1(2) requires an intention to commit the offence and an act which is more than merely preparatory. But it is not clear what constitutes an *intention* to commit an offence involving recklessness as to a consequence which does not itself form part of the offence—in this case, death. Can one intend such an offence although only reckless as to the consequence? The argument for regarding such recklessness as insufficient is weaker than in the case of recklessness as to a factor which does form part of the full offence, and even the latter is probably sufficient in some cases (*viz.* where the factor in question is a circumstance rather than a consequence);[86] but the position remains obscure.[87] In this particular instance it may be possible to avoid the problem by treating a defendant who *knows* that his act involves a risk of death as *intending* to endanger life.[88] But this solution is not available if his recklessness lies not in recognising the risk and going ahead regardless, but in failing to consider whether there is a risk at all.[89]

Burglary

6.77 Under section 9(1)(*a*) of the Theft Act 1968 a person commits burglary if he enters a building or part of a building as a trespasser and with intent to commit an offence of unlawful damage to the building or anything therein. This offence is discussed elsewhere.[90]

---

81 Criminal Attempts Act 1981 s. 1(1).
82 *Supra,* paras 6.14 ff.
83 *Millard and Vernon* [1987] Crim.L.R. 393.
84 *Supra,* para. 6.18; *cf. infra,* para. 7.31.
85 *Shivpuri* [1987] A.C. 1.
86 *Supra,* para. 6.18; *cf. infra,* para. 7.31.
87 See *O'Toole* [1987] Crim.L.R. 759.
88 *Supra,* para. 6.70.
89 *Supra,* paras 6.22 ff.
90 *Infra,* paras 7.02 ff.

Possession

6.78 Section 3 of the Criminal Damage Act 1971 creates an offence of possessing an article with intent that it be used for the commission of an offence under section 1. It provides:

"A person who has anything in his custody or under his control intending without lawful excuse to use it or cause or permit another to use it:
(*a*) to destroy or damage any property belonging to some other person; or
(*b*) to destroy or damage his own or the user's property in a way which he knows is likely to endanger the life of some other person;
shall be guilty of an offence."

The offence is triable either way[91] and is punishable on conviction on indictment with ten years' imprisonment.[92] The thing possessed may be of any description, provided that the defendant intends to use it (or to cause or permit someone else to use it) as provided. The intent may be to use it at any time in the future, and may be a conditional intent to use the thing only if necessary.[93] There must be no lawful excuse for the intended use; the statutory excuses provided by section 5(2)[94] are available, *mutatis mutandis*, unless the defendant intends the thing to be used to damage property in a way which he knows is likely to endanger the life of another.[95]

Nuclear material

6.79 Section 2(2) of the Nuclear Material (Offences) Act 1983 provides that a person of any nationality commits an offence if, in the United Kingdom or elsewhere,[96]

". . . he receives, holds or deals with nuclear material[97]—
(*a*) intending, or for the purpose of enabling another, to do by means of that material an act[98] which is an offence [under section 1 of the Criminal Damage Act 1971];[99] or
(*b*) being reckless as to whether another would do such an act."

The Act has not yet been brought into force. When it is, a person guilty of the offence under section 2(2) will be liable on conviction on indictment to imprisonment for a term not exceeding fourteen years *and* not

---

91 Magistrates' Courts Act 1980 s. 17(1), Sch. 1.
92 Criminal Damage Act 1971 s. 4(2).
93 *Buckingham* (1976) 63 Cr.App.R. 159.
94 *Supra*, para. 6.40.
95 s. 5(1).
96 s. 2(1).
97 See *supra*, para. 1.165.
98 Including an omission: s. 1(2).
99 Including an act outside the jurisdiction which is an offence under that Act by virtue of s. 1(1)(*b*) of the 1983 Act (*supra*, para. 6.65): s. 2(7).

exceeding the term of imprisonment to which a person would be liable for the offence constituted by doing the contemplated act[1] at the place where the conviction occurs and at the time of the offence to which the conviction relates.[2] Proceedings for an offence under the 1983 Act which would not be an offence apart from that Act[3] may not be begun except by or with the consent of the Attorney-General.[4]

THREATS TO DAMAGE PROPERTY

6.80   Section 2 of the Criminal Damage Act 1971 provides, with an interesting disregard for syntax:

> "A person who without lawful excuse makes to another a threat, intending that that other would fear it would be carried out,
> (*a*)   to destroy or damage any property belonging to that other or a third person; or
> (*b*)   to destroy or damage his own property in a way which he knows is likely to endanger the life of that other or a third person;
> shall be guilty of an offence."

The offence is triable either way[5] and is punishable on conviction on indictment with ten years' imprisonment.[6]

6.81   There must be no lawful excuse for the threat. The statutory excuses provided by section 5(2)[7] are available unless the threat is to damage property in a way which the defendant knows is likely to endanger the life of another.[8] For the purposes of the defence under section 5(2)(*b*) he must have "threatened to . . . damage the property in question . . . in order to protect property . . .". It is not clear whether it is the threat which must be intended to protect property, or the damage threatened. A person might attempt to deter another from damaging the former's property by threatening to retaliate in kind: the retaliation would not in itself help protect the threatener's property, but the threat might. It has several times been held that a person does not *damage* property "in order to protect property" if the damage is not intended to have that effect directly, but only by inducing another person or persons to act in a particular way;[9] it would seem to follow that one cannot make a threat

---

1   *i.e.* the act intended or as to the doing of which the person convicted was reckless, as the case may be: s. 2(6)(*a*).
2   s. 2(5).
3   Disregarding the provisions of the Internationally Protected Persons Act 1978 and the Suppression of Terrorism Act 1978.
4   s. 3(1)(*a*).
5   Magistrates' Courts Act 1980 s. 17(1) and Sch. 1.
6   Criminal Damage Act 1971 s. 4(2).
7   *Supra*, para. 6.40.
8   s. 5(1).
9   *Supra*, para. 6.46.

in order to protect property at all, because a threat in itself can have no such effect. It serves *only* to induce the person threatened to act in a particular way. The question is of importance only insofar as section 5(2)(*b*) is more generous to the defendant than are the general principles of private defence, in that it takes account of what he *believes* to be a reasonable means of protection and not just what is in fact reasonable.

EXPLOSIONS AND EXPLOSIVES

Causing explosions

6.82 Section 2 of the Explosive Substances Act 1883 provides:[10]

"A person who in the United Kingdom or (being a citizen of the United Kingdom and Colonies) in the Republic of Ireland unlawfully and maliciously causes by any explosive substance an explosion of a nature likely to endanger life or to cause serious injury to property shall, whether any injury to person or property has been actually caused or not, be guilty of an offence and on conviction on indictment shall be liable to imprisonment for life."

Proceedings for this offence may not be instituted except by or with the consent of the Attorney-General,[11] and are invalid if instituted without such consent.[12] But the absence of consent does not prevent the arrest of any person or his remand in custody or on bail,[13] and the consent may therefore be obtained between the time when the defendant is charged and the time when he appears in court to answer the charge.[14] Moreover it need not relate to the specific allegations appearing in the indictment but may simply permit the prosecutor to pursue any charge under the Act which is justified by the evidence.[15]

Explosions

6.83 The essence of the offence is the causing of an explosion. In *Bouch*[16] the appellant had made a number of petrol bombs, and was charged with making explosive substances with intent to endanger life or cause serious injury to property.[17] It was argued that a petrol bomb is not an explosive

10 As substituted by Criminal Jurisdiction Act 1975 s. 7(1), (3).
11 Explosive Substances Act 1883 s. 7(1), as substituted by Administration of Justice Act 1982 s. 63(1). If the Attorney-General is unable to give consent or there is a vacancy in the office the consent of the Solicitor-General will suffice: s. 9(1).
12 *Bates* [1911] 1 K.B. 964.
13 Prosecution of Offences Act 1985 s. 25.
14 *Elliott* (1984) 81 Cr.App.R. 115.
15 *Cain and Schollick* [1976] Q.B. 496.
16 [1983] Q.B. 246.
17 Explosive Substances Act 1883 s. 3(1)(*b*); *infra*, para. 6.92.

substance because when ignited it usually produces a fireball rather than a blast effect. The Court of Appeal took the view that a blast effect is not a necessary element of an explosion and that the generation of a fireball is enough. This conclusion was reached on the basis of a definition appearing in the 1886 edition of the *Encyclopaedia Britannica*:

> ". . . 'explosion' may for our purpose be defined as the sudden or extremely rapid conversion of a solid or liquid body of small bulk into gas or vapour, occupying very many times the volume of the original substance, and, in addition, highly expanded by the heat generated during the transformation. This sudden or very rapid expansion of volume is attended by an exhibition of force, more or less violent according to the constitution of the original substance and the circumstances of explosion."

The court did not think that this definition could be improved upon for the purposes of the 1883 Act.

Risk to life or property

6.84 The explosion caused must be of a nature likely to endanger life or to cause serious injury to property, though it need not in fact cause any injury at all. It is perhaps arguable that an explosion may be *of a nature* likely to endanger life or property without actually *being* likely to do so, if it is the sort of explosion which might have done so had it occurred in different circumstances (*e.g.* had there been any people or fragile property nearby). But this could hardly be sufficient if the defendant knew that the explosion was in fact safe; and if he did not know, it might in any event be said that the explosion *was* in fact "likely" to endanger life or property, in the sense that an ordinary bystander would have thought there was a risk.[18]

6.85 Where the risk is to property it must be a risk of *serious* injury. The seriousness of an injury to property depends not only on its extent but also on the value (economic or otherwise) of the property injured. A minor injury to a great work of art might be "serious", whereas the total destruction of a worthless article would not. Presumably this is a matter for the common sense of the jury. There is no express requirement that the property thus endangered should belong to another, but this must be implied. A person may not endanger *life* by damaging his own property,[19] but in the absence of any such danger he can hardly be guilty of an offence merely because he inflicts the damage by means of an explosion. Such an act would doubtless not be "unlawful".

---

18   *Cf. Sangha* [1988] 1 W.L.R. 519; *supra*, para. 6.71.
19   Criminal Damage Act 1971 s. 1(2); *supra*, paras 6.66 ff.

Explosive substances

6.86 The explosion must be caused by an explosive substance. It is admittedly difficult to imagine an explosion *not* so caused, but the meaning of the term "explosive substance" is important for the offences of making and possessing such substances.[20] The term "explosive" means the same as it does in the Explosives Act 1875,[21] section 3 of which defines it as

"... gunpowder, nitro-glycerine, dynamite, gun-cotton, blasting powders, fulminate of mercury or of other metals, coloured fires, and every other substance, whether similar to those above mentioned or not, used or manufactured with a view to produce a practical effect by explosion or a pyrotechnic effect[22] . . . [including] fog-signals, fireworks, fuzes, rockets, percussion caps, detonators, cartridges, ammunition of all descriptions, and every adaptation or preparation of an explosive as above defined."

Section 9(1) of the 1883 Act extends the definition so as to include, unless the context otherwise requires:

(a) any materials for making any explosive substance;
(b) any apparatus, machine, implement or materials used (or intended to be used) for causing (or aiding in causing) any explosion in or with any explosive substance;
(c) any apparatus, machine, implement or materials adapted for causing (or aiding in causing) any such explosion; and
(d) any part of any such apparatus, machine or implement.

This has been held to include a shotgun[23] and any part of a vessel which, when filled with an explosive substance, is adapted for causing an explosion.[24] A petrol bomb consists of materials for the making of an explosive substance, because although the contents are not themselves explosive (the mixture of petrol and air being too rich) the breaking of the container produces a vapour which is.[25]

Malice

6.87 The explosion must be caused "maliciously". Where an offence consists in the doing of some harm, a requirement of malice means that the defendant must either intend the particular kind of harm done or be reckless whether it occurs (in the traditional sense of acting in the

20 *Infra*, paras 6.92 ff.
21 *Wheatley* [1979] 1 W.L.R. 144.
22 A fireball would be a "pyrotechnic effect" even if it were not an "explosion": *Bouch* [1983] Q.B. 246.
23 *Downey* [1971] N.I. 224.
24 *Charles* (1892) 17 Cox 499.
25 *Bouch* [1983] Q.B. 246.

knowledge that it may).[26] In the present context it is not clear whether he must foresee the endangering of life or the causing of serious injury to property (as the case may be), or merely the explosion itself. Probably he must realise that the explosion might cause *some* personal injury (though not necessarily danger to life) or *some* injury to property (though not necessarily serious injury).

Unlawfulness

6.88 The requirement that the explosion be caused "unlawfully" appears to add little. It can hardly mean that the defendant's act must amount to some legal wrong apart from the provisions of the 1883 Act, but it probably serves to exclude the case where there is no danger to life and the only property endangered is the defendant's own. Presumably it also recognises the possibility of general defences such as duress and self-defence, though circumstances in which it would be both feasible and reasonable to cause a dangerous explosion by way of self-defence are hard to imagine.[27]

Jurisdiction

6.89 Section 2 itself refers only to acts done in the United Kingdom and to acts done by citizens of the United Kingdom and Colonies in the Republic of Ireland. The Suppression of Terrorism Act 1978, however, renders a person liable to prosecution for the offence in England and Wales if he

(a) does *in a convention country* any act[28] which would have amounted to the offence had he done it in England or Wales,[29] or

(b) being a national of a convention country but not a citizen of the United Kingdom and Colonies, does *outside* the United Kingdom and that convention country any act which makes him guilty of an offence in that convention country and which, had he been a citizen of the United Kingdom and Colonies, would have made him guilty of the offence in England and Wales.[30]

A convention country is a country[31] for the time being designated in an order made by the Secretary of State as a party to the European

---

26 *Cunningham* [1957] 2 Q.B. 396.
27 *Cf. Attorney-General's Reference (No. 2 of 1983)* [1984] Q.B. 456; *infra*, para. 6.94.
28 Including an omission: s. 8(1).
29 s. 4(1)(*a*), Sch. 1. If the act would have amounted to an attempt to commit the offence he may be charged with the attempt: s. 4(1)(*b*).
30 s. 4(3), Sch. 1.
31 Including any territory: s. 8(1).

Convention on the Suppression of Terrorism signed at Strasbourg on 27 January 1977.[32]

Intent to cause explosions

6.90 Section 3(1) of the Explosive Substances Act 1883 provides:[33]

"A person who in the United Kingdom or a dependency[34] or (being a citizen of the United Kingdom and colonies) elsewhere unlawfully and maliciously—
(a) does any act with intent to cause, or conspires to cause, by an explosive substance an explosion of a nature likely to endanger life, or cause serious injury to property, whether in the United Kingdom or the Republic of Ireland, or
(b) makes or has in his possession or under his control an explosive substance with intent by means thereof to endanger life, or cause serious injury to property, whether in the United Kingdom or the Republic of Ireland, or to enable any other person so to do,
shall, whether any explosion does or does not take place, and whether any injury to person or property is actually caused or not, be guilty of an offence and on conviction on indictment shall be liable to imprisonment for life, and the explosive substance shall be forfeited."

The offence under paragraph (a) extends to any act done with intent to cause a dangerous explosion, whereas a charge of attempting to commit the offence under section 2 would require an act which was more than merely preparatory.[35] It seems odd that a person who has privately resolved to cause an explosion should commit an offence by consulting the Yellow Pages for a supplier of explosives. The offence under paragraph (b) is somewhat narrower in two respects: it requires the making or possession of an explosive substance (not just the doing of an act), and it requires an intention that life shall be endangered or serious injury to property caused (not just an intention to cause an explosion *likely* to do these things). Proceedings for these offences may not be instituted except by or with the consent of the Attorney-General.[36]

Jurisdiction

6.91 Section 4(1) and (3) of the Suppression of Terrorism Act 1978[37] apply to offences under section 3(1) of the Explosive Substances Act 1883.

32 s. 8(1). Countries so far designated include Austria, Denmark, West Germany and Sweden (S.I. 1978 No. 1245), Cyprus (S.I. 1979 No. 497), Norway (S.I. 1980 No. 357), Iceland (S.I. 1980 No. 1392), Spain and Turkey (S.I. 1981 No. 1389), Luxembourg (S.I. 1981 No. 1507), Belgium, the Netherlands, Portugal and Switzerland (S.I. 1986 No. 271), Italy and Liechtenstein (S.I. 1986 No. 1137) and France (S.I. 1987 No. 2137).
33 As substituted by Criminal Jurisdiction Act 1975 s. 7(1), (3) and amended by Criminal Law Act 1977 s. 65(4), Sch. 12.
34 i.e. the Channel Islands, the Isle of Man or any colony other than one for whose external relations a country other than the United Kingdom is responsible: s. 3(2).
35 Criminal Attempts Act 1981 s. 1(1).
36 s. 7(1); *supra*, para. 6.82.
37 *Supra*, para. 6.89.

Making and possessing explosive substances

6.92   Section 4(1) of the Explosive Substances Act 1883 provides:

"Any person who makes or knowingly has in his possession or under his control any explosive substance, under such circumstances as to give rise to a reasonable suspicion that he is not making it or does not have it in his possession or under his control for a lawful object, shall, unless he can show that he made it or had it in his possession or under his control for a lawful object, be guilty of felony, and on conviction, shall be liable to imprisonment for a term not exceeding fourteen years, and the explosive substance shall be forfeited."

Proceedings may not be instituted except by or with the consent of the Attorney-General.[38] Broadly speaking the effect of the offence is to create a rebuttable presumption that a person who makes or knowingly possesses explosives for no obviously lawful purpose does so for the purpose of unlawfully causing an explosion; but since he is not presumed to intend a *dangerous* explosion the maximum penalty is 14 years' imprisonment, whereas proof of such an intention would render him liable to imprisonment for life.[39]

Raising the presumption

6.93   In order to invoke this presumption the prosecution must prove:

(a) that the defendant either made an explosive substance or knowingly had it in his possession or under his control, and

(b) that the circumstances were such as to give rise to a reasonable suspicion that he did not make it, or have it in his possession or under his control (as the case may be), for a lawful object.

Where the prosecution rely on possession rather than manufacture they must prove that the defendant knew he was in possession of an explosive substance. An indictment failing to allege such knowledge is defective,[40] though the defect need not result in the quashing of a conviction if knowledge is admitted in the course of the trial.[41] More precisely, the defendant must be proved to have known both that he had the substance in his possession or under his control *and* that it was an explosive substance; but if the prosecution can establish (as they must) a reasonable suspicion that the possession was not for a lawful object, this in itself may justify the inference that he knew it was an explosive.[42]

38   s. 7(1); *supra*, para. 6.82.
39   s. 3(1)(*b*); *supra*, para. 6.90.
40   *Stewart and Harris* (1959) 44 Cr.App.R. 29.
41   *McVitie* [1960] 2 Q.B. 483.
42   *Hallam* [1957] 1 Q.B. 569 at p. 573.

Lawful object

6.94 If the prosecution can establish these facts it is for the defence to prove, on the balance of probabilities, that the object of the manufacture or possession was a lawful one. An intention that the explosives be used in a manner involving no risk to others, or to the property of others, would presumably be a lawful object. But it cannot be sufficient merely to show that the intended use would not have amounted to an offence under section 2, because that offence requires an explosion of a nature likely to endanger *life* or to cause *serious* injury to property. The causing of explosions likely to result in some personal injury (though not danger to life), or in some minor damage to the property of others, can hardly be a lawful object unless justified by special circumstances. If special circumstances do exist, however, the defendant may be able to justify not only his intended use of the explosives but also his manufacture or possession of them. In *Attorney-General's Reference (No. 2 of 1983)*[43] the defendant's shop had been attacked by rioters and he made petrol bombs in order to defend himself against further attack. The Court of Appeal rejected the suggestion that this could not amount to a lawful object, and that self-defence could only justify spontaneous actions and not the premeditated preparation of violence. If the defendant could satisfy the jury on the balance of probabilities that his object was to protect himself (or his family or property) against imminent apprehended attack, and to do so by means which he believed were no more than reasonably necessary to meet the force used by the attackers, he would have established that his object was lawful. This was so even though the manufacture and storage of the explosives without a licence involved the commission of offences under the Explosives Act 1875: the object might be lawful although the means were not. But the defence was available only as long as an attack was imminently apprehended. If the defendant kept the explosives after the immediate threat had passed, his object would cease to be lawful and his possession would become an offence.

6.95 The offence under section 4 (unlike those under sections 2 and 3) extends only to acts done within the jurisdiction. But if the defendant makes or possesses explosives in England with a view to causing explosions abroad, he cannot establish that his object is lawful merely by pointing out that the causing of the explosions would not be an offence under English law. He must prove, by means of expert evidence if necessary, that it would be lawful in the country or countries where it is intended to take place.[44]

43 [1984] Q.B. 456; following *Fegan* (1971) 78 Cr.App.R. 189.
44 *Berry* [1985] A.C. 246.

Accessories

6.96 Section 5 of the Explosive Substances Act 1883 provides:

"Any person who within or (being a subject of Her Majesty) without Her Majesty's dominions by the supply of or solicitation for money, the providing of premises, the supply of materials, or in any manner whatsoever, procures, counsels, aids, abets, or is accessory to, the commission of any crime under this Act, . . . shall be liable to be tried and punished for that crime, as if he had been guilty as a principal."

This appears to add nothing to the general principles relating to the liability of accessories.[45] In *McCarthy*[46] one of the defendants had been charged with possessing an explosive contrary to section 4,[47] and the other with aiding and abetting that offence—*i.e. not* under section 5. The Court of Criminal Appeal rejected the suggestion that it is impossible to aid and abet an offence of possession: although nearly all such cases will amount to joint possession, in which case all those involved will be principal offenders, it is possible for a person who is not himself in possession or control of an explosive to encourage or assist a person who is. The prosecution must prove that the alleged accessory

(a) knew that the principal offender had explosives in his possession or under his control,

(b) knew facts giving rise to a reasonable suspicion that the principal offender did not have them in his possession or under his control for a lawful object, and

(c) was present actively encouraging or in some way helping the principal offender in the commission of the offence.

Dangerous acts in explosives stores

6.97 Section 77 of the Explosives Act 1875 provides, in part:

"Any person other than the occupier[48] of or person employed in or about any factory, magazine,[49] or store[50] who is found committing any act which tends to cause explosion or fire in or about such factory, magazine, or store, shall be guilty of an offence."

The offence is punishable on conviction on indictment with an unlimited fine and on summary conviction with a fine of the statutory maximum.[51]

---

45 Accessories and Abettors Act 1861 s. 8.
46 [1964] 1 W.L.R. 196.
47 *Supra,* para. 6.92.
48 Including any number of persons and a body corporate, and, in the case of any manufacture or trade, any person carrying on such manufacture or trade: s. 108.
49 Including any ship or other vessel used for the purpose of keeping any explosive: s. 108.
50 *i.e.* a gunpowder store existing when the Act was passed or a place for keeping an explosive licensed by a local authority under the Act: s. 108.
51 Health and Safety at Work Act 1974 s. 33(3), Sch. 1.

CONVEYANCES

6.98 There are many offences of damaging specific types of property, and no attempt will be made to compile a comprehensive list here; but some of these offences merit special mention. Probably the type of property best protected in this respect, for obvious reasons, is the conveyance. The causing of damage or danger to motor vehicles, trains, aircraft or vessels will often be an offence under legislation other than the Criminal Damage Act.

Motor vehicles

6.99 Section 29 of the Road Traffic Act 1972 provides:

"If, while a motor vehicle[52] is on a road[53] or on a parking place provided by a local authority, a person otherwise than with lawful authority or reasonable cause gets on to the vehicle or tampers with the brake or other part of its mechanism, he shall be guilty of an offence."

The offence is punishable on summary conviction with a fine of level 3 on the standard scale.[54] The drafting invites an argument based on the *ejusdem generis* rule, that tampering with a part of the mechanism other than the brake will not suffice unless the part tampered with is somehow *like* the brake; but it is hard to imagine how a part other than the brake might resemble the brake, and such an interpretation would clearly be too narrow. Nor, it is submitted, is the term "mechanism" necessarily to be construed in the light of the definition of a motor vehicle as a "mechanically propelled" vehicle: it must be possible to commit the offence by tampering with a mechanical part which serves some function other than that of making the vehicle go. This would seem to follow from the use of the expression "the brake or other part of its mechanism": apparently the brake is itself part of the mechanism, but making the vehicle go is precisely what it does *not* do. "Tampering" with a part is clearly a broader notion than damaging it, and indeed would seem to cover any unauthorised movement. If both this and the previous suggestion are correct, it follows that the common practice of inserting advertising material under the windscreen wipers of parked cars is in fact an offence.

---

52 *i.e.* a mechanically propelled vehicle intended or adapted for use on roads: s. 190(1).
53 *i.e.* any highway and any other road to which the public has access, including a bridge over which a road passes: s. 196(1).
54 Sch. 4 as amended by Criminal Justice Act 1982 ss. 38, 46.

Trains

Intent to obstruct or damage

6.100 Section 35 of the Malicious Damage Act 1861 provides, as amended:[55]

> "Whosoever shall unlawfully and maliciously put, place, cast or throw upon or across any railway[56] any wood, stone, or other matter or thing, or shall unlawfully and maliciously take up, remove, or displace any rail, sleeper, or other matter or thing belonging to any railway, or shall unlawfully and maliciously turn, move, or divert any points or other machinery belonging to any railway, or shall unlawfully and maliciously make or show, hide or remove, any signal or light upon or near to any railway, or shall unlawfully and maliciously do or cause to be done any other matter or thing, with intent, in any of the cases aforesaid, to obstruct, upset, overthrow, injure, or destroy any engine, tender, carriage, or truck using such railway, shall be guilty of an offence, and being convicted thereof shall be liable to imprisonment for life."

The deliberate obstruction or attempted obstruction of trains is "malicious" even if done in a spirit of mischief rather than malice in the ordinary sense.[57] Indeed the requirement of intent appears to render that of malice redundant: one cannot intend consequences without foreseeing them, which is all that malice technically involves.[58]

Obstruction by unlawful act or wilful neglect

6.101 Section 36 of the Malicious Damage Act 1861 provides, as amended:[59]

> "Whosoever, by any unlawful act, or by any wilful omission or neglect, shall obstruct or cause to be obstructed any engine or carriage using any railway or shall aid or assist therein, shall be guilty of an offence and being convicted thereof shall be liable . . . to be imprisoned for any term not exceeding two years."

This offence is triable either way.[60] Unlike the more serious offence under section 35, it requires that an engine or carriage (not, it seems, a tender or truck) should actually be obstructed: an act done with intent to obstruct is not sufficient. But the obstruction may be caused either by an unlawful act, such as one of those described in section 35,[61] or by wilful omission or neglect. Thus the offence can be committed not only by

---

55 Statute Law Revision Act 1892; Criminal Justice Act 1948 s. 83(3), Sch. 10.
56 Including a private railway: *O'Gorman v. Sweet* (1890) 54 J.P. 663.
57 *Upton and Gutteridge* (1851) 5 Cox 298.
58 *Cunningham* [1957] 2 Q.B. 396.
59 Criminal Justice Act 1948 s. 1(2).
60 Magistrates' Courts Act 1980 s. 17(1), Sch. 1.
61 *Hardy* (1871) L.R. 1 C.C.R. 278.

actively obstructing the line but also by passively allowing it to be obstructed, *e.g.* by failing to keep livestock off it. In *Gittins*[62] the appellant had driven a tractor across a level crossing in the path of a train, and was held to have obstructed the train by wilful neglect: the term "wilful" did not imply that the obstruction had to be deliberate. It was sufficient if the appellant knew that his conduct involved the risk of obstruction unless he took reasonable care, but deliberately fell short of exercising such care. This decision may have implications for the alternative form of the offence (which might well have been relied upon in *Gittins* itself), *viz.* obstruction by an unlawful act. If an act of obstruction also requires foresight of the risk of obstruction and a deliberate failure to take the necessary care, this amounts to a requirement of malice—in which case it is surprising that that requirement is not expressly stated, as it is in section 35 (where it is redundant). It may therefore be that where the obstruction is caused by a positive act something less than a deliberate failure to take care will suffice.

Throwing missiles

6.102 Section 56(1) of the British Transport Commission Act 1949 provides, as amended:[63]

> "Any person who shall unlawfully throw or cause to fall or strike at against into or upon any engine tender motor carriage or truck used upon or any works or apparatus upon any railway or siding now or hereafter belonging or leased to or worked by any of the Boards[64] any stone matter or thing likely to cause damage or injury to persons or property shall on conviction be liable to a penalty not exceeding level 3 on the standard scale . . ."

Aircraft

6.103 Part I of the Aviation Security Act 1982 creates a number of offences against the safety of aircraft. Most of them (*e.g.* hijacking,[65] interfering with air navigation facilities[66] and the possession of firearms, explosives *etc.* in aircraft, aerodromes or air navigation installations)[67] are primarily offences of terrorism and only incidentally offences against property. More directly relevant for present purposes are the provisions of section 2. Section 2(1) provides, in part:

---

62 [1982] R.T.R. 363.
63 Transport Act 1962 Sch. 2; Criminal Justice Act 1982 s. 46.
64 *i.e.* the British Railways Board, the British Transport Docks Board and the British Waterways Board (Transport Act 1962 s. 1(1)), any wholly-owned subsidiary of any of them (Transport Act 1968 s. 156(2), Sch. 16), and London Regional Transport and any of its subsidiaries (London Regional Transport Act 1984 s. 67(3), Sch. 4).
65 s. 1(1).
66 s. 3(1).
67 s. 4(1).

"It shall, subject to subsection (4) below, be an offence for any person unlawfully[68] and intentionally—
(*a*) to destroy an aircraft in service[69] or so to damage such an aircraft as to render it incapable of flight or as to be likely to endanger its safety in flight . . ."

Section 2(2) provides, in part:

"It shall also, subject to subsection (4) below, be an offence for any person unlawfully and intentionally to place, or cause to be placed, on an aircraft in service any device or substance which is likely to destroy the aircraft, or is likely so to damage it as to render it incapable of flight or as to be likely to endanger its safety in flight . . ."

These offences are punishable on conviction on indictment with life imprisonment.[70] Proceedings may not be instituted except by or with the consent of the Attorney-General.[71] Under section 2(4) an act committed in relation to an aircraft used in military, customs or police service does not amount to either offence unless it is committed in the United Kingdom or by a United Kingdom national; but, with that exception, the act may be committed in the United Kingdom or elsewhere, whatever the nationality of the person committing it and whatever the State in which the aircraft is registered.[72]

Vessels

6.104 Section 47 of the Malicious Damage Act 1861 provides:

"Whosoever shall unlawfully mask, alter, or remove any light or signal, or unlawfully exhibit any false light or signal, with intent to bring any ship, vessel or boat into danger, or unlawfully and maliciously do anything tending to the immediate loss or destruction of any ship, vessel, or boat, and for which no punishment is hereinbefore provided, shall be . . . liable, at the discretion of the court, to imprisonment for life . . ."

Section 48 provides:

"Whosoever shall unlawfully and maliciously cut away, cast adrift, remove, alter, deface, sink, or destroy, or shall unlawfully and maliciously do any act with such intent, or shall in any other manner unlawfully and maliciously injure or conceal any boat, buoy, buoy-rope, perch or mark, used or intended for the guidance of seamen or for the purpose of navigation, shall be . . .

---

68 An act committed in the United Kingdom is unlawful for the purposes of section 2 if (apart from the 1982 Act) it constitutes an offence under the law of the part of the United Kingdom where it is committed. An act committed elsewhere is unlawful if it would (apart from the Act) have been an offence under the law of England and Wales, or Scotland, had it been committed there: s. 2(6).
69 An aircraft is in service from the time of pre-flight preparation until 24 hours after landing: s. 38(3)(*b*).
70 s. 2(5).
71 s. 8(1)(*a*).
72 s. 2(3).

liable, at the discretion of the court, to imprisonment for any term not exceeding seven years . . ."

A person acts "maliciously" if he actually foresees the kind of harm in question,[73] which in this context presumably means damage to a vessel. The malice required need not be conceived against the owner of the property.[74]

PROTECTED MONUMENTS

6.105 Section 28(1) of the Ancient Monuments and Archaeological Areas Act 1979 provides:

"A person who without lawful excuse destroys or damages any protected monument—
(*a*) knowing that it is a protected monument; and
(*b*) intending to destroy or damage the monument or being reckless[75] as to whether the monument would be destroyed or damaged;
shall be guilty of an offence."

The offence is triable either way and is punishable on conviction on indictment with two years' imprisonment or a fine or both.[76]

6.106 A "monument" is defined as

(a) any building,[77] structure or work, whether above or below the surface of the land, and any cave or excavation;
(b) any site comprising the remains[78] of any such building, structure or work or of any cave or excavation; or
(c) any site comprising, or comprising the remains of, any vehicle, vessel,[79] aircraft or other movable structure or part thereof, which neither constitutes nor forms part of any work which is a monument within (a) above,[80] provided that the situation of that object or its remains in that particular site is a matter of public interest.[81]

Any machinery attached to a monument is regarded as part of the monument if it could not be detached without being dismantled,[82] and refer-

---

73 *Cunningham* [1957] 2 Q.B. 396.
74 s. 58.
75 For intention and recklessness see *supra*, paras. 6.11 ff.
76 s. 28(4).
77 But not an ecclesiastical building for the time being used for ecclesiastical purposes: s. 61(8).
78 Including any trace or sign of the previous existence of the thing in question: s. 61(13).
79 Other than one protected by an order under s. 1 of the Protection of Wrecks Act 1973 designating an area round the site as a restricted area: s. 61(8)(*b*).
80 s. 61(7).
81 s. 61(8)(*a*).
82 s. 61(1), (7).

ences to a monument include references to the site of the monument.[83] A "protected" monument is a monument for the time being included in the schedule of monuments maintained by the Secretary of State under section 1 of the Act,[84] or one under the ownership or guardianship of the Secretary of State, the Historic Buildings and Monuments Commission or a local authority[85] by virtue of the Act.[86] It is not a defence that the damage is done by the owner of the monument or under his authority, unless it is done for the execution of works for which scheduled monument consent has been given under section 2 or 3 of the Act.[87] It follows that the defence of lawful excuse will very rarely be available.

MAIL

6.107   Section 11(1) of the Post Office Act 1953 provides, in part, as amended:[88]

> "A person shall not send or attempt to send or procure to be sent a postal packet[89] which—
> (a)   save as the Post Office may either generally or in any particular case allow, encloses any explosive, dangerous, noxious or deleterious substance, any filth, any sharp instrument not properly protected, any noxious living creature, or any creature, article or thing whatsoever which is likely to injure either other postal packets in course of conveyance or a person engaged in the business of the Post Office . . ."

Contravention of this provision is an offence triable either way and is punishable on conviction on indictment with twelve months' imprisonment.[90] The detention by the Post Office of a postal packet on the grounds of a contravention of section 11, or of any provisions of a scheme made under section 28 of the Post Office Act 1969, does not exempt the sender from any proceedings which might have been taken if the packet had been delivered in due course of post.[91]

6.108   Section 60(1) of the Post Office Act 1953 provides, as amended:[92]

---

83   s. 61(10)(*a*). The site of a monument includes not only the land in or on which it is situated but also any land comprising or adjoining it which appears to the Secretary of State or the Historic Buildings and Monuments Commission or a local authority, in the exercise in relation to that monument of any of their functions under the Act, to be essential for the monument's support and preservation: s. 61(9).
84   s. 1(11).
85   *i.e.* a county, district or London borough council or the Common Council of the City of London: s. 61(1) as amended by Local Government Act 1985 Sch. 17.
86   ss. 28(3), 61(1).
87   s. 28(2).
88   Post Office Act 1969 s. 76, Sch. 4.
89   Including any packet or article transmissible by post: s. 87(1).
90   s. 11(2).
91   s. 11(4).
92   British Telecommunications Act 1981 s. 89, Sch. 6.

"A person shall not place or attempt to place in or against any post office letter box[93] any fire, match, light, explosive substance, dangerous substance, filth, noxious or deleterious substance, or fluid, and shall not commit a nuisance in or against any post office letter box, and shall not do or attempt to do anything likely to injure the box, or its appurtenances or contents."

Contravention of this provision is an offence triable either way and is punishable on conviction on indictment with twelve months' imprisonment.[94]

ELECTRICAL SUPPLY LINES

6.109 Section 22 of the Electric Lighting Act 1882 provides, as amended:[95]

"Any person who unlawfully and maliciously cuts or injures any electric line[96] or work[97] with intent to cut off any supply of electricity shall be guilty of an offence, and be liable to imprisonment for any term not exceeding five years . . ."

The offence is triable either way.[98]

ENDANGERING PROPERTY BY BREACH OF CONTRACT

6.110 Under section 5 of the Conspiracy and Protection of Property Act 1875 it is an offence for a person wilfully and maliciously to break a contract of service or of hiring, knowing or having reasonable cause to believe that the probable consequences of his so doing, either alone or in combination with others, will be (*inter alia*) to expose valuable property, whether real or personal, to destruction or serious injury. The offence is punishable on summary conviction with three months' imprisonment or a fine of level 2 on the standard scale.[99]

93 *i.e.* any pillar box, wall box, or other box or receptacle provided by the permission or under the authority of the Post Office for the purpose of receiving postal packets, or any class of postal packets, for transmission by or under the authority of the Post Office: s. 87(1).
94 s. 60(2).
95 Criminal Justice Act 1948 s. 1(2); Criminal Law Act 1967 s. 10, Schs. 2, 3.
96 *i.e.* a wire or wires, conductor, or other means used for the purpose of conveying, transmitting, or distributing electricity with any casing, coating, covering, tube, pipe, or insulator enclosing, surrounding, or supporting the same, or any part thereof, or any apparatus connected therewith for the purpose of conveying, transmitting, or distributing electricity, electric currents or any like agency: s. 32.
97 Including any building, machinery, engine, work, matter or thing of whatever description required to supply electricity and to carry into effect the object of the undertakers under the Act: s. 32.
98 Magistrates' Courts Act 1980 s. 17(1), Sch. 1.
99 Criminal Law Act 1977 s. 31, Sch. 13; Criminal Justice Act 1982 s. 46.

JURISDICTION OF MAGISTRATES

6.111   Section 7(2) of the Criminal Damage Act 1971 provides:

"No rule of law ousting the jurisdiction of magistrates' courts to try offences where a dispute of title to property is involved shall preclude magistrates' courts from trying offences under this Act, or any other offences of destroying or damaging property."

CHAPTER 7

Trespass

7.01 Warning notices to the contrary notwithstanding, trespass in itself is not generally a criminal offence; but additional factors may turn it into one. Such factors may include (*inter alia*) the trespasser's purpose, the commission of other offences, the possession of weapons, the use or threat of violence, refusal to leave on request, and the nature of the premises in question.

BURGLARY

7.02 Section 9(1) of the Theft Act 1968 provides:

"A person is guilty of burglary if–
(a) he enters any building or part of a building as a trespasser and with intent to commit any such offence as is mentioned in subsection (2) below;[1] or
(b) having entered any building or part of a building as a trespasser he steals or attempts to steal anything in the building or that part of it or inflicts or attempts to inflict on any person therein any grievous bodily harm."

These offences are punishable on conviction on indictment with 14 years' imprisonment.[2] In general they are triable either way but in certain circumstances they are indictable only: the relevant factors are considered below.[3]

Buildings

Ordinary meaning

7.03 Both offences require an entry into a building or part of a building.[4] The word "building" is extended to include certain objects falling outside its basic meaning,[5] but that meaning is not itself defined. In the occasional

---

1 *i.e.* theft, inflicting grievous bodily harm, rape or unlawful damage: *infra*, paras. 7.24 ff.
2 s. 9(4).
3 *Infra*, para. 7.40.
4 Obviously one cannot enter part of a building without entering the building; but it may be that the original entry into the building does not satisfy the other requirements of the offence, while a subsequent entry into part of the building does. See *infra*, paras. 7.21 ff.
5 *Infra*, para. 7.04.

borderline case it may therefore be necessary to consider whether a particular structure qualifies as a building in the ordinary sense of the word. Relevant factors would seem to include the structure's permanence or otherwise and (which comes to much the same thing) the manner of its construction. It seems reasonable to suppose that a building must at least be a part of the land on which it stands, and not merely a chattel;[6] this would raise a presumption against the inclusion of structures without foundations or other annexation to the land,[7] a presumption which could however be rebutted by evidence as to the permanence of the structure and the occupier's purpose in having it there.[8] But even a structure forming part of the land may not be a building if it lacks other essential characteristics. It probably has to be more or less enclosed: a bus shelter or a car port would hardly qualify. If it is to be the scene of a burglary it must obviously be the sort of structure which can be entered and not just trespassed upon; but, subject to that requirement, there is no reason to suppose that it must be of any minimum size.[9] A brick-built privy would clearly suffice.

Inhabited vehicles and vessels

7.04   Section 9(3) extends the scope of the offences by providing:

> "References in subsections (1) and (2) above to a building shall apply also to an inhabited vehicle or vessel, and shall apply to any such vehicle or vessel at times when the person having a habitation in it is not there as well as at times when he is."

Such vehicles and vessels are obviously not buildings, but the law of burglary applies to them as if they were. The word "inhabited" is very loose. Vehicles and vessels are put to a wide range of uses, and between the extremes which clearly do or do not constitute habitation there is a grey area. Probably the alleged inhabitant of the vehicle or vessel must at least sleep there, if not every night then fairly often; but is it sufficient if he goes there *only* to sleep? If the question ever arises it will doubtless be left to the jury. If a vehicle or vessel is used for habitation at certain times only, *e.g.* in the summer, it is arguable that by virtue of the second clause of section 9(3) it is protected by the law of burglary at other times too. But the subsection says that a vehicle or vessel which is inhabited is protected when the inhabitant is not there, not that a vehicle or vessel which is sometimes inhabited is protected when it is not inhabited as well as when it is. It is submitted that a caravan used only in summer cannot be burgled in winter.

6 For this distinction see *supra*, para. 1.06.
7 *Cf. Norfolk Constabulary v. Seekings and Gould* [1986] Crim.L.R. 167.
8 *Cf. B. and S. v. Leathley* [1979] Crim.L.R. 314.
9 *Pace* Byles J. in *Stevens v. Gourley* (1859) 7 C.B.(N.S.) 99 at p. 112.

Entry

Partial entry

7.05   The requirement that the defendant should have entered the building, or part of it, presents some difficulty where the only entry effected is that of part of his body. At common law the insertion of even a finger was enough.[10] But an ordinary word in a reforming statute should arguably be construed according to its ordinary meaning and without reference to the old authorities; and there comes a point where an intrusion is so minor as not to be, in the ordinary meaning of the word, an "entry" at all. This view is supported to some extent by dicta in two modern cases. In *Collins*,[11] the appellant had climbed up a ladder and through a young woman's bedroom window in a state of undress and with intent to rape; but this proved unnecessary, since at some stage in the course of his arrival (it was not clear precisely when) the occupant woke up, mistook him for her boy-friend and welcomed him into her bed—a turn of events of which the appellant, unaware of the mistake, proceeded to take full advantage. He was convicted of burglary by entering as a trespasser with intent to rape.[12] The Court of Appeal took the view that he would not be entering "as a trespasser" if at the moment of entering the building he thought that the occupant was inviting him in.[13] It was therefore crucial whether the entry preceded the invitation; and in view of the possibility that he might have inserted *part* of his anatomy through the window before his intended victim woke up and invited him in, it was said that he would be entering for the purposes of burglary only when he made an "effective and substantial" entry.[14]

7.06   This remark was not explained, and in *Brown (Vincent)*[15] was modified. The Court of Appeal there upheld a conviction of burglary where the appellant had leant through a shop window so that the upper half of his body was inside it. The dictum in *Collins* did not imply that there is no entry until the whole of the defendant's body is inside. Indeed it was said that the word "substantial" did not materially assist; if there is such a thing as an entry which is effective but not substantial, it is enough. But *Collins* was right in requiring the entry to be "effective", and a jury should be directed to that effect. This cannot mean that the offence under section 9(1) (*a*), the form of burglary which consists of entry with intent to commit an offence, can be committed only by an entry which is

10   *Davis* (1823) Russ. & Ry. 499.
11   [1973] Q.B. 100.
12   *Cf. infra*, para. 7.30.
13   *Infra*, para. 7.19.
14   At p. 106.
15   [1985] Crim.L.R. 212.

"effective" in the sense of enabling the entrant to commit that offence. An entry with the whole body is sufficient even if the project is doomed to failure,[16] and where the defendant has walked into the building it would be absurd to ask whether he thereby made an effective entry. But where he has only reached through a window with an arm, this may or may not be an effective entry. Perhaps it would be effective if it were sufficient to enable the defendant to steal, or to attempt to steal, but not if it were no more than an unsuccessful attempt to make a complete entry by opening a door from the inside. Even the inclusion of the former case might go beyond what most people would think of as burglary, and the latter could be more appropriately charged as an attempt.

Entry with an object

7.07 A similar approach might be appropriate to the issue, as yet undecided under the Theft Act, of whether it is possible to enter a building by inserting an object other than one's own body. It would be absurd if it were burglary to reach through a window with a human arm but not with a mechanical one. Similarly, whether or not the offence extends to an intrusion by way of an attempt to gain access, it can hardly make any difference whether such intrusion is effected with a hand or a crowbar, a trained monkey or a mechanical device under remote control. But the analogy cannot be stretched too far. It would seem excessively technical to include the propulsion into the building of a missile such as a bullet or a bomb, even one intended to cause injury or damage immediately on arrival; and if these are excluded it seems illogical to include devices programmed to explode or otherwise cause injury or damage at some later stage. A relevant factor might perhaps be whether the defendant remained in control of the device after its entry into the building or whether his role in the proceedings was then complete. It might be marginally more natural to describe him as having "entered" the building in the former case than in the latter.

Entry as a trespasser

7.08 The defendant must not only enter the building, or part of it, but must do so as a trespasser. This requirement involves both an objective element and a subjective one: the defendant's entry must in fact be a trespass, and he must realise that it is or that it may be. Further difficulties arise where it is not his entry into the building as a whole which is relied upon, but a subsequent trespassory entry into part of the building.

16 *Walkington* [1979] 1 W.L.R. 1169.

Trespass

7.09   In the absence of any overriding legal right to enter the building, even without the licence of the occupier (such as an easement or a statutory warrant), a person entering it without a licence will be a trespasser. But he may be a trespasser even if a licence apparently *has* been granted: the licence may be invalid, owing either to want of authority or to vitiating factors such as fraud or mistake, or it may not extend to the entry actually effected.

Licence unauthorised

7.10   Trespass is a wrong against the occupier of property. A licence will render lawful what would otherwise be a trespass only if it is granted by or with the authority of the occupier, who for this purpose is the person with exclusive possession of the building.[17] A licence purportedly granted by a person who is himself only a licensee ought in principle to be immaterial unless the original licensee is authorised by the occupier to grant further licences; but *Collins*[18] suggests otherwise. It will be recalled that on one view of the facts the young woman whom the appellant intended to rape had already invited him into her bedroom before he made his entry. Strictly speaking the point might have been regarded as immaterial, because the person in possession of the building (including the bedroom) was not the young woman but her mother; but this point was dismissed as unduly technical.

> "The point was raised that, the complainant not being the tenant or occupier of the dwelling house and her mother being apparently in occupation, this girl herself could not in any event have extended an effective invitation to enter, so that even if she had expressly and with full knowledge of all material facts invited the defendant in, he would nevertheless be a trespasser. Whatever be the position in the law of tort, to regard such a proposition as acceptable in the criminal law would be unthinkable." [19]

In other words, a purported licence granted by a person who is himself a licensee of the occupier may prevent the purported sub-licensee from being a trespasser even if the licensee has no authority to grant such sub-licences in the circumstances or at all. Unfortunately the court neglected to explain the extent of this discrepancy between the law of tort and that of burglary. Arguably it is confined to adult licensees who are resident in the building as members of the occupier's family, but it may extend to any licensee who is effectively in a position to let other people in. The reason for the rule is equally obscure. If the point is simply that a person invited in by a member of the occupier's family may reasonably

17   *Cf. supra*, para. 1.09.
18   [1973] Q.B. 100; *supra*, para. 7.05.
19   At p. 107.

suppose that this gives him a right to enter, it is adequately met by the court's decision that even a person who *is* a trespasser does not commit the offence if he has no idea that that is what he is.[20] If he knows that the person inviting him in has no right to do so, it is hard to see why the invitation should assist him.

Licence vitiated

7.11 A licence is simply the occupier's consent to another person's entry; and as in other cases where consent is a defence,[21] there is consent and consent. Even a licence granted by a person authorised to grant it may be invalid if it is not granted voluntarily and with full knowledge of the facts. A person who threatens the occupier into letting him in may obviously be a trespasser, though this will depend on the nature of the threat: a threat of immediate violence clearly vitiates any apparent consent, but one of a sanction not involving force probably does not.

7.12 Similarly a licence may or may not be invalidated by the fact that it is procured by fraud or otherwise granted under a misapprehension. A person who obtains admission to a building by means of a deception as to his own identity is clearly a trespasser. This is implicit in the reasoning in *Collins*.[22] In that case the complainant's mistake as to the appellant's identity was self-induced, but it was assumed to have had the effect of vitiating the licence which she purported to grant him and which (as we have seen) the court thought her somehow empowered to grant.[23] Had that licence been valid in spite of her mistake, it would have been unnecessary to investigate the effect of the appellant's ignorance of the mistake. He would not have been a trespasser at all, so the question whether it made any difference that he did not *know* he was a trespasser would not have arisen. It is submitted with respect that this assumption was clearly correct: the person on whom the licence was conferred was not in truth the appellant but the young woman's boy-friend. The same reasoning would apply *a fortiori* if the appellant had deliberately impersonated the boy-friend, except that in that case he would not only *be* a trespasser but would obviously also know that he was. Similarly he would have been guilty if, not having set out to deceive the complainant, he had realised before entering the building that she had mistaken him for someone else.

7.13 Where the mistake is as to a matter other than the identity of the licensee, the position is less clear. Certain attributes of a person are so

20   *Infra*, para. 7.19.
21   *e.g. supra*, paras. 1.73 ff.
22   [1973] Q.B. 100; *supra*, para. 7.05.
23   *Supra*, para. 7.10.

important where a licence to enter premises is concerned that a false claim
to possess such attributes may well be regarded as inducing a mistake of
identity. A person who procures admission to a house by falsely
pretending to be an official of the gas board is probably a burglar if his
intention is to steal or rape. It might be otherwise if he made no claim to
be what he is not, but deceived the occupier only as to his motives for
desiring admittance, *e.g.* by claiming to be interested in buying antiques.
It is submitted that a licence procured by such a deception would
nonetheless be a valid licence to enter;[24] *a fortiori* if the entrant *were*
interested in buying antiques, albeit only at prices far below their real
value.[25] But the question may be academic if a licence procured by a
deception as to the intending entrant's purposes is regarded as authorising
only an entry for the purpose for which it is granted. To this possibility
we now turn.

Licence abused

7.14 Even if the defendant has a valid licence to enter the building, or
the part of it in question, it does not follow that his entry is not a trespass.
It may be that the entry he actually makes is not the sort of entry which
is permitted by the licence. As Scrutton L.J. once said:

"When you invite a person into your house to use the staircase, you do not
invite him to slide down the banisters . . . "[26]

Similarly, no doubt, a licence to enter a building through a door would
not extend to an entry through a window. This is not in itself a point of
great significance. It has however been invoked so as to bring within the
law of burglary an entry effected in an authorised manner but for an
unauthorised purpose.[27] In *Jones and Smith*[28] the appellants had entered
the house of Smith's father and stolen two television sets. Smith *père*
gave evidence (albeit inconsistent with his previous statements) to the
effect that his son had unreserved permission to enter the house and
would not be a trespasser there at any time. It was argued that if this
were so then Smith *fils* could not have entered the house as a trespasser
even if his purpose in entering were such that his father would not have
allowed him to enter for that purpose. The argument was rejected:

" . . . it is our view that a person is a trespasser for the purpose of section
9(1) (*b*) of the Theft Act 1968 if he enters premises of another knowing that

24 *Cf. Whittaker v. Campbell* [1984] Q.B. 318; *supra*, para. 5.12.
25 Even if this were a deception at all (which is debatable), an intention to obtain property
by deception is not sufficient for burglary. It would have to be proved in addition that
the defendant intended, for example, to steal if he got the chance.
26 *The Carlgarth* [1927] P. 93 at p. 110.
27 See P.J. Pace, "Burglarious Trespass" [1985] Crim.L.R. 716.
28 [1976] 1 W.L.R. 672.

he is entering in excess of the permission that has been given to him, or being reckless as to whether he is entering in excess of the permission that has been given to him to enter." [29]

7.15 As a matter of civil law the defence argument may well be right. In *Byrne v. Kinematograph Renters Society Ltd* [30] it was held not to be a trespass to enter a cinema, having bought a ticket, for the purpose not of watching the film but of counting the audience. It would be remarkable if the law were otherwise. In *Jones and Smith* the court did not question this decision but distinguished it on the ground that the alleged trespassers in the cinema, unlike Smith, had done nothing that they were not invited to do. But this, with respect, is immaterial: Smith may have *become* a trespasser when he stole a television, but it does not follow that he entered as one. The civil doctrine of trespass *ab initio* has no application to the law of burglary. [31] Similarly the point is not borne out by authorities to the effect that a person is a trespasser if he has permission to hunt for rabbits but hunts for hares instead, [32] or if he uses a highway to seek game [33] or to interfere with a shoot: [34] some of the reasoning in these cases admittedly suggests that such a person is a trespasser as soon as he enters the land in question, solely by virtue of his unauthorised purpose, but in none of them was this actually decided. [35] In *Jones and Smith* the court relied on a passage in the speech of Lord Atkin in *Hillen and Pettigrew v. I.C.I. (Alkali) Ltd,* [36] on the extent of the duty of care owed by an occupier of premises to a person invited into them:

" . . . this duty . . . only extends so long as and so far as the invitee is making what can reasonably be contemplated as an ordinary and reasonable use of the premises by the invitee for the purposes for which he has been invited. He is not invited to use any part of the premises for purposes which he knows are wrongfully dangerous and constitute an improper use."

But again this does not establish the point at issue, since Lord Atkin was clearly referring to an invitee who not only enters with the intention of using the premises in an unauthorised manner but actually does so. If this were not obvious from his Lordship's own words, it would be apparent from the fact that he immediately proceeded to illustrate them with the dictum of Scrutton L.J. quoted above. It is submitted with respect that the view taken by the court in *Jones and Smith* derives little support from the English authorities.

29 At p. 675.
30 [1958] 1 W.L.R. 762.
31 *Collins* [1973] Q.B. 100 at p. 107.
32 *Taylor v. Jackson* (1898) 78 L.T. 555.
33 *Pratt* (1855) 4 E. & B. 860.
34 *Harrison v. Duke of Rutland* [1893] 1 Q.B. 142.
35 *Barker* (1983) 153 C.L.R. 338 at pp. 358 and 372, *per* Brennan and Deane JJ. and Dawson J. respectively.
36 [1936] A.C. 65 at p. 69.

7.16 The only other authority relied upon was *Collins*,[37] but the court did not explain how its reasoning was assisted by that decision; on the contrary, it was said that *Collins* had "added to the concept of trespass as a civil wrong only the mental element of *mens rea*".[38] It is submitted that, far from supporting the decision in *Jones and Smith*, *Collins* is actually inconsistent with it. Even if Collins had the young woman's apparent consent to his entry at the moment when he entered, the jury found that he had entered with the intention of raping her. Her unexpected reaction doubtless raised his hopes that she might welcome his advances, but according to the jury's verdict he intended to rape her if she did not.[39] Obviously she did not invite him in for the purpose of raping her. Therefore, even if he entered with her permission, he entered for a purpose other than that for which her permission was granted. If Smith entered "in excess of" his licence, so did Collins. But the court which allowed the latter's appeal clearly did not accept that his intentions would have precluded him from relying on any licence which he might validly have been granted. On the contrary, it assumed that had the circumstances been as he supposed them to be (*i.e.*, had the complainant's invitation been extended to him, rather than the person she thought he was), he would not have entered as a trespasser, even if he realised that she might yet withhold her consent to intercourse and in that event he intended to rape her anyway. Admittedly the point does not appear to have been argued in precisely the same way as in *Jones and Smith*, but it is unlikely that an argument along those lines would have fared any better. The court rejected the contention that a man who enters a woman's bedroom with the intention of raping her is a burglar even if he wrongly supposes that she has invited him in. It would hardly have accepted the bolder contention that he is a burglar even if she *has* invited him in. The case decides, implicitly but *a fortiori*, that he is not. In treating it as authority only for the proposition that the defendant must *realise* he is trespassing,[40] and not on the logically prior question of whether he *is*, it is submitted with respect that the court which decided *Jones and Smith* fell into error.

7.17 A further objection to the decision is that it leaves the requirement of entry as a trespasser almost redundant, at any rate in the case of burglary contrary to section 9(1) (*a*). That form of the offence requires

---

37 [1973] Q.B. 100; *supra*, para. 7.05.
38 On this point see *infra*, para. 7.19.
39 In *Barker* (1983) 153 C.L.R. 338 at p. 345, Mason J. said that this could not be assumed: the appellant's original intention to rape may have lapsed when the prospective victim invited him in. But the jury were directed that they must be satisfied that he entered with intent to rape, and they convicted.
40 See p. 675.

an entry which is both a trespass *and* effected with intent to commit theft, rape, unlawful damage or grievous bodily harm. Clearly it is envisaged that some persons who enter with the necessary intent will not be burglars because their entry is not a trespass. But according to *Jones and Smith* a person who enters for the purpose of committing one of the specified offences must also be entering as a trespasser unless he has not just a right to enter but a right to enter irrespective of his purpose in doing so. Sometimes this may indeed be the case: *e.g.* where he is himself the occupier, or he has the occupier's permission to enter for precisely the purpose for which he does enter, or he enters in order to commit a specified offence *and* to carry out a different purpose for which he has permission to enter.[41] But in the great majority of cases the effect of *Jones and Smith* is that a person who enters with the requisite intent is automatically entering as a trespasser even if his entry would otherwise be authorised. It may be doubted whether the additional requirement of trespass was really intended to come into play only in comparatively unusual situations.

7.18   The whole question was considered by the High Court of Australia in *Barker.*[42] The appellant had been authorised to enter a house for the purpose of keeping an eye on it while the occupier was away, but entered it with intent to steal. It was held by a majority that this was burglary contrary to the Victorian equivalent of section 9(1) (*a*). But even the majority insisted that a licensee does not go beyond his permission to enter merely because he enters for a purpose of which the occupier would not approve: this is so only if the licence is expressly or impliedly limited to an entry for purposes other than those for which the entry is in fact made. Had Smith's father been asked by an officious bystander whether the invitation he had extended to his son was confined to visits made in a spirit of filial piety, he might have thought the matter worthy of consideration, but he would scarcely have testily suppressed the enquirer with a common "Oh, of course". Indeed the actual decision in *Jones and Smith* was doubted in *Barker.*[43] But the dissenting member of the court, Murphy J., pointed out the difficulties involved in distinguishing between a licence which is impliedly limited in scope and one which is not. When a shopkeeper invites the public into his shop, is the invitation implicitly confined to those who intend to buy, or does it extend to browsers with no money, or is it entirely general (subject of course to the shopkeeper's

---

41 *Barker* (1983) 153 C.L.R. 338 at p. 347, *per* Mason J. *Sed quaere*: would Smith have escaped liability if he had had a cup of tea with his father as well as stealing the television sets?
42 (1983) 153 C.L.R. 338.
43 By Mason J., at p. 344.

right to exclude any particular person)? Only on the last assumption would the *Barker* test avoid the conclusion that a person who enters the shop with intent to steal is a burglar. Whether this would be a sensible conclusion is a matter of opinion, but it would certainly be a surprising one.

Awareness of trespass

7.19 Reference has already been made to a further element of the offence, which was established by *Collins*.[44] As we have seen, the court proceeded on the assumption that even if the complainant had apparently invited the appellant into her bedroom before he entered it, his entrance was still a trespass because the invitation was in fact extended not to him but to someone else. But, it was held, this did not mean that he had entered as a trespasser within the meaning of section 9(1).

> "We hold that, for the purposes of section 9 of the Theft Act, a person entering a building is not guilty of trespass if he enters without knowledge that he is trespassing or at least without acting recklessly as to whether or not his in unlawfully entering . . .
> In the judgment of this court there cannot be a conviction for entering premises 'as a trespasser' within the meaning of section 9 of the Theft Act unless the person entering does so knowing that he is a trespasser and nevertheless deliberately enters, or, at the very least, is reckless as to whether or not he is entering the premises of another without the other party's consent." [45]

Recklessness in this context clearly means actual awareness of the possibility of facts which would render the entry a trespass: the extended scope subsequently given to the concept of recklessness in *Caldwell*[46] applies where that term appears in the statute itself, not where it is used in the course of judicial exposition to denote an implied requirement of *mens rea* in the traditional sense. Where the defendant is charged under section 9(1) (*a*) with entering as a trespasser with intent to commit an offence, it must therefore be proved either that he knew he had no licence or other authority to enter, or that he at least realised that that *might* be the case; and he must have known or realised this at the moment when he entered.

7.20 In the case of a charge under section 9(1) (*b*), of first entering as a trespasser and then stealing or inflicting grievous bodily harm, or attempting to do so, the position is less clear. Must it again be proved that the defendant realised *when he entered* that he was or might be a

---

44 [1973] Q.B. 100; *supra*, para. 7.05.
45 At pp. 104 f.
46 [1982] A.C. 341; *supra*, para. 6.23.

trespasser, or is it sufficient that he had become aware of this possibility
by the time of the subsequent act relied upon? Suppose Collins had realised
after entering the bedroom that the complainant's invitation had not been
meant for him after all, and he had stolen her watch before leaving.
Would he have been guilty under section 9(1) (*b*)? The answer depends
whether the requirement of knowledge or recklessness is implied by virtue
of the general principle of *actus non facit reum nisi mens sit rea* or by way
of construction of the phrase "enters [or 'having entered'] . . . as a
trespasser". If the former, it must be satisfied at the moment of the alleged
offence; if the latter, at that of the entry. The question did not arise in
Collins itself because the charge was laid under section 9(1) (*a*), but the
wording of the judgment suggests that it was the latter approach which
the court had in mind. In the first sentence quoted above it is said that a
person who has no idea that he may be a trespasser is not only not guilty
of burglary but (for the purposes of section 9) is not even guilty of
trespass; and in the second sentence it is said that he does not enter "as
a trespasser". It is true that the two sentences are separated in the
judgment by quotations from two writers[47] who argue that such a person
should be acquitted on grounds of principle although he does enter
as a trespasser, but the court did not express unqualified approval of these
passages. It merely preferred them to the alternative view that ignorance
of the fact of trespass is not a defence at all. Section 9(1) (*b*), it should be
noted, is designed only to ensure that where the defendant has actually
done one of the acts specified the prosecution need not prove that he
intended to do it at the time when he entered.[48] The object is to catch those
who are probably guilty under paragraph (*a*) but whose guilt under that
paragraph may be hard to prove. *Collins* decides that paragraph (*a*) was
never intended to apply to a person who enters under the impression that
he is not a trespasser, even if he intends to commit one of the specified
offences; there is no reason to suppose that paragraph (*b*) *is* intended to
catch him merely because he discovers, before carrying out his intentions,
that he is a trespasser after all. It is submitted with respect that the court's
words can and should be taken at face value, and that a person who does
not realise that he may be a trespasser is not entering "as a trespasser"
for the purpose of either form of the offence.

Entering part of a building as a trespasser

7.21 In view of the decision in *Collins*[49] there are two reasons why a
person entering a building may not be entering as a trespasser: he may

47 J.C. Smith and E. Griew.
48 *Infra*, para. 7.35.
49 [1973] Q.B. 100; *supra*, paras. 7.05, 7.19.

have a licence or other authority to enter, or he may not realise that he has no such authority. In neither case can he be guilty of burglary by virtue of his entry into the building, even if he enters with the intention of committing an offence[50] and even (it is submitted)[51] if he actually does so. But in either case he may still commit burglary if, having entered the *building* otherwise than as a trespasser, he then proceeds to enter *part* of the building as a trespasser. The difference may be due to one or more of a number of factors. It may be that his authority to be in the building at all has been revoked, or that only since entering the building has he realised that he has no such authority; if in either case he then enters another part of the building he will be doing so as a trespasser. Or it may be that he first enters a part of the building where he is allowed to go but then proceeds to one where he knows he is not. In any of these cases he is entering part of the building as a trespasser, and he commits burglary if he does so with the intention of committing one of the specified offences in that part or if he does one of the specified acts there. Alternatively it may be that he did enter the building as a trespasser: in that case he is guilty of burglary not only if when he entered the building he intended to commit one of the specified offences, or if he does one of the specified acts, but also if he enters *part* of the building (still as a trespasser) with the intention of committing one of the specified offences in that part.

7.22 It may therefore be crucial whether two given points in a building are in different "parts": only if they are will the defendant have entered a part of the building by moving from one to the other. There are at least two possible criteria. On the one hand two such points may be regarded as being in different parts if they are separated by some form of physical barrier. On this view different floors are different parts, and so are different rooms. A cupboard is probably a different part of the building from the room off which it opens. Alternatively, two points not so separated may nevertheless be regarded as falling within different parts of the building if they are differentiated by the fact that the defendant has authority to be at one but not at the other. These alternative criteria may perhaps apply to different situations. If the defendant's original authority to enter the building has been revoked, or he has realised since entering that he never had such authority, or he entered the building as a trespasser but has only now decided to commit a specified offence, he cannot be entering part of the building as a trespasser merely because he moves in a direction which does not take him towards the nearest exit. In these

---

50 But it may be that he has no authority to enter with such an intention, and knows it: *supra*, paras. 7.14 ff.
51 The contrary is arguable where he is in fact a trespasser but does not realise that he is until after he has entered: *supra*, para. 7.20.

cases the only possible ground for saying that he has entered another part of the building is that he has crossed some physical barrier, *e.g.* by going through a door. But if there is one area where he is allowed to go and another where he is not, it seems that he may be entering part of the building as a trespasser merely by going from one to the other. In *Walkington*[52] the appellant had entered a counter area in a department store with intent to steal from the till. The area in question was partially enclosed by a movable counter forming three sides of an irregular quadrilateral. It was argued that even if the appellant had no business to be within that area it was not a separate part of the building. The court referred with apparent approval to a suggestion by Professor J. C. Smith that for this purpose a building has only two parts, *viz.* the part where the person in question is entitled to be and the part where he is not,[53] and went on:

> "One really gets two extremes, as it seems to us. First of all you have the part of the building which is shut off by a door so far as the general public is concerned, with a notice saying 'Staff Only' or 'No admittance to customers.' At the other end of the scale you have for example a single table in the middle of the store, which it would be difficult for any jury to find properly was a part of the building into which the licensor prohibited customers from moving." [54]

7.23   There was ample evidence on which the jury could find that the management had impliedly prohibited customers from entering the counter area and that the appellant knew they had; and that was all that was required. This seems to imply that as long as the defendant knows he is going out of bounds he need not cross any physical barrier or even any visible line of demarcation. The court did say that in *Walkington* itself there was "a physical partition", but that was true only of the three sides marked out by the counter. The existence of a partition on those three sides cannot have been crucial, since the appellant had entered the forbidden area from the fourth and unpartitioned side. It is submitted that where the defendant has strayed from a permitted area to a forbidden one the absence of partitions or other visible boundaries is not fatal to the prosecution's case. Since *Walkington* establishes that a forbidden area is *per se* a different part of the building from the permitted area, the issue is simply whether the defendant knowingly entered such an area. The prosecution may well find it easier to prove that he did so if the borderline between permitted and forbidden territory is somehow marked out; but if they can prove that the point he reached was out of bounds and that he knew it was, it can hardly be a defence that they would have found

52   [1979] 1 W.L.R. 1169.
53   See now *The Law of Theft* (5th ed.) para. 347.
54   At pp. 1175 f.

this more difficult to prove if he had not gone quite as far as he did. The reason why it might not be burglary to go to "a single table in the middle of the store" with intent to steal from it is not (as the judgment implies)[55] that there is no physical partition, but that there may be no point in the area surrounding such a table to which customers are clearly not allowed to go.

Intent or subsequent action

Intent to commit a specified offence

7.24 The offence under section 9(1) (*a*) is committed if the defendant enters the building (or part of it) as a trespasser with intent to commit one of certain specified offences there. It must be proved that at the time of his entry he intended to do certain things, and that what he intended to do (including any consequences which he intended to result from his acts)[56] would have amounted to one of the specified offences had he done it. But it is no defence that it was in fact impossible for him to do it (*e.g.* because the property he intended to steal was not there), nor that he intended to do it only if certain conditions should prove to be fulfilled (*e.g.* that there should be some property there which was worth stealing); and the latter intention is sufficient whether or not the condition was in fact fulfilled.[57] This rule does not sit easily with the principle that a person intends to commit an offence only if he has made up his mind to do so.[58]

Specified offences

7.25 The course of conduct which the defendant intends to pursue must be one which would involve one of the offences listed in section 9(2), *viz.*

" . . . offences of stealing anything in the building or part of a building in question, of inflicting on any person therein any grievous bodily harm or raping any woman therein, and of doing unlawful damage to the building or anything therein."

7.26 *Stealing.* Stealing means theft, which obviously includes aggravated theft.[59] Whether the intended course of conduct would have amounted to theft if the defendant had carried it out will depend on a multitude of factors discussed above.[60]

---

55 At p. 1175.
56 Thus it would not be sufficient that he intended to inflict an injury which he expected to be minor but which in view of the victim's medical condition would in fact be serious.
57 *Walkington* [1979] 1 W.L.R. 1169; *Attorney-General's References (Nos. 1 and 2 of 1979)* [1980] Q.B. 180.
58 *Supra*, para. 1.123.
59 s. 1(1); *supra*, para. 1.01.
60 Ch. 1. An intent to use electricity, for example, is not an intent to steal: *Low v. Blease* [1975] Crim.L.R. 513.

7.27 *Unlawful damage.* An offence of doing unlawful damage to the building or anything therein will almost invariably be one of damaging property belonging to another, contrary to section 1(1) of the Criminal Damage Act 1971,[61] or section 1(3) in the case of damage by fire.[62] An intention to damage the defendant's own property in a way which he knows may endanger life, contrary to section 1(2) of the 1971 Act,[63] would presumably suffice even if it did not amount to an intent to inflict grievous bodily harm; but such a case is perhaps unlikely to arise.[64] An intention to commit one of the other offences of property damage discussed in the previous chapter would doubtless be sufficient too, provided that the intention is actually to *damage* the property in question and not merely to endanger it.

7.28 *Inflicting grievous bodily harm.* The infliction of grievous bodily harm, if done in accordance with a previously formed intention, would automatically be an offence of causing grievous bodily harm with intent to do so contrary to section 18 of the Offences against the Person Act 1861; but it is not entirely clear what constitutes the "inflicting" of harm. In *Wilson (Clarence)* [65] it was held that, for the purposes of the offence of maliciously inflicting grievous bodily harm contrary to section 20 of the 1861 Act, it is possible to "inflict" harm by an act which, though not itself a direct application of force to the body of the victim (and therefore not an assault), directly *results* in force being violently applied to his body–*e.g.* the laying of a booby-trap.[66] In *Jenkins (Edward John)*[67] the same construction was given to the word "inflicts" in section 9(1)(*b*) of the Theft Act, and the court accepted that that word presumably means the same in section 9(2) as in section 9(1)(*b*).[68] Both decisions were reversed by the House of Lords, but not on this point.[69] Their Lordships were "content to accept" that there can be an infliction of grievous bodily harm without an assault.[70] It therefore seems that an intent to cause grievous bodily harm to a person by means of an act which will directly result in the application of violent force to his body, but which will not

---

61   *Supra*, paras. 6.02 ff.
62   *Supra*, para. 6.63.
63   *Supra*, paras. 6.66 ff.
64   It would be less unlikely if the offence extends to a trespasser whose intention is to damage property which he has himself brought with him: *infra*, para. 7.34.
65   [1983] 1 W.L.R. 356.
66   *Cf. Martin* (1881) 8 Q.B.D. 54.
67   [1983] 1 All E.R. 1000.
68   At p. 1004.
69   [1984] A.C. 242.
70   At p. 260, *per* Lord Roskill. But where the House of Lords holds that an issue decided by the Court of Appeal did not arise for decision, the Court of Appeal's decision is persuasive only: *R. v. Secretary of State for the Home Department, ex p. Al-Mehdawi,* The Independent 6 December 1988.

amount to an assault, is an intent to inflict grievous bodily harm for the purposes of section 9(2). An intent to *kill* in such a way must *a fortiori* be sufficient.

7.29 It is less clear whether an intent to cause grievous bodily harm in some way *not* involving the application of violent force, *e.g.* by poisoning, will suffice. The reasoning in *Wilson*, and the acceptance of that reasoning in *Jenkins*, would suggest not.[71] If this were right then even an intent to kill in such a way would not suffice. On the other hand the court which decided *Jenkins* supported its view that an assault is not essential by posing the example of a defendant whose entry into a building causes a person inside the building to suffer a stroke brought on by shock. The implication was that this would amount to an infliction of grievous bodily harm within the meaning of section 9(1) (*b*), and that an *intent* to cause grievous bodily harm in such a way would therefore be an intent to inflict grievous bodily harm within the meaning of section 9(2). Clearly the court did not regard the application of violent force, or indeed any force, as essential. Even in the 1861 Act the use of the word "inflict" does not always imply a requirement of force: under section 23 it is an offence unlawfully and maliciously to administer to another person any poison so as thereby to inflict upon such person any grievous bodily harm. This is obviously not confined to the *forcible* administration of poison. It is therefore entirely possible that, when the point arises for decision, the courts will regard an intent to cause grievous bodily harm (or to kill) in *any* manner as amounting for the purposes of burglary to an intent to inflict grievous bodily harm.

7.30 *Rape.* Rape is an offence under section 1(1) of the Sexual Offences Act 1956 and is defined by section 1(1) of the Sexual Offences (Amendment) Act 1976:

". . . a man commits rape if:
(*a*) he has unlawful sexual intercourse with a woman who at the time of the intercourse does not consent to it; and
(*b*) at the time he knows that she does not consent to the intercourse or he is reckless as to whether she consents to it . . ."

Since this form of burglary involves an *intent* to commit rape, it constitutes a particular example of a more general problem which may be stated as follows. Where an offence requires the existence of certain circumstances, but can be committed by a person who does not know that those circumstances exist and is merely reckless whether they do, what does it mean to speak of an *intention* to commit that offence? Does

71 And *cf. Clarence* (1888) 22 Q.B.D. 23.

such intent necessarily involve knowledge that those circumstances do or will exist, or is recklessness enough for the intent as well as for the full offence? Rape involves an act (*viz.* sexual intercourse) performed in specified circumstances (*viz.* in the absence of the woman's consent). But the man need not know that the woman does not consent: it is enough that he is reckless whether she does or not, which in this context means that he realises she may not be consenting but goes ahead regardless.[72] What then is an *intent* to rape? Must it be an intent to have intercourse with a woman who the man *knows* will not consent, or can it be an intent to have intercourse with a woman who he realises *may or may not*?

7.31   In the context of attempted rape,[73] which required an intent to rape even at common law,[74] it was assumed in *Pigg*[75] that the latter state of mind (*i.e.* recklessness) was sufficient; and it is submitted with respect that the assumption was correct. In the context of *attempted* rape a requirement of knowledge would not be unworkable, because by the time the man has done an act which is "more than merely preparatory"[76] to intercourse the woman will almost inevitably be aware of his intentions and will have had a chance to decide whether she is willing to comply. If she is not, it makes sense to ask whether the man *knows* she is not. But burglary requires only the *intent* to rape, and nothing need be done in pursuance of that intention beyond the entry into the building or part of a building. Since the offence of burglary will normally be committed at an earlier stage than the attempt to rape, it is less likely that at that stage the woman can be said (or known) to be willing or unwilling. When Collins[77] formed his plan of campaign he cannot have *known* that his prospective partner would not consent. He may have had a fair idea what her answer was likely to be, but he could not be sure until he asked her. A requirement of knowledge would be impossible to satisfy in such a case. A more workable test would be whether he thought there was any substantial possibility that she might consent; but such refinements are hardly necessary when the statute itself does not refer to knowledge at all[78] but only to intention. In *Collins* it seems to have been assumed that a man intends to rape if his intention is to have intercourse with a woman

---

72 *Satnam* (1983) 78 Cr.App.R. 149.
73 See G. Williams, "The Problem of Reckless Attempts" [1983] Crim.L.R. 365; R. Buxton, "Circumstances, Consequences and Attempted Rape" [1984] Crim.L.R. 25.
74 See now Criminal Attempts Act 1981 s. 1(1).
75 [1982] 1 W.L.R. 762.
76 Criminal Attempts Act 1981 s. 1(1).
77 [1973] Q.B. 100; *supra*, para. 7.05.
78 *Cf.* s. 1(2) of the Criminal Law Act 1977, which provides that conspiracy to commit an offence of strict liability (and *a fortiori* one of *mens rea* such as rape) is not committed unless two or more parties "intend or know" that the circumstances essential to the full offence shall or will exist at the time when the intended conduct is to take place.

whether or not she consents. Perhaps the solution is to regard this as a kind of conditional intention:[79] *if* she does not consent, the man intends to have intercourse with her anyway.

Place of the intended offence

7.32 *Part of a building.* Where the defendant enters a building as a trespasser with intent to steal, it is sufficient that he intends to steal anywhere in the building; but if he only enters *part* of the building as a trespasser, he must intend to steal in that part. It must therefore be proved not only that his movements after deciding to steal included an entry into a part of the building where he knew he was not allowed to go,[80] but also that he intended to steal in the *same* part. Where he has authority to enter some areas of the building but not others, it seems that any forbidden area is a "part" of the building.[81] If two or more physically distinct forbidden areas (*e.g.* rooms) are adjacent to one another, it is arguable that they can together be regarded as one part of the building. If a person enters a room which he knows he is not entitled to use, from a corridor which he is, he is entering part of the building as a trespasser. If he intends to steal in that room, he is therefore guilty of burglary. If his intention is to steal not in that room but in a second room to which the first room gives access, it may seem not unreasonable to treat the two rooms together as forming one (forbidden) part of the building, which he has entered with intent to steal therein. But this would seem less natural if he were already a trespasser before he entered the first room, although he had not entered the building as a trespasser with intent to steal: in that case it would be the physical barrier between the first room and the corridor, not the difference between permitted and forbidden territory, which would make it possible to treat his entry into the first room as an entry into another part of the building. The contention that the first room and the corridor are different parts of the building, because they are separated by a partition, would be inconsistent with the contention that the two rooms (also separated by a partition) together form only one part. And this approach would seem to be ruled out altogether if the two rooms were neither connecting nor adjacent but were separated by other areas *not* out of bounds to the defendant. If a person lawfully in a corridor enters one room without authority in order to get the key to a second room on the other side of the corridor, from which he intends to steal, he is clearly entering one part of the building as a trespasser with intent to steal in *another* part.[82]

79 *Supra*, para. 1.117.
80 *Supra*, paras. 7.21 ff.
81 *Walkington* [1979] 1 W.L.R. 1169; *supra*, para. 7.22.
82 Unless, of course, he intends to keep the key.

7.33 Similar considerations apply where the defendant's intention is not to steal but to inflict grievous bodily harm or to rape. It may perhaps be just arguable that in the phrase ". . . inflicting on any person therein any grievous bodily harm or raping any woman therein . . ." the word "therein" means simply "in the building", a construction which would avoid the difficulties discussed above; but it must surely mean "in the building or part of a building in question". Where the defendant's intention is to do unlawful damage, however, his intended target may be either the building itself or anything in it. This is so whether he enters the building as a trespasser or only part of the building. Thus it is burglary to enter part of a building as a trespasser with intent to damage property in another part, but not with intent to steal it. The reason for the distinction is not apparent. Similarly it is burglary to enter part of a building as a trespasser with intent to damage a different part of the building itself; an intent to *steal* some of the fabric of the building[83] in a part other than that entered as a trespasser would not be sufficient *qua* intent to steal, but would inevitably involve an intent to damage the building.

7.34 *Bringing in and taking out.* It is doubtful whether a person entering a building intends to damage "anything therein" if he brings with him something which he intends to damage once he is inside the building. Must the property he intends to damage be in the building at the time of his entry, or is it enough that he intends it to be there by the time he damages it? It is submitted that the first construction is correct. Burglary is essentially an offence designed for the protection of people and property inside a building against attack from outside, and there seems little reason to stretch it so as to catch people who bring with them the property which they intend to damage. On the other hand it can hardly be a defence that the intruder's intention is to take the occupier's property outside before damaging it. It is submitted that it is both necessary and sufficient that the property which the defendant intends to damage should be in the building or part of a building in question immediately before he enters, or at any rate that he should hope or believe that it is. A similar point might of course arise in the case of an intent to rape or to inflict grievous bodily harm, though hardly in the case of an intent to steal.

Doing a specified act

7.35 The Criminal Law Revision Committee originally intended that there should be only one form of burglary, that which now appears in

---

83 See s. 4(2)(*b*); *supra*, para. 1.08.

section 9(1) (*a*) (*viz*. entering as a trespasser with intent to commit one of the offences specified in section 9(2)), but later decided to include the alternative of entering as a trespasser and actually committing one of those offences. This addition was intended to ensure that, where the defendant has in fact committed an offence in the building or part of a building in question, the prosecution need not undertake the potentially onerous task of proving that he decided to do so before entering and not after.[84] Burglary is therefore not one offence but two, one of them an inchoate form of certain other offences and the other consisting of (or at any rate intended by the Committee to consist of) an offence aggravated by the element of entry as a trespasser; and the charge must make it clear which one is alleged. Unfortunately the final version of paragraph (*b*) is not that proposed by the Committee. In one respect it is narrower, in that it refers to some but not all of the offences specified in section 9(2). A person who steals or inflicts grievous bodily harm after entering as a trespasser can be convicted of burglary even if it cannot be proved that he intended to do so when he entered; a person who commits rape or criminal damage cannot. The distinction is hard to justify. On the other hand the amended version may be wider than the original, in that on a literal reading it does not require the commission of an *offence* at all.

Specified acts
7.36 The definition of the offence under section 9(1) (*b*) requires that the defendant should first enter as a trespasser, with or without any criminal intent, and then do one of the following:

(a) steal;
(b) attempt to steal;
(c) inflict grievous bodily harm; or
(d) attempt to inflict grievous bodily harm.

Stealing again means theft,[85] and an attempt to steal is presumably an attempt within the meaning of section 1(1) of the Criminal Attempts Act 1981.[86] The infliction of grievous bodily harm, on the other hand, need not strictly speaking be an offence at all: it can be done by accident, or in lawful self-defence. It was never intended that a person who lawfully inflicts grievous bodily harm should be guilty of burglary merely because he happens to be a trespasser.[87] But the Court of Appeal's judgment in *Jenkins*[88] appears to imply that this is indeed the effect. The applicants

84 Cmnd. 2977 para. 76.
85 s. 1(1).
86 *Supra*, paras. 1.184 ff.
87 The original draft of s. 9(1)(*b*) would have made this clear.
88 [1983] 1 All E.R. 1000.

had been convicted of assault occasioning actual bodily harm[89] on an indictment containing one count of burglary. The particulars of offence were that the applicants, having entered a building as trespassers, had inflicted grievous bodily harm upon a person therein. The actual decision, subsequently reversed on other grounds,[90] was that the alternative verdict was not available because the words "inflicts . . . any grievous bodily harm" in section 9(1) (*b*) do not require an assault.[91] But the court appears to have thought that they do not even require an offence. First it referred to one of the proposed grounds of appeal, that the recorder should have granted an application to quash the indictment because it did not allege that the grievous bodily harm was inflicted "unlawfully" or "maliciously".

> "The basis of this submission would have been that section 9 of the Theft Act 1968 refers to 'offences' (see the words of section 9(1) (*a*) and (2) of that Act). Although section 9(1) (*b*) does not contain the word 'offence', that word must be implied by reason of its association with the subsections immediately preceding and following it. Therefore, it being possible that 'to inflict grievous bodily harm' might not be an offence in extreme circumstances such as self-defence or some other lawful excuse, the particulars relating to 'inflicting grievous bodily harm' *simpliciter* disclosed no offence. Rightly, if we may say so, counsel who now appears for both applicants abandoned this ground as part of his application for leave to appeal."[92]

The court did not explain its grounds for thinking that counsel had been right to abandon the point. They may have been either that the infliction of grievous bodily harm within the meaning of section 9(1) (*b*) need not be an offence at all, or that, although the infliction must indeed be an offence and the words "unlawfully and maliciously" are therefore implied, words which are implied in the statute can equally be implied in the indictment. The latter view would be less radical and in the absence of further explanation it would be reasonable to assume that that is what was meant.

7.37 However, a further and less equivocal indication of the court's meaning may be found in the passage, already referred to,[93] where it was suggested that the causing of serious injury by shock could amount to the infliction of grievous bodily harm within the meaning of section 9(1) (*b*). In the court's hypothetical example the victim is a person "of whom [the defendant] may not even be aware".[94] If the defendant does not know

89 Offences against the Person Act 1861 s. 47.
90 [1984] A.C. 242.
91 *Supra*, para. 7.28.
92 At p. 1003.
93 *Supra*, para. 7.29.
94 At p. 1004.

that someone may suffer some injury as a result of his actions, he is not "malicious", and in causing the injury he therefore commits no offence.[95] Yet the whole point of the example is that he ought to be, and is, guilty of burglary. It is submitted with respect that this passage goes too far, and that the accidental or justifiable infliction of injury does not turn a trespasser into a burglar. The infliction of grievous bodily harm may amount to the offence of causing grievous bodily harm with intent to do so (contrary to section 18 of the Offences against the Person Act 1861)[96] or that of maliciously inflicting grievous bodily harm (contrary to section 20) or possibly even that of administering poison so as to inflict grievous bodily harm (contrary to section 23), but it is submitted that it cannot be sufficient if it amounts to no offence at all. Similarly, it is submitted, a person does not *attempt* to inflict grievous bodily harm for this purpose merely by trying to do so, but only by committing the offence of attempt. In this case there can be no question of accident, but defences such as self-defence may still be available. A further argument for the view here advanced arises out of the provisions regarding mode of trial, and will be referred to in that context.[97] Unfortunately that argument is valid only if the interpretation of those provisions there advanced is wrong; fortunately the conclusion is not affected even if that interpretation is right.

Place of the act

7.38   If the defendant enters the *building* as a trespasser, he need only do one of the specified acts somewhere in the building; if he only enters *part* of the building as a trespasser, he must do it in that part.[98] But it is submitted that it ought to be sufficient if he does one of those acts to someone or something which *was* in the building when he entered, *e.g.* if he pursues his victim out of the building and inflicts grievous bodily harm on him outside.[99]

Alternative verdicts

7.39   Under section 6(3) of the Criminal Law Act 1967 a person tried on indictment for one offence may be convicted of another if the allegations in the indictment amount to or include, expressly or by implication, an allegation of that other offence. In *Wilson*,[1] it was held by the House of Lords that for this purpose an allegation of one offence may include an

---

95 *Cunningham* [1957] 2 Q.B. 396.
96 But the harm must be "inflicted" and not merely "caused": *cf. supra*, paras. 7.28 f.
97 *Infra*, para. 7.42.
98 *Cf. supra*, para. 7.32.
99 *Cf. supra*, para. 7.34.
 1 [1984] A.C. 242.

allegation of another even if the latter requires an element not essential to the former.[2] Therefore a person indicted for burglary by entering as a trespasser and inflicting grievous bodily harm may be convicted instead of assault occasioning actual bodily harm, although it is possible to inflict grievous bodily harm without committing an assault;[3] and a person indicted for burglary by entering as a trespasser and stealing may instead be convicted of burglary by entering with intent to steal, although it is obviously possible to enter and steal without intending to steal at the time of the entry.[4] The judge is merely required to ensure that, bearing in mind the way in which the issues have been argued in the course of the trial, there is no risk of injustice in leaving the alternative to the jury. But an allegation of entering and inflicting grievous bodily harm obviously does not include an allegation of entering with intent to steal, or *vice versa*. Nor, it is submitted (though under *Wilson* almost anything is possible), does an allegation of entering with intent to steal include an allegation of entering and stealing. If the prosecution are in any doubt as to which offence they will be able to prove, they should of course include alternative counts. But they now have little incentive to charge paragraphs (*a*) and (*b*) of section 9(1) as alternatives, because even if they only charge paragraph (*b*) they can always fall back on paragraph (*a*).

Mode of trial

7.40 Burglary is triable either way, except that the following variations are indictable only:[5]

(a) burglary comprising an intention to commit an offence triable only on indictment;

(b) burglary comprising the commission of an offence triable only on indictment; and

(c) burglary committed in a dwelling, if any person in the dwelling is subjected to violence or the threat of violence.

Type (a) clearly refers to burglary contrary to section 9(1) (*a*) (because only that form of the offence requires an *intention* to commit another offence) and type (b) refers to section 9(1) (*b*). Type (c) could be either, because the violence or threat need not be *comprised* in the burglary at all. Burglary by entering as a trespasser with intent to rape, or to inflict grievous bodily harm (which would necessarily be an intent to commit the offence of causing grievous bodily harm with intent to do so, contrary

2 *Supra*, para. 1.197.
3 *Wilson* [1984] A.C. 242.
4 *Whiting* (1987) 85 Cr.App.R. 78, overruling *Hollis* [1971] Crim.L.R. 525.
5 Magistrates' Courts Act 1980 Sch. 1.

to section 18 of the Offences against the Person Act 1861) would be indictable only, because those offences are themselves indictable only. Burglary by entering with intent to steal or to do unlawful damage would normally be triable either way.

7.41 It is arguable, however, that if a charge under section 9(1) (*a*) were framed as involving an intent not just to steal but to rob,[6] or not just to damage property but to do so being reckless whether life were endangered,[7] it would be triable only on indictment. This would depend whether it could be said that the burglary actually alleged "comprises" an intent to commit the more serious offence, given that an intent to commit the less serious offence would still have been sufficient to convert the entry into a burglary (albeit a less serious one). Similarly it is arguable that burglary contrary to section 9(1) (*b*) is triable only on indictment not only where it involves an *attempt* to inflict grievous bodily harm[8] but also where it involves robbery or the infliction of grievous bodily harm with intent,[9] even though simple theft or the merely reckless[10] infliction of grievous bodily harm contrary to section 20 of the 1861 Act (which is also triable either way) would have been sufficient. It would be odd if the deliberate infliction of grievous bodily harm by a trespasser (if charged as burglary and not simply under section 18 of the 1861 Act) were triable either way, whereas an attempt to do so would be indictable only– particularly since the former necessarily includes the latter. Doubtless the question is largely academic because it is unlikely that any bench would accept jurisdiction in such a case. But this might be less unthinkable if the charge were one of burglary by entering as a trespasser with intent to rob. It is submitted that an allegation of robbery, or of inflicting grievous bodily harm with intent to do so, or of entry with intent to rob, or with intent to damage property so as to endanger life, will render a burglary charge indictable only. Where an offence can be committed in two ways, one of them an aggravated form of the other, it does not seem unnatural to say that when the aggravating factor is present the offence "comprises" the aggravated form.

7.42 If this view is wrong, however, and burglary "comprises" only those elements without which the defendant would not be guilty of burglary at all, it would follow that a trespasser "inflicts or attempts to

6 *Supra*, para. 1.170.
7 Criminal Damage Act 1971 s. 1(2); *supra*, para. 6.66.
8 Which is indictable only, because it is by definition an attempt to commit the offence under s. 18: Criminal Attempts Act 1981 ss. 1(1), 4(1)(*b*).
9 Or, perhaps, administering poison so as to inflict grievous bodily harm contrary to s. 23 of the 1861 Act: *cf. supra*, para. 7.29.
10 See *Cunningham* [1957] 2 Q.B. 396.

inflict . . . grievous bodily harm" within the meaning of section 9(1) (*b*) only if he thereby commits an offence.[11] Otherwise burglary could never "comprise" the commission of an offence triable only on indictment, as these rules envisage that it can, because some variations of the offence under section 9(1)(*b*) would comprise the commission of an offence triable either way (*viz.* theft and attempted theft) while the rest (*viz.* inflicting and attempting to inflict grievous bodily harm) would not "comprise" any offence at all.

Going equipped

7.43 A person who, when not at his place of abode, has with him an article for use in the course of or in connection with burglary is guilty of an offence under section 25(1) of the Theft Act 1968. This offence is discussed elsewhere.[12]

ARMED TRESPASS

Aggravated burglary

7.44 Section 10(1) of the Theft Act 1968 provides:

"A person is guilty of aggravated burglary if he commits any burglary and at the time has with him any firearm or imitation firearm, any weapon of offence, or any explosive . . ."

The offence is punishable on conviction on indictment with life imprisonment.[13]

Weapons

Firearms and explosives
7.45 The word "firearm" is not defined, except that it includes an airgun or air pistol;[14] the definition laid down in section 57 of the Firearms Act 1968 does not apply for this purpose, but a borderline case will almost inevitably be a weapon of offence in any event. An imitation firearm is defined as anything which has the appearance of being a firearm, whether capable of being discharged or not.[15] The test is whether the thing looked like a firearm at the time when the defendant had it with him.[16] An

11 *Cf. supra*, paras. 7.36 f.
12 *Supra*, paras. 1.192 ff.
13 s. 10(2).
14 s. 10(1)(*a*).
15 s. 10(1)(*a*).
16 *Morris and King* (1984) 79 Cr.App.R. 104.

"explosive" is defined as any article manufactured for the purpose of producing a practical effect by explosion, or intended by the person having it with him for that purpose.[17]

Weapons of offence

7.46 Clearly the broadest of the terms employed is "weapon of offence", which is defined as any article made or adapted for use for causing injury to or incapacitating a person, or intended by the person having it with him for that purpose.[18] This definition is almost identical to that of an "offensive weapon" in section 1(4) of the Prevention of Crime Act 1953, section 1(1) of which prohibits the possession of such a weapon in a public place without lawful authority or reasonable excuse, except that the definition in the Theft Act refers to incapacitation as well as injury. Thus the following are included:

(a) an article *made* for use for causing *injury* to a person (*e.g.* a dagger, flick-knife,[19] cosh or knuckleduster);
(b) an article *adapted* for such use (*e.g.* a sock filled with sand);
(c) any article *intended* for such use by the person having it with him;
(d) an article *made* for use for *incapacitating* a person (*e.g.* an electric "stun-gun");[20]
(e) an article *adapted* for such use (*e.g.* a rag soaked in chloroform);
(f) any article *intended* for such use by the person having it with him.

Articles of types (a), (b), (d) and (e) are (for the purpose of section 10) offensive *per se*, and a burglar who has such an article with him is guilty of the aggravated offence even if he has no intention of using it for one of the purposes described or at all. But an article which is neither made nor adapted for causing injury or incapacitation is not offensive *per se* just because it would make an effective weapon if its possessor were minded so to use it.[21] Some categories of article (*e.g.* sheath knives) may or may not be offensive *per se*, depending on the precise nature of the article in question, and in that case the issue must be left to the jury;[22] others are necessarily offensive, and judicial notice may be taken of the fact and the jury directed accordingly.[23]

---

17 s. 10(1)(*c*); *cf.* the definition in s. 3 of the Explosives Act 1875 (*supra*, para. 6.86), which is wider in including substances designed or intended to produce a practical effect by a *pyrotechnic* effect.
18 s. 10(1)(*b*).
19 *Gibson v. Wales* [1983] 1 W.L.R. 393; *Simpson* [1983] 1 W.L.R. 1494.
20 Which is a "firearm" within the meaning of the Firearms Act 1968 (*Flack v. Baldry* [1988] 1 W.L.R. 393) but probably not within the ordinary meaning of that word.
21 *Southwell v. Chadwick* (1987) 85 Cr.App.R. 235 (heavy machete with 12 in. steel blade, "almost razor sharp", and powerful "Black Widow" catapult).
22 *Williamson* (1977) 67 Cr.App.R. 35.
23 *Simpson* [1983] 1 W.L.R. 1494 (flick-knife).

7.47 Where the article is not offensive *per se* it must be proved that the defendant intended it to be used for the causing of injury or incapacitation. This clearly includes an intention to use the article for such a purpose if necessary, and it includes an intention so to use it which is entirely unconnected with the burglary: the mischief struck at by the offence is the carrying by burglars of weapons which they may be *tempted* to use if challenged.[24] But it would probably not be sufficient if the article were not offensive *per se* and the defendant originally had no intention to cause injury or incapacitation with it at all, whether in the course of the burglary or otherwise, and decided so to use it only a moment before actually doing so.[25]

Availability of weapon

7.48 The defendant must have the article in question "with him", which means that it must be "either on his person or readily and immediately available to him".[26] There must therefore be evidence of the whereabouts of the article, and, although it is then a question of fact and degree for the jury whether the evidence establishes sufficient proximity, there must come a point where the article is so far from the scene of the burglary that it cannot possibly be said that the defendant has it with him.[27] It may be enough that the article is carried by another party to the burglary, provided always that the burglar who is not carrying the article knows that the other one is;[28] but, depending on the circumstances, this situation might not confer on the former a sufficient degree of control. He might of course be an accessory to an aggravated offence by the other party; but if the article is not offensive *per se* (and is not a firearm, imitation firearm or explosive) then that offence will require proof that the party with the article intended to use it for causing injury or incapacitation. The party without the article cannot therefore be guilty as an accessory unless he realises not only that the other party may use it but that he may be carrying it with the intention of doing so.

Time of burglary

7.49 The defendant must have the article in question with him "at the time" of committing the burglary. In the case of burglary contrary to section 9(1) (*a*), which is committed when the defendant enters as a

24 *Stones*, [1989] 1 W.L.R. 156.
25 *Cf. Ohlson v. Hylton* [1975] 1 W.L.R. 724.
26 *Browning* 8 June 1984, Criminal Appeal Office transcript no. 280/A/83; applying *Kelt* [1977] 1 W.L.R. 1365.
27 *Browning, supra.*
28 *Cf. Cugullere* [1961] 1 W.L.R. 858.

trespasser and with the requisite intent, this means that he must have the article with him when he enters. In the case of burglary contrary to section 9(1) (*b*), which is committed when he steals (or inflicts grievous bodily harm, or attempts to do either) after entering as a trespasser, he must have the article with him when he does that act: it is not enough that he has it with him when he enters if he abandons it before he steals.[29] Conversely it was held in *O'Leary*[30] that it is sufficient if he finds the article inside the building and keeps it with him until he steals. But there is much to be said for the view that, since section 9(1) (*b*) exists only to dispense with the need for proof that the defendant intended all along to do what he later did,[31] its aggravated form ought not to be available unless the defendant has the article with him when he enters as well as when he steals.[32] In *O'Leary* the court asserted that this view was wrong, but omitted to explain why.

Burglary with a firearm or imitation firearm

7.50 A person who commits burglary (or attempts to do so, or aids or abets another to do so), and at the time of doing so, or of being arrested for doing so, has in his possession a firearm or imitation firearm, is guilty of an offence under section 17(2) of the Firearms Act 1968 unless he shows that he had it in his possession for a lawful object.[33] The offence is punishable on conviction on indictment with life imprisonment.[34] It is somewhat wider than aggravated burglary in that it may be committed by someone who has committed burglary without a firearm but who has one in his possession when he is arrested. On the other hand it is open to the defendant to show that his possession of the firearm was for a lawful object.

Trespass with a firearm

7.51 Section 20 of the Firearms Act 1968 creates two offences of trespassing with a firearm. For the first offence the trespass must be in a building; for the second it may be on any land. In this context a "firearm" includes not only a weapon falling within that term for the purposes of the offence under section 17(2)[35] but also any component part of such a

---

29 *Francis* [1982] Crim.L.R. 363.
30 (1986) 82 Cr.App.R. 341.
31 *Supra*, para. 7.35.
32 E. Griew, *The Theft Acts 1968 and 1978* (5th ed.) para. 4–42.
33 *Cf. supra*, para. 1.180.
34 Sch. 6, as amended by Criminal Justice Act 1988 s. 44(3). The penalty for offences committed before s. 44 came into force on 29 September 1988 (s. 171(6)) remains at 14 years: s. 44(4).
35 *Supra*, para. 1.180.

weapon and any accessory designed or adapted to diminish the noise or flash caused by firing the weapon.[36]

Trespass in a building

7.52 Section 20(1) provides:

"A person commits an offence if, while he has a firearm with him, he enters or is in any building or part of a building as a trespasser and without reasonable excuse (the proof whereof lies on him)."

The offence is punishable on conviction on indictment (unless the firearm is an air weapon)[37] with five years' imprisonment; with that exception it is triable either way.[38] A person "has a firearm with him" if he has a degree of immediate control over it.[39] By contrast with the law of burglary, he need not *enter* the building or part of a building as a trespasser and with a firearm: it is sufficient if he is *in* the building (or the part of the building in which he is) as a trespasser and with a firearm. Thus it need not be proved that he had the firearm at the time when he entered. Presumably he must at least realise that he may be a trespasser.[40] Once it is proved that he was in a building (or part of a building) as a trespasser and that he had a firearm with him, it is for him to prove that he had reasonable excuse. The words "and without reasonable excuse" appear to apply only to the requirement of trespass: if so, it is a defence that he has a reasonable excuse for trespassing (though not for doing so with a firearm), but not that he has a reasonable excuse for having a firearm—unless the excuse also justifies his trespassing with it.

Trespass on other land

7.53 Section 20(2) provides:

"A person commits an offence if, while he has a firearm with him, he enters or is on any land[41] as a trespasser and without reasonable excuse (the proof whereof lies on him)."

The offence is punishable on summary conviction with three months' imprisonment or a fine of level 4 on the standard scale or both.[42]

---

36 s. 57(1).
37 An air weapon is an air rifle, air gun or air pistol not of a type declared by the Firearms (Dangerous Air Weapons) Rules 1969, S.I. 1969 No. 47, or other rules made by the Secretary of State under s. 53 of the Act, to be specially dangerous: ss. 1(3)(b), 57(4). A weapon whose ammunition is propelled by a compressed gas other than air (*e.g.* carbon dioxide housed in disposable cylinders) is not an air weapon although the gas is compressed by mechanical means rather than by an explosion: *Thorpe* [1987] 1 W.L.R. 383.
38 Sch. 6 as amended.
39 *Kelt* [1977] 1 W.L.R. 1365.
40 *Cf. Collins* [1973] Q.B. 100; *supra*, para. 7.19.
41 Including land covered with water: s. 20(3).
42 Sch. 6 as amended.

Trespass with a weapon of offence

7.54   Section 8(1) of the Criminal Law Act 1977 provides:

"A person who is on any premises[43] as a trespasser, after having entered as such, is guilty of an offence if, without lawful authority or reasonable excuse, he has with him on the premises any weapon of offence."

The offence is punishable on summary conviction with three months' imprisonment or a fine of level 5 on the standard scale or both.[44] A constable in uniform may arrest without warrant anyone who is, or whom he with reasonable cause suspects to be, in the act of committing the offence.[45] "Weapon of offence" means the same as it does for the purposes of aggravated burglary.[46] The defendant must have entered the premises as a trespasser, which arguably means that he must then have known he might be trespassing,[47] and he must still be a trespasser when he has the weapon with him. He is a trespasser if he enters or is on the premises by virtue of any title derived from a trespasser, or of any licence or consent given by a trespasser or by a person deriving title from a trespasser;[48] and he does not cease to be a trespasser by virtue of being allowed time to leave the premises.[49]

VIOLENT ENTRY

7.55   Section 6(1) of the Criminal Law Act 1977 provides:

"Subject to the following provisions of this section, any person who, without lawful authority, uses or threatens violence for the purpose of securing entry into any premises for himself or for any other person is guilty of an offence, provided that–
(a) there is someone present on those premises at the time who is opposed to the entry which the violence is intended to secure; and
(b) the person using or threatening the violence knows that that is the case."

The offence is punishable on summary conviction with six months' imprisonment or a fine of level 5 on the standard scale or both.[50] A constable in uniform may arrest without warrant anyone who is, or whom he with reasonable cause suspects to be, guilty of the offence.[51]

---

43   "Premises" includes not only a building but also a part of a building under separate occupation, any land ancillary to a building and the site comprising any building or buildings together with any land ancillary thereto: see *infra*, para. 7.56.
44   s. 8(3) as amended by Criminal Justice Act 1982 s. 46.
45   s. 8(4).
46   s. 8(2); see *supra*, para. 7.46.
47   *Cf. supra*, para. 7.20.
48   s. 12(6).
49   s. 12(7).
50   s. 6(5) as amended by Criminal Justice Act 1982 s. 46.
51   s. 6(6).

Premises

7.56 "Premises" are defined for this purpose as including:

(a) any building;[52]
(b) any part of a building under separate occupation;[53]
(c) any land ancillary to a building;[54] and
(d) the site comprising any building or buildings together with any land ancillary thereto.[55]

Thus the offence can be committed not only where part of a building is under separate occupation (*e.g.* a flat) and the use or threat of violence is intended to secure entry to that part alone, but also (by virtue of (d) above) where it is intended to secure entry into the grounds of a building and there is someone in the building itself who is opposed to the entry into the grounds.

Entry opposed

7.57 The defendant's purpose must be to secure entry into the premises, either for himself or for another person. But it is immaterial whether the entry he intends to secure is for the purpose of acquiring possession of the premises in question or for any other purpose.[56] The question may therefore arise whether he must intend to enter (or to enable someone else to enter) in the fullest sense of that word, or whether it is sufficient, for example, if he intends merely to reach through a window. A similar question arises in the context of burglary and is discussed above.[57] The defendant's purpose need not be to secure *immediate* entry: it is apparently sufficient if he uses or (more likely) threatens violence with a view to ensuring that his entry will be unopposed at some later stage. Such a rule may yield curious results when combined with the requirement that there must be someone present on the premises, at the time of the alleged offence, who is opposed[58] to the entry which the defendant intends

---

52 "Building" includes any structure other than a movable one, and any movable structure, vehicle or vessel designed or adapted for use for residential purposes: s. 12(2). This clearly includes an immovable "structure" which would not fall within the ordinary meaning of the word "building": *cf. supra*, para. 7.03.
53 Part of a building is under separate occupation if anyone is in occupation or entitled to occupation of that part as distinct from the whole: s. 12(2)(*a*). *Quaere* whether this refers to *exclusive* occupation: would it include a lodger's bedroom? On the expression "part of a building", *cf. supra*, paras. 7.22 f.
54 Land is ancillary to a building if it is adjacent to it and used, or intended for use, in connection with the occupation of that building or any part of it: s. 12(2)(*b*).
55 s. 12(1)(*a*).
56 s. 6(4)(*b*).
57 Paras. 7.05 f.
58 "Opposed" is not defined. Presumably it means merely that the intended entry, if effected, would be against that person's will. There is no requirement that he should be ready to oppose the entry by physical force.

to secure, and whom the defendant knows to be so opposed. Since the offence consists in the use or threat of violence for the purpose of securing entry, and not in the entry itself, the crucial time at which there must be someone present on the premises and opposed to the entry (and known to be opposed to it) is the time not of the entry but of the use or threat of violence. If a person intends to enter premises next week and expects his entry to be then opposed, and threatens violence in order to deter such opposition, it is hard to see why his liability should depend on whether one of the likely objectors is on the premises at the time of the threat; and if he is nowhere near the premises when he makes the threat (and not in direct contact with them, *e.g.* by telephone), he can hardly know whether anyone is there. Recklessness is not enough.

Use or threat of violence

7.58 In order to overcome the opposition of the person present on the premises, whom he knows to be opposed to the entry which he intends to secure, the defendant must use or threaten "violence". The violence may be directed (or, presumably, threatened to be directed) against property as well as against the person.[59] But it must in all cases be an act which can (or, where there is only a threat, could if the threat were carried out) be described as "violence". Not every assault involves violence: it is a question of degree. Similarly it would be a use of violence to smash a door with an axe, but not to unscrew the hinges.

Lawful authority

7.59 The use or threat of violence must be without lawful authority. But it is not a defence merely that there is lawful authority for the entry which the use or threat of violence is intended to secure, *e.g.* because the defendant or some other person has a proprietary interest in the premises to be entered or a right to possession or occupation of them.[60] In other words even the owner of premises is not entitled to use or threaten violence for the purpose of securing entry against the opposition of a trespasser.[61] The keeping of the peace is regarded as a higher priority than the protection of property. Presumably a person has lawful authority for the *use* of violence only if he would have a defence to a charge of assault or criminal damage, as the case may be. This would exempt violence justified by such factors as the need to prevent crime or to save life.

59 s. 6(4)(*a*).
60 s. 6(2).
61 Unless he is a displaced residential occupier: *infra*, para. 7.60.

Presumably, too, there is lawful authority to threaten violence if there is lawful authority to use it. But there may be cases where the threat is justified although its execution would not be: the one may be more reasonable than the other. In this case the question cannot be determined simply by asking whether the threat would be an offence apart from section 6, because even an unjustified threat of violence is not necessarily an offence. Clearly a threat is not made with lawful authority for this purpose merely because it does not amount to any other offence. The defendant must be able to point to some concrete justification. There may be room for an analogy with the law of blackmail: perhaps a threat of violence to secure entry is justified if the defendant thinks that he is entitled to secure entry and that the use of the threat is a proper means of securing it.[62] But the phrase "lawful authority" probably denotes a less subjective test.

The displaced residential occupier

7.60 Although an entitlement to the premises in question is not in general a defence,[63] there is an important exception for a "displaced residential occupier". This privileged person is immune from liability under section 6, whether or not his object in securing entry to the premises is to resume residential occupation, and even if he uses more force than is reasonably necessary (though in that case he may of course be guilty of some other offence such as assault or criminal damage). Section 6(3) provides:

> "In any proceedings for an offence under this section it shall be a defence for the accused to prove—
> (*a*)   that at the time of the alleged offence he or any other person on whose behalf he was acting was a displaced residential occupier of the premises in question; or
> (*b*)   that part of the premises in question constitutes premises of which he or any other person on whose behalf he was acting was a displaced residential occupier and that the part of the premises to which he was seeking to secure entry constitutes an access[64] of which he or, as the case may be, that other person is also a displaced residential occupier."

A displaced residential occupier of premises is a person who was occupying them as a residence (otherwise than as a trespasser)[65] immediately before[66] being excluded from occupation by anyone who

---

62   *Cf. supra*, para. 3.19.
63   s. 6(2).
64   *i.e.* any part of any site or building within which the premises are situated which constitutes an ordinary means of access to the premises (whether or not that is its sole or primary use): s. 12(1)(*b*).
65   s. 12(4). In effect, *jus tertii* excludes the defence.
66   It is not enough that he had previously occupied them as a residence if that occupation had already ceased before he was excluded.

entered them[67] (or any access[68] to them) as a trespasser; and he continues to be a displaced residential occupier for as long as he continues to be excluded from occupation of the premises by the original trespasser or by any subsequent trespasser.[69] Anyone on the premises by virtue of any title derived from a trespasser (or of any licence or consent given by a trespasser, or by a person deriving title from a trespasser) is himself treated as a trespasser.[70] A displaced residential occupier of any premises is regarded also as a displaced residential occupier of any access to them.[71]

SQUATTING

7.61 Squatting is not theft of the land, even if the squatter hopes to acquire an unimpeachable title to it by adverse possession and thus permanently to deprive of it the person to whom it currently belongs.[72] But it may involve such offences as burglary[73] or violent entry;[74] and, whether or not a squatter's initial entry is an offence, he may be guilty of an offence if he fails to leave on request.

Failing to leave residential premises

7.62 Section 7(1) of the Criminal Law Act 1977 provides:

"Subject to the following provisions of this section, any person who is on any premises as a trespasser after having entered as such is guilty of an offence if he fails to leave those premises on being required to do so by or on behalf of—
(a) a displaced residential occupier of the premises; or
(b) an individual who is a protected intending occupier of the premises by virtue of subsection (2) or subsection (4) below."

The offence is punishable on summary conviction with six months' imprisonment or a fine of level 5 on the standard scale or both.[75] A

---

67 It is not enough that he is excluded by someone who was originally a tenant or a licensee. *Quaere* whether this would include someone who obtains a licence by fraud, or who enters for a purpose (*e.g.* that of excluding the occupier) other than that for which the licence was granted: *cf. supra,* paras. 7.12 ff.
68 See n. 64, *supra.* The effect is that a residential occupier does not commit the offence by forcing his way into an occupied access to his home even if the home itself has not been occupied by trespassers.
69 s. 12(3).
70 s. 12(6). A trespasser does not cease to be a trespasser merely because he is allowed time to leave, nor does anyone cease to be a displaced residential occupier because he allows a trespasser time to leave: s. 12(7).
71 s. 12(5).
72 *Supra,* para. 1.04.
73 *Supra,* paras. 7.02 ff.
74 *Supra,* paras. 7.55 ff.
75 s. 7(10) as amended by Criminal Justice Act 1982 s. 46.

constable in uniform may arrest without warrant anyone who is, or whom he with reasonable cause suspects to be, guilty of the offence.[76]

Entry onto premises as a trespasser

7.63 The defendant must have entered premises as a trespasser and must still be a trespasser on them when he is required to leave. In this case it is hardly relevant whether he knew he might be trespassing at the time he entered, provided that he knows it when he fails to leave.[77] "Premises" means the same as it does for the purposes of the offence of violent entry,[78] except that for the purposes of section 7 (other than the definition of a protected intending occupier)[79] premises include any access to them, whether or not the access would otherwise constitute premises within the meaning of the Act.[80] The premises in question need not be wholly residential, but it is a defence for the defendant to prove that they are (or form part of) premises used mainly for non-residential purposes and that he was not on any part of the premises used wholly or mainly for residential purposes.[81] He enters or remains upon the premises "as a trespasser" if he does so by virtue of any title derived from a trespasser, or of any licence or consent given by a trespasser or by a person deriving title from a trespasser;[82] and once he is on the premises as a trespasser he does not cease to be one merely because he is allowed time to leave.[83]

Requirement to leave

7.64 The defendant must have been required[84] to leave the premises by (or on behalf of) either a displaced residential occupier or a protected intending occupier. It is a defence for him to prove that he believed that the person requiring him to leave was not, and was not acting on behalf of, such a person.[85] The definition of a displaced residential occupier has already been discussed.[86] An individual[87] is a protected intending occupier

---

76 s. 7(11).
77 *Cf. supra*, para. 7.20.
78 *i.e.* it includes not only a building but also a part of a building under separate occupation, any land ancillary to a building and the site comprising any building or buildings together with any land ancillary thereto: see *supra*, para. 7.56.
79 *Infra*, para. 7.64.
80 s. 7(9).
81 s. 7(7).
82 s. 12(6).
83 s. 12(7).
84 s. 7(8) refers to his being *requested* to leave. The difference is probably inadvertent and of no significance.
85 s. 7(6).
86 *Supra*, para. 7.60.
87 *i.e.* not a corporation; but the distinction is unnecessary because a corporation could not require the premises as its residence.

of premises[88] if at the time in question he is excluded from occupation of the premises by a person who entered them (or any access[89] to them) as a trespasser, and *either*

(1) (a) he has in those premises a freehold interest or a leasehold interest with not less than 21 years still to run, and he acquired that interest as a purchaser for money or money's worth, and

(b) he requires the premises for his own occupation as a residence, and

(c) he (or a person acting on his behalf) holds a written statement which—

(i) specifies his interest in the premises, and

(ii) states that he requires the premises for occupation as a residence for himself, and

(iii) is signed by him and by a justice of the peace or commissioner for oaths as a witness to his signature;[90]

or

(2) (a) he has been authorised to occupy the premises as a residence by one of the following authorities:

(i) a body mentioned in section 14 of the Rent Act 1977,[91]

(ii) the Housing Corporation, or

(iii) a registered housing association within the meaning of the Housing Associations Act 1985,[92] and

(b) there has been issued to him, by or on behalf of that authority, a certificate specifying which type of authority it is and stating

---

88 In the definition of a protected intending occupier, "premises" does *not* include an access to the premises, but a person who *is* a protected intending occupier of any premises is regarded as a protected intending occupier of any access to those premises too: s. 7(9).

89 *i.e.* any part of any site or building within which the premises are situated which constitutes an ordinary means of access to the premises (whether or not that is its sole or primary use): s. 12(1)(b).

90 s. 7(2), (3). A person is guilty of an offence if he makes a statement for this purpose which he knows to be false in a material particular, or if he recklessly makes such a statement which is false in a material particular: s. 7(3). This offence is punishable on summary conviction with six months' imprisonment or a fine of level 5 on the standard scale or both: s. 7(10).

91 Currently including a county, district or London borough council, the Common Council of the City of London, the Inner London Education Authority, a joint authority established by Part IV of the Local Government Act 1985, the Commission for the New Towns, a development corporation established by an order made (or having effect as if made) under the New Towns Act 1981, the Development Board for Rural Wales, and an urban development corporation within the meaning of Part XVI of the Local Government, Planning and Land Act 1980: Local Government Act 1985 ss. 84, 102(2), Schs. 14, 17; New Towns Act 1981 s. 81, Sch. 12; Local Government, Planning and Land Act 1980 s. 155(1).

92 Criminal Law Act 1977 s. 7(5) as amended by Housing (Consequential Provisions) Act 1985 Sch. 2.

that he has been authorised by that authority to occupy the premises as a residence.[93]

Where the person requiring the defendant to leave the premises claims to be (or to act on behalf of) a protected intending occupier, it is a defence for the defendant to prove that when he was requested to leave he asked that person to produce such a statement or certificate and that person failed to do so.[94]

Failure to leave

7.65 The trespasser commits the offence if he fails to leave on being validly required to do so. It is not necessary that he should *refuse* to leave: it is sufficient if he simply ignores the request. Nor is there any qualification to the effect that he is permitted a reasonable time to leave. Strictly speaking, and subject no doubt to *de minimis*, he commits the offence unless he leaves at once.

Failing to leave land

7.66 Section 39(1) of the Public Order Act 1986 empowers the senior police officer[95] to direct any person or persons to leave any land if he reasonably believes:

(a) that two or more persons (including the person or persons so directed) have entered the land as trespassers,[96] and
(b) that they are present there with the common purpose of residing there for any period,[97] and
(c) that reasonable steps have been taken by or on behalf of the occupier[98] to ask them to leave, and
(d) (i) that any of them has caused damage to property[99] on the land, or
  (ii) that any of them has used threatening, abusive or insulting words or behaviour towards the occupier, a member of his family or an employee or agent of his, or

---

93 s. 7(4). A document purporting to be such a certificate is admissible in evidence, and is deemed to have been issued by or on behalf of the authority stated unless the contrary is proved: s. 7(8)(b).
94 s. 7(8)(a).
95 i.e. the most senior in rank of the police officers present at the scene: s. 39(5).
96 sc. as against the occupier of the land: s. 39(5).
97 A person may be regarded as having such a purpose notwithstanding that he has a home elsewhere: s. 39(5).
98 i.e. the person entitled to possession of the land by virtue of an estate or interest held by him: s. 39(5).
99 i.e. property within the meaning of s. 10(1) of the Criminal Damage Act 1971 (*supra*, para. 6.03): s. 39(5).

(iii) that they have between them brought twelve or more vehicles[1] on to the land.

"Land" does not include buildings,[2] nor land forming part of a highway.[3]

7.67 Section 39(2) then provides:

"If a person knowing that such a direction has been given which applies to him—
(a) fails to leave the land as soon as reasonably practicable, or
(b) having left again enters the land as a trespasser within the period of three months beginning with the day on which the direction was given, he commits an offence . . ."

The offence is punishable on summary conviction with three months' imprisonment or a fine of level 4 on the standard scale, or both.[4] A constable in uniform who reasonably suspects that a person is committing the offence may arrest him without warrant.[5] It is a defence for the defendant to show that his original entry on the land was not in fact as a trespasser, or that he had a reasonable excuse for failing to leave the land as soon as reasonably practicable or for again entering it as a trespasser (as the case may be).[6] The offence is not committed if it is not in fact reasonably practicable for him to leave within the time allowed by the officer giving the direction, even if the officer thinks it is.[7]

Obstructing court officers

7.68 Section 10(1) of the Criminal Law Act 1977 provides:

" . . . a person is guilty of an offence if he resists or intentionally obstructs any person who is in fact an officer of a court engaged in executing any process issued by the High Court or by any county court for the purpose of enforcing any judgment or order for the recovery of any premises or for the delivery of possession of any premises."

The offence is punishable on summary conviction with six months' imprisonment or a fine of level 5 on the standard scale or both.[8] A constable in uniform or any officer of a court may arrest without warrant

---

1 Including caravans as defined in s. 29(1) of the Caravan Sites and Control of Development Act 1960: s. 39(5).
2 Other than agricultural buildings within the meaning of s. 26(4) of the General Rate Act 1967, or scheduled monuments within the meaning of the Ancient Monuments and Archaeological Areas Act 1979.
3 s. 39(5).
4 s. 39(2).
5 s. 39(3).
6 s. 39(4).
7 *Krumpa v. D.P.P.*, [1989] Crim.L.R. 295.
8 s. 10(4) as amended by Criminal Justice Act 1982, s. 46.

anyone who is, or whom he with reasonable cause suspects to be, guilty of the offence.[9]

Judgment or order for recovery or possession

7.69   The person resisted or obstructed must be attempting to enforce a judgment or order for the recovery of premises or for the delivery of possession of premises. "Premises" includes not only such buildings and land as would constitute premises for the purposes of the other offences under the 1977 Act[10] but also "any other place".[11] But the offence can be committed only where the judgment or order in question was given or made in proceedings brought under R.S.C. O. 113 or C.C.R. O. 26, or any other provisions of rules of court applicable only in similar circumstances.[12]

Officer of a court

7.70   The person resisted or obstructed must be an officer of a court, *i.e.*

(a) a sheriff, under sheriff, deputy sheriff, bailiff or officer of a sheriff, or

(b) a bailiff or other person who is an officer of a county court within the meaning of the County Courts Act 1984.[13]

It is a defence for the defendant to prove that he believed that the person he was resisting or obstructing was not an officer of a court,[14] but apparently not that he did not know that that person was engaged in executing process.

Resistance and obstruction

7.71   The defendant must either resist the officer or intentionally obstruct him. If there is such a thing as resistance which does not amount to obstruction, it apparently need not be deliberate. Clearly some assistance may be derived from the authorities on the phrase "resists or wilfully obstructs a constable" in section 51(3) of the Police Act 1964, although a court officer's function is not the same as a police officer's and therefore the possible ways of resisting or obstructing him need not be the same either. Moreover the court officer must not only be acting in the execution

---

9   s. 10(5).
10   *Supra*, para. 7.56.
11   s. 12(1)(*a*).
12   s. 10(2). These provisions are applicable where the person claiming possession of the premises alleges that they are occupied solely by a person or persons (not being a tenant or tenants holding over after the termination of the tenancy) who entered or remained in occupation without the licence or consent of the person claiming possession or of any of his predecessors in title.
13   s. 10(6).
14   s. 10(3).

of his duty but actually engaged in executing process; it may be doubted, for example, whether the offence would be committed by resisting a court officer's attempts to exercise the power of arrest conferred by section 10(5). It has been said that a person "obstructs" a constable if he makes it more difficult for the constable to carry out his duty,[15] and in general this is doubtless true of court officers too. But it does not impose a general duty to assist an officer,[16] only to refrain from getting in his way.

POACHING

7.72 Poaching is a large subject and an exhaustive account would occupy a disproportionate amount of space. What follows is no more than an outline of the major offences.

Game and birds' eggs
Poaching by night
7.73 The Night Poaching Act 1828 creates offences of taking or destroying game or rabbits by night, or trespassing for that purpose. For the purposes of this Act "game" includes hares, pheasants, partridges, grouse, heath or moor game, black game and bustards,[17] and "night" is the period between the expiration of the first hour of sunset and the beginning of the last hour before sunrise.[18]

Taking game and trespass
7.74 Section 1, as amended,[19] provides:

"If any person shall by night, unlawfully take[20] or destroy any game or rabbits in any land, whether open or enclosed,[21] or shall by night unlawfully enter or be in any land, whether open or enclosed, with any gun, net, engine, or other instrument, for the purpose of taking or destroying game, he shall be liable on summary conviction to a fine not exceeding level 3 on the standard scale."

15 *Hinchcliffe v. Sheldon* [1955] 1 W.L.R. 1207 at p. 1210, *per* Lord Goddard C.J.
16 *Rice v. Connolly* [1966] 2 Q.B. 414.
17 s. 13.
18 s. 12.
19 Statute Law Revision (No. 2) Act 1888; Criminal Law Act 1977 ss. 15, 30, Sch. 1; Criminal Justice Act 1982 s. 46.
20 To "take" means to catch, not necessarily to take away: *Glover* (1814) Russ. & Ry. 269.
21 Or on any public road, highway or path, or the sides thereof, or at the openings, outlets or gates from any such land into any such public road, highway or path: Night Poaching Act 1844 s. 1.

Trespass in armed groups

7.75 Section 9, as amended,[22] provides:

> "If any pesons, to the number of three or more together, shall by night unlawfully enter or be in any land whether open or enclosed,[23] for the purpose of taking or destroying game or rabbits, any of such persons being armed with any gun, crossbow, fire arms, bludgeon, or any other offensive weapon, each and every of such persons shall be . . . liable on summary conviction to imprisonment for a term not exceeding six months or to a fine not exceeding level 4 on the standard scale, or to both."

It is not necessary that the whole group should enter the land, provided that at least one enters in pursuance of the common purpose of all of them.[24]

Poaching by day

7.76 The Game Act 1831 creates several offences of poaching in the daytime, which is defined as the period between the beginning of the last hour before sunrise and the expiration of the first hour after sunset.[25] A prosecution for one of these offences must be commenced within three calendar months after the commission of the offence.[26]

Trespass in search of game

7.77 Section 30, as amended,[27] provides:

> "If any person whatsoever shall commit any trespass by entering or being in the daytime upon any land in search or pursuit of game,[28] or woodcocks, snipes or conies, such person shall, on conviction thereof before a justice of the peace, forfeit and pay such sum of money, not exceeding level 1 on the standard scale, as to the justice shall seem meet . . . "

A person does not "enter" upon land for this purpose merely by sending a dog on to it: the section envisages a personal and not just a constructive entry.[29] It is provided, somewhat unnecessarily, that the defendant may rely by way of defence on any matter which would have been a defence to an action for trespass at law; but where some person other than the occupier has the right of killing the game upon the land, an entry without that person's consent is deemed to be a trespass and the consent of the occupier is no defence.

---

22 Statute Law Revision (No. 2) Act 1888; Criminal Justice Administration Act 1962 s. 20(2), Sch. 5; Criminal Law Act 1977 ss. 30(3), 65, Sch. 12; Criminal Justice Act 1982 s. 46.
23 s. 1 of the Night Poaching Act 1844 applies: *supra*, n. 21.
24 *Whittaker* (1848) 1 Den. 310.
25 s. 34.
26 s. 41.
27 Statute Law Revision (No. 2) Act 1888; Protection of Birds Act 1954 s. 15(2), Sch. 6; Game Laws (Amendment) Act 1960 s. 5(1); Criminal Justice Act 1982 ss. 38, 46.
28 Including hares, pheasants, partridges, grouse, heath or moor game and black game: s. 2.
29 *Pratt v. Martin* [1911] 2 K.B. 90.

Failure to leave or to give name and address

7.78 Section 31 of the Game Act 1831 provides in part, as amended:[30]

"Where any person shall be found on any land, in the daytime, in search or pursuit of game, or woodcocks, snipes, or conies, it shall be lawful for any person having the right of killing the game upon such land, by virtue of any reservation or otherwise, as hereinbefore mentioned, or for the occupier of the land (whether there shall or shall not be any such right by reservation or otherwise), or for any gamekeeper or servant of either of them, or for any person authorised by either of them,[31] to require the person so found forthwith to quit the land whereon he shall be so found, and also to tell his christian name, surname, and place of abode; and in case such person shall, after being so required, offend by refusing to tell his real name or place of abode, or by giving such a general description of his place of abode as shall be illusory for the purpose of discovery, or by wilfully continuing or returning upon the land, it shall be lawful for the party so requiring as aforesaid, and also for any person acting by his order and in his aid, to apprehend such offender, and to convey him or cause him to be conveyed as soon as conveniently may be before a justice of the peace; and such offender (whether so apprehended or not), upon being convicted of any such offence before a justice of the peace, shall forfeit and pay such sum of money, not exceeding level 1 on the standard scale, as to the convicting justice shall seem meet . . . "

Trespass in groups

7.79 Section 30 of the Game Act 1831 continues, as amended:

". . . if any persons to the number of five or more together shall commit any trespass, by entering or being in the daytime upon any land in search or pursuit of game, or woodcocks, snipes, or conies, each of such persons shall, on conviction thereof before a justice of the peace, forfeit and pay such sum of money, not exceeding level 3 on the standard scale, as to the justice shall seem meet . . . "

Again the consent of the occupier is no defence if someone else has the right of killing the game upon the land.

7.80 *Intimidation by armed groups.* Section 32 of the Game Act 1831 creates an offence of violence or intimidation by armed groups of poachers against a person attempting to exercise the powers granted by section 31.[32] As amended,[33] it provides:

30 Statute Law Revision (No. 2) Act 1888; Protection of Birds Act 1954 s. 15(2), Sch. 6; Game Laws (Amendment) Act 1960 s. 1(2); Wild Creatures and Forest Laws Act 1971 s. 1, Sch.; Criminal Law Act 1977 s. 31(6); Criminal Justice Act 1982 s. 46; Police and Criminal Evidence Act 1984 Sch. 7.
31 Or a police constable: s. 31A, inserted by Police and Criminal Evidence Act 1984 Sch. 6.
32 *Supra*, para. 7.78.
33 Statute Law Revision (No. 2) Act 1888; Protection of Birds Act 1954 s. 15(2), Sch. 6; Wild Creatures and Forest Laws Act 1971 s. 1; Criminal Law Act 1977 s. 31(6); Criminal Justice Act 1982 s. 46; Criminal Justice Act 1988 s. 64(1).

"Where any persons, to the number of five or more together, shall be found on any land, in the daytime, in search or pursuit of game, or woodcocks, snipes, or conies, any of such persons being then and there armed with a gun, and such persons or any of them shall then and there, by violence, intimidation, or menace, prevent or endeavour to prevent any person authorised as herein-before mentioned from approaching such persons so found, or any of them, for the purpose of requiring them or any of them to quit the land whereon they shall be so found, or to tell their or his christian name, surname, or place of abode respectively, as herein-before mentioned, every person so offending by such violence, intimidation, or menace as aforesaid, and every person then and there aiding or abetting such offender, shall, upon being convicted thereof before two justices of the peace, forfeit and pay for every such offence such penalty, not exceeding level 4 on the standard scale,[34] as to the convicting justices shall seem meet . . . "

Birds' eggs

7.81 Section 24 of the Game Act 1831, as amended,[35] provides:

"If any person not having the right of killing the game upon any land, nor having permission from the person having such right, shall wilfully take out of the nest or destroy in the nest upon such land the eggs of any bird of game,[36] or of any swan, wild duck, teal, or widgeon, or shall knowingly have in his house, shop, possession, or control, any such eggs so taken, every such person shall, on conviction thereof before two justices of the peace, forfeit and pay for every egg so taken or destroyed, or so found in his house, shop, possession, or control, such sum of money, not exceeding level 1 on the standard scale, as to the said justices shall seem meet . . ."

Possession of game or birds' eggs

7.82 Section 2 of the Poaching Prevention Act 1862 (as amended)[37] empowers a constable to search, in any highway, street or public place, any person whom he has good cause to suspect of coming from any land where that person has been unlawfully in search or pursuit of game[38] ("or any person aiding or abetting such person"),[39] and having in his possession any game unlawfully obtained, or any gun, part of a gun or cartridge or other ammunition, or any net, trap, snare or other device of a kind used for the killing or taking of game.[40] The constable may also

---

34 Raised from level 1 by Criminal Justice Act 1988 s. 64(1), but only in respect of offences committed on or after 29 September 1988 (ss. 64(2), 171(6)).
35 Statute Law Revision (No. 2) Act 1888; Criminal Law Act 1977 s. 31(6); Criminal Justice Act 1982 s. 46.
36 *i.e.* pheasants, partridges, grouse, heath or moor game or black game: s. 2.
37 Statute Law Revision Act 1893; Game Laws (Amendment) Act 1960 ss. 3(2), (3); Criminal Justice Act 1982 ss. 38, 46.
38 Which for the purposes of this Act includes hares, pheasants, partridges, woodcock, snipe, rabbits, grouse, and black and moor game, and eggs of pheasants, partridges, grouse, and black and moor game: s. 1.
39 This presumably means a person whom he has good cause to suspect of aiding and abetting a person unlawfully going on land in search or pursuit of game.
40 Game Laws (Amendment) Act 1960 s. 3(2).

stop and search a conveyance in or upon which he has good cause to suspect that any such game, article or thing is being carried by any such person, and to seize and detain any such game, article or thing so found. The section then goes on to create offences:[41]

". . . if such person shall have obtained such game by unlawfully going on any land[42] in search or pursuit of game, or shall have used any such article or thing as aforesaid for unlawfully killing or taking game,[43] or shall have been accessory thereto, such person shall, on being convicted thereof, forfeit and pay any sum not exceeding level 3 on the standard scale."

Deer

Poaching deer

7.83 Deer are not "game" within the meaning of the Night Poaching Act 1828 and the Game Act 1831,[44] but are protected by separate offences under the Deer Act 1980. Section 1(2) provides:

". . . if any person while on any land—
(a) intentionally takes, kills or injures, or attempts to take, kill or injure, any deer;[45]
(b) searches for or pursues any deer with the intention of taking, killing or injuring it; or
(c) removes the carcase of any deer,
without the consent of the owner or occupier of the land or other lawful authority, he shall be guilty of an offence."

Each offence under this section is punishable on summary conviction with three months' imprisonment, or with a fine of level 4 on the standard scale for each deer in respect of which the offence is committed,[46] or with both.[47]

Lawful authority

7.84 It is a defence that the defendant has the consent of "the owner or occupier of the land", or other lawful authority for his conduct. The "owner" is presumably the holder of the legal fee simple:but it is not clear what relevance his consent has if he is not the occupier and the defendant knows he is not. The consent of a person who is neither the owner nor the occupier, but who has the right to take or kill deer on the land, is not expressly included. Perhaps such a person's consent is "other lawful

---

41 The earlier part of the section creates no offence: *Lundy v. Botham* (1877) 41 J.P. 774; *Garman v. Plaice* [1969] 1 W.L.R. 19.
42 It need not be proved *what* land: *Brown v. Turner* (1863) 13 C.B.N.S. 485.
43 *i.e.* for the purpose of such killing or taking. The attempt need not have been successful: *Jenkin v. King* (1872) L.R. 7 Q.B. 478.
44 *Inglewood Investment Co. Ltd v. Forestry Commissioners* [1988] 1 W.L.R. 959 at p. 963, *per* Harman J.
45 Including deer of any species and the carcase of any deer or any part thereof: s. 8.
46 s. 1(6).
47 s. 1(5).

authority"; but it is strange that he is not referred to, whereas it is expressly provided that he is an "authorised person" entitled to require a poacher to give his name and address and to leave.[48]

Belief that authority does or would exist
7.85 Section 1(3) provides:

"A person shall not be guilty of an offence under subsection . . . (2) above by reason of anything done in the belief that—
(*a*) he would have the consent of the owner or occupier of the land if the owner or occupier knew of his doing it and the circumstances of it; or
(*b*) he has other lawful authority to do it."

It is immaterial whether there are any grounds for such belief.

Trespass in search or pursuit of deer
7.86 Section 1(1) of the Deer Act 1980 provides:

". . . if any person enters any land without the consent of the owner or occupier or other lawful authority in search or pursuit of any deer with the intention of taking, killing or injuring it, he shall be guilty of an offence."

The offence is punishable on summary conviction with three months' imprisonment or a fine of level 4 on the standard scale or both.[49] If a person trespassing in search or pursuit of two or more deer can be said to commit the offence "in respect of" more than one, the maximum fine may be imposed in respect of each one.[50] The defence under section 1(3), that the defendant thinks he has lawful authority or would have it if the owner or occupier knew the circumstances, is equally available here.

Failure to leave or to give name and address
7.87 Section 1(4) provides:

"If any authorised person suspects with reasonable cause that any person is committing or has committed an offence under subsection (1) or (2) above on any land, he may require that person—
(*a*) to give his full name and address; and
(*b*) to quit that land forthwith;
and any person who fails to comply with a requirement under this subsection shall be guilty of an offence."

The offence is punishable on summary conviction with three months' imprisonment or a fine of level 4 on the standard scale or both.[51] "Authorised persons" include not only the owner or occupier of the land[52]

---

48 s. 1(7); *infra*, para. 7.87.
49 s. 1(5).
50 s. 1(6).
51 s. 1(5).
52 *Cf. supra*, para. 7.84.

and any person authorised by the owner or occupier but also any person having the right to take or kill deer on the land in question.[53]

Fish

7.88 Section 32(1) and Schedule 1 of the Theft Act 1968 preserve with modifications certain offences, formerly existing under the Larceny Act 1861, of unlawfully taking or destroying fish. Paragraph 2(1) of Schedule 1 provides, as amended:

"Subject to subparagraph (2) below, a person who unlawfully takes or destroys, or attempts to take or destroy, any fish in water which is private property or in which there is any private right of fishery shall on summary conviction be liable to imprisonment for a term not exceeding three months or to a fine not exceeding level 3 on the standard scale or to both."

Any person may arrest without warrant anyone who is, or whom he with reasonable cause suspects to be, committing the offence.[54] Paragraph 2(2) provides that a person unlawfully taking or destroying fish by angling in the daytime (*i.e.* between one hour before sunrise and one hour after sunset), or attempting to do so, commits not this offence but a less serious one, punishable on summary conviction with a fine of level 1 on the standard scale.

7.89 In the case of salmon there is a special offence, closely analogous to that of handling stolen goods, and discussed in that context.[55]

DUMPING

7.90 Unauthorised dumping can in certain circumstances amount to an offence of criminal damage,[56] but is perhaps more appropriately charged as a distinct offence. Section 2(1) of the Refuse Disposal (Amenity) Act 1978 provides:

"Any person who, without lawful authority—
(a) abandons on any land in the open air, or on any other land forming part of a highway, a motor vehicle or anything which formed part of a motor vehicle and was removed from it in the course of dismantling the vehicle on the land; or
(b) abandons on any such land any thing other than a motor vehicle, being a thing which he has brought to the land for the purpose of abandoning it there,
shall be guilty of an offence . . . "

53 s. 1(7).
54 Para. 2(4).
55 *Supra*, paras. 4.93 f.
56 *Supra*, para. 6.09.

The offence is punishable on summary conviction with three months' imprisonment or a fine of level 3 on the standard scale or both.[57] A person who leaves any thing on any land, in such circumstances or for such a period that he may reasonably be assumed to have abandoned it, is deemed to have abandoned it there unless the contrary is shown.[58] Except where the thing abandoned is a motor vehicle,[59] or part of a motor vehicle removed from it in the course of dismantling it on the land, the offence is not committed unless the defendant brought the thing on to the land for the purpose of abandoning it there; but if he leaves it there in such circumstances or for such a period that he may reasonably be assumed to have brought it there for that purpose, he is deemed to have done so unless the contrary is shown.[60]

PARTICULAR PREMISES

Enclosed premises

7.91 Section 4 of the Vagrancy Act 1824 creates a number of offences, one of which is relevant here. It provides, in part:

". . . every person being found in or upon any dwelling house,[61] warehouse, coach-house,[62] stable, or outhouse, or in any inclosed yard, garden, or area, for any unlawful purpose . . . shall be deemed a rogue and vagabond, . . . and . . . it shall be lawful for any justice of the peace[63] to commit such offender . . . to [imprisonment] for any time not exceeding three calendar months . . ."

Alternatively a fine of level 3 on the standard scale may be imposed.[64]

7.92 A "yard" or "garden" within the meaning of the section is a relatively small area, contiguous or attached to a building or used for purposes ancillary to those of a building; and the word "area" is to be construed *ejusdem generis*.[65] An "inclosed" yard, garden, or area is one

---

57 s. 2(1) as amended by Criminal Justice Act 1982 ss. 35, 46.
58 s. 2(2).
59 *i.e.* a mechanically propelled vehicle intended or adapted for use on roads (whether or not it is in a fit state for such use), including a trailer intended or adapted for use as an attachment to such a vehicle, a chassis or body (with or without wheels) appearing to have formed part of such a vehicle or trailer, and anything attached to such a vehicle or trailer: s. 11(1).
60 s. 2(2).
61 This includes being in a common entrance hall: *Hollyhomes v. Hind* [1944] K.B. 571.
62 *Quaere* whether this includes a garage.
63 But if the conviction is before a single justice (other than a stipendiary magistrate: Justices of the Peace Act 1979 ss. 16(3), 33(4)) the maximum term of imprisonment is 14 days and the maximum fine is £1: Magistrates' Courts Act 1980 s. 121(5).
64 Magistrates' Courts Act 1980 s. 34(3) as amended by Criminal Justice Act 1982 s. 46.
65 *Knott v. Blackburn* [1944] K.B. 77; *Quatromini v. Peck* [1972] 1 W.L.R. 1318.

surrounded by walls, buildings or fences, but it need not be *wholly*
surrounded in the sense that there is no access through spaces between
the surrounding structures. Nor need there be any means of closing any
such access, such as a gate, and if there is a gate it need not be closed.
Whether the accesses are so large or numerous as to prevent the yard,
garden, or area from being "inclosed" is a question of degree.[66] The
requirement that the defendant be in the place in question for an
"unlawful purpose" means that he must intend to commit a criminal
offence,[67] though not necessarily in that place or at the time when he is
found there.[68]

Railways

7.93   Under section 16 of the Railway Regulation Act 1840, as amended,
it is an offence wilfully to trespass upon any railway, or any of the stations
or other works or premises connected therewith, and to refuse to quit the
same upon request made by any officer or agent of the railway company.
The offence is punishable on summary conviction with one month's
imprisonment or a fine of level 3 on the standard scale in the case of
property of the British Railways Board; in other cases the maximum fine
is one of level 1.[69]

7.94   Under section 55(1) of the British Transport Commission Act 1949,
as amended, it is an offence to trespass upon any of the lines of railway
or sidings, or in any tunnel, or upon any railway embankment, cutting
or similar work belonging or leased to or worked by any of a number of
specified bodies,[70] or to trespass upon any other lands of any of those
bodies in dangerous proximity to any such lines of railway or other works
or to any electrical apparatus used for or in connection with the working
of the railway. The offence is punishable on summary conviction with a
fine of level 3 on the standard scale. It must be proved that a notice had
been clearly exhibited (and renewed if obliterated or destroyed) at the
station nearest to the place of the alleged offence, warning the public not
to trespass upon the railway.[71]

7.95   Under section 23 of the Regulation of Railways Act 1868, as

---

66   *Goodhew v. Morton* [1962] 1 W.L.R. 210.
67   *Hayes v. Stevenson* (1860) 25 J.P. 39.
68   *Re Joy* (1853) 22 L.T.Jo. 80.
69   British Railways Act 1977 s. 13(1) as amended by Criminal Justice Act 1982 s. 45.
70   *i.e.* the British Railways Board, the British Transport Docks Board and the British
     Waterways Board (Transport Act 1962 s. 1(1)), any wholly-owned subsidiary of any of
     them (Transport Act 1968 s. 156(2), Sch. 16), and London Regional Transport and any
     of its subsidiaries (London Regional Transport Act 1984 s. 67(3), Sch. 4).
71   s. 55(3).

amended, it is an offence for a person to be or pass upon any railway, except for the purpose of crossing the same at any authorised crossing, after having once received warning by the company which works the railway (or any of its servants or agents) not to go or pass thereon. The offence is punishable on summary conviction with a fine of level 1 on the standard scale.

Licensed aerodromes

7.96   Under section 39(1) of the Civil Aviation Act 1982 it is an offence to trespass on any land forming part of an aerodrome[72] licensed in pursuance of an Air Navigation Order.[73] The offence is punishable on summary conviction with a fine of level 1 on the standard scale.[74] It must be proved that, at the material time, notices warning trespassers of their liability under the section were posted so as to be readily seen and read by members of the public, in such positions on or near the boundary of the aerodrome as appear to the court to be proper.[75]

Explosives factories

7.97   Section 77 of the Explosives Act 1875 provides, in part, as amended:[76]

"Any person who enters without permission or otherwise trespasses upon any factory,[77] magazine,[78] or store,[79] or the land immediately adjoining thereto which is occupied by the occupier[80] of such factory, magazine, or store, or on any wharf[81] for which byelaws are made by the occupier thereof under this Act, shall be guilty of an offence, and may be forthwith removed from such factory, magazine, store, land, or wharf, by any constable, or by the occupier of such factory, magazine, store, or wharf, or any agent or servant of or other person authorised by such occupier."

---

72   *i.e.* any area of land or water designed, equipped, set apart or commonly used for affording facilities for the landing and departure of aircraft, including any area or space, whether on the ground, on the roof of a building or elsewhere, which is designed, equipped or set apart for affording facilities for the landing and departure of aircraft capable of descending or climbing vertically: s. 105(1).
73   *i.e.* an Order in Council under s. 60: s. 105(1).
74   s. 39(1) as amended by Criminal Justice Act 1982 s. 46.
75   s. 39(2).
76   Explosives Acts 1875 and 1923 (Repeals and Modifications) Regulations 1974, S.I. 1974 no. 1885, regulations 2, 9, Sch. 2.
77   In its context this must presumably be confined to explosives factories.
78   Including any ship or other vessel used for the purpose of keeping any explosive: s. 108.
79   *i.e.* a gunpowder store existing at the time of the passing of the Act or a place for keeping an explosive licensed by a local authority under the Act: s. 108.
80   Including any number of persons and a body corporate, and, in the case of any manufacture or trade, any person carrying on such manufacture or trade: s. 108.
81   Including any quay, landing-place, siding, or other place at which goods are landed, loaded, or unloaded: s. 108.

The offence is punishable on conviction on indictment with an unlimited fine and on summary conviction with a fine of the statutory maximum.[82]

Diplomatic missions

7.98 Section 9(1) of the Criminal Law Act 1977 provides:

". . . a person who enters or is on any premises to which this section applies as a trespasser[83] is guilty of an offence."

The offence is punishable on summary conviction with six months' imprisonment or a fine of level 5 on the standard scale or both.[84] Proceedings may not be instituted except by or with the consent of the Attorney-General.[85] A constable in uniform may arrest without warrant anyone who is, or whom he, with reasonable cause, suspects to be, in the act of committing the offence.[86]

7.99 The section applies to any premises[87] which are or form part of—

(a) the premises of a diplomatic mission within the meaning of the definition in Article 1(*i*) of the Vienna Convention on Diplomatic Relations signed in 1961 as that Article has effect in the United Kingdom by virtue of section 2 of and Schedule 1 to the Diplomatic Privileges Act 1964;

(b) the premises of a closed diplomatic mission;[88]

(c) consular premises within the meaning of the definition in paragraph 1(*j*) of Article 1 of the Vienna Convention on Consular Relations signed in 1963 as that Article has effect in the United Kingdom by virtue of section 1 of and Schedule 1 to the Consular Relations Act 1968;

(d) the premises of a closed consular post; [89]

(e) any other premises in respect of which any organisation or body is entitled to inviolability by or under any enactment; or

---

82 Health and Safety at Work Act 1974 s. 33(3), Sch. 1.
83 For entry "as a trespasser" see *supra*, para. 7.54.
84 s. 9(5) as amended by Criminal Justice Act 1982, s. 46.
85 s. 9(6).
86 s. 9(7).
87 "Premises" includes not only a building but also a part of a building under separate occupation, any land ancillary to a building and the site comprising any building or buildings together with any land ancillary thereto: see *supra*, para. 7.56.
88 *i.e.* premises which fall within Article 45 of the Vienna Convention on Diplomatic Relations signed in 1961 as that Article has effect in the United Kingdom by virtue of section 2 of and Schedule 1 to the Diplomatic Privileges Act 1964: s. 9(2A), inserted by Diplomatic and Consular Premises Act 1987 s. 7(2).
89 *i.e.* premises which fall within Article 27 of the Vienna Convention on Consular Relations signed in 1963 as that Article has effect in the United Kingdom by virtue of section 1 of and Schedule 1 to the Consular Relations Act 1968: s. 9(2A), inserted by Diplomatic and Consular Premises Act 1987, s. 7(2).

(f) any premises which are the private residence of a diplomatic agent (within the meaning of Article 1(*e*) of the Convention mentioned in paragraph (a) above) or of any other person who is entitled to inviolability of residence by or under any enactment.[90]

A certificate issued by or under the authority of the Secretary of State, stating that any premises were or formed part of premises of any of the descriptions above at the time of the alleged offence, is conclusive evidence to that effect.[91] But it is a defence for the defendant to prove that he believed that the premises in question were not premises to which the section applies.[92]

JURISDICTION OF MAGISTRATES

7.100 The jurisdiction of magistrates over an offence triable either way may be ousted if the defence is a *bona fide* assertion of title to real property.[93] But the rule does not apply to the offences created by Part II of the Criminal Law Act 1977 (*viz.* trespass with a weapon of offence, failing to leave residential premises, and trespass in diplomatic missions).[94]

---

90 s. 9(2) as amended by Diplomatic and Consular Premises Act 1987 s. 7(1).
91 s. 9(4).
92 s. 9(3).
93 *Burton v. Hudson* [1909] 2 K.B. 564; *R. v. Holsworthy JJ., ex p. Edwards* [1952] 1 All E.R. 411.
94 Criminal Law Act 1977 s. 12(8). Title to the premises is not a defence to a charge of violent entry: s. 6(2).

Specimen Indictments and Informations

Theft: Theft Act 1968 s. 1(1)

John Doe, on the 1st day of January 1989, stole cash to the sum of £50 belonging to Richard Roe.

Robbery: Theft Act 1968 s. 8(1)

John Doe, on the 1st day of January 1989, robbed Richard Roe of cash to the sum of £50.

Attempted theft: Criminal Attempts Act 1981 s. 1(1)

John Doe, on the 1st day of January 1989, attempted to steal some or all of the contents of a wallet belonging to [or attempted to steal from] Richard Roe.

Going equipped to steal (etc.); Theft Act 1968 s. 25(1)

John Doe, on the 1st day of January 1989, when not at his place of abode, had with him an article for use in in the course of or in connection with a burglary [or theft or cheat], namely a crowbar [etc.].

Obtaining property by deception: Theft Act 1968 s. 15(1)

John Doe, on the 1st day of January 1989, dishonestly obtained a motor car registration number A123 XYZ belonging to[1] Richard Roe with the intention of permanently depriving the said Richard Roe thereof by deception, namely by falsely representing[2] by words or conduct that a cheque number 123456 for the sum of £500 tendered by the said John Doe in payment for the said motor car was a good cheque.

---

1 The wording "obtained . . . *from* Richard Roe" is usually adequate but is not strictly correct, since it is possible to obtain property *from* a person which does not *belong to* that person as the offence requires: see *supra*, para. 2.04.
2 This is the usual wording. It is submitted however that the allegation of a misrepresentation is unnecessarily confusing and that the alternative wording ". . . by inducing the said Richard Roe by words or conduct falsely to believe . . ." would be preferable: see *supra*, paras. 2.13 f.

Blackmail: Theft Act 1968 s. 21(1)

John Doe, on the 1st day of January 1989, with a view to gain for himself [*or* for Jane Jones, *or* with intent to cause loss to Richard Roe], made to Richard Roe an unwarranted demand with menaces.

Handling stolen goods (receiving): Theft Act 1968 s. 22(1)

John Doe, on the 1st day of January 1989, dishonestly received [*or* arranged to receive] a stolen video-cassette recorder knowing or believing it to be stolen.

Handling stolen goods (other than receiving): Theft Act 1968 s. 22(1)

John Doe, on the 1st day of January 1989, dishonestly undertook or assisted in [*or* arranged to undertake or assist in] the retention, removal, disposal or realisation of a stolen video-cassette recorder by or for the benefit of Jane Jones, knowing or believing it to be stolen.

Taking a conveyance without authority: Theft Act 1968 s. 12(1)

John Doe, on the 1st day of January 1989, without having the consent of the owner Richard Roe or other lawful authority, took a conveyance, namely a motor car registration number A123 XYZ, for his use [*or* for the use of Jane Jones].

Driving (or allowing oneself to be carried in or on) a conveyance taken without authority: Theft Act 1968 s. 12(1)

John Doe, on the 1st day of January 1989, drove [*or* allowed himself to be carried in (*or* on)] a conveyance, namely a motor car registration number A123 XYZ, without having the consent of the owner Richard Roe or other lawful authority and knowing that the said conveyance had been taken without such authority.

Removing an article on public display: Theft Act 1968 s. 11(1)

John Doe, on the 1st day of January 1989, without lawful authority removed from [the grounds of] a building known as the Anytown Municipal Museum, to which the public [on that day][3] had access in order

---

3 This allegation must be included where the article removed was in the building (or its grounds) otherwise than as forming part of, or being on loan for exhibition with, a collection intended for permanent exhibition to the public: see *supra,* para. 5.43.

to view it [*or* part thereof, *or* (part of) a collection housed therein], an article displayed [*or* kept for display] to the public therein, namely a brick forming part of a work entitled "A Pile of Bricks" by Richard Roe.

Making off without payment: Theft Act 1978 s. 3(1)

John Doe, on the 1st day of January 1989, knowing that payment on the spot of the sum of £15 was required or expected from him for a quantity of petrol supplied to him [*or* a service done for him] by Acme Petrol plc, dishonestly made off without having paid as required or expected and with intent to avoid payment of the amount due.

Damaging property belonging to another: Criminal Damage Act 1971 s. 1(1)

John Doe, on the 1st day of January 1989, without lawful excuse destroyed [*or* damaged] a window belonging to Richard Roe, intending to destroy [*or* damage] property belonging to another or being reckless whether any such property would be destroyed [*or* damaged].

Arson: Criminal Damage Act 1971 ss. 1(1) and 1(3)

John Doe, on the 1st day of January 1989, without lawful excuse destroyed [*or* damaged] by fire a building belonging to Richard Roe, namely 13 Acacia Avenue, Anytown, intending to destroy [*or* damage] [by fire][4] property belonging to another or being reckless whether any such property would be [so] destroyed [*or* damaged].

Damaging property with disregard for danger to life: Criminal Damage Act 1971 s. 1(2)

John Doe, on the 1st day of January 1989, without lawful excuse destroyed [*or* damaged] a building belonging to Richard Roe [*or* to the said John Doe], namely 13 Acacia Avenue, Anytown, intending to destroy or damage property or being reckless whether property would be destroyed or damaged and intending by the said destruction or damage to endanger the life of Jane Jones [*or* of another] or being reckless as to whether the life of the said Jane Jones [*or* of another] would be thereby endangered.

---

4 This allegation ought in principle to be essential, but it is doubtful whether it is: see *supra,* para. 6.63.

Possession with intent to damage property:
Criminal Damage Act 1971 s. 3

John Doe, on the 1st day of January 1989, had in his custody or under his control a can of petrol, intending without lawful excuse to use it [*or* to cause or permit Jane Jones to use it] to destroy or damage a building known as 13 Acacia Avenue, Anytown, belonging to Richard Roe [*or* belonging to himself (*or* to the said Jane Jones) in a way in which he knew was likely to endanger the life of another].

Causing explosions: Explosive Substances Act 1883 s. 2

John Doe, on the 1st day of January 1989, unlawfully and maliciously by an explosive substance caused an explosion of a nature likely to cause serious injury to property [*or* to endanger life].

Acting with intent to cause explosions:
Explosive Substances Act 1883 s. 3(1)(*a*)

John Doe, on the 1st day of January 1989, unlawfully and maliciously did an act with intent to cause [*or* conspired with Jane Jones to cause] by an explosive substance an explosion of a nature likely to cause serious injury to property [*or* to endanger life].

Making or possession of an explosive substance with intent:
Explosive Substances Act 1883 s. 3(1)(*b*)

John Doe, on the 1st day of January 1989, unlawfully and maliciously made [*or* had in his possession or under his control] an explosive substance with intent by means thereof to cause serious injury to property [*or* to endanger life] [*or* to enable Jane Jones to cause serious injury to property *or* to endanger life].

Burglary: Theft Act 1968 s. 9(1)(*a*)

John Doe, on the 1st day of January 1989, entered [part of] a building known as 13 Acacia Avenue, Anytown, as a trespasser with intent to steal [*or* to do unlawful damage *or* to inflict grievous bodily harm on a person *or* to rape a woman] therein.

Burglary: Theft Act 1968 s. 9(1)(*b*)

John Doe, on the 1st day of January 1989, having entered [part of] a building known as 13 Acacia Avenue, Anytown, as a trespasser stole cash to the sum of £50 belonging to Richard Roe [*or* attempted to steal, *or* inflicted (*or* attempted to inflict) grievous bodily harm on Richard Roe] therein.

Aggravated burglary: Theft Act 1968 s. 10(1)

John Doe, on the 1st day of January 1989, entered [part of] a building known as 13 Acacia Avenue, Anytown, as a trespasser with intent to steal [*or* to do unlawful damage *etc.*] therein, and at the time of the said entry had with him a firearm [*or* an imitation firearm *or* a weapon of offence *or* an explosive].

or

John Doe, on the 1st day of January 1989, having entered [part of] a building known as 13 Acacia Avenue, Anytown, as a trespasser stole cash to the sum of £50 belonging to Richard Roe [*or* attempted to steal *etc.*] therein, and at the time of the said offence[5] had with him a firearm [*or* an imitation firearm *etc.*]

---

5   This wording assumes that the act done by the defendant in the building (or part of a building) in question is itself an offence. It is submitted that this must indeed be the case, but the contrary is arguable—at any rate where the act in question is the infliction (or attempted infliction) of grievous bodily harm (*supra*, para. 7.37). In that case the charge would have to read ". . . at the time of the said infliction [*or* attempted infliction] . . .".

Index

aerodromes (*see also* aircraft)
  trespass on, 7.96
agents, *see* fiduciaries
aggravated burglary, 7.44–7.49
air force stores, acquisition and
  disposal of, 4.91–4.92
aircraft, damaging and endangering
  (*see also* conveyances; damage),
  6.103
alternative verdicts
  burglary, 7.39
  handling stolen goods and theft,
  4.77–4.78
  stealing, and offences of, 1.197
animals, taking (*see also* poaching),
  5.03
appropriation, 1.63–1.107
  bona fide purchaser, by, 1.105
  company controllers, by, 1.93–1.94
  consent of owner, and (*see also*
    consent), 1.73–1.103
  deprivation and, 1.64–1.67
  duration of, 1.107, 1.176, 4.73
  effect on property, and, 1.68–1.72
  fiduciaries, by, 1.91–1.94
  keeping, by, 1.104–1.105
  subsequent to initial acquisition,
    1.104–1.105
  successive, 1.106
arson (*see also* damage), 6.63, 6.74
assault with intent to rob, 1.190
attempts, *see* damage; handling stolen
  goods; intention; theft
authority, *see* consent

bank accounts (*see also* cheques,
    intangibles)
  credit balance as property, 1.12
  mistake, payments made by, 1.44
  overdraft facility as property,
    1.12
  stolen money and, 4.13–4.19

belonging to another, property (*see
    also* property; theft)
  belief that not, 1.149–1.150
  companies, property of, 1.26
  corporations sole, property of, 1.60
  damage, in offences of, 6.05
  deception, in obtaining by (*see also*
    deception), 2.03–2.05
  equitable interests and, 1.22–1.25
  fiduciary obligations and (*see also*
    fiduciaries), 1.30–1.39
  mistake, property got by (*see also*
    mistake), 1.40–1.59
  possession or control and, 1.27–1.28
  proprietary interests and, 1.21–1.26
  theft, in, 1.17–1.62
  trust property as, 1.22–1.25, 1.29
  wild creatures as, 1.61–1.62
bilking, *see* making off without
    payment
birds' eggs and game, 7.73–7.82
blackmail (*see also* threats), 3.02–3.25
  demand with menaces, 3.12–3.17
  duress and, 3.23
  ineffectual threats as, 3.09
  jurisdiction in, 3.24–3.25
  making a demand, 3.18
  menaces, 3.03–3.11
  nuclear material, in relation to, 3.25
  offences, threats to commit,
    3.21–3.22
  propriety of menaces, belief in,
    3.21–3.23
  reasonable grounds for demand,
    belief in, 3.20
  scale of demand, relevance of,
    3.05–3.08
  third party, threat of action by,
    3.11
  timidity of victim, 3.10
  unwarranted demand with
    menaces, 3.19–3.23

363